D1554053

INNOVATIONS AND TECHNOLOGY
IN THE WORLD ECONOMY

Editors

Martin Kenney, University of California, Davis / Berkeley Roundtable on the
International Economy

Bruce Kogut, Wharton School, University of Pennsylvania

The Triumph of Ethernet

Technological Communities
and the Battle for the LAN Standard

Urs von Burg

Stanford University Press
Stanford, California

Stanford University Press
Stanford, California

© 2001 by the Board of Trustees of the Leland Stanford Junior University

Printed in the United States of America on acid-free, archival-quality paper

Library of Congress Cataloging-in-Publication Data

Burg, Urs. von.
  The triumph of Ethernet : technological communities and the battle for the LAN standard / Urs von Burg.
    p.   cm.
  Includes bibliographical references and index.
  ISBN 0-8047-4094-1 (alk. paper) — ISBN 0-8047-4095-X (pbk. : alk. paper)
  1. Ethernet (Local area network system)   2. Data transmission equipment industry.   I. Title.

TK5105.8.E83 B87 2001
004.6'8—dc21   2001020909

Original printing 2001

Last figure below indicates year of this printing:
10 09 08 07 06 05 04 03 02 01

Designed and typeset by Princeton Editorial Associates, Inc.,
Scottsdale, Arizona, and Princeton, New Jersey

Contents

Tables and Figures

Preface

This is the story of the rise of Ethernet, of its remarkable transformation from one of several competing technological standards for connecting computers in local area networks (LANs) into the undisputed industry and market standard. That story is fascinating in itself, but it is especially interesting for what it tells us about how technologies—and the products that embody them—become dominant in today's economy.

In fact, Ethernet's victory was far from being predetermined. Between the late 1970s and early 1980s dozens of established computer companies and specialized start-ups backed by venture capital introduced almost as many different technologies to network computers locally. Confronted with so many alternatives, the market flirted with different technologies at various times, since each had its own merits in the different environments in which they were put to use. After several years of intense competition, in the mid- to late 1980s the market chose Ethernet for an ever-increasing variety of uses, with the result that it began to drive the other alternatives from the market. As this book explains in great detail, Ethernet's victory originated from a number of intersecting factors, including an inherent potential for technological improvements, random and largely minor events, major shifts in the computer market, and the misguided business strategies of the sponsors of competing technologies. But ultimately Ethernet's victory resulted from the clever strategy of its sponsors of opening the technology, in order to create profitable business opportunities for other firms as well, and thereby to assemble an entire cottage industry around their preferred technology. It is this explanation that allows us to gain a better understanding of the relative success of a number of recent technologies, such as the Linux operating system.

The story of Ethernet's rise and the parallel growth of the data networking industry are also of interest because they tell how a handful of visionary entrepreneurs, supported by a few venture capitalists, created an entirely new industry and in the process changed the world. In fact, the LAN and network technology in general, despite their modest beginnings, have become a central part of the way people all over the world work and communicate. In the late 1970s and early 1980s, most entrepreneurs and venture capitalists held only modest expectations for the market growth of their companies, hoping eventually to reach $50 million in sales. But the market picked up momentum with remarkable rapidity. The data networking industry, virtually nonexistent in the late 1970s, reached annual sales of many billions of dollars by the mid-1990s. Even more important, by providing new means of communication between users, data networks (of which LANs are an important component) provided the infrastructure for today's Internet economy. It is already evident that computer networks and the electronic marketplaces that they make possible have provoked changes as fundamental as those brought about by the telephone and railroad networks. In fewer than two decades, LANs and their vendors have become critical parts of what has come to be known as the New Economy.

Of course, the buildup of networks and the accompanying business revolution did not result solely from the advent of LAN technology; many other elements had to fall into place as well, including the privatization and explosion of the Internet, the shipment of millions of PCs, and the continuous expansion of network capacity through fiber optic technology, as well as the establishment of thousands of dot-coms, ISPs, and business-to-business marketplaces. In fact, despite the aggressive exploitation of the underlying network infrastructure by the dot-coms and business-to-business marketplaces, the dynamism of the New Economy did not result primarily from the LAN—by now a well-established technology. But in many ways the origins, as well as the patterns and dynamism, of today's New Economy can be traced back to similar patterns of entrepreneurialism and venture capital investments that were already apparent in the creation of the LAN industry two decades ago.

In fact, in 1970–71, when LAN technology was invented, several other, more prestigious network technologies already existed. In 1958 the U.S. Air Force built a network for its SAGE air defense system, connecting radar installations and other devices to a central computer, and in 1969–70 the Advanced Research Projects Agency (ARPA) established the ARPANET, the Internet's legendary precursor, in an attempt to interconnect the computer science elite at universities and research centers. These early networks were huge wide area networks (WANs), spanning thousands of miles throughout North America and connecting a few large mainframe computers. At roughly the same time, the major computer manufacturers began using networks to build time-sharing systems.

Although these (wide area) networks, especially the ARPANET and the Internet, were critical steppingstones in the network buildup, none led to the explosive growth of computer networks nor sparked the development of an actual network component industry. Throughout most of the 1970s, the mainframe and minicomputers, the principal computer types at that time, were still too few to create a significant market, while the computer manufacturers carefully controlled their networks, thereby preventing specialized producers of network components from entering the market. Besides, ARPANET (and later the Internet) grew too slowly within the academic world—their main field of application before being privatized—to spark the interest of entrepreneurs and venture capitalists.

By contrast, the novel LAN technology quickly took off. Many entrepreneurs saw in it considerable business opportunities, because by the early 1980s thousands of computers had been installed within corporations, while the existing computer firms remained hesitant to provide solutions for linking customers to their competitors' devices. And although the minicomputer still dominated as the principal computer resource within corporations, some envisioned networks connecting the emerging class of microcomputers. The concept was still visionary in the early 1980s, because PCs were still in their infancy. But many entrepreneurs acted in the same spirit as the early microcomputer builders, realizing that networks would not only empower the individual office worker but also mean good business by turning the infant standalone microcomputers into powerful office systems. As a result, between the late 1970s and the early 1980s, dozens of firms were established in Silicon Valley or along Route 128 near Boston—many owing their beginnings to infusions of venture capital.

The LAN's intersection with the PC revolution proved fortunate. In the 1980s, as the PC became the primary office automation tool and millions of PCs were sold, the market for LANs, as well as network traffic itself, exploded, thereby allowing several LAN producers to grow rapidly, reaching sales of hundreds of millions of dollars by the end of the decade. In the middle of the 1990s, when the Internet was finally privatized, corporate LANs quickly became important on-ramps to it, and thus tightly interconnected with the rest of the world. In addition, many LAN companies eventually became important suppliers of Internet technology. For example, Cisco, today's giant in the data networking industry, has its roots in providing the technology for interconnecting geographically dispersed LANs. Nortel, a leading telecommunications company and strong competitor of Cisco's, bought its way into the data networking market by acquiring a leading LAN company, Bay Networks.

Such entrepreneurial dynamism did not remain confined to the LAN, but gradually swept over to the WAN side, reaching unprecedented levels. As corporations, the main adopters of LANs, increasingly desired to interconnect their dispersed local networks in corporate-wide networks and as the volume of data traffic took off, enormous opportunities arose for new technologies on the WAN side, and thus for another wave of specialized start-ups. Encouraged by their previous LAN investments, during the late 1980s and the 1990s venture capitalists funded dozens of start-ups focusing on WANs, including Ascend, Ciena, Juniper, StrataCom, and Sycamore. In many ways, this investment cycle proved even more successful, as many of these WAN start-ups reached market capitalizations in the billions instead of the hundreds of millions of dollars. Simultaneously, with the privatization of the Internet, venture capitalists heavily invested in so-called dot-com companies, thereby laying the foundation for today's New Economy. In this sense, the interconnected patterns of entrepreneurial dynamism, venture capital investment, and commercialization of new technologies apparent in the LAN space were repeated again and again, though on an ever-escalating scale. By describing the birth of the LAN industry two decades ago, this book not only analyzes an important part of this network build-up but also provides critical insights into the underlying principles and origins of today's New Economy.

Although this is not strictly a history of technology, readers not versed in network architecture will benefit from a brief overview of the technology, since some technical terms will of necessity arise throughout the book. In the early 1970s, when LAN technology was first invented, it differed from existing networks in two major ways. First, LANs were fast. Whereas the existing networks transmitted at speeds of up to 50 kilobits per second (kbps) but quite often no faster than 9 kbps, early LANs operated in the megabit-per-second (Mbps) range—that is, at speeds a thousand times faster than the earlier networks. Although relatively slow by today's standards—especially when compared with the speed ranges of Internet backbones—in 1971 these LANs were on the cutting edge. Second, as already mentioned, LANs spanned only short distances—between a couple of hundred yards and two miles—whereas SAGE, the ARPANET, and many of the other early networks covered hundreds or even thousands of miles.

Speed and distance are not the only parameters for networks. LAN technology also defines a wiring structure (or topology), the mechanisms for transferring data over the wire, how computers gain access to the wire, and how they share the network. To make LANs operational, all these concepts and parameters had to be implemented in actual devices. Thus the most important devices invented in the 1980s were adapters, repeaters, local and remote bridges, hubs, and routers. Adapters connect computers and other nodes (like printers) to the network and perform the LAN's access and transmission functions. Repeaters amplify the electrical signals after a certain distance. Local bridges can be used for the same purpose, but they have the additional function of dividing a network into segments and reconnecting them. Remote bridges perform a function similar to that of local bridges, but they do their jobs over long distances. Routers are also used to interconnect various LANs over long distances, but they are capable of selecting a particular transmission path, whereas bridges broadcast network traffic over every segment. Network hubs are similar to the hubs of wheels: they connect the various nodes of the network over a single point. It was these devices that ultimately created the economic opportunities for LAN companies—and eventually an entire industry.

There is no single best way to choose a LAN topology, no single best way to design transmission and access methods. Different network environments require different topologies, transmission methods, and access methods, and entrepreneurs and engineers devised numerous designs. But the various devices connected to a network can only operate together (interoperate) if they are compatible or adhere to the same technical specifications. As the number of networks within corporations grew, this requirement made standardization crucial in the evolution of the LAN industry. It is for this reason that this book focuses on the standardization battle in its account of the evolution of LAN technology and the industry that was born from it.

Acknowledgments

Like most people who devote considerable time and energy to a long-term project, I have a long list of persons to acknowledge.

I am greatly indebted to all the entrepreneurs, venture capitalists, engineers, and managers who helped create the subject of my research in the first place, and who so willingly shared their knowledge and time with me during the interviews. They are Jon Bayless, James Breyer, Neil Brownstein, Craig Burton, Werner Bux, Bandel Carano, Howard Charney, Eric Cooper, Ronald Crane, Michael D'Addio, William Davidow, Wally Davis, Dixon Doll, Robert Donnan, John Dougery, Judith Estrin, David Farber, Marc Friend, Samuel Fuller, Robert Galin, Jennifer Gill-Robertson, Maris Graube, Sonja Hoel, Richard Kramlich, David Liddle, Donald Loughry, Robert Love, David Mahoney, John Morgridge, Leo Nikora, Michael Pliner, Kanwal Rekhi, David Rodgers, Harry Saal, Jerome Saltzer, Howard Salwen, Jonathan Schmidt, Ronald Schmidt, William Seifert, Leonard Shustek, Larry Stephenson, Patricia Thaler, Donald Valentine, Andrew Verhalen, Paul Wythes, and especially Robert Metcalfe, Ralph Ungermann, Thomas Bredt, and James Swartz.

I also acknowledge Nathan MacBrien and Laura Comay of Stanford University Press. They provided superb editorial assistance and excellent suggestions as they transformed the original manuscript into this book. Their cheerful support made the final stage of this project a positive experience indeed.

Furthermore, I am grateful to the University of St. Gallen, Switzerland, my alma mater, and the University of California, Davis, where I spent most of my research time and whose hospitality I deeply appreciate. There, special thanks go to the fine staffs of Services for International Students and Scholars and the Department of Human and Community

Development, and to the many dedicated research assistants in Professor Martin Kenney's office, especially Kimmie Lee, Kalela McConnell, and Kimmy Pang.

Particular recognition goes to the Swiss National Science Foundation, which provided financial assistance for a significant part of this project at the outset. I also acknowledge the Sloan Foundation's grant to Martin Kenney for a study of the television and PC industries, which indirectly provided support.

On a more personal level, I recognize Jery and Chinh Le, who generously let me use their house in Davis during the week while making me part of their family on weekends. Furthermore, I thank the many friends I have made in Davis. There are too many to be named, but I acknowledge Andy Draper, John Bric, Tina Castillo, Sonja Streuber, Troy Carliss, Eric Hays, and Haeran Lim.

Among all those in Davis, my deepest gratitude, however, goes to Anne Liston, climbing partner and best friend. Anne naturally understood the situation of a foreign Ph.D. and was more than willing to share her life and circle of friends with me. Without her friendship, humor, encouraging words, and love for outdoor activities, I could not have gone through the many lonely hours of writing and rewriting the many drafts of this book.

In Switzerland, I recognize my sister, Esthi, and my friends Wilfried Oehry, Fredi Schmidli, and Rafael Stieger.

My greatest thanks, however, must go to four individuals without whose help I simply could not have finished the project. Martin Kenney, my adviser and sponsor at UC Davis, provided much guidance and inspiration. His unfailing advice and constant willingness to make time for discussions were unsurpassed. During these insightful and stimulating conversations, he became far more than an adviser—he became a good friend. Emilia Curtis crossed my path several times and continuously gave generous moral support. But, most important, my parents, Rolf and Vreni von Burg, showed extraordinary patience, provided much financial support, and believed in me far more than I ever did. To them I dedicate this work.

Abbreviations

AMD	Advanced Micro Devices Corporation
ANSI	American National Standards Institute
ARC	Attached Resource Computing
ARPA	(U.S. Department of Defense) Advanced Research Projects Agency
ATM	automatic teller machine
AUI	attached unit interface
CD	collision detection
CSMA/CD	Carrier Sense Multiple Access with Collision Detection
DEC	Digital Equipment Corporation
DIX	DEC, Intel, and Xerox
ECMA	European Computer Manufacturers Association
ENIAC	Electronic Numerical Integrator and Computer
ERA	Engineering Research Associates
FDDI	Fiber Distributed Data Interface
GI	General Instruments
H-P	Hewlett-Packard
IBM	International Business Machines Corporation
IC	integrated circuit
IEEE	Institute of Electrical and Electronic Engineers
IMP	interface message processor
IPTO	(ARPA) Information Processing Techniques Office
kbps	kilobits per second
LAN	local area network
MAN	metropolitan area network
MAU	multistation access unit
MAXC	Multiple Access Xerox Computer
Mbps	megabits per second
MCA	Multiprocessor Communications Adapter

MIS	management information system
MIT	Massachusetts Institute of Technology
MITS	Micro Instrumentation Telemetry Systems
NBS	National Bureau of Standards
NCR	National Cash Register Corporation
NEC	Nippon Electric Corporation
NOS	network operating system
OA	office automation
OEM	original equipment manufacturer
OSI	Open Systems Interconnection
PARC	(Xerox) Palo Alto Research Center
PBX	private branch exchange
PDP	Programmable Data Processor
PROWAY	process control data highway
PUP	PARC Universal Packet
RCA	Radio Corporation of America
SABRE	Semi-Automatic Business-Related Environment
SAGE	Semi-Automated Ground Environment
SIGnet	Simonyi's Infinitely Glorious Network
SMC	Standard Microsystems Corporation
SNA	Systems Network Architecture
STP	shielded twisted-pair
TCP/IP	Transmission Control Protocol/Internet Protocol
TI	Texas Instruments
U-B	Ungermann-Bass
UC	University of California
UTP	unshielded twisted-pair
VLSI	very-large-scale integration
WAN	wide area network
WWW	World Wide Web
XNS	Xerox Network System

The Triumph of Ethernet

Introduction

In 1978, Robert Metcalfe, the inventor of Ethernet, a local area networking technology for connecting computers to enable them to share information, quit his job at Xerox's Palo Alto Research Center (PARC). Xerox PARC was soon to become famous worldwide as the laboratory that spawned many of the important technological innovations that drove the rise of numerous Silicon Valley high-tech businesses. Eager to see Ethernet prosper beyond its implementation at PARC and dissatisfied with its slow commercial development by Xerox, Metcalfe left the research lab to become a consultant and to promote his invention.

Metcalfe soon signed on at MIT as a visiting researcher.[1] While there, he witnessed two early developments that would prove crucial in making his Ethernet technology the industry standard in the LAN marketplace. The first was the codification of Ethernet as an open technological standard. Its technical specifications would eventually be available to anyone who wanted to develop and sell products that would conform to them. Unlike a proprietary technology, which is kept under tight control by the firm responsible for its development in the interest of locking buyers in to that firm's products, an open standard would permit any firm that was willing to make the commitment to manufacture, sell, and resell hardware and software for Ethernet LANs.

The second development was even more significant. Around this open standard there began to grow a community of technology firms, entrepreneurial innovators, and venture capitalists. It was this community, as much as the potential inherent in the actual technology itself, that would in the end account for the triumph of Ethernet. The technology that Metcalfe had invented would prevail not just over various proprietary LAN technologies put forth by a variety of start-ups, but over the competing

Token Ring LAN technology developed by the International Business Machines Corporation (IBM).

While he was at MIT, Metcalfe tirelessly championed Ethernet, and he found a willing audience at nearby Digital Equipment Corporation (DEC). DEC had hired him as a consultant to evaluate its own LAN development.[2] In the late 1970s, the market for computers was divided into three principal classes: mainframes, the giant enterprise-wide computers whose chief supplier was IBM; minicomputers, newer, smaller, and with potentially many more sales and applications; and microcomputers, then largely the concern of hobbyists, but also the predecessors of today's desktop PCs. DEC, the world's leading vendor of minicomputers, and soon to be the second-largest computer manufacturer, needed a high-speed LAN for its forthcoming generation of VAX computers.[3] The VAX series, DEC's main product line throughout the 1980s, consisted of a wide range of compatible, though completely proprietary, computers that DEC intended to connect into clusters, forming a homogeneous, distributed computing environment.[4] Since these clusters made the individual minicomputers more powerful, DEC expected to gain leverage in its competition with the mainframes of IBM—its principal competitor and, with sales of $21.3 billion, also the unquestioned giant in the computer industry.[5]

Convinced of Ethernet's advantages, DEC initially considered developing an Ethernet-like network, but Xerox held the patent rights to the underlying Ethernet technology and DEC was worried about infringing on them. What could have been a dead end for Ethernet technology resulted instead in a development that ultimately gave the entrepreneurs, engineers, and firms who committed themselves to Ethernet technology a major competitive advantage over those who supported other LAN technologies: the opening of the Ethernet standard.

Metcalfe contended that compatibility was critical in the networking market and that companies should first collaborate in the creation of a standard, thus enlarging the marketplace before competing in it. So he suggested that DEC simply contact Xerox about licensing its Ethernet. DEC agreed, and in 1979 Metcalfe drafted a letter to David Liddle, the head of the Systems Development Division at Xerox PARC, in which DEC inquired about such a possibility.[6] In an unusual step for a company whose core business had been based on technology protected by patents, Liddle agreed to license Ethernet.[7] But he made it clear that he intended to open the technology not just to DEC, but to any firm interested in Xerox's LAN. As he explained in an interview with me, he intended to establish Ethernet as a standard, rather than to collect royalty fees. After some thought, DEC accepted this condition.[8]

Another major high-technology company, Intel, joined the alliance through a coincidence. In April 1979, while visiting the National Bureau of Standards (NBS), Metcalfe heard of a semiconductor engineer who had visited NBS the day before, talking about a high-speed chip and wondering what kind of local-net chips to build. Metcalfe tracked the engineer down at Intel and made an appointment to see him. In a meeting attended by forty Intel engineers and executives, Metcalfe presented the same argument that he had made at DEC.[9] Knowing that achieving high-volume production was the key in developing semiconductor technology, Intel's managers agreed with Metcalfe's argument and decided to join the effort to create an open technological standard for Ethernet. The result was what came to be known as the DIX alliance—for DEC, Intel, and Xerox.

The DIX group in turn soon realized that, as individual firms, they would be unable to produce all the necessary specialty hardware and software components and specialized semiconductors economically enough to drive down Ethernet's costs and effectively build Ethernet networks. They concluded that the best strategy would be to open the Ethernet standard to all comers, effectively outsourcing the manufacturing of many of these components by attracting third-party suppliers for whom designing and producing such components could be a viable business. Initially the three firms had planned to write the Ethernet specifications without inviting other firms and then to offer them as an industry standard. In 1980, however, the DIX group was forced to join the parallel standardization efforts undertaken by the Institute of Electrical and Electronics Engineers (IEEE); after long and intense debates Ethernet became one of the IEEE's LAN standards.

In 1979, the mere prospect of an open technological standard was enough to bring together a community of competing companies that were nevertheless united by their commitment to the success of Ethernet technology as the basis for a family of networking products. Metcalfe initially attempted to persuade two friends of his to establish a joint network company: Ralph Ungermann, the founder of Zilog, an early semiconductor start-up that was also working on Z-Net, a proprietary technology for networking microcomputers or small business computers, and Michael Pliner, who worked at Ford Aerospace and Communications Corporation in Silicon Valley, which had also experimented with LAN technology.[10] This plan never materialized, but while organizing the DIX alliance, on June 4, 1979, Metcalfe started his own firm, 3Com, in Menlo Park, California.[11] Through 3Com (which stands for "computer communication compatibility") Metcalfe intended to manufacture

Ethernet components for the DIX group and other end users and ultimately to establish his invention as the industry standard.

Only five weeks later, Ralph Ungermann made a similar move. On July 11, 1979, he and Charles Bass, who had previously worked with him at Zilog and who was also a good friend of Metcalfe's, established their company, Ungermann-Bass (U-B).[12] Metcalfe had started 3Com primarily to exploit his farsighted vision of networked microcomputers, but Ungermann and Bass had broader and yet more immediately focused interests.

Both had gained ample experience in data communications even before working on Zilog's Z-Net, and they were well aware of the many data communication problems plaguing large firms.[13] These problems resulted from the widespread incompatibility of the firms' computer equipment in terms of network speed and data format, which made it difficult to exchange data, as well as from the large number of terminals (often in the hundreds) that they needed to connect to a mainframe or minicomputer host and from the low throughput rate of the telephone lines used to make the connections. All of these limitations conspired to render the interconnection of hundreds of devices highly inefficient.[14] Eager to solve these problems, Ungermann and Bass decided to build "a company that focused strictly on building the network."[15] At that time, this was a revolutionary idea.

To avoid aggravating their customers' incompatibility problems, the two entrepreneurs decided to adopt the nascent Ethernet standard. Though the DIX group had not yet announced its plans, Ungermann recalls, he and Bass were very much "aware of what was going on" thanks to their friendship with Metcalfe, and "that was one of reasons we formed the company."[16] Having established firms devoted to Ethernet over a year before the DIX group released its specifications in 1980, Metcalfe, Ungermann, and Bass had launched the race for Ethernet's commercialization well before its official start.[17] This head start would allow theirs to become the leading Ethernet firms by the mid-1980s.

By founding their firms well before Ethernet's official release, Metcalfe, Ungermann, and Bass planted the seed for the later Ethernet supplier community. But very soon other firms were established as well, with the goal of manufacturing Ethernet components. In 1981 and 1982, three entrepreneurial teams left their employers and started their own firms: Interlan, Bridge Communications, and Excelan. They were encouraged by Ethernet's progressing de jure standardization at the IEEE and the opportunities that the DEC market offered. But they also took the step because they belonged to the tightly knit community of early Ethernet supporters. Some had been friends of Ungermann and Bass and had worked at Zilog, while others had been on Ethernet's development team at DEC. It was not long before DEC and Hewlett-Packard (H-P), as well as several semi-conductor manufacturers, began offering their first Ethernet products. Within a few years after the publication of its specifications as an open standard, Ethernet had attracted over two dozen suppliers—specialized LAN start-ups dedicated to the Ethernet business, semiconductor firms, and existing computer manufacturers—all producing parts for the system. It was by far the largest and most diversified supplier base that any technology had attracted up to that time.

This large supplier base proved quite beneficial for the evolution of the Ethernet technology. Thanks to its broad supplier support, Ethernet enjoyed the benefits of ongoing steep price declines as the existence of so many suppliers created intense competitive pressure. Ethernet also enjoyed the benefits of the highest innovation rates in the LAN business, because innovation was one of the principal ways by which suppliers could at least temporarily escape the competitive pressure to lower prices. The large number of Ethernet suppliers produced an unequaled variety of products because many firms could easily specialize in certain parts of the system, relying on others to offer complementary components. And Ethernet's large supplier base gave it a comparably large base of distributors, thereby increasing its market reach. Not surprisingly, these technical, market, and price advantages made Ethernet attractive to end users, and as more and more users adopted Ethernet, the technology's increasing market size in turn made it even more attractive to manufacturers and distributors of network components.

But Ethernet was not the only technology on the market. While a wave of entrepreneurs had started firms dedicated to the Ethernet standard, an even larger number had started companies that produced proprietary LANs. One of these start-ups was Corvus. Located in Silicon Valley, Corvus was established by Michael D'Addio during the West Coast Computer Fair in May 1979 and was a supplier of some of the first hard disk storage systems for the Apple II.[18] Unlike today's hard disks, his were not integrated within the computer, but were configured as external devices comparable to a server. Since Corvus storage systems cost $5,000, whereas the microcomputers to which they were connected ranged in price between $1,000 and $2,000, customers demanded the means to share a hard disk among several microcomputers; in response, in late 1979 and early 1980, Corvus developed a LAN called CONSTELLATION.[19] But the CONSTELLATION network was obsolete almost from its debut, and Corvus immediately began looking for an alternative.[20] The disk vendor considered the recently released Ethernet standard. But Ethernet's boards were too large to fit into an Apple II, and its price per node was too high for the most popular microcomputer at that time.[21] So Corvus decided to develop a second proprietary LAN, Omninet, which it introduced in May 1981.[22] The more powerful Omninet was soon to become one of Ethernet's fiercest competitors in the PC LAN market.[23]

Omninet had technical features that were similar to Ethernet's, but to meet the tight cost restrictions in the Apple II market, it included several technical compromises that gave it a major price advantage. In 1981 an Omninet adapter cost only $495, compared with $3,000–$4,000 for an Ethernet minicomputer board; thus Omninet rapidly penetrated the Apple LAN market while Ethernet remained excluded for reasons of price and size.[24] Because the IBM PC, which soon became the standard in the microcomputer market, would require network characteristics similar to those of the Apple II, Corvus was well positioned to conquer the PC LAN market, which was to emerge with the introduction of the IBM PC.

It didn't happen. Instead Corvus was one of the first makers of proprietary LANs to fall, as Ethernet began its rise. There were firm-specific reasons for its demise, but the more systemic reason it lost its competitive opportunity was its failure to develop a strong technological community to support it. Corvus had licensed its proprietary technology to interested firms, so despite the large number of firms involved with Omninet— approximately thirty in 1985—the Omninet "community" was not so much a community as a group of opportunistically associated enterprises. It primarily consisted of licensees, original equipment manufacturer (OEM) dealers, resellers, and second-rank PC clone makers.[25] These firms were neither independent innovators nor technological contributors, but merely passive adopters of Omninet. Since their core businesses did not depend on LAN technology, they had few incentives to make asset-specific investments in the form of innovations, and thus they developed only weak ties to Omninet. As a result, they could easily switch to a different technology when Omninet ceased to serve their interests—and they did.

Corvus was not the only proprietary LAN vendor to disappear. The other proprietary networking technologies, including those produced by Sytek and Proteon, among many others, failed as well despite some initial advantages over Ethernet. The underlying reason for their disappearance, as this book explains at length, was their failure to attract similarly large supplier communities. The earliest networking firms, which had entered the field before the establishment of the open standard for Ethernet, as well as those that marketed advanced proprietary LANs, all suffered from the absence or relatively small size of the technological communities that might have supported and promoted them. As a result, they could not keep pace with Ethernet's steep price declines and rapid technological progress.

Even developing another supposedly open technological standard that competed with the Ethernet standard was not enough to enable those who backed the competing technology to prevail in the absence of a large and vital technological community. As we will see, IBM was able to insist that the IEEE create a standard for its Token Ring LAN technology in addition to the Ethernet standard that the IEEE had promulgated. But whereas Token Ring was supposedly an open standard, IBM did what it could to retain proprietary control over its development, and these efforts interfered with the formation of a robust technological community.

Such a community must be nurtured and constructed. It requires an unconditional commitment to full interoperability by its principal proponents, as well as an absence of monopolistic control and the opportunity for many firms to build a profitable business. DEC and Xerox, Ethernet's main proponents in the early 1980s, pursued such a community-friendly strategy from the beginning. They were committed to attracting suppliers and did not intend to monopolize the Ethernet market. In fact, both provided a market for start-ups, both purchased components from the fledgling Ethernet start-ups, and both licensed their technology. As a result of their endeavoring to nurture a supplier community, both firms lost their leadership in the marketplace rather quickly, but the technology they promoted ultimately became not just a technological, de jure standard— a set of specifications established by the IEEE—but the dominant technology in the marketplace—the de facto industry standard as well.

IBM, in contrast, had a more "selfish" plan for making its Token Ring the industry standard. From the outset, IBM undermined the rise of a Token Ring community by controlling the chip supply and manipulating the interoperability of its products. Instead of nurturing a supplier community and winning the standardization race, IBM preferred to reap high profits by controlling the market and avoiding the tendency toward commodification that plagued the Ethernet suppliers. This strategy was viable as long as IBM could claim that Token Ring was technologically superior to Ethernet, but the vitality of the Ethernet community, and the inability of IBM to respond quickly enough to that community's capacity for finding rapid solutions to Ethernet's technological shortcomings, meant that Token Ring soon lost its technological edge. In the long run, the Ethernet community was able to prevail even over the efforts of IBM.

None of this was supposed to happen. The success of Ethernet as a LAN technology in becoming a marketplace standard ran contrary to the conventional wisdom of the time, which strongly favored keeping technological innovations proprietary in order to derive as much profit as possible from them, rather than sharing them with other firms. It also runs contrary to much of what current standardization theory suggests should happen to innovating firms when technological standards become industry-wide standards as well. This book examines what the creation of open standards in the LAN industry and the creation of technological communities that they enable can tell us about the ways in which social structures, as well as technological innovations, contribute to or hinder the success of high-technology firms.

The Economic Theory of Standardization

Battles between technologies to become industry standards are not a recent phenomenon. At the end of the nineteenth century and the beginning of the twentieth, significant standardization battles occurred among different firms and technologies in electric power and telephone systems. Despite the wide-reaching roles of these two technologies and the clear dominance of the winning technology and firm, economists did not develop an explicit theory of standardization until their attention was drawn to the prominent standardization battles in video systems and PCs in the late 1970s and early 1980s. What fascinated them was the fact that in all these cases, a single system had emerged as the market-dominant winner, even though it did not possess overwhelming techno-logical advantages. In fact, in some instances, an inferior technology had prevailed.

These winner-take-all outcomes seemed at odds with the neoclassical theory based on constant or decreasing rates of return. Under these con-ditions, the ascendancy of a technology would have been slowed and even stopped by growing diseconomies of scale, and a market equilib-rium with several technologies would have been more likely. As a result, several economists began developing models that could explain such an unusual outcome. In the process, they created an economic theory of standardization.

"TIPPING" AND LOCK-INS

In the course of their studies, economists found that the technolo-gies whose standardization they studied had distinct characteristics. They were all networks—that is, product systems that interlink components and/or users, either directly, like the telephone network, or indirectly, via the supply of complementary components, such as videocassettes and VCRs, or PC hardware and software.[26] Unlike non-network goods— such as those produced by, say, the furniture or automobile industries— networks entail network externalities in the sense that "the actions of a market participant affect others without compensation being paid." Externalities can be negative or positive (water pollution by a factory, for instance, often adversely affects anglers downstream), but fortunately, where networks are concerned, the externalities are typically positive.[27] In other words, when a user joins a network, her adoption creates positive effects to the incumbent users.[28]

In direct communication networks, positive network externalities result from the direct linkage between users. If new users connect to the telephone network, all existing users benefit without having to make payments to the new users because they can now dial a greater number of individuals or organizations. In indirect, software/hardware-based networks, however, positive network externalities arise through a market-mediated process. As new users join the virtual network, more complementary goods (software applications, for instance) will be developed and become available to all users adhering to that platform.[29] Most conventional goods, by contrast, do not exhibit externalities. If someone else purchases a table, I do not benefit.

Externalities are not unique to networks. They underlie many pollution phenomena, for example. But in networks, externalities take on an unusual twist. As new users join the network, it is usually assumed that its value increases not just proportionately, but exponentially. In other words, the value of a network with, say, two million users is far greater than double that of a network with, say, one million.[30] All things being equal, this means that being connected to a bigger network is better than being connected to a small one.[31] This attribute has been called by many names, but the terms "increasing rates of return" or Metcalfe's Law are most commonly used.[32]

The concept of increasing rates of return leads directly to the principal explanation for industry-wide standardization. According to standardization theory, if several network technologies compete, a single winner is likely to emerge because as a network becomes larger and exponentially more beneficial, positive feedback mechanisms kick in, with the result that the leading network drives out smaller rivals. Economists call these positive feedback mechanisms "network effects." The leading technology attracts an ever-increasing number of adopters, which prompts manufacturers to increase the production of complementary goods. The users' and manufacturers' adoption of the technology makes it even more attractive, setting in motion a virtuous circle of increasing adoption and an increasing supply of complementary goods, thereby solidifying the leading technology's value and nurturing its continuing success in the marketplace. Rivals lose their attractiveness and their shares of the market by means of a vicious circle that is the mirror image of the process

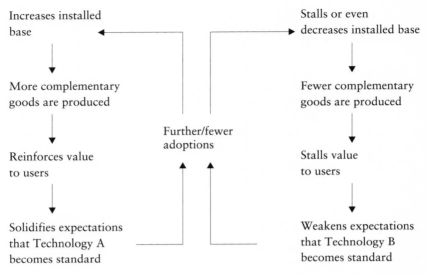

FIGURE I.1   Increasing rates of return, or virtuous and vicious circles. (Adapted from Grindley 1995: 27.)

that brings success to the increasingly dominant technology. Eventually, in economists' parlance, the entire market "tips" toward the leading technology, which finally becomes dominant, setting the standard for the industry.[33] Thus, according to standardization theory, by magnifying an initial lead, the increasing rates of return and the feedback mechanisms inherent in networks make it likely that a single winner will arise when several incompatible technologies compete (figure I.1).[34]

Such "tipping" clearly occurred in PCs and video systems. Once the IBM PC and JVC's VHS system had gained an initial lead in number of users and complementary goods over their rivals—the microcomputers of Apple and the Beta system of Sony, respectively—a self-reinforcing process cemented that lead. As a result, the market "tipped" almost completely toward the leading PC and VHS systems.[35] Occasionally—very occasionally—"tipping" may be prevented. This can occur if "consumers care more about product attributes than about network size," for example.[36] Consumer differences and consumers with strong preferences based on product differentiation may sustain an equilibrium with several networks.[37] This clearly worked in favor of the relatively small network formed around Apple's Macintosh computers, which prospered throughout the 1980s partly because a minority of computer users cherished the Macintosh's user-friendly interface, a feature that Microsoft's DOS operating system did not provide.

Economists also found that these self-reinforcing processes are subject to much unpredictable, external influence and can lead to troublesome outcomes. "Tipping" is very sensitive to small events at the outset, the architects of standardization theory claim, because of the amplifying power of network effects.[38] Because small events are often of random origin, standardization becomes unpredictable and unstable at the outset of the process, and early adopters carry disproportionate weight in the selection of the standard. Their adoption may suffice to trigger a self-reinforcing process and convince other users to jump on the bandwagon. Moreover, standardization battles are frequently won or lost in the early period because of the pivotal role of small events. Once a network has gained a certain momentum, countermeasures at a later time may be in vain or too costly to stop the momentum of a virtuous circle. The pivotal role of small events also creates path dependence "in the sense that the 'emergent standard' depends on the details of the historical sequence in which individual choices occurred, that is, on the path the adoption took," as Paul David and Shane Greenstein put it.[39] Put differently, in an environment in which small events can make a big difference, the sequence in which they occur matters.

Finally, the "tipping" mechanism risks selecting an inferior technology as the standard. A technology does not need to be superior to take over the market.[40] Because the benefits of a large network often exceed those created by technological advantages by several orders of magnitude, an inferior technology may succeed in "tipping" the market if it has a sufficient first-mover advantage, allowing it to initiate a virtuous circle.

Even worse, once any technology has "tipped" the market, its reign may persist. The market "locks in," as economists say.[41] This occurs because of the prohibitive costs of switching from the incumbent network, with its huge network effects, to a superior technology without a large installed base and without an abundant supply of complementary goods. Because users forgo the adoption of the fledgling newcomer, it cannot generate a virtuous circle of adoption, price reductions, production of complementary goods, and innovation. This locks out the superior newcomer and cements the reign of the inferior incumbent.[42]

Because of their lesser sophistication, inferior technologies have a systematic advantage in reaching the market ahead of more advanced technologies, which require more time to be developed. In addition, the dominance of a single standard in so many network technologies—ranging from PCs and video systems to telephones, electrical supply, Internet protocols, and stereo systems—indicates the overwhelming power of net-work effects.[43] Such effects might allow a mildly inferior technology to lock out a mildly superior newcomer. In fact, a rule of thumb among ven-ture capitalists suggests that the replacing technology should be five to ten times better than the entrenched technology or else offer a compelling new feature.[44] Besides, high transaction costs may make it prohibitively expensive to coordinate the move to a superior standard with only minor technological advantages. Arguably, the possibility of a long-term lock-in to an inferior technology is standardization theory's strongest, as well as most pessimistic, claim.

PROPRIETARY STANDARDS VERSUS OPEN STANDARDS

In pursuit of a way to lock in their products at the time LANs first began to appear, many technology companies followed what at the time seemed to be the ultimate lock-in strategy: they made their technology proprietary. Proprietariness allows the vendor of a network technology to extract monopoly rents because of the switching costs users face once they have invested in a proprietary system.[45] In fact, if users want to switch to a different system, they would not only have to bear the costs of purchasing the new system but also lose any previous hardware invest-ment that might not yet have been written off. What is more, since the two systems are incompatible, users would also lose previous investments in complementary goods—such as data, software, and human training—while having to pay for employee retraining and software conversion.[46] As a result, once a user has invested in a proprietary network, the user remains locked into the system, with the consequence that the supplier gains considerable market power for any later upgrades and repeat pur-chases.[47] Worse, if the vendor succeeds in "tipping" the entire market, the resulting lock-in stifles competition and innovation while exacerbat-ing the exploitation of users.

Keeping a technology proprietary also allows for strategic actions aimed at rapidly enlarging the installed base of its network to ignite "tip-ping" while simultaneously retarding the network growth of rivals.[48] The proprietary owner may expedite product launches to preempt successful commercialization by its rivals, or it may lure consumers by means of aggressive pricing and subsidizing early adopters.[49] In addition, the owner may make preannouncements to influence users' expectations in its favor. Vendors often deploy this strategy when they are unable to deliver products and want to discourage users from purchasing a competitor's product.[50] This tactic is rampant in the computer industry, given its manifold network effects.[51]

To be sure, a completely proprietary strategy presents problems for the firm that uses it. To offer a proprietary system, a firm is obliged to undertake extensive investments, since it cannot rely on third-party vendors for the supply of complementary goods. The provision of an entire network consisting of many hardware and software components can overburden the vendor financially, especially if it has to cross-subsidize unprofitable components. Also, since users attempt to avoid a disadvantageous lock-in, a proprietary network may remain small, thereby preventing economies of scale and increasing the costs of components. Finally, fierce competition for future monopoly rents may dissipate these very profits.[52] These drawbacks reduce the appeal of a completely proprietary strategy, but from a theoretical point of view the big prize of a successful proprietary standard remains tempting. In the heyday of its domination of the mainframe computer business, IBM provided a glowing example of the benefits accruing to making technologies proprietary, and many firms sought to emulate its success by pursuing this tactic.

A variation of the proprietary strategy that effectively overcomes some of its weaknesses is the less monopolistically oriented strategy of sponsoring a new technology. As we will see in more detail, it was this strategy that IBM ultimately pursued in the market fight to make its Token Ring technology the LAN standard. In this strategy, as in the case of the proprietary strategy, the sponsoring firm upholds its ownership rights over the technology and thus can take certain strategic actions. But in contrast to the proprietary vendor, the sponsor licenses its technology. The goal of this strategy is not so much to give access to the technology to competitors as to increase the number of suppliers of complementary goods and so exacerbate network effects. It was this strategy that made Microsoft so successful. While Microsoft continued to keep tight control over the PC software market, the licensing of its operating system attracted a myriad of hardware makers that fiercely competed with each other and in the process made the PC system very attractive. Not accidentally, the share of software costs continued to rise over the PC's life cycle.[53]

Finally, instead of pursuing the strategy of proprietariness, with or without the variations on that strategy provided by sponsorship, a firm may decide that the theoretical benefits of adhering to an open technological standard for its products outweigh the apparent competitive drawbacks. From the point of view of the user, the benefits of an open standard are clear. In direct communication networks, the compatibility between products that an open standard provides means that users can communicate with a greater number of other users without having to duplicate equipment or purchase gateways. In indirect, hardware/software-based networks, it means that users can choose from a larger pool of software. In addition, openness intensifies price competition because it relaxes the potential monopoly lock enjoyed by the proprietary vendor. Thus most users prefer compatibility or openness to proprietariness. A compatible or open system is therefore likely to emerge if users have greater market power than vendors.[54]

The incentives pushing vendors toward openness or compatibility are more ambiguous. Compatibility relieves a vendor from the burden of having to develop the entire system, since the firm can now rely on other vendors for the supply of complementary products. Compatibility also enlarges a firm's market, since the combined network attracts additional users and ignites network effects, an outcome that benefits competitive vendors.[55] Some have even argued that compatibility increases users' willingness to pay for constituent components and hence augments vendors' profits.[56] However, compatibility forces vendors to give up the substantial monopoly profits discussed previously.

From a theoretical perspective, whether firms prefer compatibility and openness to proprietariness depends mainly on the conditions they initially face in the market.[57] The firm with the smaller network will be more likely to prefer compatibility with the larger rival, who in turn will be likely to oppose such openness. By tapping into the larger rival's network, the smaller firm can significantly increase the value of its own network. In contrast, the addition of a small network does not compensate the large vendor sufficiently for the erosion of its profits under the increased competition of an open system. Consequently, with increasingly equal initial conditions, the vendors will more likely agree on compatibility.[58] In this case, they need to decide whose technology to adopt. If the vendors' vested interest in their technology is low, they will coordinate their actions without much friction. But if the vendors have a high vested interest in their technology, then the outcome takes the form of a "battle-of-the-sexes" game.[59] In this case, the outcome depends on the relative power of the contestants.

Because the outcomes depend on particular and contingent conditions, standardization theory provides no general answer to the question whether firms ought to prefer proprietariness to compatibility or openness.[60] One might argue that, at least in theory, the potentially huge profits of a successful proprietary system wielded by a large firm appear to outweigh the compatibility benefits to vendors. Repeated attempts by Apple and IBM to replace the open Apple II and PC, respectively, with more proprietary computers, such as the Lisa, Macintosh, and PS/2, underline the firms' strong, continuous penchant for proprietariness. In addition, the erection of some proprietary "toll roads" remains a crucial business strategy of many high-tech start-ups in Silicon Valley.

But the actual answer also depends on the historical context. Historically, proprietary standards succeeded when no open systems competed with them in the marketplace. Thus, in the early history of computing, proprietary systems dominated. Throughout the 1960s and 1970s, most vendors, including IBM, DEC, and Wang, offered vertically integrated, proprietary packages attempting to capture the lock-in benefits that the proprietary strategy seems to promise.[61] Deprived of any open alternatives, users had little choice but to purchase such systems. Since the mid-1980s, however, the computer market has increasingly shifted toward open systems.[62] Under the pioneering leadership of Sun Microsystems, computer manufacturers began using openness as a competitive weapon to lure users away from proprietary rivals.[63] Once offered open alternatives, users insisted on openness as a purchase criterion, and they now avoid proprietary systems that fail to provide compelling advantages. Ethernet, PC hardware, and Unix are some of the principal examples of the way in which open systems have advantages in the high-technology marketplace over proprietary and sponsored technologies. The economic theory of standards therefore must take this phenomenon into account.

MORE SHORTCOMINGS AND UNANSWERED QUESTIONS

In 1981, when IBM introduced its PC, Apple appeared already to have "tipped" the market. The Apple II had about 15,000 to 16,000 applications available, and with 171,000 units sold in 1981, amounting to a global market share of 20 percent, it clearly outnumbered the 20,000 PCs shipped in the same period.[64] But, as we know today, within a few years the IBM PC replaced Apple as the dominant technology in personal computing. Apple lost its appeal when it abandoned the Apple II's openness and migrated to the more proprietary successor models Lisa and Macintosh.[65] This strategy not only contracted the third-party supply of complementary goods such as peripherals and software, it also coincided with IBM's open-PC strategy, which attracted myriad peripheral and software suppliers, as well as clone makers. In addition, IBM addressed the vast business market, a market that Apple had not tapped at that time.[66]

Standardization theory, however, fails to identify the thresholds of "tipping" and lock-ins, either in this case or in general. Nor does it, in large measure, address the issue of which technological or market discontinuities (such as the appearance of new technologies and new products) unravel a possible lock-in, or, more generally, which factors terminate a lock-in. These questions are critical to understanding why Ethernet succeeded in becoming the standard despite the earlier market entry of some propriety LANs and their domination of certain market niches.

The impact of technological and market discontinuities on firm success has been intensively examined by the dominant-design theory.[67] Several of its adherents have pointed to the devastating effects of certain technological discontinuities. One could therefore assume that such discontinuities might mitigate, or even terminate, lock-in. But in large measure, the dominant-design model has not addressed what happens when such discontinuities occur under the conditions governing high-tech communications firms such as those in the LAN industry—the conditions of network externalities and increasing rates of return.[68] Hence it remains an open question whether the benefits of a large, well-accepted network protect it from the technological discontinuities that such innovations can cause. The early LAN market was tiny compared with its final size, and small initial advantages did not matter; this situation allowed latecomers to catch up. But as we will see, technological and market discontinuities indeed affected LAN standardization, ending the life cycle of some technologies abruptly while favoring those that could more easily adapt.

Standardization theory also leaves unanswered some issues that arise from various idiosyncrasies of LAN technology, which deviate from the rigorous assumptions undergirding existing standardization theory. These deviations question the explanatory power of the conventional economic theory for comprehending LAN standardization, and beyond that, for comprehending the dynamics behind the economic development of other emerging technologies that share LAN's characteristics—for example, as we will eventually see, the Linux operating system. Standardization theory often assumes quite implicitly that network technologies are prone to great "tippiness." A small lead, as well as mere expectations about the final outcome and other mechanisms honed to influence adopters' expectations, such as preannouncements, often suffice to trigger "tipping," in quite the same way as a small snowball can lead to an unstoppable avalanche.

Technically, the great impact from such small events results from the theory's assumption of strong network externalities. Clearly, LAN technology gave rise to network effects from the LAN's direct linkage of users, as well as from the various intra-technological, complementary components of LAN technology, including boards, transceivers, adapters, hubs, repeaters, local and remote bridges, and routers. In addition, network effects could result from the various additional complementary goods on which LANs depended. For instance, the LAN had to interoperate with the computer and network operating system (NOS) or file server software. An additional complementary relationship resulted from the cabling, because LANs typically require exact and specified wires for proper transmission. Though these complementary relationships indeed created network effects, the effects were rather small in some instances, at least initially. In contrast to the telephone or power networks, which span hundreds of miles and connect hundreds of thousands or even millions of users, the early LANs often connected fewer than a dozen users, as they were installed merely to share an expensive hard disk or laser printer in an office. What is more, only a few LANs were interconnected in the early 1980s when such networks were first installed. Network externalities from this source increased only in the late 1980s as the size of the LANs grew and corporations began to interconnect their various LANs. Similarly, NOS or file server software failed to create network effects, because Novell, the leading supplier of such systems, made its software compatible with any LAN type, thereby neutralizing the competitive effect it would have had if it had supported only specific LAN types.

One may then ask to what extent these idiosyncrasies alter the standardization process. The theory gives little guidance, but hypothetically one could argue that they soften or annihilate "tipping" effects, first-mover advantages, and the importance of small events. By the same token, one could expect that such softening might increase the role of manufacturing and traditional cost-based strategies in the standardization of LANs. The empirical research on standardization of PCs and video recorders suggests that the alleged role of expectations and small events may indeed be exaggerated. Although adopters' expectations contributed to the victory of the IBM PC and JVC's VHS system, mass adoption occurred only *after* the suppliers had manufactured their technologies and the advantages had unfolded.[69] For instance, consumers abandoned Beta only when VHS offered longer playing time and a greater variety of prerecorded tapes.[70] In other words, actual delivery, rather than promises and expectations, prompted users to opt for a particular system. Most theoreticians would not refute this claim, but they would insist that the actual delivery of promised advantages is not a necessary condition to lure adopters. Expectations may suffice.

This contradiction in emphasis touches on the issue of the role of manufacturing in standardization, as opposed to that of adopters' expectations. It raises the question to what extent mere beliefs can outweigh actual advantages, such as a cost advantage achieved by more efficient manufacturing methods and economies of scale. If traditional cost advantages do not play an important role, then "tipping" may indeed be the typical process of standardization, but if traditional cost and product advantages are critical in the adoption decisions of users, markets might be less "tippy" than standardization theory suggests. It certainly was the case that Ethernet's actual, realized price and technological advantages far outweighed the small leads of its contenders and proved far more important for its adoption than any favorable expectations that emerged from its standardization by the IEEE.

Moreover, standardization theory does not adequately account for the power of open systems or standards, especially the dynamics that occur on the supply side. The economic theory of standards reduces a standardization battle to the skirmish of two strategically acting firms. As a result, the theory's models fail to recognize the powerful momentum that develops when a community of dozens or even hundreds of suppliers unites to exploit a particular standard.

Indeed, standardization theory has not yet come to terms with the dynamism that open systems can create when technological communities form around them. Richard Langlois, for example, found that the PC's openness developed a market momentum that no single firm could match. The PC's openness as a technological standard engendered a vigorous, competitive system that attracted myriad component suppliers and clone makers, led to vast specialization economies, and reduced prices dramatically, all the while amplifying market size by several orders of magnitude. The hundreds of peripheral makers, software writers, and clone manufacturers nurtured a self-reinforcing process—an irresistible force that overwhelmed its proprietary rivals, especially Apple.[71] Although video technology did not evolve as rapidly as PCs, a study conducted by Michael Cusumano and his colleagues draws a similar picture.[72] By attracting a greater number of suppliers, the more open VHS standard quickly defeated Sony's more proprietary Beta system.[73] Economic theory has failed not only to capture this dynamism but also to develop a theoretical model of such technological communities and open systems.

Without such a model, the theory does not allow us to compare the different supply structures of different standards: open, multifirm standards such as the PC's or Ethernet's, completely proprietary technologies such as Apple's operating system, and proprietary but licensed standards such as Microsoft's Windows. Hence we do not know from a theoretical perspective which supply structure gives those who support different standards the advantage in standardization battles. In view of the continuous struggle between the proponents of proprietary, vertically integrated, and open systems, a theoretical model for such comparative analyses would be helpful. Such a model should predict under what circumstances one of these supply structures would prevail over the other forms. If the model proved that one supply structure entailed an inherent competitive advantage, this could have implications for a firm's standardization strategy.

Above all, despite the accumulating body of work on the role of sociological factors in the development of technological innovations, standardization theory has turned a blind eye to the social forces shaping standardization and to the phenomenon of a technological community forming around a standard. (An exception is the work of James Wade.)[74] As mentioned, economic theory sees standardization as a relatively mechanistic process of virtuous and vicious circles, thereby neglecting the fact that standardization is ultimately a very social process. In fact, users as well as manufacturers must agree on a commonly shared technology. In the real world, such agreements require a great deal of social interaction, through which differences are resolved and supporters are won. In fact, it is a commonly observed phenomenon that successful standards are promoted by a hard-core group of individuals and companies before they attract a large following of specialized manufacturers, industry associations, and user groups—all supporting and nurturing the technology.

This myopia closely correlates with the theory's neglect of the dynamism of open systems. By condensing standardization to a conflict between two strategically acting firms, the economic theory of standardization ignores the influence of a supplier community and the many interactions within it. Hence the question of what role a community of individuals and companies plays in standardization completely lacks a theoretical answer. This book begins to lay some of the groundwork for answering that question, as well as the other questions on which standardization theory has until now remained silent.

A Brief Outline of This Book

To understand the role of a technological community and the different structures of such communities, the theoretical concept of a technological community is developed in the first chapter. Based on different degrees of openness and proprietariness, different community structures are identified and then compared by using the recently developed "capability" approach of strategic management. It is found that under ideal conditions, open technologies indeed entail a systematic advantage over proprietary and sponsored technologies, not just on the demand side but also on the supply side.

This discussion is followed by an economic history of the development of the LAN industry between the early 1970s, when the first LANs were developed, and the mid-1990s, when the standardization process came to an end and a fast-growing, multibillion-dollar networking industry was established. In the early 1970s nothing predicted this dynamism. Networks were not yet an integral part of computing technology, and the level of network activities was still modest. Many of the first and most important early networks were one-time projects funded by the U.S. government, while the commercial (wide area) networks were too few to trigger a commercial boom and the creation of many firms. In addition, LAN technology was a relatively late network development; the first LANs were developed by university professors and researchers, often as by-products of distributed computing systems. Chapter 2 describes this precommercial phase of network development, occurring in the 1960s and 1970s. It conceptualizes the early network developments within the evolution of computing and gives a brief overview of the network developments preceding LANs. Its main focus, however, is on the invention and precommercial evolution of Ethernet and token ring technology, the earliest invented LAN technologies and the principal rivals in the marketplace. Despite some technological differences neither had gained a clear (technological) edge by the end of the 1970s. Hence the precommercial stage left ample space for market forces, business strategies, and random events to determine the outcome of later competition.

In the late 1970s and early 1980s, several firms began rushing their own LAN technologies to market. Among the early market entrants were Network Systems, a specialized start-up offering a high-end network for mainframes and corporate data centers; Zilog, a microprocessor manufacturer pursuing an ambitious strategy of forward integration; Nestar, a specialized LAN start-up addressing the novel Apple II market; and Datapoint, an innovative midsize computer manufacturer. According to standardization theory, their head start should have given these pioneers a significant advantage in the race for a LAN standard, but in reality their early entry into the market disadvantaged rather than advantaged them. Entering a nonexistent market, they were quickly overburdened with too many of the tasks that inevitably fall to industry pioneers, while being exposed to the myriad shifts in the computer market in the early 1980s. As a result, with the exception of Datapoint, they quickly fell away. This earliest stage in the commercialization of the novel LAN technology is analyzed in chapter 3.

Network Systems, Zilog, Nestar, and Datapoint were not the only firms to see the business opportunities created by the novel technology.

In fact, numerous entrepreneurs were also about to establish start-ups, while most computer manufacturers were preparing for the commercialization of LAN technology as a means for achieving connectivity among their machines. In the late 1970s, a few forward-looking individuals realized the necessity of creating standards if widespread communication chaos was to be avoided. Their foresight produced two independent standardization initiatives, one led by the DIX group and the other by the IEEE. Though the two initiatives were later united, the participating firms failed to create a single standard. Instead, they created three: Ethernet, Token Ring, and Token Bus. Chapter 4 examines these standardization efforts and focuses on two issues: (1) the reasons most incumbent computer manufacturers joined the efforts to create an open standard despite their earlier proprietary strategies in computing, and (2) their inability to agree on a single standard, apparently contradicting their stated desire for openness and compatibility.

Ethernet's standardization quickly attracted numerous manufacturers of Ethernet components. As chapter 5 recounts, many of these suppliers were established semiconductor firms and computer manufacturers adopting the open Ethernet technology, such as DEC and H-P. But the most important catalysts in jumpstarting the Ethernet community were the specialized start-ups, such as 3Com, established by Robert Metcalfe, or U-B, established by his friends Ralph Ungermann and Charles Bass. They not only expedited Ethernet's market introduction and improved it technologically, but also widened the product variety and introduced it from the initial minicomputer market to the PC market, thereby prolonging the life span of the technology. The chapter further examines the various interactions and synergies among the Ethernet suppliers and concludes that by the mid-1980s Ethernet had gained a substantial supplier community. This positioned Ethernet well in the standards race.

But, as already mentioned, in the early 1980s Ethernet was not the only technology offered on the market; various additional start-ups—including Corvus, as well as Sytek, Proteon, and Datapoint—had emerged as strong contenders. Many challenged Ethernet and its supporters by offering (proprietary) LANs that were either less expensive or more capable in some respects than the leader. Hence they could penetrate market segments that Ethernet was unable to serve. Yet despite considerable initial success, the proprietary LANs all waned in the mid- to late 1980s. Many failed for quite idiosyncratic reasons, such as strategic blunders or the financial problems of their sponsors, but the underlying reason for their failure must be seen as their inability to attract a strong supplier base. Without such a base, they could not keep pace with Ethernet's relentless price reductions and continuously expanding product variety. The rise and fall of Ethernet's proprietary contenders is examined in chapter 6.

The following chapter discusses the final stage in the standardization battle: the competition between Ethernet and Token Ring. It begins with an analysis of the competitive situation at the outset of the battle and then proceeds to analyze the reasons for Ethernet's victory and Token Ring's defeat. It describes how the Ethernet community, under the leadership of a new start-up, SynOptics, fixed Ethernet's gravest technical shortcomings, thereby catching up with Token Ring technologically. Once Ethernet had closed the technology gap, Token Ring came under great pressure to close its price gap. But because IBM's power over the Token Ring standard retarded the emergence of a competitive supplier community, Token Ring's prices remained significantly higher than those of Ethernet. Unable to close the price gap and falling behind technologically, Token Ring could not avoid lapsing far behind Ethernet in its installed base, especially with the completion of the networking of the millions of PCs in the corporate sector.

The final chapter draws lessons from Ethernet's victory for contemporary standardization battles. In particular, it compares the Ethernet story with the initial development of the Linux technology. Whether these two technologies will indeed gain significant momentum is still unclear, but the chapter shows that the sponsors of the two emerging standards have applied the lessons of the early, community-based Ethernet supporters quite well.

1 Technological Communities and Open Standards

It is a commonplace that the high-tech businesses of Silicon Valley succeed or fail in an atmosphere of intense, unremitting cutthroat competition. But there is more involved in the ways that these firms pursue success than simple competitive rivalry. In the early 1980s, for example, Ronald Crane, an innovative engineer at 3Com who helped that company realize Robert Metcalfe's vision of networking desktop PCs, would frequently assist engineers at competing firms to implement the Ethernet standard in their products. He could do so because he, the engineers he assisted, and the firms for whom they all worked were more than just competitors. They also were members of a technological community.

"We [at 3Com] saw our growth linked to the growth of Ethernet as a whole, and anything that made Ethernet look bad would hurt us," Crane explained. "So, it was in our interest that all of our competitors at least got their interfaces right so that the standards worked out. If the rest of their products failed, that was fine, but we did not want their product to fail because Ethernet failed."[1] As a result of such collaboration and information sharing, the Ethernet community was not just a techno-economic phenomenon based on the competing firms' adherence to a technological standard. It was also a social phenomenon because of the dense web of personal and business interactions that grew up around that standard.

A technological community includes all those firms, organizations, and individuals that are directly or indirectly involved in the development, manufacturing, and distribution of a particular technology or standard. It thus is the social matrix within which a technology or standard is embedded, and the community's economic, social, cultural, and political forces shape the technology's evolution. Depending on the specific technology, the participating organizations may vary significantly, and they may include not just manufacturers, suppliers, and resellers, but also standards-setting bodies, universities, and professional organizations.

A technological community is not just an aggregation of firms, organizations, and individuals attracted by self-interest to the same technology or standard, however. As is the case with other communities, from neighborhoods to small towns to large cities, technological communities are cemented by allegiances, strong or weak, to a common ethos or identity, to common standards or values, and to common ends—allegiances held by people who interact and communicate to develop and benefit from symbiotic relationships.[2] A variety of such communities came into being in the LAN industry. Some were not really communities at all, just aggregations of autonomous firms associated only by virtue of temporarily shared interests in a proprietary or sponsored technology. Others were genuine communities but never became strong ones because they remained small, or because their ties remained weak, or both. In many ways, the paradigm of a strong and vibrant technological community was the one that grew up around a common commitment to the Ethernet standard, a commitment engendered by that standard's open status.

The kind of technology community that the Ethernet community exemplifies exhibits the same characteristics as other kinds of communities. They are far from homogeneous. The mere existence of a community does not ensure Edenic harmony, as anyone who has lived in a small town knows. Competition, of course, is one of the principal motives driving activity within a technological community. Its members compete for the same customers, often with similar products. Although competition is one of the principal sources of a technological community's vitality, it is not the only one.

Technological communities also can display a remarkable amount of collaboration because of their members' commitment to a common standard. Firms, for instance, may collaborate directly on the development of a new component, or they may have reseller agreements. And like many communities, technological communities derive much of their vitality from differentiation and specialization, enabling the community to adapt and survive in ways a more homogeneous aggregation cannot, but also requiring collaboration and cooperation so that the different specialized parts supplied by a variety of firms complement each other and can be assembled into a complete network. This can result either from direct negotiation or as a natural consequence of firms' efforts to seek unoccupied, lucrative market niches.

Not all communities are similarly structured, and this is true of technological communities as well. In general, the larger the community becomes, the more differentiated it becomes, in the same way that large cities tend to have more specialty shops than small towns. In addition, the larger and more differentiated the community, the more competition there is within it. The more firms that offer the same component, for example, the more intense the competition becomes and the more radically prices decline in relation to the prices of comparable components of a different technology. And the larger, more differentiated, and more specialized the community becomes, the greater the variety in the products that it offers.

In technological communities, one of the principal determinants of how the community is structured is the kind of technological standard around which the community is constituted. In particular, communities constituted around an open technology tend to have a different structure than those that grow up around more closely held or proprietary technologies. They tend to be decentralized and nonhierarchical, because no single company controls the technology, and thus no company can exclude other firms from manufacturing the technology and from proposing innovations. Communities that arise around more proprietary technologies are more hierarchically structured, because a single company may exert strong or absolute control over whether and in what manner other firms are allowed to employ the technology.

These differences in community structure have a definite effect on the outcomes of battles to become market standards. As will become clear, less hierarchically structured technological communities often have the advantage over more hierarchically structured communities. In hierarchically structured communities, a single entity regulates the way in which new knowledge and innovations are produced. As a result, different and even conflicting strategies can rarely be pursued simultaneously. In nonhierarchically structured communities, such as those that arise around an open technological standard, by contrast, different, specialized firms pursue different paths, and as a result the technology does not easily become locked in to a declining market.

The mere creation of an open standard, however, does not guarantee that a technology will prevail over more closely held technologies and become the market standard. As will be shown in more detail, like the DIX alliance, IBM turned its Token Ring technology into an open IEEE standard, but unlike Ethernet, Token Ring did not attract a large, vital, nonhierarchically structured community. Because IBM sought to be and to remain the principal player in the Token Ring realm, especially in terms of market share, and thus was the principal competitor of other Token Ring suppliers, the resulting Token Ring community had severe hierarchical characteristics, and there were few incentives for other firms to join it. What proves more important than creating a de facto open standard is creating attractive business opportunities for a large number of suppliers. Open technologies quite often fulfill this prerequisite, but as the case of IBM shows, dominant firms may possess sufficient leverage to violate it, to the eventual detriment of their own dominant position.

Standardization is thus indeed a deeply social process, and in the emergence of Ethernet as the market standard in the LAN industry, as we will see, socioeconomic factors stand out as determinants of standardization battles, especially at their outset. The history of the LAN industry suggests that, all other things being equal, the technology with the broadest and most diversified social support has the best chance to prevail.

All other things are never equal, however. Technical factors, in particular, differ; otherwise there would be no basis for competition between technologies. But in the LAN industry technical factors, in and of themselves, were not ultimately decisive in shaping the outcome of the standards battle. Instead, they were quite malleable, set and readjusted by their sponsors in response to market exigencies. What proved more important than any short-term technical advantage was the relative size and diversity of the technological communities involved. It would be erroneous to conclude that the underlying technology played no role, and that social factors were all that mattered. But the technology proved to be the raw material on which the technological communities worked to achieve the outcomes they desired, not the fundamental basis on which one outcome was determined.

Standardization cannot be understood without examining the role of users. There is no standardization if users do not adopt the technology, and users often provide crucial feedback to the producers, as von Hippel has pointed out.[3] Moreover, users are an important group of actors participating in the social processes that shape the technological outcome. Hence, it seemed only logical to include users in the technological community as well.

In the present community concept, however, users are not included. This exclusion not only follows the convention of the literature[4] but also is justified by the goal of explaining the advantages of open technologies that accrue on the supply side. Besides, the exclusion of users results partly from empirical difficulties in finding original material on users' experiences and locating individuals who can be interviewed. This approach does not seem to be a significant drawback in explaining Ethernet's success, however. As will be described, during the very early standardization

efforts Ethernet was primarily championed by its inventor, Robert Metcalfe, and the DIX group. Similarly, users played a negligible role in the
de jure standardization by the IEEE. The ones casting the votes at the
IEEE were the representatives of the firms producing LAN technology,
not the users. Once Ethernet had become a de jure IEEE standard, most
users simply followed the LAN recommendation of their computer manufacturers, as this created the least amount of compatibility problems.
Since Ethernet had gained support from some of the most powerful computer manufacturers at that time, especially DEC and H-P, it had a clear
edge in this regard. In other words, the manufacturers clearly took the
end users' preferences into consideration and created a standard. But there
was little inherent demand for a technology that possessed the particular
characteristics of Ethernet. The end users strongly demanded a standard,
but a somewhat different technology could also have solved their networking needs. Consequently, the users granted the manufacturers much
leeway in shaping the technology and simply adopted their eventual
offering, as long as it suited their needs and as long as it was in fact a
standard.

Capabilities and Communities

Many alternative approaches to explaining technological evolution
have qualified the initial insights of economic standardization theory and
gone beyond the assumptions of neoclassical economics on which those
insights were based. Today, a broader conception of a technology's social
and institutional embeddedness seems better suited to grasp the processes
by which technologies become market standards. The social and geographic dimensions of innovation and standardization have received considerable attention over the past thirty years. Innovating firms often
draw from knowledge accumulated by users and suppliers, we now recognize.[5] In the approach stressed by adherents to the paradigm of the
social construction of technology, the concept of a "network of actors"
is employed to explain what shapes technology.[6] Other scholars have
contended that firms often incorporate knowledge that is "stored" in a
regional district such as Silicon Valley,[7] whereas others have drawn the
geographic line of the knowledge repository even more broadly, suggesting the framework of a "national system of innovation."[8]
Certainly, the regional advantages of Silicon Valley and Boston's
Route 128 played an important role in the creation of the LAN industry.
In fact, it comes as no surprise that most LAN companies were established in these two areas. However, looking at how people cluster around

a particular place, rather than around a particular technology, has the drawback of not permitting us to focus on factors that are clearly relevant to that technology as well. The emphasis on geographic space makes it difficult to compare the effect of social and institutional factors on the evolution of those technologies that reside within the same geographic space.

That is why several researchers have proposed the concept of a technological community as the appropriate way to conceptualize the social dimension of technological innovation and standardization. Edward Constant, for example, argues that turbojet technology was in the possession of and advanced within a "community of practitioners" comprising both individual engineers and organizations like firms.[9] Leonard Lynn, Mohan Reddy, and John Aram have developed the concept of an "innovation community" to link the corporate development process of a technology to its institutional environment. Such a community comprises universities, unions, trade associations, and professional societies.[10] Embarking from a research tradition in population ecology, James Wade claims that "each technology can be thought of as being supported by a community of organizations that have a stake in the technology or design."[11] Although these scholars differ in their definition of a technological community, they all draw the institutional line around a particular technology, instead of a region.

Because the evolution of technology in the LAN industry revolved around issues posed by open and proprietary standards, classifying the technological communities to be found there in those terms makes the most sense. One could of course classify communities otherwise, along dimensions such as the type and numbers of members (that is, the involvement of universities, the military complex, or standards-setting bodies, in addition to firms), the nature of functional integration, the forms of interaction, or geographic scope. But classifying the LAN communities in terms of their relative openness emphasizes what is key to the processes by which each was able to compete and by which the proponents of Ethernet eventually triumphed: the different capabilities possessed by its firms and the advantages that accrued to the technology because its firms possessed those capabilities.

CAPABILITIES

Although the concept of capabilities as a way to understand the ways in which businesses grow—or fail to grow—was originally applied to factors at work within individual firms, the concept has evolved so that it is applicable to the successes and failures of technological communities as well.[12] In a seminal work first published in 1959, *The Theory of the Growth of the Firm,* Edith Penrose approached the firm not as an abstract production function, as it had been treated in neoclassical theory, but as an administrative, planning organization endowed with real people and a collection of productive resources. According to her, the growth of firms mainly depends on the efforts of managers whose job it is to find opportunities for further growth and to remove obstacles. But managerial efforts may also limit a firm's growth. Although a (growing) firm can hire new managers, they need firm-specific experience and must function as a team to be effective. These requirements cannot be met in a market transaction; instead they must be built through a time-consuming learning process within the firm.

Although Penrose did not use the term "capability"—it was coined in this context by G. B. Richardson in 1972[13]—these claims became the cornerstone of the capability approach to explaining how and why economic growth occurs within firms. The capability approach begins with the notion that the sources of competitive advantage must be built within the firm and cannot be acquired through market transactions. In other words, firms, rather than the environments in which they operate (such as the market), are responsible for their own competitive advantages.

Economists long ignored the ideas of Penrose, but in the 1980s and 1990s various scholars discovered, extended, and refined her work.[14] David Teece, Gary Pisano, and Amy Shuen, in particular, have developed a useful, integrative framework that explains how strategic advantage emerges in this paradigm. In their view, a firm's competitive advantage depends on its capabilities, as well as on its endowment with assets such as specialized plant and equipment, reputation, skilled personnel, financial assets and so on, factors that they call the "asset position" of a firm.[15] Capabilities and asset position, in large measure, determine what a firm is capable of in terms of production, knowledge creation, innovation, and market adjustments.

For a firm to reach a zone of strategic advantage, its capabilities and asset position typically must be unique. A firm's competitive edge further depends on its future strategy or path and on the market and technological opportunities that lie ahead. Whereas neoclassical economics suggests that firms can choose from an infinite range of technologies, strategies, and markets, Teece and his colleagues claim that a firm's choice range is rather narrow. What a firm can achieve in the future depends on its past and present capabilities and assets. The less a firm's future product and market strategies are related to the firm's current capabilities and assets, the less likely it is to succeed. This is because a firm is subject to a costly, time-consuming, and highly path-dependent learning process. In a metaphorical sense, if a firm has traveled in a two-wheel-drive vehicle, it cannot suddenly conquer off-road terrain requiring a four-wheel-drive vehicle. Finally, a firm's strategic advantage depends on the ability of its competitors to replicate its capabilities and asset position. If competitors can easily imitate them, then the firm's profits will evaporate quickly.[16] Consequently, a firm's capabilities and asset position must be not only unique, but also difficult to imitate and nontradable if they are to create a competitive edge.

To gain a strategic advantage, then, a firm must cultivate those capabilities that allow it to produce superior products at lower unit costs, products that competitors cannot easily imitate. Such capabilities may be based on organizational and execution skills, on R&D and manufacturing facilities, and on technological know-how. A firm also must carefully match its capabilities to the market opportunities and environment. Finally, a firm needs luck, since the efforts of competitors in building similar capabilities can rapidly render its investments obsolete. The capability approach claims that a firm secures a competitive advantage if it manufactures efficiently and if it can adjust swiftly to changing environments, abilities that Teece and his colleagues term "dynamic capabilities."[17] These abilities, in turn, depend on unique firm-internal assets and capabilities honed to learning, knowledge creation, coordination, and the integration and transformation of internal and external resources.

In many instances, however, firms do not manufacture and innovate an entire product in-house. Instead, they rely on input from other firms. Such market reliance exists partly because the larger and more diversified the market becomes and the more complex the product becomes, the more unlikely it becomes that a single firm can possesses all the capabilities required to conceive of, develop, and bring to market such a product.[18] Hence, firms begin to specialize and become dependent on the capabilities of other specialists whose input they purchase. Capabilities therefore may reside not only within a firm, but also outside the firm, in markets, industries, or regions. For instance, drawing from Alfred Marshall's concept of an industrial district, Richard Langlois argues that the enormous growth in the PC industry occurred through reliance on "external" capabilities, that is, capabilities that are "produced by and reside within a network of competing and cooperating firms rather than within the boundaries of large vertically integrated organizations."[19]

These capabilities can include what Nicolai Foss has called "higher-order capabilities."[20] These are bodies of productive knowledge that reside not only within a firm, but also within a collectivity of firms residing either in a particular industry or in a particular region. Higher-order capabilities are not proprietary to one firm but are shared among the collectivity. They have the characteristic of "semiprivate" goods and yield rents only to the firms participating in that collectivity. Examples of higher-order capabilities include standards, knowledge sharing in R&D networks, trust, or a regional pool of trained engineers from which firms can draw. Like firm capabilities, these higher-order capabilities must be built within the particular industry or region and must be unique, inimitable, and nontransferable through market transactions if they are to render a competitive advantage to that collectivity of firms.[21] Hence, if a firm wants to draw upon Silicon Valley's capabilities, it must locate there and become part of one of its communities.

It should thus be clear how powerfully the concept of capabilities, as it has evolved, contributes to our understanding of the processes by which technological communities succeed or fail. In a nutshell, capabilities are a way of understanding the overall ability of an institution—a firm, market, or community—to manufacture and commercialize a technology efficiently, to generate technological innovations, and to adjust to technological and market discontinuities on a timely basis. Capability thus refers to what a technological community can do and to what it might be able to do in the future. This ability depends on the community's resources—that is, on its tangible assets, such as plant and production equipment—as well as on its competence, skills, and experience, and on the knowledge of its members.[22]

THREE TYPES OF TECHNOLOGICAL COMMUNITIES

The capabilities of different kinds of technological communities become evident when the communities are classified according to their degree of openness. When that is done, the competitive advantages and disadvantages that result from these capabilities become clear. Although most theoretical standardization models treat openness and proprietariness as a dichotomy, a more accurate approach is to treat openness and proprietariness as relative terms.[23] They may be understood as endpoints of a range along which various degrees of a standard's ownership and accessibility to third-party suppliers exist. As figure 1.1 illustrates, at one end of the range is a completely proprietary standard. Such a standard is owned by a single firm, which holds unrestricted private property rights and refrains from licensing it to other vendors. At the opposite end of the range is a de jure and therefore maximally open standard. No vendor possesses private property rights in an open standard, and the standard is in the public domain, accessible to any vendor at any time and on a nondiscriminatory basis.[24]

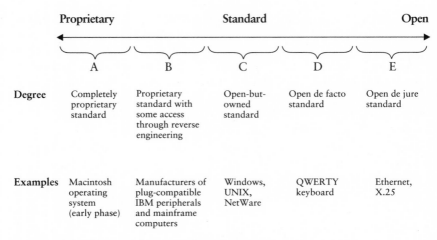

FIGURE 1.1   Degrees of openness and proprietariness.

Between these two extremes, a standard might be completely open, yet lack de jure status, as in the case of the QWERTY keyboard. Another middle degree emerges when third-party vendors succeed in gaining access to a completely proprietary technology through reverse engineering. But most important is the case in which a single firm possesses private property rights to a standard but decides to make it available to other vendors through, say, a license. Borrus and Zysman term such a standard "open-but-owned."[25] Such status means that third-party suppliers can adopt the technology, but the proprietary firm often reaps the principal economic benefits. The mixed regime exposes the licensees to the risk of unilateral, discriminatory actions by the proprietor. All other things being equal, open-but-owned standards appeal to a lesser degree than de jure standards to third-party vendors.[26] Microsoft's Windows or Novell's NetWare exemplify this case.

Across this spectrum, three major types of technological community can be discerned: the proprietary community, the sponsor community, and the open community (figure 1.2).[27] The proprietary community forms around a completely proprietary standard. Because, by definition, the proprietor refrains from licensing its technology, this community comprises only the proprietary firm and its practitioners, as well as any resellers and suppliers of its technology. Whereas the proprietor obviously forms the core of this community, many resellers build only weak ties to the community because they forgo asset-specific investments and therefore can relatively easily abandon the community and switch to a rival's product.[28] Though the proprietor may actively attempt to involve

Proprietary community   **Sponsor community**

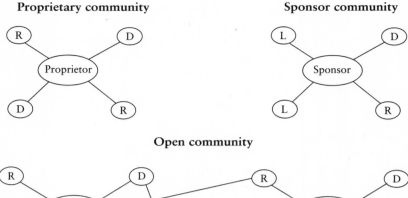

Open community

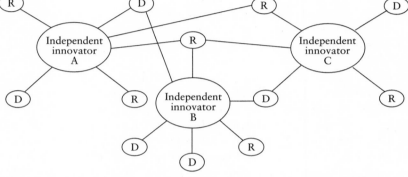

FIGURE 1.2   Structures of the three types of communities. R, reseller; D, distributor; L, licensee.

suppliers in the innovation process, it usually retains principal responsibility for the development and upgrading of its technology.[29] This reliance on a single firm constitutes a bottleneck in the innovation process and a severe handicap in modular systems requiring a great diversity of capabilities. In addition, the communal interactions and symbiotic relationships remain concentrated on the sponsor. In terms of size, this community may remain relatively small, but it can become quite substantial, as did the community of manufacturers of plug-compatible peripherals and computers formed around IBM's mainframes.[30] Most early entrants in the LAN market gathered within such a community.

The sponsor community, which forms around an "open-but-owned" standard, has the following structure: Like the proprietary community, its membership consists of the sponsor and its practitioners, as well as of resellers, distributors, suppliers, and their practitioners. But because the proprietor licenses its technology, a sponsor community is also composed of the various licensees. This structure is similar to that of the proprietary

community, but there are differences as well. As in the case of the proprietary community, a single firm, the proprietor, tends to be solely responsible for developing and upgrading the entire technology. Hence, the
sponsor community may face the same limitations on the generation of
innovations as the proprietary community. The main difference between
the proprietary community and sponsor community lies in the latter's
inclusion of licensees. These might simply resell the technology, the way
PC clone makers license and resell Microsoft's Windows. In that case, the
structure of the sponsor community does not fundamentally differ from
that of the proprietary community. But licensees might also engage in
actual manufacturing—for example, as a second source of integrated
circuits—or make other asset-specific investments in the licensed technology. If licensees undertake such investments, they tend to develop strong
ties to the community. As a result, the communal interactions and specialization may extend beyond the sponsor.

The size of a sponsor community also varies. Since the proprietor often
collects the principal profits, and since its control exposes the licensees
to the risk of unilateral, discriminatory actions by the proprietor (as happened, for example, when Apple withdrew its license to the Macintosh
shortly after granting it), a sponsor community may remain relatively
small.[31] But (as the cases of Microsoft's Windows and Novell's NetWare
exemplify) a sponsor community can also grow to vast size, especially if
the sponsor possesses a market-critical technology. Most communities of
Ethernet's proprietary contenders resembled this type. In fact, even Token
Ring's community, despite its open de jure status, had a similar structure.

The maximum degree of openness characterizes the open technological community. Although de jure standards do not inherently attract
numerous independent suppliers, they often do. De jure status not only
provides vendors with a technology for a nominal fee, it also protects
them from unilateral manipulations by requiring a democratic process
for the approval of any changes in technical specifications. In addition,
de jure status prevents a single vendor from accumulating profits simply
on the basis of its property rights, thereby leveling the playing field among
competitors—at least from a legal standpoint. As a result, the community of a de jure standard comprises the several independent manufacturers, their practitioners, as well as any resellers and distributors.

This structure differs in some subtle but critical ways from the structures of the other two community types. Whereas the proprietary and
sponsor communities include a single innovating firm that propagates
its technology to resellers and licensees, the open community, lacking a
controlling proprietor, must be less hierarchically structured. Even more
important, it encompasses several innovators that stand on equal legal

terms and are independent of each other. This means that communal interactions and a division of labor can extend over several firms and take on more complex forms than would be possible if there were only a single sponsor. Finally, the open community is quite elastic in its particular institutional form. It might consist mainly of a few large, vertically integrated firms, but it could also gravitate toward a decentralized network of small, specialized suppliers, resembling a Marshallian industrial district in economists' parlance.[32] In short, the open community possesses not only additional means of production and innovation, but also a chameleonlike flexibility in its institutional manifestations.

The concept of a technological community and the distinctions just drawn among the various types of community structures have direct methodological implications for the economic theory of standardization. They take us beyond the shortcomings of standardization theory's method of viewing competition between the proponents of two technologies in terms of the strategic actions of two contending firms. Because the economic theory of standardization neglects the community phenomenon, it provides no insight into the role that the technological community plays in standardization. As we will see, although the strategic actions of the community's firms continue to play an important role, and although a community may even follow a coherent course similar to that of an individual firm, the community does not act as an autonomous entity. Instead, its course results from the aggregate of its firms' actions and encompasses systemic effects that an individual firm does not exhibit.

The recognition of the role played by communities in technological evolution requires that the competition between standards be seen not as a clash between firms, but as a contest between communities and their respective members. Viewing it in these terms allows us to understand the ways in which the differences in communal structures affect standardization by endowing the different communities with different capabilities.

Technological Communities and Their Capabilities

Does one of the three community types have capabilities that endow it with a competitive advantage in a standards race? As figure 1.3 illustrates, the three community types permit six possible comparisons: three among equal types and three among different types of communities.

For purposes of comparison, we make the following assumptions. The three community types, all competing to set the standard, start with a roughly equal technology. The contenders also enter the market at roughly

	Proprietary community A	Sponsor community B	Open community C
Proprietary community D	Situational I	B prevails over D II	C prevails over D III
Sponsor community E	—	Situational IV	C prevails over E V
Open community F	—	—	Situational VI

FIGURE 1.3 Competition between community types: expected outcomes under ideal conditions.

the same time. These assumptions exclude "tipping" effects resulting from first-mover advantages. All compete for the same market. Moreover, let us assume that all community types are of similar size—at least at the time of their market entry—and can obtain sufficient (financial) resources to grow with the market. Of course, as the standards race progresses, their sizes would start to diverge. Finally, since this is what is of interest, only qualitative differences will be considered. In other words, if the market volume is $30 million, it is assumed that in the case of a proprietary community this sales volume would be concentrated in a single firm, whereas in the open community the $30 million sales volume would be divided up among several firms.

If two equal types of communities compete, the outcome depends on the concrete factors—that is, capabilities, asset positions, and so on—and hence little can be predicted from a theoretical perspective. The competition between two proprietary communities (quadrant I) is, of course, largely the comparison between two individual firms. The competitive outcome in this case depends on the firms' capabilities; their present asset positions; the match of their capabilities with the technological and market requirements, present and future; and the ability of the competitor to replicate any unique positions and capabilities.[33] Because the specific outcome depends on particular historical factors, the analysis must be situational. Therefore, from a theoretical perspective little can be said about the expected outcome.

However, a few general predictions seem possible. Because the outcome depends on the contenders' current capabilities, positions, and ability to match technological and market requirements, the larger a firm's pool of capabilities and the closer these capabilities match the technological and market requirements, the more likely it is to win the race to establish its technology as the market standard. Thus, everything else being equal, a large firm should outrun a smaller firm because large size implies a larger pool of the required capabilities. However, if the small firm is a dedicated specialist, while the large firm has only a tangential interest in the technology, the small specialist might be able to outmaneuver its rival, especially if it acts swiftly and can mobilize enough resources to grow. This outcome clearly occurred in the minicomputer market, where DEC managed to conquer the new economic space despite IBM's overall domination of the computer industry.[34]

Regarding the competition between two sponsor or two open communities (quadrants IV and VI), little can be said about the expected outcome theoretically. Again, the outcome depends on the communities' specific capabilities and positions, and their actual match with the technological and market requirements. However, a few general statements seem possible as well. All things being roughly equal, the community with the most extensive network of licensees and resellers is likely to triumph over smaller rivals. This is because possession of an edge in distribution channels may be instrumental in growing the installed base at a fast pace, and such growth can in turn prompt a market to "tip." Such an edge clearly influenced the battle over video systems. Although Sony's Beta was not completely proprietary, Sony initially hesitated to license Beta and refrained from OEM manufacturing. In contrast, JVC, sponsor of the victorious VHS system, aggressively recruited large manufacturers that had extensive distribution networks. As a result, VHS gained the upper hand in the distribution channels and therefore contributed to the larger installed base of prerecorded tapes that caused the market to "tip."[35]

The comparison between different types of communities yields clearer theoretical answers than the comparison of equal types. If the proprietary and the sponsor communities compete with each other (quadrant II), the sponsor community holds a competitive advantage under the conditions we have assumed. Although little can be said about the internal capabilities of the sponsors, the sponsor community possesses a structural advantage in the distribution channels, thanks to its licensees. Often, these licensees not only make asset-specific investments and therefore develop a strong vested interest in the technology's success, they also cultivate their own distribution channels. This means that the single innovator of the proprietary community competes with several firms, all pushing the technology through their distribution channels. Everything else being equal, this situation should allow the sponsor community to accumulate a larger installed base and thus to "tip" the market. Such a dynamic clearly worked against Apple in its competition with the PC platform. In the distribution channels, Apple confronted not only IBM but also myriad clone makers, including Compaq, Dell, AST, Gateway, Packard Bell, and no-name firms. By the same token, and for the same reasons, an open community tends to outcompete a proprietary community (quadrant III).

In a competition between a sponsor community and an open community (quadrant V), the two communities differ mainly in the number of independent innovators they embody. While the sponsor community depends solely on the proprietor for the development of the technology, the open community may include several independent manufacturers and innovating firms. One might thus interpret this comparison as the classical question of the market versus the firm.[36] Numerous particular factors would determine the outcome, including transaction and production costs, types of innovations, institutional structure, industrial life cycle, and environment. A few of the general points raised by the debate over the market versus the firm, however, are worth considering in connection with the competition between a sponsor community and an open community.

Several economists have vehemently argued that the firm—especially the large, vertically integrated firm—is superior to the market in terms of economic efficiency and the power to generate innovations. One of the most prominent proponents of this view is business historian Alfred Chandler, who has analyzed the evolution of the institutional organization of production and distribution in the United States between the 1840s and the 1920s.[37] He found that in this historical context, the modern multiunit business enterprise managed by a hierarchy of salaried executives superseded the market mechanism in the coordination of economic activities and the allocation of resources across most industries. In Chandler's view, the rise of large, integrated firms occurred because administrative control proved far more efficient than market coordination based on the price mechanism in accommodating the high production volume and speed that emerged with the development of railroad and telephone systems. In fact, administrative control allowed goods to flow from one productive unit to another at much higher speed and hence in much greater volume than market-mediated coordination of product flow. Because high throughput rate and high volume increased the utilization of capital investments, enormous reductions in unit costs resulted. In Chandler's view, firms thus continuously expanded the range of administrative control through forward and backward integration, mainly to maintain the steady flow of input materials and the efficient sale of manufactured goods.

The large firm outperforms the market mechanism, according to William Lazonick, because vertical integration provides the firm with privileged access to key resources for the generation of innovations—for example, by hiring trained personnel. Such privileged access initially requires high fixed costs, but once the innovation succeeds on the market, the firm can defray those costs over a large volume of product, thereby allowing it to offer a high-quality product at low unit costs. In contrast, the market, with its unprivileged access to innovative resources, faces constant or even increasing variable costs. As a result, Lazonick believes the large firm has a structural advantage over the market mechanism.[38]

However, as Richard Langlois and Paul Robinson point out, the large, vertically integrated firm prevails over a network of suppliers only if the necessary capabilities are not cheaply available in the market and if innovations are systematic, requiring changes in other parts of the system, and not autonomous.[39] Systematic innovations favor a vertically integrated firm over a network of suppliers because the firm, with its integrated ownership, can redirect resources and renegotiate changes more cheaply than the market mechanism, with its separate input ownership. This is so not only because input holders whose capital might become obsolete in the wake of a systematic innovation may resist changes and hold up renegotiations,[40] but also because of informational transaction costs. In fact, spatial centralization of different production stages (for instance, in a factory) allows the firm to conceive of opportunities that might escape distant, specialized suppliers. Even more important, it may be difficult to convey tacit knowledge and to persuade outside contractors about still-evolving, qualitatively new aspects of a systematic innovation.[41]

Although the reasoning behind the claim for the supremacy of the firm over the market mechanism and hence of the sponsor community over the open community can seem convincing, this conclusion is premature. The work of scholars such as Chandler and Lazonick has focused mainly on large enterprises, but as the case of the incipient LAN industry shows, not all firms can be expected to start as large ones. In fact, many LAN firms were tiny start-ups lacking the resources to immediately pursue a large-scale strategy of forward and backward integration. In addition, the open community exhibits a chameleonlike flexibility in its institutional manifestations. It may be a network of small, specialized suppliers, but if a few large firms dominate, it may well gravitate toward a structure of vertical integration. In other words, in a $30 million market, the open community could include firms worth $25 million, $3 million, and $2 million. Thus the open community can match the advantages of vertical integration inherent in the sponsor community. In short, in terms of internal capabilities, sponsor communities and open communities are equally matched.

But since an open community consists of several independent manufacturers and thus can muster not only internal but also additional, external capabilities, it has resources that a sponsor community lacks. One has thus to ask under what circumstances external capabilities or (in terms of the firm-versus-market debate) the ability to use the market mechanism provides the open community with a competitive advantage. Put differently, under what conditions is the market mechanism more powerful than the large firm?

The answer is that a network of suppliers, coordinated by the market mechanism, can be more powerful than the large, vertically integrated firm if innovations are autonomous instead of systematic. Innovations are autonomous when changes in one stage of production do not necessitate simultaneous changes in other stages. Most prominently, autonomous innovations occur in modular systems such as the PC, in which consumers assemble the product from a set of interchangeable modules according to their individual preferences. In such systems, innovations can proceed autonomously. That is, several firms can simultaneously experiment with a particular component or module. Even more important, autonomous innovation can occur not only in one module, but also across several modules. Langlois and Robertson thus assume that the simultaneous, autonomous pursuit of innovation by multiple firms surpasses the innovation capacity of a single firm, especially if market and technological conditions change rapidly and if the required capabilities, as well as market size, surpass the capacity of an individual firm.[42]

The autonomous and simultaneous pursuit of innovations by a network of suppliers advances the technology more rapidly because it overcomes the innovative barriers inherent in a single firm. Ostensibly, a single innovator's most critical limitation lies in the fact that it must generate all innovations alone. This can create a bottleneck, since all informational input must be channeled through one firm. In addition, from a knowledge creation standpoint, when informational input originates from a wide range of sources, it is more likely to result in genuinely new knowledge and insights. A single firm, even though it may be big, may be unable to fulfill this requirement.[43] Finally—with the exception of very large firms that can pursue different or even contradictory technological and market directions simultaneously—most firms are limited in this regard. For these reasons, the open community has an advantage over the sponsor community in the generation of innovations if the product system is modular and if innovations proceed autonomously.

There are two other reasons that a market-based system, such as a supplier network or an open community, can be more potent than a system based on vertical integration, such as a sponsor community. First, a system with several independent innovators is likely to be better suited to overcome corporate path dependencies than a system relying on a single firm. Strong path dependencies restrict a firm's future path.[44] Corporations cannot select any path from an infinite range of future markets, technologies, and strategies; instead they are bound by their present capabilities and positions. For an individual firm in an open community, these path dependencies are as strong as those for the single innovator of the sponsor community. But as a collective, an open community may face weaker path dependencies than an individual firm, including the sponsor of the sponsor community. In fact, since firms differ in their capabilities and positions because of natural heterogeneity and specialization, an open community possesses several distinct firm capabilities and asset positions.[45]

This variety allows an open community (though not its individual firms) to move into several markets simultaneously (figure 1.4). If a market or technological discontinuity occurs, (say, F in the figure), an open community with its many specialists is more likely than a sponsor community with its single innovator to have a firm that is closely positioned to take advantage of F. In this case, the firms in the closest position quickly exploit the opportunity, and as a result the technology moves into the new direction, too. In contrast, if the innovator of a sponsor community (like firm M or P in figure 1.4) happens not to be positioned close to F, it must undertake costly and time-consuming adjustments. In the meantime, a better-positioned innovating firm of the open community (such as firms B, O, and Q) may already have captured the emerging market opportunity, possibly locking out the sponsor community.[46]

For the same reason, the existence of various independent innovating firms reduces the open technology's dependence on the success of a single vendor. If the market or technology approach of a particular firm fails, the other firms of the open community are likely to compensate for the failure. In contrast, if the market or technology approach of the proprietor in the sponsor community fails, the technology collapses with it.

Second, a network of independent suppliers can be more efficient than a large, vertically integrated firm when the industry matures. In novel

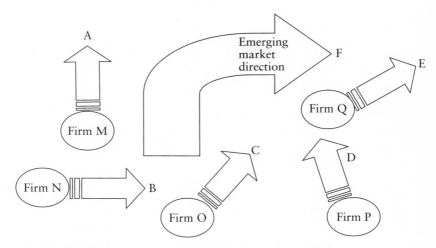

FIGURE 1.4   Breaking through corporate path dependencies.

industries, the capabilities necessary for large-scale integration are not
cheaply available on the market, and the transaction costs of using the
market are high. In the long run, however, these rationales evaporate.
Outside suppliers learn, and capabilities diffuse into the market. Likewise, actors learn to reduce the transaction costs of using the market
system. Then the market system becomes more efficient than vertical
integration because it allows for greater economies of division of labor,
faster adjustments, and more rapid learning.[47] This is especially the case
when size, diversity, and the uncertainty of the market, as well as the
pace of technological development, preclude a single firm from developing and upgrading all necessary capabilities.

Thus there are strong reasons to conclude that a market-based system
such as a decentralized supplier network or a Marshallian industrial district is economically more powerful than vertical organization under
certain conditions. In particular, a system with market elements may
outperform the large, vertically integrated firm in modular systems, in
rapidly changing markets, and in mature industries. Hence, an open
community, which can include market-based mechanisms and rely on
several firms, can have significant advantages over a sponsor community
in the competition to establish a market standard.

Three qualifications should be mentioned regarding the claimed superior advantages of open communities. The first revolves around the issue
of the appropriability of profits from innovations. So far, the analysis has
assumed that firms of the open community do in fact produce innovations,

thereby outperforming communities with a single innovator. But do the members of the open community have enough incentives to engage in innovative activities? This question arises because, by definition, openness deprives an innovating firm of the legal means (such as a patent) to protect its innovation. As a result, its communal peers may be able to use its innovation for a free ride, thereby preventing the innovator from reaping the profits from its investments. Unable to appropriate profits, the firms of the open community may therefore lack the necessary incentives to engage in costly innovative activities. It was exactly this appropriability issue that handicapped the X/Open movement.[48] If this problem is a general one, the competitive advantage of the open community may deteriorate compared with the proprietary or sponsor community, whose constituency (a single innovator) precludes such a handicap.

However, there are mechanisms that may allow a firm participating in the open community to appropriate profits from its innovations. Appropriability of profits from innovations depends on co-specialized assets.[49] If imitating competitors lack the necessary co-specialized assets, the innovating firm may succeed in securing the principal profits.[50] Moreover, as the example of Sun Microsystems shows, it is possible to succeed in appropriating profits despite licensing technology to competitors.[51] Sun relied partly on transient monopolies, during which it harvested the profits from its R&D investments. Because of the tacit component of technological knowledge, imitators must also invest in their own capabilities to assimilate innovations. If they forgo such investments, they may find themselves unable to imitate an innovation on a timely basis.[52] This barrier may shield the innovator from immediate imitation by its fellow competitors.

In addition, open standards often enlarge markets to such an extent that the profits from a smaller piece of a larger market outweigh the profits from a larger piece of a smaller market.[53] In conjunction with the profits from a transient monopoly, increased market size may provide a firm with sufficient incentives to pursue innovations. Even if competitors ultimately succeed in imitating the innovation, the innovating firm may still be better off by developing a market-enlarging innovation. In short, various mechanisms seem to mitigate the potential appropriability problem of open communities.

A second, somewhat related, problem plagues open technologies: balkanization. Because the open community does not have a designated innovator, but leaves innovation open to all vendors, different firms may produce slightly varying and thus not fully compatible innovations. Balkanization occurred in the UNIX world and could threaten any other open source standard.[54] The division of the open community into competing factions can severely weaken the power and attractiveness of open technologies. To assess the severity of this problem, one might have to distinguish between different degrees of openness, however. In fact, both the UNIX and Java standards, though quite open, lack de jure status. This might permit the conclusion that standards that are open but not de jure—standards that consequently have less stringent rules—are more susceptible to balkanization than de jure standards, which allow for a more clear-cut definition of standard adherence.

The third qualification to the potential superiority of the open community revolves around the assumptions made in order to undertake this analysis. If one relaxes the assumption that roughly equal initial conditions pertain and that the competing communities enter the market with an equivalent technology at about the same time, the outcome might differ, although it would not necessarily do so. For example, a single firm entering the market well ahead of an open community may have "tipped" the market before the strengths of the open community come into play. Or a very large vendor with a superior technology and a well-established distribution network might crush a fledgling open community. The markets' "tippiness" and the role of small events may override the potential competitive advantage of open systems. Consequently, the theoretical superiority of an open community still remains subject to historical forces. The history of the LAN industry, which is recounted beginning in the next chapter, provides a testing ground for these claims.

2 *The Invention of the LAN*

The history of digital computing began in November 1945, when Presper Eckert and John Mauchly of the Moore School at the University of Pennsylvania put the first computer, a mainframe called ENIAC (Electronic Numerical Integrator and Computer) into operation.[1] ENIAC and the subsequent mainframes were gigantic machines. They contained thousands of vacuum tubes, weighed tons, filled entire rooms, and ranged in price between several hundred thousand and several million dollars.[2] Because of these high prices, in the 1950s and 1960s annual shipments of mainframes remained fairly small; in fact their installed base reached only 800 units in 1956 and 6,000 units in 1960.[3] Even in the late 1980s (that is, at the end of the period of LAN standardization), annual shipments did not exceed 20,000 units.[4] This meant that despite their head start, mainframes would not constitute the principal LAN market. Owing to their exorbitant prices, mainframes were used only for central computing tasks—tasks that could justify their high costs. As a result, they were deployed mainly by large institutions, such as the government, the military, universities (often in connection with defense-related research), and Fortune 1000 companies, which used them for corporate accounting and transaction processing.[5]

The early development of electronic computers in the mid-1940s and early 1950s took place at university research centers under contract to government agencies. But gradually the novel computing technology led to the founding of new firms and growing commercial interest, and eventually to the formation of a completely new industry. One of the first computer companies was the Eckert-Mauchly Computer Corporation, established in 1946, when the two builders of ENIAC left the Moore School to commercialize their invention. Their effort eventually resulted in the UNIVAC machine, which became well known as a result of its installation and use at the U.S. Census Bureau.

Another early start-up was Engineering Research Associates (ERA), which was formed at about the same time as Eckert and Mauchly's company, to carry out computer projects under contract to the U.S. Navy. But high capital costs, as well as the experimental nature of the early machines and widely held skepticism as to the commercial viability of computers, made the commercialization efforts of these start-ups not only difficult but also unprofitable. As a result, in the early 1950s both of the computer start-ups were acquired by Remington Rand, a major office equipment supplier. These two acquisitions made Remington Rand (which allowed the two firms to operate as independent subsidiaries) the early leader in the fledgling computer industry. Throughout the mid-1950s UNIVAC was recognized as one of the best large-scale computers then in use for data processing, whereas the computers developed by ERA, the ERA 1101 and 1103, became the leading scientific computers.[6]

Remington Rand may have been the early leader, but the company that would come to dominate the emerging computer industry and play a major role in LAN technology was IBM. Like Remington Rand, IBM was a vendor of office equipment, dominating the tabulating market with a market share of 90 percent. After being overtaken by Remington Rand, which owned the remaining 10 percent of the tabulating market, IBM's management began to appreciate the business opportunities the novel technology offered. Supported by several generous military contracts, IBM made entry into the computer market a high strategic priority and eventually surpassed Remington Rand thanks to a variety of technological innovations, the penetration of new market segments, and superb marketing to its existing customer base. By the end of the 1950s, IBM dominated all three main segments of the computer market at that time—scientific computers, large-scale data processing computers, and medium-scale business computers.[7] In the mid-1960s, IBM further strengthened its grip on the computer industry with the introduction of the IBM 360 series, an entire family of compatible computers.

There were other computer manufacturers, including Burroughs, the Radio Corporation of America (RCA), Honeywell, and National Cash Register (NCR), who had all bought themselves into the market by acquiring computer and electronics start-ups. But with a market share of 74 percent by the mid-1960s, IBM dwarfed all its competitors, effectively controlling the global computer industry—as it would until the late 1980s.[8] IBM's stranglehold on the computer industry meant that any LAN that would not enjoy its support was doomed to fail as a standard.

Or so it appeared from the perspective of the late 1970s and early 1980s, when LANs were first being commercialized.

For almost one and a half decades mainframes remained the only class of computers, but in the early 1960s a second class was introduced, effectively coexisting with mainframes: minicomputers. Minicomputers were much smaller—approximately the size of a refrigerator—and cost much less than mainframes.[9] The first minicomputer was the Programmable Data Processor 1 (PDP-1), introduced in 1959 by DEC, a start-up that had been established in 1957. Instead of costing millions like many mainframe computer models, the PDP-1 cost only $120,000.[10] Many subsequent models cost even less. DEC's PDP-7, introduced in 1965, cost approximately $60,000; its successor, the PDP-9, introduced in 1966, $35,000; and the PDP-8, introduced in 1965, an unheard-of $18,000.[11] This pricing meant that most minicomputers were still too expensive to be used by a single individual, and thus they had to be shared like mainframes; however, minicomputers were an important step toward the goal of a true personal computer.

The low prices of minicomputers resulted from various cost-saving innovations, but they also reflected what became known in computer component or semiconductor development as the "miniaturization trajectory." The idea behind the miniaturization trajectory is that the density of electric circuits per area is ever increasing, while the prices of electric circuits are continuously falling—a concept also known as Moore's Law. An important step along this trajectory was the invention of the transistor by Bell Laboratories in 1947. Like the vacuum tube or valve, which was used in the early computers like ENIAC, the transistor was a device that amplified or switched an electrical signal.[12] But unlike a vacuum tube, the transistor used semiconductor material and was much smaller than the vacuum tube, while also consuming less power. Transistors were used in mainframes, but they became especially closely linked with the minicomputer. Because price reductions were so crucial to the commercialization of minicomputers, transistors were first implemented in this computing class.[13]

As in computing, the development of the transistor led to the formation of many new firms, all producing discrete components and chasing each other down the price curve. Many of these firms were located in Santa Clara County south of San Francisco—an area that soon became known as Silicon Valley.

Despite their low price and reasonably high performance, minicomputers did not replace mainframes. Instead, they carved out previously untapped market niches, quite different from those served by mainframes.[14]

In the 1960s, minicomputers were first used for laboratory instrumentation and for the monitoring and control of industrial processes. But they were soon being employed for a broader variety of tasks. Though some minicomputers were sold as general-purpose machines, many were designed for highly specialized applications and particular business functions, such as engineering, industrial process control, CAD/CAM applications, communications switching, and word processing.[15] Minicomputers and mainframes also differed in that minicomputers were often deployed outside the corporate computing center. In other words, minicomputers often served as the computing resource for departments, while the larger and more powerful mainframes served the computing needs of the entire corporation.[16]

These differences in application fields and user base were to play a critical role in the LAN market. Because of their different user bases, mainframes and minicomputers were initially not interconnected—a fact that kept the mainframe and minicomputer LAN markets quite separate and ensured that the two computer types required quite different LAN characteristics. LANs designed for the departmental minicomputer market could be simpler, whereas corporate needs demanded LANs of higher complexity and greater robustness. These different requirements were largely responsible for LAN firms' inability to create a single standard. Given the minicomputers' low prices and new markets, annual unit shipments in this class surpassed those of mainframes by far. In 1980 more than 100,000 machines were shipped as compared with 9,900 mainframes; in the mid- to late 1980s this number increased to approximately 200,000 compared with some 12,000 mainframes (figure 2.1).[17] The far more numerous minicomputers would thus play a greater role in LAN standardization than mainframes, thereby giving the minicomputer manufacturers considerable clout.

Following what had already become a familiar pattern in the (mainframe) computer industry, the development of the new class of minicomputers created new economic opportunities that were quickly exploited by a fresh set of start-ups. DEC, which had pioneered the first commercial minicomputer, quickly succeeded in becoming the leading vendor, dominating the scientific and engineering market, although it later moved into the business market. Other leading companies pursuing similar segments and strategies were Silicon Valley-based H-P and Data General, which was spun off from DEC in 1968. The specialized character of the minicomputer created additional business segments. For instance, Prime, which was spun off from Honeywell in 1971, aimed at the general-purpose OEM market; Tandem specialized in fault-tolerant computing systems; and Wang, established in 1951, became a leader in the word

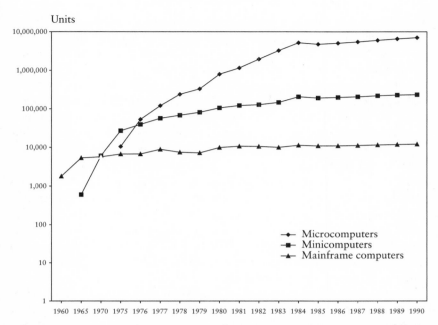

FIGURE 2.1   Yearly shipments of computers in the United States, 1960–1990.

processing market. Between the early 1970s and the mid-1980s, thirty-five to fifty firms occupied the minicomputer space at any given time.[18] Though the top six or eight firms claimed a market share of approximately 80 percent, the minicomputer industry became less concentrated than the mainframe market, still dominated by IBM.[19] However, DEC remained the clear leader, with a market share of never less than 30 percent throughout the 1980s.[20]

In the mid-1970s, a third computer class was introduced: microcomputers. Like the minicomputers of the 1960s, microcomputers resulted from the ongoing pursuit of the miniaturization trajectory of semiconductor technology. In 1959, twelve years after the invention of the transistor, Jack Kilby of Texas Instruments had made another important breakthrough: the development of the integrated circuit (IC). The IC integrated a number of discrete transistors on a single chip of semiconductor material, thereby continuing to nurture the miniaturization trajectory of ever-increasing circuit density and ever-falling prices.[21] The IC paved the way for the development of memory chips, and in 1970–71, also utilizing IC technology, Silicon Valley–based Intel invented the microprocessor, an entire programmable computer on a single chip.[22] The microprocessor was a significant development, because it made possible computers that cost between several hundred and several thousand dollars—far below what minicomputers cost.[23] Such low prices meant that computers would no longer need to be shared like minicomputers and mainframes; they could now be used economically by individuals.

One of the first companies to produce a computer based on Intel's microprocessors was now-defunct MITS (Micro Instrumentation Telemetry Systems) in Albuquerque, New Mexico. Established by electronics tinkerer Ed Roberts, in 1975 MITS introduced the Altair computer. The Altair cost $379 and was a skeleton machine. It lacked a monitor, a keyboard, and useful software; users had to enter programs by flipping switches, only to see a few lights on the front panel blink. What was more, the Altair was sold as kit, forcing buyers to assemble their own machines. To the general public, as well as the established computer companies, the Altair was of no interest, but it took the world of electronics hobbyists by storm. For the first time, they could have their own personal computer. Within a few months, MITS had received 4,000 orders and was completely overwhelmed.[24]

MITS did not long remain the exclusive manufacturer of such microcomputers; within a few years numerous firms began producing their own proprietary machines. Many of them were located in Silicon Valley, where there was an especially large number of hobbyists because of the many semiconductor firms located there. In fact, the level of interest among Silicon Valley's hobbyists became so great that in the mid- to late 1970s the region became the epicenter of the microcomputer revolution. Competition among the various manufacturers was fierce, and as a result microcomputer technology evolved rapidly. By the late 1970s and early 1980s microcomputers were equipped with faster processors and more memory, as well as monitors, keyboards, and floppy disk drives. Among the leading models were the Commodore PET and the Radio Shack TRS-80, but the frontrunner was the Apple II from Apple Computer Corporation in Cupertino, California.[25]

In 1981, a fundamental shift occurred in the microcomputer industry. Having watched the beginning of the microcomputer revolution in Silicon Valley from the sidelines, in August of that year IBM introduced its version of a microcomputer, the IBM PC. As a result of IBM's domination of the mainframe computer industry and the PC's open architecture, the IBM PC quickly replaced the Apple II as the market leader, and in the process Silicon Valley lost its dominance in the manufacturing of microcomputers to IBM and the PC clone industry scattered around the United States. Simultaneously, offices displaced hobbyists as the main market for microcomputers, thanks to IBM's focus on the office market and the development of word processing and spreadsheet software. The vast new office market allowed yearly shipments of IBM PCs and clones to swell to approximately five million in 1986.[26] Indeed the term "PC" rapidly supplanted "microcomputer" as the designation for this newest class of computer, owing to the ubiquity of the IBM machines. PCs now presented the largest potential market for LAN technology. IBM continued to dominate PC production for many years, but because of the machine's openness, Big Blue could not prevent the rise of the clone makers Compaq, AST, Gateway, Packard Bell, and Dell, which eventually took over the PC market.

Although mainframes, minicomputers, and microcomputers constituted the principal classes of computers, in the late 1970s a fourth, hybrid computer class emerged: workstations. Developed primarily by Apollo and Sun Microsystems, workstations were desktop computers that fit roughly between minicomputers and personal computers. Though used as personal devices, workstations were considerably more expensive than PCs, costing at least $10,000.[27] This made them too expensive for general office use, but because they were optimized to perform intensive calculations they competed in the same markets as minicomputers, namely engineering departments.

In 1980, these various classes of computers coexisted without too much competition, but during the 1980s important shifts took place in the computer industry. As already mentioned, PCs soon outnumbered the installed base of any other computer class. Furthermore, PCs and workstations began to invade the traditional minicomputer markets. In the early to mid-1980s, PCs replaced minicomputer-based word-processing systems, leading to the fall of minicomputer powerhouse Wang.[28] In the mid- to late 1980s, workstations edged minicomputers out of their core engineering and scientific markets. As a result, most minicomputer firms, including DEC, stumbled and were relegated to second-tier status or even disappeared completely.[29] This meant that any LAN entrenched in the minicomputer market would have to make the transition to PCs and workstations if it was to survive.

Early Network Technologies

For the first two decades after the invention of the ENIAC mainframe machine, computers and networks evolved separately, because networks were not yet an integral part of computing technology. Between the 1970s and the early 1990s, however, networks were gradually integrated into the technology, and with the arrival of client/server-based computing they became an indispensable part of it. The first step of this integration occurred with the deployment of time-sharing systems in the late 1960s and early 1970s, when users began interacting with computers through terminals. A further step toward ever-tighter integration was taken in the early to mid-1970s with the development of the first distributed computing systems, that is, systems that distributed the processing of data and programs over several specialized computing units. In fact, in 1970–71, while experimenting with a distributed computing system based on minicomputers, David Farber of the University of California, Irvine, invented the first high-speed LAN technology, a token ring LAN. But the most important step in this integration occurred in 1973, when Xerox PARC, even before the arrival of microcomputers, built a system that distributed office computing tasks over many small, specialized units, including personal workstations. It would take more than a decade before such distributed computing systems—by then on the so-called Wintel standard (employing the Microsoft Windows operating system on devices built around Intel microprocessors)—became part of the mainstream computing architecture for offices. But if it was to link large numbers of personal computers for computing in offices, PARC would need a powerful network—a fact that not only led to the development of the second important LAN type, Ethernet, but also reinforced the complementary relationship between computers and networks.

Though computing technology and networks evolved on different paths for many years, computing technology clearly influenced the evolution of networks and the types of networks that were initially built. In fact, the early networks were mostly WANs, not LANs (figure 2.2). The initial focus on WANs, as well as the slow pace of growth in network installations, resulted primarily from the exorbitantly high prices of mainframes (the only computer class before the arrival of minicomputers in the mid-1960s), which made it uneconomical for most organizations to install several computers at one site—an obvious requisite for a LAN. At the same time, because computing power was so expensive, computers were used for only the most critical tasks, such as air defense and reservation systems—applications that depended on large-scale data collection. Such expensive computers, covering large geographic areas and used for central computing tasks, would naturally be linked by WANs rather than LANs. It was only when computer prices began to fall, and corporations as well as universities could afford to install several computers at one location, that LANs came into their own.

Although the first electronic computers were built in the mid-1940s, the era of computer networks did not begin until the late 1950s for several reasons. Most mainframe computers of the late 1940s and early 1950s were one-of-a-kind, experimental machines; they completely lacked any

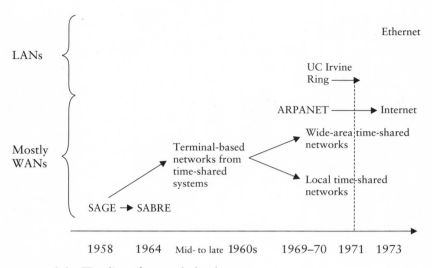

FIGURE 2.2   Timeline of network development.

built-in communications capability. Even the more numerous commercial mainframes of the mid- and late 1950s were designed as standalone machines and thus had only limited communications capabilities as well.[30] Computer networking was also slow to develop because in the 1950s most mainframe models, even if they were built by the same manufacturer, were incompatible in terms of hardware, data formats, and software.[31] Although incompatibility does not preclude the linking of computers via networks—in time, incompatible computers would indeed be linked—it greatly complicated data communication in the early years.[32] Aside from these technical reasons, data networks emerged only slowly in the 1950s because the installed base of computers was still very small. The several hundred mainframes installed in the late 1950s in the United States were simply not numerous enough to encourage extensive networking. And corporations, the most important purchasers of mainframes together with universities and government agencies, saw little commercial value in interconnecting their computers. In fact, firms mostly used their computers for central computing tasks, such as corporate accounting, making their data either too sensitive or too uninteresting to be shared with other firms.[33] This meant that corporate networks could not evolve from the total installed base of computers; instead they had to grow from the firms' *internal* installed bases. But because of the novelty and high prices of mainframe computers, in the late 1950s most firms had either only one machine or at best a very few, thereby further impeding network growth.

The computing paradigm of the 1950s, based on high-cost mainframes, was simply not conducive to networking.

Despite these obstacles, in 1958 the U.S. Air Force installed the first large-scale data network as part of its air defense system, SAGE (Semi-Automated Ground Environment).[34] SAGE was a centralized command and control system that used telephone lines to connect radar stations and other devices scattered all over North America to central mainframe computers.[35] The SAGE system, resulting from an $8–12 billion research effort, was revolutionary for its time.[36] Thanks to its powerful mainframes, SAGE was able to maintain an overall picture of the North American airspace in (almost) real time—a critical innovation. If it detected alien aircrafts, it calculated trajectories for counterattacks and communicated them to human operators through the use of terminals, another important innovation.[37] SAGE eventually included over a million miles of telecommunication lines, becoming a huge WAN.[38]

Its special-purpose nature made SAGE an isolated networking event in the 1950s, but its control and coordination concept, as well as its network-friendly innovations (including the use of terminals and modems, as well as its real-time operation) spurred the development of similarly structured networks in the civilian sector.[39] One of the first SAGE-based civil systems was SABRE (Semi-Automatic Business-Related Environment), an airline reservation system installed in 1964 by American Airlines.[40] Instead of tracking the movement of aircrafts, SABRE coordinated seat reservations, which were entered from remote terminals. When put into operation, SABRE connected over 1,200 terminals distributed throughout the United States to a central mainframe computer via 12,000 miles of telephone lines, making it, like SAGE, a large-scale WAN.[41] Similar transaction processing and reservation systems were installed in the hotel and banking industries, among other sectors.[42] Though SABRE and the SABRE-like reservation and transaction systems did not really surpass SAGE technologically, their civilian applications led to a modest increase in the installation of (terminal) networks during the 1960s.

A SAGE-related development with a more significant impact on network growth was the advent of time-sharing, a novel concept in user-computer interaction. First suggested in 1959, time-sharing still required multiple users to share a single computer, mainly because the relatively high (albeit declining) computer prices of the day continued to block the ultimate goal, a computer for each individual user. Yet time-sharing was a significant improvement over batch processing, the previous mode of using a computer. In batch processing, users were deprived of direct access to the computer and had to write programs off line before submitting them to an operator.[43] This was very inconvenient, because users

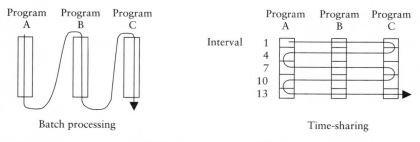

FIGURE 2.3   Execution of programs in batch processing and time-sharing.

received their output only after a delay of several hours or sometimes days.[44] Developed to remove this bottleneck, time-sharing, in contrast, gave the user direct access to the computer through a terminal. Although multiple terminals were connected to one computer, users nevertheless gained the illusion of having exclusive and immediate access to the machine. This was because a time-sharing system divided the mainframe's processing time into tiny intervals, allocated one interval to one program at a time, and cycled rapidly among all the programs running at the time (figure 2.3). Users appeared to receive almost instant response from the computer.[45] Given this drastic improvement, time-sharing became the principal mode of computer-user interaction in the early to mid-1970s and continued to prevail throughout the mid- to late 1980s, after which time distributed computing systems based on PCs finally replaced time-sharing systems.[46]

Since time-sharing, first implemented in the early 1960s, required terminals, it had a positive impact on the extent of network installations.[47] Initially, most terminal networks were local ones, because many users installed their terminals in close proximity to the host computer. Yet these local terminal networks did not immediately require high transmission speeds, because the relatively brief, text-based messages sent back and forth between the host and its terminals were not very data intensive. Low-speed telephone lines and wires based on twisted-pair cable, the underlying medium of telephone lines, entirely sufficed. Only in the late 1970s and early 1980s, when organizations began connecting hundreds of terminals to a single host computer, did the higher network speeds of LANs become necessary.[48]

Time-sharing also led to wide-area terminal networks. In fact, users quickly began installing their terminals in more convenient places than the immediate surroundings of the host computer, and some corporations even began selling access to their systems to those remote users who could not afford their own computers.[49] As in the case of local terminal networks, low-speed telephone lines served as the principal transmission medium for these wide-area terminal networks.[50] Given the low speeds of telephone lines, this meant that the initial networks transmitted at far slower speeds than the later LANs.

Before long, network installations resulting from time-sharing surpassed the network growth spurred by SABRE and the SABRE-like systems, for two reasons. In contrast to these reservation and transaction systems, time-sharing computers were general-purpose machines that executed any type of application, not just specific, predefined applications. And time-sharing was implemented not only on mainframes but also on the more numerous minicomputers.[51] Time-sharing was thus responsible for most of the network growth that took place in the late 1960s and the 1970s.[52]

From a technological perspective, however, the most important network development preceding LANs was the ARPANET, built by the U.S. Department of Defense's Advanced Research Projects Agency. ARPANET's construction must be viewed within the context of ARPA's mission. Established in response to the shock of the Sputnik launch in 1957, ARPA was initially commissioned to advance scientific progress in military-related fields, such as space and missile research, by funding research projects at universities.[53] But given the importance of computing technology for these projects, the agency quickly became involved with this new technology, and in the early 1960s it established an office to provide overall guidance for research in computing: the Information Processing Techniques Office (IPTO). Before long, the agency became the main sponsor of computer research at U.S. universities and was responsible for the development of various one-of-a-kind supercomputers, including MAC at the Massachusetts Institute of Technology (MIT) and ILLIAC IV at the University of Illinois.[54] Yet despite its deep pockets, ARPA soon realized that it could no longer sustain its generous funding levels. By 1966 it had seventeen research centers under contract, each requesting ever more specialized supercomputers. Meeting such demands not only incurred high costs but also threatened to produce much wasteful duplication, as the universities often wanted to build similar systems.[55] This cost pressure, in combination with ARPA's vision of building a national research community, prompted the agency in the early 1960s to initiate design studies for a network that would connect all its research sites.[56]

After several years of careful studies, in 1969–70 ARPA began the construction of what became known as the ARPANET. By early 1970 it had connected four sites, but thereafter the network quickly expanded. By April 1971 it consisted of fifteen nodes and twenty-three host computers scattered throughout the United States, and during the mid-1970s it was expanding at a rate of one node per month, reaching approximately a hundred hosts in 1975.[57] The ARPANET spanned thousands of miles and transmitted at 50 kbps—then considered a relatively high speed but one far below the transmission speed of later LANs.

The ARPANET's hundred or so host computers failed to match the extension of network installations spurred by time-sharing; yet the ARPANET was of greater significance than time-sharing in other ways. Unlike time-sharing and earlier networks, the ARPANET connected primarily computers, not terminals, making it the first true computer-to-computer network.[58] And as other government agencies and countries built similar computer networks and as they were connected to the ARPANET, it eventually evolved into the Internet, a network of networks and the precursor to the World Wide Web (WWW).[59]

Finally, the construction of the ARPANET led to the development of many new network technologies, including packet switching, layering, and the use of a network interface. In packet switching, a message was broken into smaller units, called packets, and the network consisted of a mesh of many intermediary, permanently established links (which, in the case of the ARPANET, were leased telephone lines). As the top panel of figure 2.4 shows, the ARPANET did not connect each pair of nodes directly, but the packets eventually reached their final destinations because each node could forward (or route) a packet toward its destination.[60] Packet switching differed sharply from the telephone system's circuit switching method, which sent its (voice) messages in a continuous stream and established a direct (though only temporary) link (circuit) between any two nodes (bottom panel in figure 2.4). Packet switching proved very cost-effective in the case of the ARPANET, because the method allowed the network to interleave packets from different messages on the same line and because data communication, unlike a telephone conversation, occurs in short bursts with long pauses.[61]

ARPANET's second network innovation, layering, broke the entire communication process up into several steps, or layers, each performing a specific function in the communication process. Though adjacent layers interacted with each other, each layer operated independently of the others. This approach meant that ARPANET's designers and programmers did not need to understand the complexity of the communication process in its entirety but could focus narrowly on a specific layer.[62]

Finally, the use of a network interface, called the interface message processor (IMP) in the case of the ARPANET, simply meant that the computer was not linked to the wire directly but instead through an interface. The interface assumed responsibility for all network-related tasks,

Packet switching

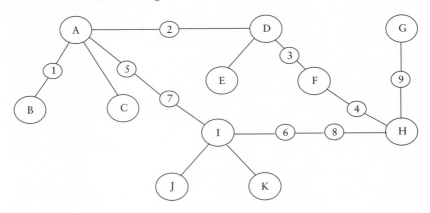

1 – 6 : Packets from node B to node H

7 – 9 : Packets from node A to node G

Circuit switching

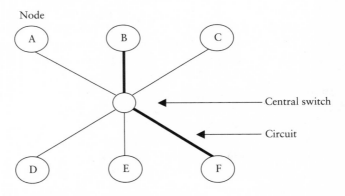

FIGURE 2.4 Packet switching and circuit switching.

such as connecting the hosts to the telephone lines, transforming messages into packets and vice versa, and routing packets over the intermediary links.[63]

It was not long before these three network innovations found their way into later networks, including LANs. Though LANs were not constructed on the basis of intermediary links, they typically broke a message into

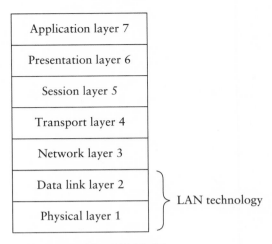

FIGURE 2.5   The OSI Model.

smaller packets, sometimes also called frames. Like the packet method, layering was also widely adopted in LAN development. Most computer vendors divided their communication protocols into various layers. In the seven-layer Open Systems Interconnection (OSI) Reference Model, the International Standards Organization's idealized model for representing data communication, LAN technology occupied the two bottom layers (figure 2.5).[64] Finally, LAN builders often used the interface method to connect a node to the LAN wire. In LANs, the interface was often referred to as adapter card. These network innovations, together with the origination of the Internet and the World Wide Web, made the ARPANET the most important network development of the 1960s and 1970s.

In summary, with the exception of some local terminal networks, the networks of the 1950s and 1960s were primarily WANs, not LANs. The early networks' long distances were to a large extent rooted in the computing paradigm of the 1950s and 1960s, one based on high-cost mainframes, the predominant computer class of the period. In fact, the high prices of mainframes, together with their novelty, depressed the installed base of computers at local sites, thereby preventing the installation of local networks. In addition, the high prices of computers made it imperative that they be accessible for remote data access and shared among as many users as possible. This situation favored WANs over LANs, simply because long network distances allowed for greater sharing and wider data collection, thereby making more cost-effective use of the expensive computers. As we have seen, these factors were the rationale behind the construction of the ARPANET, as well as of the SAGE and SABRE networks and various time-sharing networks. Despite the absence of high-speed local networks during this period, the early networks (especially the ARPANET) had a significant impact on their successors, the LANs. LAN designers were to make extensive use of several network techniques invented for the ARPANET, and the growth of terminal-based time-sharing networks eventually made it necessary to rely on the LANs' higher speeds.

The Invention and Evolution of Token Ring

In hindsight, LANs could have been invented in any one of a number of places, since at the start of the 1970s many university research laboratories had more than one computer.[65] But the transition to LANs occurred at the University of California, Irvine, in 1970–71. By the start of the new decade the prices of minicomputers had fallen so drastically that UC Irvine could now afford to install several minicomputers. One of its faculty members, David Farber, became interested in building a local distributed computing system, that is, a system that distributed computation and data processing operations over several linked but separate computing devices.[66] Though such a system obviously required a network, Farber realized that the transmission rates of existing networks, based on telephone wires, would not suffice. In contrast to time-sharing terminal-based systems, his distributed system would involve computer-to-computer communication and the transfer of entire files. Since these operations had to match the high speeds of which computer buses were already capable, and since they were far more data-intensive than text-based exchanges, they required a higher-speed network.[67] If Farber was to realize a true distributed computing system, he would have to pioneer a faster network technology.

After evaluating different network concepts, Farber decided to build what later became known as a token ring LAN; his network later became known as the UC Irvine Ring.[68] As the name suggests, a token ring network links nodes in a closed cable loop and sends a bit pattern, called a token, continuously and unidirectionally around the ring (figure 2.6). The token essentially controls transmission. If a station desires to transmit, it seizes the token as it passes by, changes the bit pattern to "busy" by adding a destination address to it, and attaches its data packets to it. The token, with its attached data packets, continues its journey to the destination node, which purges the message upon arrival. The token then returns to the sender node, which not only regenerates a "free" token but also passes it downstream before refilling it with new data. Such passing

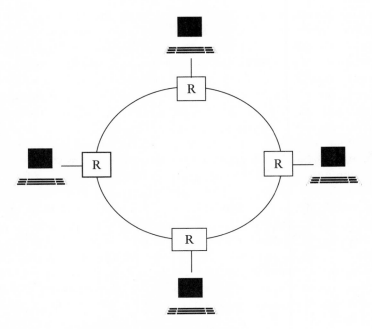

FIGURE 2.6 Ring topology. R, repeater.

ensures that no node can monopolize the network.[69] Since the maximum time interval between successive appearances of the token can be calculated, token ring technology has a deterministic element. Not only would this characteristic eventually serve to differentiate token ring-based network technologies from Ethernet, it would also be declared a technological advantage.[70]

Determinism was one reason Farber opted for a token ring, but he also liked the technology for its high reliability, easy scalability, and low cost, as well as the absence of centralized network coordination. In fact, in 1975 the connection costs per node were only $600, and since the network operated without any central (switching) components, costs grew in proportion to the number of nodes. This characteristic pleased Farber, who intended to build only a small distributed system.[71]

By 1971 Farber had operationalized his distributed computing system. It operated over twisted-pair and coaxial cable at 2.3 Mbps—that is, at a speed that exceeded that of the ARPANET, itself a fast WAN, by a factor of forty-six.[72] In 1975 the system connected five minicomputers (three Lockheed SUE computers and two Varian 620/i computers), as well as

several terminals, printers, and a magnetic tape unit. The system worked
well, and Farber published several papers about it. But since he had no
commercial interest in this "side product," the UC Irvine Ring remained
an experimental network, influencing the design of subsequent token rings
without having a direct impact on the marketplace.[73]

On the news of Farber's invention, several research laboratories quickly
imitated his token ring system, but not without making modifications in
either access method or wiring structure. One of the first imitators was
the computer laboratory at Cambridge University. Eager to replace a central mainframe with a distributed computing system consisting of several
minicomputers, in 1974 the laboratory initiated design studies for a digital communication ring.[74] This effort eventually led to the so-called
Cambridge Ring, a token ring network that in the late 1970s operated at
10 Mbps and connected a PDP-7 and two PDP-11 minicomputers, the
Cambridge CAP computer, a Data General Nova minicomputer, and a
plotter.[75] Though the Cambridge Ring preserved the UC Irvine Ring's
physical ring structure, its designers implemented a different token access
method, known as the empty slot principle.[76] This method differed from
Farber's token system in that it sent not just one but several bit patterns,
called slots (comparable to tokens), around the ring.[77] Hence the Cambridge Ring offered stations more opportunities to send a message than
Farber's token network.[78] Despite this incremental enhancement, the
market considered neither Cambridge's empty slot principle nor access
methods in general to be critical LAN attributes. As a result, despite
efforts by some British firms to commercialize it, the Cambridge Ring
joined the UC Irvine Ring as an interesting variation, but one without
market impact.[79]

A more significant modification of token ring technology occurred at
MIT. Attempting to understand the emerging LAN technology, in the
mid-1970s several researchers at MIT, including Professor Jerome Saltzer,
research staff member Kenneth Pogran, and Professor David Clark, not
only began experimenting with Ethernet technology but also built a copy
of Farber's UC Irvine Ring.[80] Convinced of the usefulness of LAN technology and satisfied with the technology underlying the UC Irvine Ring,
in the late 1970s Saltzer and Pogran, among others, decided to develop
their own token ring system. Whereas the architects of the Cambridge
Ring had modified Farber's access method, Saltzer and Pogran decided to
experiment with the LAN's *wiring structure* or *topology*. Rather than
wiring the nodes in a physical ring as Farber and the researchers at Cambridge University had done, they decided to wire them in a star-shaped
ring. Instead of sending the wire directly from node to node, after each
node they passed the wire through a device at a central location before

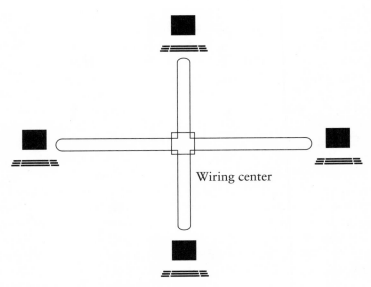

Wiring center

FIGURE 2.7   Star-shaped ring topology.

reaching out to the next node (figure 2.7). This wiring structure gave the network the appearance of a star, although in reality the network remained a ring, formed at the wiring center. The device at the wiring center later became known as a multistation access unit in the token ring realm and as a hub in the Ethernet realm.

Saltzer and Pogran abandoned Farber's "pure" ring architecture for several reasons. Observing the ongoing microcomputer revolution, they anticipated that desktop computers would soon be ubiquitous and concluded that many networks would eventually include thousands of nodes.[81] They believed that under such conditions a network wired in a physical ring would experience severe reliability, installation, and management problems. For instance, since the nodes could be expected to be scattered across different buildings and offices within those buildings, a physical ring network was likely to take on a very irregular shape; this might adversely affect the network's performance. In addition, because the insertion of a new node between two already connected stations often required the drawing of new cable, thereby leaving the old cable unused, a physical ring structure would produce many abandoned wires within ceilings and walls as stations were incrementally added to the network. But the "pure" ring structure entailed an even more serious problem. If

network administrators were to find the cause of a network failure, such as
a broken cable or a single improperly connected node, they would literally
have to follow the ring—an extremely inconvenient and time-consuming
method of troubleshooting, given that the wiring was often placed in
ceilings and behind walls. Besides, this search procedure would require the
administrators to carry test equipment from node to node and to have keys
to every office that contained a node.[82] Saltzer and Pogran concluded
that troubleshooting was likely to be difficult in a "pure" ring network,
especially if it contained many nodes. This was especially troublesome
because a single failure—either of the wire or the connectivity device
between wire and node—could stall the entire network.

They reasoned that the star-based ring topology, with its central connection point, could avoid these problems. In this topology, the installation of new nodes did not make any previous wires obsolete, because the
wires of a new spoke could easily be inserted and the ring rearranged at
the wiring center. As they wrote in 1979, "unanticipated installations
could [thus] be handled without creating a hodgepodge of wires criss-
crossing through the walls and ceilings."[83] But most important, the star
topology would simplify the troubleshooting process. With a central connection point, the troubleshooter could test the entire network from one
location, simply launching a message into the ring at the wiring center,
observing how far it got, and temporarily isolating any faulty segments.
To effect the repair, the troubleshooter needed access only to the trouble
spot.[84] For these reasons, Saltzer and Pogran believed that a network's
wiring structure was far more critical for efficient network operation than
access method and throughput rate—the very features that vendors would
later so often refer to when they bragged about LAN performance, and
whose implementation required sophisticated algorithms and ICs. Though
mundane, wiring structure had a critical impact on troubleshooting, management, and maintenance, the most costly and mission-critical issues in
networks.[85]

As the following chapters reveal, history would prove that Saltzer and
Pogran had made the right assumptions and drawn the correct conclusion.
The star topology indeed became part of the dominant design in LANs.
Both the Token Ring and Ethernet IEEE standards eventually employed
the topology—Token Ring from the beginning and Ethernet since the
late 1980s. Yet in the late 1970s Saltzer and Pogran's idea was clearly
ahead of its time, as very few sites possessed dozens, let alone hundreds,
of nodes. For that reason, subsequent LAN architects would not all use
the hub topology.[86]

The transition from the early WANs to LANs thus took place in parallel
with the proliferation of minicomputers, whose lower prices allowed user

organizations to gather several machines together at one site. Farber's invention of token ring technology at UC Irvine led quickly to the development of similar networks at other university research laboratories. Token ring technology was soon well accepted within the research community.

The Invention of Ethernet

The experimentation with LAN technology sparked by Farber's innovation did not remain confined to the realm of token rings. In the 1970s and 1980s numerous LAN technologies—with a wide variety of access methods, topologies, and technical parameters—were developed. But the most important rival to the token ring was Ethernet.

Ethernet was invented in 1973 by Robert Metcalfe at Xerox PARC, and it relied on a fundamentally different access method and topology. Ethernet's development must be considered within the historical context of PARC, one of the most productive research organizations in the history of computing. In fact, PARC did far more than develop an alternative LAN technology. By creating the first functional personal workstation for the office environment and by making the LAN an integral part of the office, PARC almost single-handedly created the principal environment in which LANs would be deployed and which would drive the phenomenal growth of the LAN industry in the late 1980s: distributed computing systems based on personal computers.

Established in 1970, Xerox PARC originated from Xerox's desire to extend its copier business to embrace computer technology. Although it had been catapulted into the Fortune 500 in fewer than ten years thanks to its revolutionary copier technology, by the late 1960s Xerox realized that computers severely threatened its core business. Whereas copiers, based on analog technology, were able only to reproduce existing information, computers' digital capability allowed them to execute far more complex and transformative information-handling operations, such as storing, communicating, processing, and computing.[87] Even more threatening to the copier vendor, computer printers allowed users to *print* computer data. Although early computer printouts were clearly of inferior quality, Xerox knew that improvements to them were inevitable. Since "both copiers and computers served the same ultimate demand for better, faster, and more powerful means to process and communicate information," Xerox's management concluded that direct competition with computer manufacturers would be unavoidable.[88]

To counter the attack of the computer vendors—some of whom were already invading Xerox's turf by developing copiers of their own—Xerox decided to produce its own line of computers.[89] To avoid competition with IBM, whose mainframes dominated the back offices of large corporations, Xerox decided to focus on the very markets in which its copiers were employed, namely the "*front offices* of sales forces, production managers, finance and planning personnel, secretaries, and executives."[90] Xerox would join the race for the "office of the future"—a much-hyped quest in the late 1970s to computerize office operations, and one expected to become a multibillion-dollar business. As the following chapters show, numerous computer manufacturers—including Wang, IBM, and Datapoint—also vied for this business, and the development of LAN technology became inextricably linked to the quest for the "office of the future" or "office automation" (OA).[91]

Since front offices required computing technology fundamentally different from that of the mainframes employed in back offices, and since Xerox lacked a significant electronics capability, in 1970 the copier vendor decided to invest part of its $100 million annual research budget in the establishment of a corporate research laboratory.[92] The research facility was commissioned to develop computer-based means for organizing the information explosion then taking place in front offices.[93] In the words of Peter McColough, CEO of Xerox, the research center was to create a new "architecture of information" for the office.[94] Exactly what this architecture was to look like was unclear to McColough, but the term incisively captured the mission of the new laboratory.

If Xerox was to succeed in creating a fundamentally new "architecture of information," it would have to locate its new research laboratory in the most stimulating environment and to hire the brightest researchers. After evaluating several sites, in 1970 the company selected Palo Alto, California, in the heart of Silicon Valley. A Palo Alto location put Xerox's research lab in close proximity to Stanford University, as well as such leading semiconductor and computer companies as Fairchild, Intel, and H-P, which were to play an important role in the burgeoning computer industry.[95] Xerox expected that this location would provide it "with dependable vendors, experienced scientists, and an intellectually rich and relevant environment."[96] A decade later, PARC's location would have another critical impact: Silicon Valley's powerful business-creating institutions would expedite Ethernet's commercialization outside PARC.[97]

To head the new facility, Xerox hired Robert Taylor, a former director of ARPA's IPTO, mainly because of his excellent contacts within the computer science community.[98] As anticipated, Taylor's hiring soon prompted many star computer engineers to join PARC, including Alan Kay, Butler Lampson, and Charles Thacker. Many came from institutions ARPA had previously funded, such as MIT, the University of Utah, and Carnegie-

Mellon University; several others came from Berkeley Computer Corporation, a defunct pioneer in time-sharing.[99] By 1971 Xerox PARC was sufficiently well established to begin the actual work of transforming the front office.

To realize the new "architecture of information," PARC's researchers embarked on a bold new course. After developing their own time-sharing minicomputer system, in 1972 they decided *not* to base Xerox's office architecture on such central computing facilities but instead to realize it by placing a personal computer on every desktop.[100] Though a ubiquitous reality today, the personal computer was still a radical idea in the early 1970s.[101] Yet PARC's researchers knew that the transition to personal computers was inevitable.[102] By 1972, rapid progress in computer technology, especially in semiconductors, had provoked such steep price reductions that a personal computer on every desk was a foreseeable reality.[103]

The vision of PARC's researchers did not stop at creating a personal computer. Inspired by the concept of Alan Kay's Dynabook—a self-contained knowledge manipulator providing all the functions of books, paper, and pencil, embracing both communication and computing—they decided to create a computer that would go far beyond the state of the art in the early 1970s.[104] Eventually their personal computer, called Alto, would be equipped with a bit map monitor, a graphical user interface, a mouse, and multitasking capability.[105] Once again, these features are ubiquitous today, but in the early 1970s they were beyond the comprehension of many computer scientists, accustomed as they were to text-based computing systems.[106] PARC began work on Alto in November 1972; when it was finished in April 1973, its parts cost $10,000, or 60 percent less than the least expensive minicomputer.[107] Although this made the Alto considerably more expensive than the later IBM PC, it was the closest thing to a personal computer available at that time.[108]

The Alto was not the only device PARC's researchers were developing for their office system. Xerox knew from its copier business about knowledge workers' appetite for hard-copy printouts, and its researchers also began developing a laser printer, called EARS, which they had in operation by 1973.[109] PARC also decided to develop a network. This too seemed indispensable, so that knowledge workers, who often worked in teams, could send e-mails and share information and files.[110] Besides, PARC's laser printer was so expensive that it had to be shared among several Altos.[111] Finally, PARC developed file servers that would store electronic files and make them available to individual computers.[112]

In short, PARC's office concept consisted of a personal computer, file servers, and a laser printer—all interlinked by a network. By distributing office operations over several small personal computers instead of concentrating them in a large time-sharing system, PARC created a huge potential market for LAN technology—not only because the smaller devices had to be "reintegrated" to match the larger systems' performance, but also because PARC's system was intended for the general office market. Eventually, such personal distributed computing systems (albeit based on the Wintel standard) would become the dominant environment for LANs, effectively replacing terminal-based systems.

When PARC's researchers decided in 1971–72 to develop a network, they took two important steps: In July 1972 they hired Robert Metcalfe, then a prospective Harvard Ph.D. with ARPANET experience, to actually build the network.[113] And they defined various requirements for their network.[114] Since the network would have to link all future Alto computers at PARC, the first requirement was that it be capable of connecting hundreds of computers over hundreds of meters.[115] The network also had to be able to operate at very high speeds, transferring data at hundreds of kilobits per second. Such a transmission rate was primarily necessary to speed up the printing of the data-intensive images generated by the Alto. In fact, the Alto and the EARS laser printer were together powerful enough to display and print a page within a second or two, but if PARC had used "what was then considered as a high-speed serial link," printing a page would have taken fifteen minutes, an unacceptable amount of time.[116] Relying on what was soon to become a general pricing target in the LAN industry, PARC researchers further determined that the network "had to cost no more than five percent of the costs" of the personal computers it connected.[117] Finally, PARC decided to employ coaxial cable for its network because of its high transmission rate of up to several thousand kilobits per second. In short, PARC's network had to be relatively powerful, yet inexpensive and simple.

PARC rejected several network alternatives it had initially considered. The MCA (Multiprocessor Communications Adapter) network accompanying its Nova minicomputers was ruled out, because it could not meet the transmission-distance requirement. PARC also dropped the idea of building a miniaturized copy of the ARPANET, viewing it as too complex.[118]

Armed with these decisions and requirements, in late 1972 Metcalfe set to work developing PARC's network.[119] He spent more than half a year on research, but on May 22, 1973, approximately two years after Farber had completed his UC Irvine Ring, Metcalfe finished the concept and algorithm for his network. He called the system the ETHER Network. The word *ether* "came from *luminiferous (a)ether,* once thought to pervade the universe as the medium for the propagation of light." This seemed an appropriate metaphor: data would flow through the coaxial cable like light through the ether. Later, Metcalfe shortened the name to Ethernet.[120]

Though Ethernet served the same function as Farber's token ring, namely connecting computers at high speeds over short distances, it operated quite differently. Instead of regulating transmission through a token, Ethernet had no control mechanism and allowed any node to initiate a transmission at any moment. But before sending data, it had to listen to the wire. If it detected an already ongoing transmission, it had to wait. But if the node did not detect a transmission, it could begin sending its data immediately. When two stations found the wire silent and thus started transmitting simultaneously, the resulting collision would cause them to back off instantly without completing their messages. They would then wait for a randomly chosen interval, after which they would try to retransmit their data.[121] In case the nodes had to reinitiate their transmissions repeatedly—for example, if too many nodes were attempting to (re)transmit at once—Metcalfe designed the network so that the random delay increased with each failed attempt.[122] This feature was the core of Ethernet's transmission and access mechanism. Later it became known as CSMA/CD (Carrier Sense Multiple Access with Collision Detection). Metcalfe disliked the term, but it succinctly described the functioning of Ethernet.[123]

With this transmission method, Metcalfe had come up with a network fundamentally different from Farber's token ring. Whereas Farber's token technology sent a token continuously around the ring and permitted nodes to send data only after having seized the token, Ethernet's cable remained silent except when transmitting, and any node was free to initiate a transmission at any moment. Another difference was that the token ring sent its messages around the ring unidirectionally, whereas Ethernet broadcast them. Most important, with its CSMA/CD feature, Ethernet contained more random elements than token ring technology. Ethernet's randomness, as well as its provision of equal but uncoordinated access to the cable, mirrored the office environment, in which the transmission of files, e-mails, and print jobs occurred at random times. Yet this distinguishing feature was soon to provoke heated debates over the relative merits of the two technologies. Ethernet's randomness prompted token ring's proponents to argue that an Ethernet node might have to postpone transmission for a long time. They also claimed that, in large networks and under heavy traffic, Ethernet's method of increasing the length of the random delay between transmission attempts considerably slowed down its actual throughput rate and in fact only exacerbated the overload problem.[124] Although the debate would later intensify, given

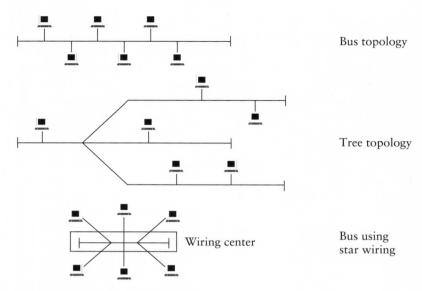

Bus topology

Tree topology

Wiring center

Bus using
star wiring

FIGURE 2.8　Ethernet topologies.

the few computers then in place at most sites, transmission speed was not a major bottleneck in the 1970s, and it ultimately did not play a major role in de facto LAN standardization.

Ethernet's topology accounted for another difference between the two technologies. Ethernet was neither a star nor a ring, but a branching bus or unrooted tree (middle panel in figure 2.8).[125] This meant that an Ethernet network could branch out at any point in several directions as long as no loops were formed. In the simplest case, Ethernet would not branch out but would remain a continuous string with the cable terminated at both ends (top panel in figure 2.8). This structure was termed a bus topology. In a more complex case, several Ethernet segments could be connected at one point (bottom panel in figure 2.8). This meant that Ethernet, in theory, could be star-wired like Saltzer and Pogran's token ring network, thereby gaining similar advantages in terms of wiring topology and network management.[126]

Developing his network several years before the development of Saltzer and Pogran's star-shaped ring, Metcalfe in the end chose a bus topology for PARC's Ethernet—a decision that would have a far-reaching impact on later competition between the two technologies. Metcalfe preferred the bus to the star in part because it saved the cost of the extra wire between the hub and the nodes. But by laying the cable in a simple string he also expected to avoid wiring complications, boost reliability, and, most important, save the cost of an active (that is, powered) hub.[127] As Saltzer himself has pointed out, an active hub would have required a large number of chips—which, of course, were still quite expensive in the early 1970s.[128] By opting for the bus topology, Metcalfe was able to save network costs in the short run. But by avoiding the hub-based star topology, his network was now open to the same potential disadvantages in terms of network management and troubleshooting as Farber's ring. In the absence of a central connectivity device, the Ethernet network administrator would also have to follow the wire to find the trouble spot and could not perform testing from a single location.

In the mid-1970s, with only few computers at any given site, the potential drawbacks of the bus topology simply did not matter. But the topology indeed posed significant disadvantages in large networks, and these would jeopardize Ethernet's survival in the late 1980s. Metcalfe's selection of the bus topology set a precedent with far-reaching consequences. Because Xerox and the other firms that commercialized Ethernet simply imitated his topology, Ethernet became locked into the bus structure for more than a decade. Only in the mid-1980s did its vendors remember and deploy the alternate star topology.

With the development of the Ethernet algorithm, Metcalfe's task was not yet complete: he still had to make Ethernet operational. Now collaborating with David Boggs, a talented amateur radio expert, Metcalfe "sweated" almost half a year before the first Altos exchanged data packets.[129] A critical part of their work was the development of a device called a transceiver (transmitter and receiver), which, similar to ARPANET's IMP, was an interface between node and cable and the main hardware device in their network.[130] Although Boggs managed to develop several prototypes, the duo was unable to manufacture "real" transceivers that could move the bits across hundreds of meters at a speed of several hundred kilobits per second. So they turned to Tat Lam, a contract worker at PARC, who later established his own company, TCL, specializing in the manufacturing of Ethernet transceivers.[131] While building the network, Metcalfe and Boggs also set the parameters of PARC's network (which later became known as Experimental Ethernet) to a distance of one kilometer, a maximum of 256 stations, and a top speed of 2.94 Mbps.[132] Thus Ethernet operated not only at a speed comparable to Farber's token ring but also almost sixty times faster than the ARPANET.[133]

The two men's hands-on work after the invention of Ethernet illustrates important aspects of LAN technology. Although Metcalfe's initial design studies consisted mainly of developing mathematical algorithms, the details of their later operationalization demonstrate that LAN technology is not purely science-based; rather its development requires much practical, knowledge-intensive tinkering with cable characteristics, transmission speeds, and device specifications. Furthermore, to make any LAN technology fully functional, numerous parameters must be defined, including network speed, cable length, cable type, and access method. Such definition was later to become an important part of the formal standard-setting process, because the interoperability of LAN components made by different manufacturers would depend on exact adherence to the parameters. Finally, a major part of LAN development consists of implementing LAN concepts, such as Ethernet's CSMA/CD mechanism, in devices and ICs. As demonstrated by Tat Lam, the manufacture of such devices was to open up an economic space for start-ups and eventually for an entire industry. The work of Metcalfe and Boggs at PARC was to be repeated in much greater complexity at the macrolevel of the LAN industry.[134]

Experimental Ethernet quickly expanded within and outside Xerox PARC. By 1974, the network had reached a hundred nodes. PARC's researchers initially used it to share files and to send e-mails between Alto computers, but Ethernet's most important application at PARC was the sharing of the expensive EARS laser printers.[135] As a result, it soon became indispensable.[136] Thanks to the use of telephone lines and gateways, in the late 1970s PARC's distributed computing system gradually expanded outside the boundaries of the center, connecting to other Xerox sites scattered all over North America.[137] These expansions within and outside PARC also anticipated future developments in the LAN industry. Although self-contained workgroups, like those at PARC, were to provide the initial nucleus for network growth, in the late 1980s corporations gradually interconnected their scattered LANs via telephone lines into private WANs.

Yet despite the successful operation of the Alto and Ethernet, Xerox's management was unable to comprehend the significance of PARC's innovations and kept delaying their commercialization.[138] Ethernet—like so many other technologies first created at PARC—would eventually escape Xerox and be commercialized by other firms.

Thus Xerox PARC developed not only the second major LAN type but also the dominant environment in which all LANs would be deployed: office systems based on personal workstations. Throughout the 1970s, this office architecture remained a vision; it was realized on a large scale only with the introduction of the IBM PC in 1981. Not surprisingly, PARC's visionary "information architects" created a network that was far ahead of its time. Although Ethernet had become extremely useful inside Xerox PARC—where personal computers and laser printers were already the norm in the mid-1970s—Ethernet's speed of 2.94 Mbps was just not required outside PARC, where modems running at 1.2 kbps (2,500 times slower than Experimental Ethernet) were considered over-kill.[139] Only in the mid-1980s, as the world caught up with PARC's vision, did Ethernet's high speed finally become a necessity.[140]

From Laboratory to Market

With the implementation of Metcalfe's invention throughout PARC and beyond, and Saltzer and Pogran's experimentation with token ring topologies, the two most important LANs had been developed and successfully deployed in a first testing phase. Though these two LAN technologies were not the only ones developed, for reasons to be explored later they became the most important ones. The IEEE standards for office networks were based on them, and they were to become the strongest competitors in the LAN marketplace.

The 1970s were clearly the precommercial trial-and-error stage for LAN technology—a decade marked by extensive technical experimentation. Once Farber had "invented" high-speed LAN technology, experimentation by other universities and research institutions led to an impressive array of LAN designs (including multiple LAN access and transmission methods, such as the token, empty slot, and CSMA/CD principles) and topologies (including ring, bus, and star-shaped ring). These differing attributes would eventually become keys to corporate strategies for product differentiation.

While the transition from WANs to LANs in the early 1970s clearly was a function of the economics of computers, experimentation within the LAN realm did not result from such "hard" restrictions. Instead, LAN developers were guided by their own beliefs and technological preferences. Of course, Farber, Metcalfe, and Saltzer and Pogran had good reasons for choosing their particular designs, such as Metcalfe's desire to keep network costs low and Saltzer and Pogran's intention to build a network well suited to accommodate large installations. Eventually all these hypothesized constraints in fact materialized, at least to some extent, and had to be taken into account by network builders. But in the 1970s they had not yet become reality. Thus it was not yet clear which combination of features would become part of the dominant LAN design, nor was it obvious to all experimenters that topology would be a more critical criterion than access method in the later market competition. As a result, the early researchers explored a variety of topologies, access methods, and other design parameters with relative freedom and little apparent predisposition to any single approach.

For the same reasons, it was unclear from the perspective of the 1970s whether Ethernet or token ring technology had gained any edge in the marketplace competition that lay ahead. Token ring's deterministic nature seemed to provide it with a slight advantage under certain conditions, but the UC Irvine Ring and Ethernet had similar speeds; lacking a central connectivity point, both had similar potential drawbacks in network management and troubleshooting. Though by the late 1970s token ring technology had evolved toward the more advantageous star-shaped ring topology—in fact, it later became part of the dominant design—this did not appear to be an overwhelming advantage, because too few sites possessed the numbers of computers that would make such a wiring structure imperative. Besides, the star-shaped topology was technologically feasible in Ethernet as well. Since the precommercialization period failed to provide either technology with a clear technical edge, there was still ample room for market forces, business strategies, and random events to determine the outcome of the later competition.

Technological experimentation is a natural phenomenon in the immediate aftermath of the development of novel technologies, as the proponents of the dominant-design theory have pointed out. But the considerable experimentation in LAN architectures during this period also resulted from the extensive involvement of universities and corporate research laboratories, which faced little immediate pressure to commercialize their inventions. MIT, Cambridge University, and Xerox PARC conceived of the emerging science of LANs as something with which to experiment, not as a technological given. They did not adopt existing designs without modification but instead used a particular design as the basis for further technical innovation. David Farber, for instance, believes that Robert Metcalfe was less interested in CSMA/CD per se than in inventing something different from Farber's UC Irvine Ring; in fact, he might have opted for a token ring architecture if it had been Farber who invented Ethernet.[141] The universities and corporate research laboratories were interested in technical innovations (which generated publications), not in creating a standard, which would be a critical issue during the later commercialization period.

In the late 1970s, as this precommercialization phase ended and LAN start-ups and computer manufacturers rushed to the market with their own technology, universities began to lose their position as important players. After Saltzer and Pogran's development of the star-shaped ring network, the flow of important LAN technical innovations from universities largely dried up. With a few notable exceptions, such as Cisco and Fore, universities failed to spin off many LAN companies.[142] The basic concepts had by then been invented; for most academics LAN technology was but a side product of their distributed computing systems, and one that did not spark sufficient theoretical interest. Corporations would dominate the further evolution of the novel technology.

With the development of Ethernet and token ring and the construction of the ARPANET on the WAN side, the foundations for the network revolution had been laid. The ARPANET gradually evolved into the Internet, which—once privatized and complemented by the WWW in the mid-1990s—was to create the enormous business opportunities of the dot-coms and the business-to-business marketplaces. The LAN side evolved in a less spectacular way. Though WANs and LANs became critical complementary parts of today's network revolution, for approximately fifteen years they evolved separately, for they served different needs and many LANs were linked neither to a WAN nor to the Internet. Only in the late 1980s and early 1990s did the evolutionary paths of LANs and WANs begin to intersect on a large scale. Corporations began to interconnect their remote LANs over leased T-1 lines, thereby creating large private WANs, and a few years later LANs became important corporate on-ramps to the (by then privatized) Internet. In the late 1970s, however, this enormous network buildup was barely foreseeable. At that time, only a very few LANs existed, and a handful of small start-ups were trying to commercialize the novel technology. But, as the following chapter shows, this proved to be a difficult business proposition.

3 Pioneers: The Beginning of Commercialization

Soon after David Farber and Robert Metcalfe had invented the first LAN technologies, in the late 1970s a handful of firms—start-ups as well as established computer manufacturers—began commercializing proprietary LAN technologies and in the process created a small market. Within a few years, the market would grow significantly, with dozens of firms selling LAN technology. But in the late 1970s, the market barely existed. Among the pioneers four stood out: Network Systems and Nestar, two LAN start-ups; Zilog, a semiconductor firm; and Datapoint, a mid-size computer manufacturer in San Antonio, Texas. Although these four vendors were not the only ones selling LANs before 1980–81, they all introduced products before the formation of the IEEE 802 standardization committee in 1980, the pivotal event in the nascent LAN industry, and were recognized as front-runners in the trade press. By introducing LAN technology before the finalization of the standardization process, these four vendors initiated what could be called the pre-dominant-design period for LAN technology.

The economic theory of standardization predicts that the head start they enjoyed could have assisted these pioneers in staking out lead positions in the impending standards race. By entering the market well ahead of their competitors, they had the chance to build up their installed base—a step that, at least in theory, could have led to a self-reinforcing momentum and possibly a "tipping" of the LAN market. Yet, with the exception of Datapoint, none of them succeeded in becoming an influential contender in the race for the standard. On the contrary, several fell quickly by the wayside, having had no impact on the race at all.

Rather than being an advantage, their head start was a problem for the earliest marketers, for two reasons. First, the LAN market of the late

1970s and early 1980s was unsettled and amorphous, and consequently industry pioneers were faced with many tasks that would not fall to their successors. Given the novelty of the market, the pioneers not only had to find customers and develop products for them but also figure out applications, convince venture capitalists of the growth potential of the fledgling market, and create new business models. Even more important, the inchoate market deprived them of suppliers, forcing them to develop almost every component of their systems themselves. For the smaller start-ups, the plethora of pioneering tasks proved too taxing.[1]

The market posed a second challenge for the pioneers. By commercializing LAN technology so early, the four firms encountered tremendously disproportionate markets. IBM had not yet introduced its PC, which would eventually become the principal LAN market, and the sizes of the four main segments of the computer market—mainframes, minicomputers, workstations, and micro- or personal computers—differed sharply from their sizes in the late 1980s, at the end of the standardization struggle. As a result, the pioneers were unable to address the "right" market from the outset, and they had to adjust their technologies and distribution channels constantly in a painstaking attempt to catch the new growth markets. For the small firms, once again, these constant market adjustments proved too burdensome financially and technically.

Not surprisingly, the only pioneer to become a significant force in LAN standardization, Datapoint, was already a successful computer manufacturer. As such, it had a well-protected market, as well as sufficient financial means and adequate technological capabilities to develop an advanced, well-functioning LAN. And Datapoint happened to design a network with price-performance characteristics similar to those that would later be required in the PC LAN market. Datapoint thus avoided many of the problems that plagued the other pioneers.

Launching Products and Firms

As we have seen, the 1950s and 1960s were not conducive to the development of LANs. However, with the proliferation of minicomputers and the continuously falling prices of computer and semiconductor technology, conditions for local networks gradually improved during the mid-1970s, leading to the development of Xerox's Ethernet and Farber's token ring. Conditions continued to improve along the same trajectory throughout the rest of the decade. The total and local installed bases of computers grew; computer prices dropped sharply; and, even more important, in the late 1970s a new class of computers, low-cost microcomputers, was introduced.[2] As a result of these LAN-friendly developments, in the mid-1970s a few forward-looking entrepreneurs conceived of market opportunities for LAN technology, prompting them to establish firms and begin developing products.

One of the first individuals to think of starting a LAN firm was James Thornton. In the 1960s and early 1970s, he had worked for the mainframe vendors Sperry Univac and Control Data, and so he naturally considered developing products for networking mainframes.[3] This was a far-sighted choice, for in the almost thirty years that mainframes had existed none of their manufacturers had considered introducing high-speed LAN technology for them; the first LANs came into being only with the arrival of minicomputers and workstations.

Nevertheless, in 1973–74 Thornton noticed various developments that seemed to offer the possibility of building a successful mainframe LAN business. Mainframes not only represented by far the largest computer market in dollars but also trailed minicomputers by a ratio of merely four to one in unit sales.[4] (In 1973–74 microcomputers did not yet exist.) Even more important, the number of connectable devices at the typical site had expanded drastically. Many corporate data centers now possessed more than one mainframe, as well as numerous peripherals, such as front-end processors, terminals, and storage devices. In fact, some data centers had become congested. The rapid falloff in speed over the telephone wires that were the principal connectivity medium meant that the centers were forced to cluster their computing devices in close proximity to one another. Thornton believed that the congestion problem signaled a business opportunity: a high-speed LAN would allow data centers to place their equipment farther apart.[5]

Thornton observed another market development as auguring well for a mainframe LAN start-up. Since data centers increasingly purchased equipment from different vendors and since computer vendors typically offered proprietary systems, the data centers were encountering growing interconnectivity problems. Because the incompatible machines employed different communication protocols and data formats, they could not easily exchange data and share peripherals. Thornton knew that the established computer manufacturers had no interest in interlinking each other's equipment because they relied on the devices' proprietariness in part to lock in users.[6] He concluded that a specialized LAN vendor without a vested interest in its own computer line would be in an excellent position to provide such a badly needed gateway function.[7] Encouraged by these trends and having been joined by several partners, in 1974 Thornton decided to establish a firm. He named the start-up, located in Brooklyn Park, Minnesota, Network Systems.

Despite the improving climate for a mainframe LAN business, raising venture capital proved difficult. Compared with Silicon Valley and Route 128, Minnesota was not a center for venture capital, and the installed base of mainframes, despite steady growth, was still quite small.[8] In addition, many industry pundits claimed that telephone lines were in fact adequate for data communication, despite their low throughput rate of 0.9–9.6 kbps.[9] Unable to obtain venture capital from typical sources, the founders of Network Systems had to rely on seed capital from wealthy individuals in the Minneapolis–St. Paul area. Only after the development of a product prototype in 1976 did they receive more conventional venture capital from Norwest Venture Capital Management of Minneapolis, among other investors.[10]

Having secured start-up capital, Network Systems introduced its mainframe LAN, called HYPERchannel, in 1977. The product quickly enjoyed considerable success. Despite the high price of a HYPERchannel adapter, by the end of 1980 annual sales had reached $12.8 million.[11] Yet, with only 676 adapters in place at a total of 101 customer sites, Network Systems' installed base remained relatively small.[12] Part of the problem was the high price of a HYPERchannel adapter, but growth was mainly restricted by the small number of data centers that had at least two mainframe computers.[13] However, Network Systems' relatively high revenues nevertheless made it the largest LAN start-up in 1980, a position the firm maintained until the middle of the decade.

Whereas in 1974 Thornton could choose between only the mainframe market and the minicomputer market, a few years later entrepreneurs had a third market from which to pick: microcomputers, which emerged in the late 1970s in Silicon Valley. Among the first to see business opportunities in this segment were Frederico Faggin and Ralph Ungermann. In 1974 the two Intel alumni had established a Silicon Valley semiconductor firm, Zilog, as a subsidiary of Exxon. The oil company was eager to invest its windfall profits from the decade's energy crisis in the fast-growing electronics and office automation markets.[14] Through Zilog, Exxon expected to participate in the creation of the "office of the future." Drawing on Faggin's illustrious background (at Intel he had been instrumental in implementing the microprocessor in silicon), Zilog began with the manufacture of ICs and quickly evolved into a leading microprocessor supplier to Silicon Valley's fast-growing microcomputer vendors.[15]

Before long, Zilog embarked on an ambitious strategy of forward integration that included not only boards but also a (proprietary) microcomputer, as well as a LAN.[16] Zilog decided to develop a LAN partly because its communication chip had been so successful in the marketplace and partly because it believed that the network was central to its

concept of the "office of the future."[17] As one of the leading figures in
the microcomputer revolution, Faggin anticipated that the very-large-
scale integration (VLSI) technology on which semiconductors were based
would radically alter the entire architecture of computing: "This new
[computer] architecture that could best take advantage of VLSI technology would be highly parallel in the sense that it would include a number
of more or less independent processors and other resources, all interconnected to permit communication among elements of the architecture."[18]
Faggin shared the belief of PARC's information architects that advances
in VLSI technology would lead to such radical price reductions in ICs
that a computer on every desk would soon become a reality. He expected
that some applications would be distributed among several computers
connected by a high-speed network—a model quite similar to today's
client/server architecture.[19] Like PARC, Zilog believed that the office of
the future would best be realized with a personal distributed computing
system based on a LAN.

To build such a system, Zilog hired several new engineers, including
Charles Bass, who had had previous experience with the ALOHANET,
Metcalfe's main inspiration for Ethernet. By 1980 they had finished
Zilog's office system. It was completely proprietary and included a microcomputer called MCZ, an operating system called Leo, and a LAN called
Z-Net.[20] Like PARC's Ethernet, Z-Net played a critical enabling role
in Zilog's office system, allowing users to network MCZ computers,
exchange e-mails, and share file and print servers.[21] Z-Net, at least on
the surface, appeared to compete head-on with Ethernet, which Xerox
introduced at about the same time.[22]

Zilog's founders were not the only ones thinking about the market
potential for LANs in the microcomputer market. While working on
large time-sharing systems at IBM's research laboratory in Santa Teresa,
California, physicist Harry Saal took a personal interest in the ongoing
microcomputer revolution.[23] In contrast to many who saw microcomputers as merely toys, he was impressed by their computing power and
responsiveness, noticing that they did not slow down in the way that
time-sharing systems often did during periods of peak usage.[24] But he
also realized that microcomputers were still in their infancy and lacked
professional, high-quality peripherals, such as printers and hard disks—
tools to which he had become accustomed while working at IBM.[25]
Moreover, Saal saw that the software available for microcomputers
failed to meet professional standards, thus locking them out of the large
office market. This intrigued him, and he became "quite interested in the
idea of building large distributive systems of personal computers by networking them."[26] Saal envisioned networking the new microcomputers,

such as the Apple II, so they could share peripherals and information and therefore be used in the office market. He wanted to develop a computing concept for the office similar to those of Xerox PARC and Zilog. But unlike these two competitors, he did not want to design his own microcomputer; instead he intended to take advantage of such existing, and rapidly proliferating, microcomputers as the Apple II.

In the late 1970s, Saal attempted to persuade IBM to let him work on these ideas, but its management declined. "They [IBM] did not get it," he recalled. "They were quite, I would say, arrogant about the possibilities [for microcomputers] and conceived that minicomputers might have some future, but surely not toy computers." Preferring to follow his own intuition, Saal resigned, and in October 1978, together with Leonard Shustek, he established his own start-up, Nestar.[27]

Though Nestar, by interlinking microcomputers, was to take the microcomputer revolution a significant step further, raising venture capital would prove very difficult—as Saal and Shustek quickly discovered. As Saal remembered,

> I had no financial background. I was not a businessperson, although I was very committed to this idea. [I] started talking to venture capitalists here in [the] San Francisco Bay Area and New York and basically got a fantastic rejection from all of them. [They said this company] would not go anywhere, that these toy computers were never going to be serious, and if they were serious, nobody would have many of them at a time together. I think they did not believe that these types of computers [Apple IIs, TRS-80s, Commodore PETs] would be ever used in a real commercial-type environment. [Also, they did not believe] that the other market for microcomputers, the education[al market], was a commercially viable business to be in. . . . If this were such a good idea, IBM already would have done it. That kind of mentality [dominated] back in 1978.[28]

Unable to overcome the skepticism of potential financial backers, Saal and Shustek were forced to undertake the development of their ambitious product line without venture capital—a limitation that was to severely undermine their success in the market. Only later did a British company (Zynar, a subsidiary of the Rank Organisation) invest in the start-up.[29]

In hindsight, the venture capitalists' refusal to invest in Nestar is not surprising. Nestar posed high risks according to all possible criteria for evaluating venture capital investments, namely management, technology, market, and business model.[30] As Saal himself pointed out, the firm's technology and management team were largely unproven.[31] But most important, Nestar appeared to lack a viable market. In 1979, the installed base of microcomputers was still fairly small, and microcomputers had barely moved from the initial, tiny hobbyist market into the vast office market. To make matters worse, most microcomputers employed in the office at that time were employed for single-user applications, such as word processing. This made it difficult to see why a LAN connecting several microcomputers would be necessary, while raising the question of how Nestar would be able to boost its revenues at a fast pace—a vital requirement for securing venture funding. Taking these risk factors into account, venture capitalists passed on investing in Saal and Shustek's start-up—even though their vision of connecting microcomputers made by third-party vendors and deploying them in the office environment ultimately proved accurate. The difficulties experienced by both Network Systems and Nestar in raising capital were typical for the fledgling industry. Many venture capitalists underestimated market growth while overestimating the competitive threat posed by computer manufacturers.

Despite its difficulties in securing capital and launching its products, in January 1980 Nestar introduced its distributed computing system, Cluster/One.[32] The Cluster/One system, which initially connected only Apple II microcomputers, included an e-mail and staff-scheduling package, file and print servers, and network-based versions of the VisiCalc and DB Master software.[33] Since Nestar closely followed Apple, Cluster/One's main market became educational institutions, Apple's stronghold. The Lawrence Hall of Science at the University of California, Berkeley, was its first adopter. Cluster/One also found its way into the office market; it was employed at engineering and software development sites, and was also used for special turnkey applications, such as travel and real estate agency systems.[34] Given Apple's disinterest in LANs and the almost complete absence of LAN competitors in the Apple II market, in 1980 and 1981 Nestar was recognized as the leading micro LAN vendor.[35] Nestar's revenues, however, failed to match those of Network Systems. Owing to the infancy of the microcomputer market and Nestar's later market entry, the start-up earned only $0.8 million in 1980 compared with Network Systems' $12.8 million.[36]

And so, despite facing considerable obstacles, by 1980 Network Systems, Nestar, and Zilog had succeeded in introducing their first networking products, thereby creating a small LAN market. Their early market entry and complete domination of their segments seemingly positioned them well for the impending standards race—at least according to standardization theory. By dominating the mainframe market and by being the largest start-up throughout the mid-1980s, Network Systems appeared—theoretically—to have a good chance to conquer the minicomputer market, the segment below mainframes and the largest source of LAN business in the early to mid-1980s. With Network Systems poised to roll up the markets from the high end, Zilog and especially Nestar (with its focus on the market-leading Apple II) had gained a foothold in the strategically important microcomputer market at the low end. Microcomputers were soon to accumulate the largest installed base of any computer class, and the early models had price-performance characteristics similar to those of the soon-to-be-dominant IBM PC. The two firms seemed to have a good chance at playing a significant role in de facto standardization.

The Problems of a Head Start

Despite these promising prospects, the three pioneers failed to set the de facto standard, and they did not play an influential role in the standards race. Each was eclipsed for quite different reasons, but, as noted earlier, their failures were ultimately rooted in the same problem: their head start.

The first pioneer to disappear was Zilog. The semiconductor firm failed mainly because of its inability to offer a well-functioning network. At first glance, Zilog was designing a modestly powerful LAN. Like Ethernet, the later standard, Zilog's Z-Net employed a proprietary CSMA/CD mechanism; it operated at a speed of 800 kbps (roughly four times slower than Experimental Ethernet) and connected as many as 255 of Zilog's MCZ microcomputers.[37] But before Z-Net could come to fruition, several leading engineers and employees—including Ralph Ungermann, Charles Bass, William Carrico, Judith Estrin, and Eric Benhamou—left the company, disdaining Exxon's quixotic quest to enter the office market, to start their own businesses.[38] One of the replacement engineers, Kanwal Rekhi, recalled: "When I joined Zilog, Z-Net was absolutely not working. It was extremely unreliable. I had to reengineer Z-Net."[39] But in late 1981 Rekhi too left to start his own company. Although he had improved Z-Net, it never became a mature, advanced system. As Ralph Ungermann concluded, "Z-Net was kind of an experimental thing that got nowhere. It was never a real product."[40]

Zilog also owed its failure to a second problem, one every bit as onerous as the technical imperfections of its Z-Net. In August 1981 IBM introduced its PC, which rapidly became the leading microcomputer standard. The PC's ascendancy had a devastating effect on Z-Net, which was intended solely to connect Zilog's proprietary MCZ microcomputers. With sales of MCZ computers hindered from the outset by the rise of the PC, Z-Net simply lacked a market. Weakened by its technical imperfections and deprived of a market, Z-Net never succeeded in the marketplace, prompting Zilog to discontinue its network in the middle of 1983 and to adopt Ethernet.[41] Without a market and a well-functioning technology,

Zilog was in no position to affect standardization, let alone "tip" the market. The theoretical advantage conferred by early market entry could not compensate for the handicap of competing with an inferior product.

Nestar, the other pioneer in the microcomputer market, fared slightly better than Zilog, managing to stay in business several years longer. Yet, like Zilog, Nestar had no impact on the standards race. After dominating the Apple II market in 1979–80, it quickly fell by the wayside, and by 1981–82 it had disappeared as a serious competitor. It lingered on for several more years, but because its peak sales of $10 million in 1984–85 were tiny compared with a market size of at least $294.1 million in 1984 and $537 million in 1985, Nestar too was in no position to play an influential role in standardization.[42] As revenues stagnated and the company failed to turn a profit, in 1986 Saal and Shustek decided to sell out to Digital Switching Corporation, which dissolved its new subsidiary the following year.[43]

Nestar's rapid fall into oblivion was rooted mainly in its head start and the inchoate nature of the market, which trapped the start-up between two conflicting forces: the lack of suppliers on the one hand and the development of an overly ambitious product on the other. As mentioned, Nestar's interest did not lie merely in providing LAN hardware for the Apple II but in building a complete office system. This meant that the firm had to offer not only LAN hardware but also file server software and LAN applications, such as e-mail and network versions of database and spreadsheet programs. In the infant LAN market, most of these components did not yet exist as readily available, off-the-shelf products offered by third-party suppliers. Nestar, like the other pioneers, was thus forced to develop most of them in house—or at least to modify a module offered by a supplier, such as a database program, for network operation.[44]

The development of such a broad product offering put an enormous strain on the technological capabilities of the small start-up. Nestar needed expertise not only in LAN concepts and hardware devices, but also in software development for file servers and network applications. It succeeded in putting together a functioning system, and its LAN hardware, the Cluster/One network, worked more reliably than Zilog's Z-Net. However, the depth of the required capabilities took its toll: Nestar failed to develop a system whose components were all state-of-the-art. For instance, the Cluster/One LAN hardware was far inferior to many other LANs, including Ethernet. Cluster/One operated only at the modest speed of 240 kbps, spanned but a kilometer, and connected a mere 65 computers; in contrast Ethernet, in its standardized version, transmitted at 10 Mbps, covered 2.5 kilometers (with the use of repeaters), and was able to connect up to 1,024 nodes.[45]

Cluster/One's low performance had no repercussions within the Apple II market, nor did it have any impact in 1979–80, at a time when no competitors existed. On the contrary, its limited performance was virtually a requisite for penetrating the Apple II segment, which would tolerate only a low-cost network and required small board size. In fact, had Nestar developed a network with Ethernet-like performance, it could not have been able to serve the Apple II market. The Ethernet board, owing to its various high-performance features, was too large to fit into an Apple II microcomputer; furthermore, a Cluster/One interface cost $595, whereas Ethernet's initial per-node price of approximately $3,000–$4,000 was far too expensive to network computers that ranged in price between $1,000 and $3,000.[46] But after 1982, as the number of competitors increased and the standardization battle intensified, Cluster/One's impoverished performance became a severe handicap.[47] In fact, as personal computers became more powerful, the demands on network performance increased as well, and Cluster/One failed to meet those demands. Its lower performance completely blocked it from entering the minicomputer market, which required even higher levels of network performance than PCs.

With its inferior Cluster/One LAN hardware, Nestar simply could not stand out among the growing number of competitors, nor could it vie with Ethernet and the numerous other, more powerful, LANs in the PC and minicomputer sector. As Saal recalled:

> In 1980, what we did was unheard of and strange and weird, and no one could understand why you would do it. Five years later, every single day, there was a new network, a new company, a new operating system, and customers were totally confused. [As a result] it was difficult for a small company to have any credibility. [Finally] IBM, Microsoft, and Apple woke up, so people wanted to do business with them. Who is Nestar? So that was really the beginning of the end, when everybody else jumped into the market.

And Nestar's inferiority surfaced not only in LAN hardware but in many other parts of its system as well, including the NOS.[48]

The development of a broadly defined product system overburdened not only Nestar's technological capabilities but also its finances. Even with adequate funding, the development of such an ambitious product system would have been challenging for a small start-up; but the lack of sufficient capital strained its financial resources too heavily. As Saal describes the situation,

> Because of the timing we had to do everything ourselves. We had to develop a [network] operating system; we had to develop the client side and server side; we had to develop print servers. We developed e-mail, gateways, SNA

[Systems Network Architecture] gateways. We had to worry about multi-user versions of single-user software [like VisiCalc]. We suffered [through] figuring out what the licensing agreement would be for putting software on a file server. In those days it was not clear to any software company whether they wanted to allow this to happen. Later, in the mid-1980s, it was possible to go into business and just build a part of the puzzle. You could be a player in a more complex infrastructure and just build an adapter card, an SNA gateway, or an e-mail system. And here we were, this tiny company that was acting like a giant in terms of the breadth and software we had. That was just inconsistent from a financial point of view. [He laughs.] So I think we just sort of collapsed as a result of all this baggage that we picked up.[49]

Inadequate financial resources and excessive product development plans were not the only reasons Nestar vanished so rapidly; the start-up also floundered because it bet on the "wrong" LAN application. In the developing microcomputer LAN market of 1979–80, no "killer" applications had yet emerged, and users as well as vendors experimented with a variety of possible applications in an attempt to find those best suited for the new technology. Citibank in New York, for example, used Nestar's Cluster/One as part of a mobile automatic teller machine (ATM), consisting of a microcomputer, file server, and cash dispenser—all networked by Cluster/One and all placed on a cart.[50] Though a creative use of the technology, mobile ATMs did not become a major application for LANs. Eager to provide a complete office system, Nestar saw the principal purpose of LANs as sharing information or, in technical terms, sharing files. As Harry Saal wrote in 1981, "Information sharing is as important as ever. Once two or more people begin to work cooperatively, they need to communicate and exchange information, whether the impetus be the joint development of a large program, several people checking on information in a common data base, or the implementation of an electronic mail system"[51]

Although Saal was ultimately right—sharing files and information did eventually drive the installation of LANs—by emphasizing file sharing Nestar was ahead of its time. File sharing required a complex technology in the form of an NOS, and neither Nestar nor the other vendors had yet completely figured out how several users could concurrently share the same file (such as a spreadsheet) without interfering with and corrupting each other's entries and updates. It was not until several years later that Novell introduced an NOS suited for file sharing and as a result built a thriving business. In the absence of such an NOS in the early 1980s, most micro LAN users simply employed their networks to connect several microcomputers to (standalone) hard disks, an application that required a far simpler NOS than file sharing. An NOS for this purpose had to be capable only of separating disk space—instead of, say, allowing the simultaneous use of a spreadsheet by several users. What was more, disk sharing solved a real economic problem, since the prices of hard disk storage systems often far exceeded the prices of microcomputers. In a word, disk sharing, not file sharing, was the "killer app" of microcomputer LANs in the early 1980s.[52]

Although Cluster/One could be used to connect microcomputers to a disk server, Nestar had no particular competitive advantage in this segment and could only stand by, as several disk vendors, including Corvus and Davong, took over the market by developing networks for their storage systems. Unable to offer the needed application in 1980–81, Nestar had great difficulty in "convincing people that networking [Apple IIs] was such a good idea."[53] As a result, its revenues grew very slowly, and its installed base remained fairly small; by the middle of 1982 it had reached only approximately 100 networks.[54] This was far too low a level of penetration to trigger "tipping" in a market that would encompass 30,000–40,000 networks by 1985.[55]

Finally, Nestar fell so quickly by the wayside because it was a victim of the same technological discontinuity that devastated Zilog's Z-Net: the introduction and rapid proliferation of the IBM PC. To avoid the fallout from the rapidly shrinking Apple II market (Nestar's principal business) and to benefit from the PC's enormous market growth, in 1981–82 Nestar decided to integrate IBM's new microcomputer into its Cluster/One office system. But since the start-up had become so deeply entrenched in the Apple II market, Nestar found it necessary to continue to support Apple's microcomputer to avoid stranding its existing customer base.[56] Although a dual-platform strategy made strategic sense, it required costly technical adjustments, mainly in the software. Unable to carry the additional burden of upgrading its rapidly obsolescing Cluster/One LAN hardware, Nestar decided to abandon its original LAN hardware and replace it with a LAN from a different vendor, namely Datapoint's ARCnet, whose chip had become available in 1981.[57] Nestar introduced its new ARCnet-based office system, now called PLAN, at the end of 1982. Since the PLAN system operated at the far higher speed of 2 Mbps and supported both the IBM PC and the Apple II on the same network, Nestar now had a far better network system to offer.[58]

On the surface, it appeared as if Nestar had survived the transition from the Apple II to the IBM PC standard, but the underlying reality was quite different. The market moved on quickly to new systems, while Nestar was forced to take care of its legacy systems. In fact, to expand its market base and to keep up with its competitors, the start-up had continually to modernize its technology and to integrate the new computers of IBM and Apple—a task that Apple (with its incompatible Lisa and Apple III) made very complicated.[59] And to satisfy its initial Apple II customer base, Nestar also had to try to maintain backward compatibility with that device. Trapped between the past and the future, Nestar fought an endless uphill battle just to maintain the functionality of its current system and consequently lacked the resources to develop new product lines. "Because we were so early in the market, we had such a tie to the past and so many products that we had to support. [At the same time] we had such a large and complex system. It was very difficult to imagine how we were going to grow the business on top of the base that we already had."[60] Stymied by its legacy, Nestar rapidly fell behind technologically and was forced to concede the future to those firms that had no such ties to the past. Like Zilog it had focused on the right market—microcomputers for the office—but it had the timing wrong. Introducing LAN technology for a previously nonexistent market and before the advent of the IBM PC, it had to contend with too many burdensome product development tasks and became locked into a microcomputer type that failed to become mainstream, preventing it from building a viable business for the long run.

Among the three pioneers, Network Systems fared best by far. Throughout the early and mid-1980s, its installed base and revenues increased sharply. Between fiscal 1980 and 1983, the firm more than doubled the installed base of its HYPERchannel network while tripling the number of customer sites.[61] Sales grew from $12.8 million in 1980 to $71.2 million in 1984, making Network Systems the largest LAN start-up.

The company owed its success to various factors. To begin with, unlike the other pioneers, Network Systems enjoyed strong market demand, because its HYPERchannel solved critical bottlenecks common to data centers, such as the aforementioned congestion and incompatibility problems.[62] It also benefited from the lack of substantial competition in the data center mainframe market. As Thornton had expected, most computer manufacturers had no interest in providing a gateway between their equipment and that of other vendors, and only a few LAN start-ups challenged Network Systems' lead.[63] Furthermore, Network Systems avoided many of Nestar's pioneer problems by relying on a clever strategy. Unlike Nestar, Network Systems did not make the mistake of creating a comprehensive product line, but instead offered a stripped-down system. It developed only LAN hardware, expecting its customers to design the necessary complementary software.[64] Hence it was never burdened with having to develop and upgrade an ever-expanding, all-encompassing product line.

Finally, Network Systems was far better capitalized than Nestar. Unlike Nestar, Network Systems had succeeded in securing venture capital, and two public offerings raised an additional $16.7 million.[65] Besides, Network Systems became profitable in 1978, accumulating total profits of $38.7 million between 1978 and 1984, whereas Nestar never turned a profit.[66] Thus Network Systems had the financial means necessary to upgrade its technology and to continue to innovate. Unlike Nestar, Network Systems was a successful, fast-growing corporation with a dominant, if not monopolistic, position in the data center and mainframe LAN market.

Yet Network Systems floundered just as badly as Nestar and Zilog when it came to setting the mainstream LAN standard. Its main problem was that, from the perspective of later standards development, it had addressed the "wrong" market, namely mainframes. Though mainframes appeared a good bet in the early 1970s, when Network Systems went into business, during the 1980s—the crucial period in LAN standardization—the computer market underwent radical transformations. While annual shipments of mainframes hovered near 12,000 units, those of minicomputers soared to approximately 200,000 units, only to be overshadowed by the millions of PCs that were shipped. These drastic shifts meant that Network Systems' core market remained too small to affect de facto LAN standardization. Several thousand mainframes were simply irrelevant compared with hundreds of thousands of minicomputers and millions of PCs.

If Network Systems had succeeded in moving from mainframes down into the minicomputer market, the relative shrinkage of the mainframe market would not have affected it as seriously. But it remained locked into mainframes, unable to push HYPERchannel into the minicomputer market, mainly for price reasons. In fact, while developing its network, Network Systems created a very-high-speed LAN. At distances of up to 2,000 feet, HYPERchannel could transmit at 50 Mbps—over thirty times faster than PARC's Experimental Ethernet and five times faster than the later Ethernet standard.[67] Network Systems perceived such high throughput as crucial to accommodate the high computing speeds of mainframes and thus avoid idling the expensive machines.[68] But HYPERchannel's high speed came at the steep price of $45,000–$50,000 for a single connection, making it at least eleven times more expensive than Ethernet.[69] HYPERchannel's exorbitant price did not limit its proliferation in the mainframe market, since mainframes often cost up to several million dollars and HYPERchannel remained within a similar *relative* price range as Ethernet, which was originally designed to link personal workstations that cost $15,000–$25,000.[70] But HYPERchannel's high price made it

simply uneconomical for networking minicomputers, whose average price
was $58,921 in 1980, with some models even costing less than $20,000.[71]
Needless to say, this price made it even more difficult for Network Systems to enter the microcomputer market, in which LAN prices had to be
even lower.

Responding to this price-based barrier to entry, in the early 1980s Network Systems launched a second LAN, called HYPERbus, aimed at minicomputers. At first glance, HYPERbus appeared to have a better chance
than HYPERchannel to succeed in the minicomputer market, since it had
price-performance characteristics similar to those of Ethernet. In fact,
HYPERbus cost between $2,000 and $6,000 per node and operated at
10 Mbps.[72] Yet, like HYPERchannel, HYPERbus failed to make inroads
into the minicomputer segment, for several reasons.[73] First, Network
Systems did not begin full-scale marketing before fiscal 1983—although
the product was already available in 1981.[74] This meant that commercialization of HYPERbus lagged up to two years behind that of Ethernet—a
critical disadvantage in industries subject to network effects. Furthermore,
HYPERbus had the handicap of being proprietary, while Ethernet became
an open standard. This not only deterred its adoption on the user side
but also resulted in substantial repercussions on the supply side. As most
minicomputer firms and several start-ups rallied behind the open Ethernet standard, Ethernet gained far greater momentum in the distribution
channels than HYPERbus. This greater supplier support in turn allowed
Ethernet to advance very rapidly in terms of technical improvements and
price reductions. Being supported by only one firm, HYPERbus, in contrast, faced greater restrictions.

Uninvolved with the construction of the minicomputer LAN standard
and competing without a supportive community, Network Systems—a
small firm compared with DEC, H-P, and the Ethernet community as a
whole—had no competitive advantage in the minicomputer market and
thus remained locked in to the profitable but ultimately irrelevant mainframe market. By addressing the wrong market, the largest LAN start-up
of the mid-1980s was paradoxically relegated to niche-player status, with
no prospects for affecting the mainstream standardization battle.

Despite their failure, two of the three early pioneers left lasting
imprints on the emerging LAN industry. Nestar's founders, Harry Saal
and Leonard Shustek, left the firm in 1986 to start Network General, a
company that became a midsize player in the LAN industry.[75] More
important, the various engineers leaving Zilog established four important LAN start-ups: Ungermann-Bass, Bridge Communications, Excelan,
and Orchid Technology (see chapter 5). These spin-offs made Zilog,

together with Xerox PARC, the most fertile seed institution in the LAN industry (figure 3.1).

Datapoint: Turning a Head Start into a Strong Position

Despite the experiences of Zilog, Nestar, and Network Systems, failure due to early market entry was not necessarily a foregone conclusion. Unlike the other pioneers, Datapoint, also an early LAN commercializer, succeeded in turning its head start into a strong position in the standards battle of the 1980s. Datapoint's greater success resulted mainly from its position as a well-established computer manufacturer. Its computer business created various synergies for its LAN business, thereby alleviating many of the problems faced by the other pioneer firms.

Established in 1968 by Phil Ray and Gus Roche in San Antonio, Texas, Datapoint began as a third-party manufacturer of computer terminals, but its business focus evolved quickly.[76] In 1970 Datapoint decided to integrate a microprocessor into its terminals, so that a single terminal could interact with several incompatible computers. This capability would relieve users from having to maintain a different type of terminal for each computer system—a necessity that arose from the computers' widespread incompatibility—and Datapoint thereby hoped to gain a competitive edge in the terminal market.[77] But once Datapoint had introduced its microprocessor-based terminal, which was equipped with 8,000 kilobytes of storage, users quickly discovered a second use for it. They began employing it as standalone computer to write business programs, such as accounting or payroll routines.[78] As the demand for this intelligent terminal–cum–small computer increased, Datapoint redefined its market focus and evolved into a vendor of small (proprietary) business computers. This market was far more lucrative than the terminal business. In 1976 sales reached $72 million, and profits grew to $15.2 million.[79] The firm's financial success was soon to play a critical role in its entry into the LAN market. Unlike Zilog and Nestar, Datapoint did not have to struggle with limited financial resources, nor did it lack the technical capabilities to develop an advanced LAN. Besides, Datapoint's computer business provided its LAN with an instant captive market.[80]

Before long, Datapoint indeed had to make the leap toward offering a computer network. As users discovered the value of Datapoint's business computer, they demanded ever-greater computing power and storage capacity from the eight-bit machine. At first Datapoint attempted to satisfy these demands with the introduction of a more powerful computer,

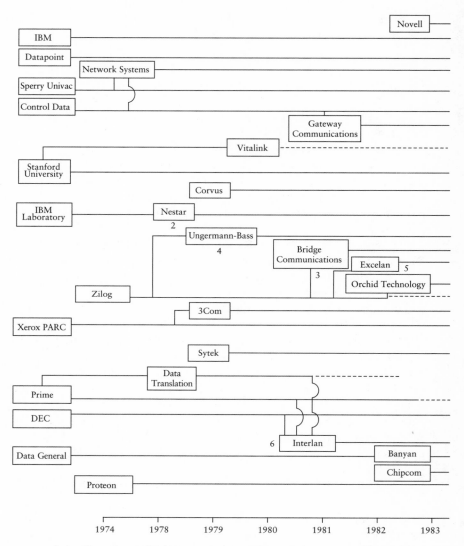

FIGURE 3.1 Genealogy of LAN companies, 1974–1990. 1, Acquired by Hughes Aircraft, subsidiary of General Motors, in 1989; 2, acquired by Digital Switching Corporation in 1986; 3, merged with 3Com in 1987; 4, acquired by Tandem in 1988; 5, acquired by Novell in 1989; 6, acquired by Micom in 1985.

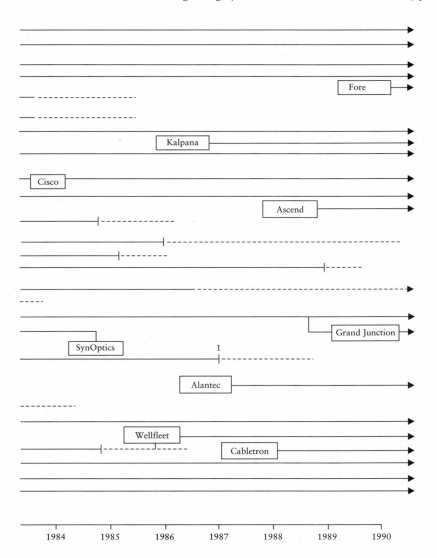

the Datapoint 6600, but eventually it had to offer a more radical remedy.[81] In 1977 the company introduced a network-based, distributed computing system called ARC (Attached Resource Computing). Like PARC's personal distributed computing system based on the Alto and Ethernet, the ARC system allowed users to network several computing and storage devices (such as word or data processors), thereby forming a

homogeneous environment. Users could then access all data, files, processors, and peripherals stored in or attached to the system.[82]

Conforming to the predominant business model of the 1970s, the
ARC system was vertically integrated and completely proprietary, that
is, it consisted of and integrated only Datapoint's computing devices.
Though consumers today shy away from proprietary systems, in the late
1970s the ARC system's proprietariness did not represent a major handicap. All of Datapoint's competitors in the office market offered proprietary
systems as well, and the ARC system was one of the most advanced office
systems available.[83] This put Datapoint not only at the forefront of the
race to actualize the "office of the future" but also in direct competition
with Xerox, which had targeted a similar market with its Alto-based distributed computing system. As a result, Datapoint's LAN, later called
ARCnet, and Xerox's Ethernet were to become direct opponents in the
race for the LAN standard.[84]

In the late 1970s both LANs were proprietary and operated at a similar speed—ARCnet at 2.5 Mbps and Experimental Ethernet at 2.94 Mbps.
However, from the perspective of the pre-IEEE period, ARCnet appeared
to be in a stronger competitive position than Ethernet.[85] ARCnet had a
head start of two to three years, since Xerox did not ship Ethernet until
1979–80.[86] Furthermore ARCnet, a token-passing network, was quite
sophisticated for its time, and, according to at least one observer, even
superior to Ethernet.[87] In fact, ARCnet operated on a cable (of the RG-
62U type) that was easy to install, allowed for foolproof attachment of
nodes thanks to its BNC connectors, and was often preinstalled in buildings, since IBM used the same wire for its 2260 terminal system.[88] Ethernet, in contrast, was difficult to install, and its method of connecting
nodes to the wire was quite cumbersome. Even more important, unlike
Ethernet, ARCnet operated on a hub topology.[89] It therefore possessed
wiring and network management advantages similar to those of Saltzer
and Pogran's star-shaped token ring, with the result that it was far more
convenient to operate than bus-based Ethernet.[90] When both LANs were
shipped, ARCnet also held the price advantage. Whereas Ethernet initially cost $3,000–$4,000, ARCnet cost only $1,397 per node.[91] These
first-mover and technical advantages allowed Datapoint to position itself
far better in preparation for the standardization battle than Zilog and
Nestar, whose demise had resulted to a large extent from the inferiority
of their technologies.

Datapoint's ARCnet had another vital advantage that the networks of
Zilog and Nestar lacked: it possessed a substantial captive market. Owing
to the proprietariness of Datapoint's system, ARCnet was the only means
to network Datapoint equipment, a substantial point of leverage since the

Datapoint market grew briskly from $72 million in 1976 to $449 million in 1981 (see appendix B). Unlike Z-Net, which was stymied by the slow sales growth of Zilog's MCZ computers, ARCnet did not have to wait for its target market to take off. As a result of this captive market, by 1980 ARCnet had accumulated the largest installed base among all LANs. With a base of 2,000 networks in 1981, it not only was far ahead of Nestar's Cluster/One but also had surpassed the scant 35 Ethernets that Xerox had installed.[92]

Of course, this lead did not mean that ARCnet was on the verge of "tipping" the entire LAN market. The other computer manufacturers would inevitably introduce LANs as well, and the proprietariness of their systems provided them with captive markets of their own. Besides, ARCnet's very proprietariness meant that it could not invade the other vendors' markets but would remain restricted to Datapoint equipment, a relatively small segment of the business compared with the IBM and DEC markets. Yet in 1980 Datapoint was clearly the market leader in office LANs.

Thus in 1980 Datapoint found itself in a far better position for the impending standards battle than either Nestar or Zilog. Thanks to its financial resources and technical capabilities, Datapoint offered a LAN that was quite powerful for its time. And thanks to its fast-growing computer business, Datapoint could sell its network into a large captive market. Designed as it was to network small business computers, ARCnet happened to have a price-performance structure similar to that required in the PC market. ARCnet could thus be applied to PCs quite easily and did not require the technical adjustments that prevented Network Systems' HYPERchannel from entering the minicomputer market. Leveraging these advantages, Datapoint avoided many of the burdens that plagued the small LAN start-ups, and it thus became one of the prime contenders to set the standard.

The Perils of Pioneering

The economic theory of standardization claims that gaining a head start is not only critical but also in many cases sufficient to win a standards race. A head start is expected to allow a technology or a firm to enlarge its installed base in such a way that network effects are unleashed, leading the market to "tip" toward the early entrant. The early stage of LAN commercialization, however, worked in exactly the opposite way. Three out of the four pioneers failed exactly *because of* their early market entry. There is a good deal of truth in the bitter Silicon Valley joke: The

pioneers are easy to spot. They're the dead guys with the arrows sticking
out of them.

The theoretical and empirical findings disagree because the theory's
abstract models ignore many of the complications that can occur in an
inchoate industry. In the case of the newborn LAN market, the pioneers
had to develop a smoothly functioning technology and to identify the
"right" markets. They also had to mobilize capital, figure out the "killer
apps," educate customers, find new distribution channels, and attract
suppliers. In addition, they had to cope with a small and slowly growing
market that required substantial investments but promised only small
initial returns. Finally, the pioneers had to survive the various technological and market discontinuities that rocked the computer market in the
early 1980s. In short, early market entry was a difficult process because
the immature market required firms to embed their technology in many
ill-defined dimensions, such as end-user and capital markets, corporate
structures, and time—dimensions the abstract models of standardization
theory neglect.[93] In this sense, the dominant design theory provides a far
better explanation than standardization theory for the fate of the earliest
pioneers.

Despite this apparent contradiction with standardization theory, its
claims are not completely refuted. The Ethernet standard indeed prevailed partly because of its relatively early commercialization. Nevertheless, this pre-dominant-design period suggests that a strategy of being the
very first pioneer in a novel market poses substantial risks. A firm following the pioneers very closely can be better off, as many dimensions
of technological embeddedness are already settled. With regard to the
struggle between the specialized LAN vendors and the computer manufacturers to set the standard, Datapoint's success does not necessarily
indicate that the computer manufacturers had a strategic advantage over
the start-ups in dominating the incipient LAN market. As the history of
computing has repeatedly shown, start-ups often move faster than
incumbent firms to seize new opportunities—opportunities that at the
outset are often too small for large firms to consider. In addition, specialized LAN start-ups were largely unaffected by the disincentive of interconnecting incompatible equipment. This gave them a fair chance in the
emerging industry.

Though excessive pioneering chores and the various market shifts in
the computer industry were principal causes of the pioneers' decline, they
also failed because they all insisted that their respective technologies
remain proprietary and thus lacked a true supplier community. Some of
them kept their systems closed as a result of a deliberate corporate strategy, while others were forced to go the proprietary route owing to the

novelty of the LAN market. In fact, Harry Saal has remarked that the inchoate market deprived Nestar of natural allies, and thus it had to develop a vertically integrated system out of necessity.[94] Whatever the reason for this proprietariness, the lack of suppliers posed a significant handicap for the firms and their networks. Without community support, the firms had to provide the entire system; hence they could not capture specialization gains nor rely on other vendors for the provision of complementary goods. Without supplier support, their networks became tightly coupled to the success of their sponsors and consequently vulnerable to market shifts. In this sense, the fate of the early pioneers confirms the thesis that a technology being supported by a single firm is doomed to fail in a rapidly changing market, especially if the firm is small and undercapitalized.

The commercialization efforts by the four pioneers described in this chapter initiated the pre-dominant-design period. By 1980, they had created a small market but not yet an entire industry—nor had they set the standard. There was still ample room for later entrants to shape the infant marketplace.

4 The Standardization of LAN Technology

In the early 1980s, the LAN market was about to take off. Numerous additional LAN start-ups were established, and most computer manufacturers began experimenting with LAN technology to prepare for its eventual commercialization (table 4.1). In fact, according to a *Business Week* article published in October 1980, over forty firms were already selling LANs.[1] In the absence of a standard, they risked creating widespread chaos in the field of LAN communication. To avoid such a Babel of incompatible protocols, in the late 1970s a few forward-looking individuals and firms had undertaken two independent initiatives to create an open standard; these quickly became united in a single standards project under the aegis of the IEEE. Although the project, called IEEE 802, attracted numerous computer vendors interested in LAN standardization, the participants quickly began battling over which technology to standardize on. Unable to work out a compromise and hopelessly deadlocked, the participants eventually yielded to their respective special interests and created not one but three standards: Ethernet, Token Ring, and Token Bus.

Despite its failure to create a single standard, the IEEE 802 project was the pivotal event in LAN standardization and industry development for two reasons. First, when most of the large computer vendors—including IBM, DEC, H-P, and Data General—adopted one of its standards, they broke with their traditional business model based on proprietariness, thus drastically curbing the proliferation of incompatible LANs. Second, as multiple LAN start-ups were established to exploit its open standards, IEEE 802 effectively laid the foundation for the emerging LAN industry.

Most participating computer vendors joined the project because their customers no longer tolerated proprietary solutions in the area of data

TABLE 4.1

Selected LAN Companies Between the Late 1970s and the Mid-1980s

Firm	Network name	Year of introduction
Datapoint	ARCnet	1977
Network Systems	HYPERchannel	1977
Xerox	Ethernet	1979–80
Zilog	Z-Net	1979–80
Amdax	Cablenet	Around 1980
Ungermann-Bass	Net/One	Around 1980
Apollo	DOMAIN	Early 1980s
Contel Information Systems	Contelnet	Early 1980s
Applitek	UniLAN	Early to mid-1980s
Fox Research	10-Net LAN	Early to mid-1980s
Orchid Technology	PCNet	Early to mid-1980s
Corvus	CONSTELLATION	1980
Nestar	Cluster/One	1980
Prime Computer	Primenet	Around 1980–81
Digital Microsystems	Hinet	1980–82
Codenoll Technology	Codelink-20	Around 1981
	Codelink-100	Around 1981
Corvus	Omninet	1981
InteCom	InteNet	1981
Proteon	Pronet	1981
Sytek	LocalNet	1981–82
Wang	Wangnet	1981–82
Kaypro	KayNet	Around 1982
Syntrex	Synnet	1982
Concord Data Systems	Token/Net	Around 1983
Gateway Communications	G/Net	Around 1983
3M	LAN/1	1983–84
Apple	AppleTalk	Around 1984
Centram	TOPS	1984–85
IBM	PC Network	1984–85
NCR	PC2PC Network	1985

NOTE: Does not include vendors of factory networks and Ethernet suppliers.

communication. They also opted for an open standard to increase market acceptance of their individual technologies—and this could be interpreted as a strategy to magnify network effects favoring their technologies. But another reason—one usually not explicitly considered by standardization theory—motivated several computer vendors, especially the principal supporters of the Ethernet standard. They saw LANs as merely a costly enabling technology, and they intended to reap profits from their core businesses in computer hardware and software, rather than from the manufacturing of LAN components. In other words, by keeping the cost of the network low, they hoped to increase the competitiveness of the products of their core businesses. They reasoned that an open standard would attract outside LAN suppliers, a development that would help them shed costs and increase the profitability of their core businesses. In this sense, they considered openness as a vehicle for attracting suppliers and "subsidizing" their key products.

As we will see, however, the participants ultimately failed to create a single standard because of market considerations that seemed every bit as compelling as those that had prompted them to seek an open standard in the first place. In the variety of markets in which the many participating vendors operated, their technological needs were too diverse to be satisfied by a single technology, and as a result they refrained from reconciling their technological differences—in what would, at any rate, have been a painstaking process.

The DIX Alliance

The first standardization effort that fed into the IEEE 802 project was the formation of the DIX alliance among DEC, Intel, and Xerox in 1979. Though the coalition did not aim at creating a de jure standard, as did IEEE 802, it pursued a similar goal: the creation of an industry-wide LAN standard.

While looking for ways to connect its new VAX computers into clusters to form a distributed computing environment, DEC experimented with a few LAN technologies internally. But Gordon Bell, chief designer of DEC's VAX strategy, encouraged his engineers to look at other firms' LANs as well, and if necessary to license one of those technologies. Having tested several existing LANs, including Datapoint's ARCnet, the Cambridge Ring, and Ethernet, DEC decided that an Ethernet-like network offered the best solution.[2] ARCnet seemed too slow, and the Cambridge Ring appeared unreliable owing to its ring topology; Ethernet, with its bus topology and lack of central control, appeared well suited for connecting a few engineering workstations along a corridor and for expanding a network incrementally.[3] DEC also liked Ethernet because it seemed possible to upgrade its 2.94-Mbps throughput. This was an important consideration for DEC, which needed high network speed for a future VAX superminicomputer, as well as for the synchronization of VAX clusters in real time and for fast access to remote hard disks.[4]

It was at this point that Robert Metcalfe, as a visiting researcher at MIT and a consultant at DEC, suggested contacting Xerox about licensing the Ethernet technology. With the participation of Xerox and the fortuitous events that led to Intel's joining, the DIX alliance was formed.

Initially the three firms kept their alliance secret to avoid scrutiny from the Department of Justice while completing the Ethernet specifications. But as soon as the specifications were finished, they planned to "announce [Ethernet] to the world as an open standard."[5] Their stated goal was to create an industry-wide de facto standard, available to any firm.[6]

In subsequent meetings, in which Metcalfe did not participate, the alliance modified Xerox's Experimental Ethernet to prepare it for commercialization. The engineers of the alliance altered various technical parameters of Xerox's original Ethernet, such as its address and frame size, frame check sequence, and electrical security. Ronald Crane of Xerox redesigned the transceivers and controllers.[7] Most important, its original speed of 2.94 Mbps was increased to 10 Mbps.[8] As Metcalfe later wrote, "10 Mbps made Ethernet tolerably expensive [in terms of ICs] yet fast enough to carry the bulk of LAN traffic through the year 2003."[9] Although this assessment ultimately proved too optimistic, the modifications improved Ethernet considerably, especially in terms of its speed. Yet two critical omissions remained to be addressed. The DIX group's engineers modified neither Ethernet's bus topology nor its use of thick coaxial cable, which required a cumbersome method to connect nodes to the cable.[10] Thus they missed the opportunity to correct two deficiencies that would later haunt the standard. Ethernet, though improved, was far from being the very best technology available—a fact that was to trigger objections when it was finally presented to the IEEE 802 group.

Standardization theory usually assumes that an open standard poses significant risks to vendors, as it exposes them to increased competition and deprives them of monopoly rents. Why then did Xerox decide to license its technology? And why did DEC and Intel join Xerox's effort to create an industry-wide standard?

First, the risks of an open LAN standard did not seem so high to the three vendors. LAN technology was not a core business for DEC. If competitors were to have taken over the LAN business, this would not have been of great significance to the company. Furthermore, openness in LAN technology did not jeopardize its core products, namely computer hardware and profession-specific software. While opening up its LAN, DEC kept all its higher-level protocols, as well as its VAX operating system (known as VMS) and professional software, proprietary. Since seamless data communication requires the sharing of *all* protocol layers, this partial proprietariness acted like a fence around DEC's product system. Competitors would not be able to offer low-cost systems that could seamlessly communicate with DEC's own. Opening LAN technology simply meant that DEC's competitors could make their machines transmit on the cable used by DEC's computers and that they could compete with DEC in the LAN component business. In fact, as will be seen later in this chapter, this was even an intended effect.

Although Xerox, like DEC, kept the core product of its office system (the Star workstation) proprietary, it faced a higher risk than DEC, because it opened not only its LAN protocols but also its higher-level XNS protocols.[11] Xerox thus faced the theoretical risk that its competitors could offer seamless communication with its Star workstations, possibly opening up an entry point for competition in its core business. What was worse, Xerox's other office products were mostly peripherals, such as printers and copiers; unlike DEC's VAX computers, these lacked strong protective mechanisms, such as a complementary, proprietary operating system and software applications. This meant that a Xerox customer could quite easily add a non-Xerox printer or copier to a Xerox-based office system. Yet this potential risk failed to stop Xerox from pursuing an open communication strategy. Like DEC, most of Xerox's competitors in the office automation market, including Wang and Datapoint, used proprietary protocols and operating systems of their own; having thus erected fences around their systems, they could not easily offer computing devices for a Xerox-based office system. Xerox also expected that it would be able to stay ahead of its competitors in the copier and laser printer markets.[12] The company was therefore not concerned about the risks inherent in its open Ethernet strategy.

As we know today, however, Xerox's office strategy proved a total failure. Its Star workstations never took off in the marketplace, since the $15,000 machines were too expensive and not versatile enough for general-purpose office automation.[13] Moreover, H-P and various Japanese manufacturers succeeded in capturing the laser printer market.[14] Once Xerox had opened Ethernet and XNS, it could not prevent its competitors and customers from using its own communication protocols to network their non-Xerox printers and PCs. Although Xerox's strategy floundered, the cause was the rise of the IBM PC—which obliterated the Star workstation—and not the openness of Ethernet and XNS.[15]

Like DEC and Xerox, Intel faced risks of its own from an open LAN strategy, since such an approach would allow other semiconductor manufacturers to compete with it in the Ethernet chip market. But given the huge learning curves inherent in semiconductor technology, Intel figured that its first-mover advantages would suffice to keep it ahead of its competitors.

Second, DEC, Intel, and Xerox opted for an open standard because such a strategy would nurture the adoption of their LAN system and increase their overall market penetration. Xerox realized that if Ethernet were to become an open standard, customers would be more likely to purchase it. Widespread adoption of Ethernet, in turn, would spur sales of its core products (Star workstations and laser printers), while stalling the proliferation of competing office products. As a later rule in the computer industry would have it: whoever owns the wire owns the account.[16] In this sense, Xerox used the open LAN strategy as a means to increase Ethernet's adoption and ultimately to augment sales of its Alto-based office system.

DEC had a similar motivation. Many of its customers had installed computers from different vendors. Since these systems typically were proprietary, DEC's customers faced an onerous incompatibility problem. They could not easily get their incompatible machines to exchange data and share peripherals, and they were therefore forced to install a separate wire for each system. DEC's customers strongly objected to its adoption of a proprietary LAN, since this would only aggravate their networking problems.[17] They could accept proprietariness in the other parts of DEC's computing system—including software, higher-level protocols, and the operating system—because they believed it increased the system's functionality; however, they believed that the LAN provided little added value and therefore had to be open.[18] Although an open LAN standard did not by itself ensure seamless communication—to accomplish this, computers would need to share compatibility at *all* protocol layers—it at least allowed computers from different vendors to transmit on the same cable, even if they deployed different higher-level protocols.[19] Since this facilitated interoperability in a multivendor environment, DEC reasoned that an open LAN standard would increase customer acceptance of its computers, thereby spurring its hardware sales.

Third, DEC, Intel, and Xerox banded together because their alliance created various synergies. Xerox depended on DEC to help it establish Ethernet as standard in the computer industry. Although Xerox was a successful Fortune 500 company with vast financial resources thanks to its copier franchise, as a relative newcomer to the computer industry it lacked the necessary clout and credibility to establish a network standard on its own.[20] It needed a powerful computer firm like DEC as an ally.[21] But the synergies between Xerox and DEC were mutual. DEC needed Xerox to gain access to Xerox's patent rights in Ethernet, its preferred technology. In addition, DEC expected that it could benefit from Xerox's lavish advertising campaign for Ethernet. Free-riding on Xerox's promotion of Ethernet was a significant side benefit for DEC, because in the late 1970s most end users were not yet familiar with LAN technology.[22]

Fourth and most important, Xerox and DEC pursued an open strategy in order to attract third-party suppliers of Ethernet components. Though Ethernet played a critical enabling role in Xerox's office system, Xerox did not see itself as being in the business of manufacturing Ethernet components. It not only lacked the necessary capabilities for producing Ethernet parts, such as transceivers, at low cost, but also believed that such components would command low margins. If Xerox had to produce these parts, it would have to cross-subsidize the network, thereby diluting the profits from its workstation and laser printer business. Xerox concluded that an open standard could help it avoid this problem, since such a standard was likely to attract specialized suppliers for whom the manufacture of Ethernet products could be a viable business.[23] This would free the copier vendor from wasting resources on a noncore business and make cross-subsidies unnecessary. To David Liddle, head of the Systems Development Division at Xerox PARC, creating an open standard was a far better alternative than simply subcontracting the production of a proprietary Ethernet network, because an open standard was likely to attract *several* suppliers, thereby spurring price competition, while freeing Xerox from any hold-up risks.[24]

DEC did not depend on outside suppliers to the same extent as Xerox, since its capability set was better tuned to the production of Ethernet components. In fact, from the outset DEC planned to manufacture at least some (basic) Ethernet parts, such as transceivers, and in the mid-1980s it indeed became a leading Ethernet manufacturer.[25] Yet DEC shared Xerox's belief that outside suppliers would be useful.[26] By relying on additional Ethernet manufacturers, DEC could focus on the development of its higher-level protocols (that is, DECnet), which allowed for the introduction of more value-added features (and hence higher profit margins) than basic LAN technology. Besides, third-party Ethernet suppliers would be helpful because they could provide specialty products, such as bridges and routers, which DEC did not intend to manufacture. Most important, DEC, like Xerox, depended on the semiconductor firms to supply Ethernet chips. The two vendors realized that aggressive use of ICs would be vital to push Ethernet's initial price of approximately $3,000–$4,000 per node down to their target price of $500.[27] Although DEC had recently built its own IC manufacturing facilities, it did not have the competence to achieve this price goal.[28] DEC understood that semiconductor firms would be much less inclined to develop an IC for DEC if its LAN was proprietary.[29] Therefore, like Xerox, DEC opted for an open standard partly as a means to attract third-party Ethernet suppliers, especially IC manufacturers.

From this perspective, Intel was their first supplier. And as a supplier, Intel benefited from the open Ethernet standard as much as Xerox and DEC. If Xerox or DEC had ordered a proprietary network IC from Intel, Intel would have had a smaller market and thus fewer sales over which to spread the IC's high manufacturing and design costs. A proprietary IC would also have absorbed many scarce resources (e.g., design engineers, fabrication facilities) in the pursuit of a marginal LAN project, potentially at the cost of more lucrative opportunities. Besides, a proprietary chip would have exposed Intel to higher asset-specific risks.[30] To reduce both risks and costs, Intel preferred an open-standard IC, which it could produce in high volume and sell to any vendor adopting the standard. Conversely, the open standard freed Xerox and DEC from the need to compensate Intel for the higher costs and risks associated with producing for a proprietary LAN, while attracting IC vendors in competition with Intel.[31]

For all these reasons, the three firms complemented each other very nicely. Xerox had the technology; DEC provided market clout, credibility, and some Ethernet components; and Intel brought the chips, so vital in achieving steep price reductions. In this sense, the capability theory explains the open-LAN-standard strategy of DEC and Xerox as well as standardization theory. Though the two firms opted for an open standard to increase the market penetration of their preferred technology, they also pursued an open strategy to attract firms with complementary capabilities and assets. Their open strategy can be understood as a clever outsourcing strategy.

The IEEE Standard

The DIX group was not the only one thinking about standardization of the novel LAN technology. In fact, in the early to mid-1970s the IEEE, as well as other standards organizations, had already created a few de jure networking standards. But since these standards were inadequate for the requirements of general-purpose local networks, in the late 1970s a few individuals began looking for an alternative. Their efforts eventually resulted in the IEEE 802 project, the second principal strand in the fiber of LAN standardization.

One of the earliest network standards, which preceded the IEEE 802 specification, was the IEEE 488 standard. Created between 1971 and 1974 under the leadership of Donald Loughry of H-P, IEEE 488 was the specification for a rather simple network.[32] Intended for industrial process control, it was a digital interface bus designed to connect programmable instruments so they could be controlled remotely. Although this network was widely adopted and allowed users to connect instruments from different vendors, its maximum distance of only 20 meters made it unsuitable as a general-purpose LAN.[33]

The success of the IEEE 488 standard made H-P and Loughry (who later chaired the Ethernet subgroup of IEEE 802) staunch believers in open standards, but IEEE 802 was initiated mainly through a solo effort by Maris Graube, who was an engineer with Tektronix and later became the group's chairman. Realizing the severe distance limitation of IEEE 488, in the late 1970s Graube began looking for an alternative network standard. He located a group at Purdue University involved with PROWAY (short for process control data highway), an international standardization effort focused on networks for industrial process control. Though intended to cover longer distances than the IEEE 488 standard, PROWAY appeared to Graube to be as ill suited for general-purpose LANs as the IEEE 488 network.[34] PROWAY was intended to provide extremely reliable data communications well suited for, say, nuclear and petrochemical facilities, but at the cost of requirements that were too stringent for a general-purpose LAN.[35] Unable to find a standards organization engaged in the development of such a LAN standard, in the middle of 1979 Graube submitted to the IEEE a project authorization request, which was necessary to initiate such a standardization effort. The IEEE approved Graube's request in late 1979, and the first meeting of what came to be called IEEE Project 802 was scheduled for February 1980 in San Francisco.[36]

The IEEE's new standards project attracted considerable interest. The first meeting in February 1980 was attended by approximately seventy-five individuals representing a diverse set of vendors (figure 4.1).[37] Among the companies represented (in addition to the members of the DIX alliance) were (1) leading computer manufacturers, including IBM, H-P, Data General, Honeywell, Burroughs, Prime, and Apollo; (2) vendors of office automation products, including Wang; (3) vendors of factory automation systems, such as Allen-Bradley, Fisher-Porter, and Gould; and (4) several recently formed LAN start-ups, including 3Com and U-B.[38] Despite the participation of a few LAN start-ups, it was clear that the large computer manufacturers, not the start-ups, would be the driving actors in IEEE 802.

Given this diversity of backgrounds, it is not surprising that the vendors participated in the IEEE standards project for quite different reasons. Some, like H-P, were truly interested in an open LAN standard. As Loughry explained, the overwhelming success and market-enlarging effect of the IEEE 488 standard had convinced H-P of the importance of open standards.[39] H-P had no doubt that it had to adopt an open standard in LANs as well. Other vendors participated primarily to learn about the novel LAN technology. Its successful development and commercialization would require detailed knowledge in many different areas, such as cabling, transmission and access methods, chip design, and electrical

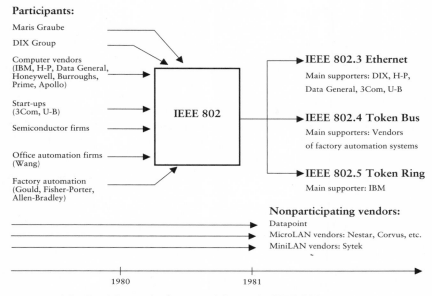

FIGURE 4.1 Participants and nonparticipants in IEEE 802.

safety, as well as careful assessment of market needs, applications, and cost-performance trade-offs. None of the participating engineers understood all these issues; hence many "conceded that they were there to learn rather than to support any particular position."[40] To these vendors, IEEE 802 was an educational forum, from which knowledge fed back into their specific product development efforts.

But other vendors, including the manufacturers of factory automation systems, participated because they already had strong preferences for certain technologies. In fact, several vendors had already experimented with their own LAN technologies, while others (like Apollo and Prime) had even commercialized their first LAN products. Each attended the meetings to defend its interests and to ensure that its preferred technology would become the standard.

IBM—which was soon to become one of the main actors in the standardization negotiations—also participated to learn about the novel technology and to defend its interests, as it had already experimented with token ring technology at its Zurich research laboratory. But it joined the IEEE project for other reasons as well: like DEC, it faced significant customer pressure. Even loyal IBM customers were no longer willing to tolerate a proprietary data network.[41] Not only would an IBM-only network have precluded them from mixing computing devices from different vendors, it would also have made them captives in the same way that they had become locked in to Big Blue's mainframes.[42] If IBM offered a proprietary LAN, many customers might defect to the IEEE standard. To avoid losing customers, IBM, like many other vendors, had at least to consider adopting an open LAN technology.

IBM's decision making was also influenced by scrutiny from the Antitrust Division of the U.S. Department of Justice, whose long-standing investigation of the firm had placed it under great pressure. Realizing that its LAN products would be delayed until the mid-1980s, IBM could not preannounce a proprietary LAN without incurring further scrutiny from the Justice Department. Since IBM had calculated that its market clout and technical expertise would allow it to control IEEE 802 anyway, joining the group provided a practical way to circumvent antitrust attacks.[43] Besides, an open LAN standard would not jeopardize IBM's mainframe business, since the company continued to rely on many proprietary higher-level protocols and did not intend to use the LAN for linking its mainframes.[44] Hence IBM, in common with DEC, faced little risk from an open LAN standard.

IBM, like many other vendors, thus had a variety of reasons for participating in the meetings and considering an open LAN standard. Many of its reasons resembled those of the DIX group, including customer pressure and vested interest in a particular technology. But IBM and the DIX group differed in one significant respect (table 4.2). IBM did not consider an open standard as a means of attracting outside suppliers. In fact, as Werner Bux has pointed out, IBM intended to build its own LAN business.[45] As the following chapters will show, this difference was to have a significant impact on the outcome of the standards race.

Three Standards

The two standard-setting efforts, in conjunction with the broad vendor participation in IEEE 802, were positive developments for the concepts of standardization and openness. But the existence of two competing efforts also led to an inability to create a single standard, even when the two efforts eventually merged.

The first IEEE 802 meeting, in February 1980, took place without much contentiousness, as it was mainly devoted to sorting out preliminary issues.[46] While initially unable to decide on the exact market focus of the standard—whether office or factory automation—the participants agreed to follow the OSI Reference Model, that is, to define layers 1 and 2 of the model as they applied to LANs.[47] This meant that they would

TABLE 4.2

Why Xerox, DEC, and IBM Chose an Open Standard

	To attract semiconductor firms	To attract other suppliers	To enhance de facto standardization	Customer pressure and interoperability in multivendor environments
Xerox	+++	+++	+++	++
DEC	+++	++	+++	+++
IBM	+	+	+++	+++

have to specify the cable type for the LAN, its access and transmission mechanism, its topology, and the parameters of the data packets.[48] Since many of these attributes were to be implemented in ICs, the state of the art in semiconductor technology would affect their standard, thereby giving semiconductor firms significant influence over the project.[49]

The participants set several additional requirements their LAN had to meet:

1. The standard, a peer-to-peer network, was only meant for commercial and light industrial applications; networks with extreme reliability requirements would not be addressed.

2. Nevertheless, the network had to operate fairly reliably, tolerating only one undetected data transmission error per year.

3. The network had to span up to 2 kilometers, connect up to 200 devices, and operate at a speed ranging from 1 to 20 Mbps.

4. The standard was to be media-independent; that is, its cable access and transmission mechanism had to operate over a variety of cable types.[50]

With these requirements set, the standards committee had neither implied a specific LAN technology nor yet decided whether to focus on office or factory automation.

During these meetings Graube (who had by now been elected chair of the project) hoped to create a single, ideal standard. But the computer vendors quickly succeeded in dominating the agenda and in the process transformed the meetings into a struggle among special interests.[51] The earliest interference came from the DIX group. Initially, the three firms had intended to keep their alliance secret in order to finish drafting their Ethernet specifications without outside interference. However, when IEEE 802 began meeting in early 1980, they were forced to show their hand. Realizing that collaboration with IEEE 802 would help them establish Ethernet as a standard, just prior to the group's first working meeting, on May 27–31, 1980, Gordon Bell of DEC, David Liddle of Xerox, and Robert Noyce, co-founder of Intel, announced their alliance and their intention to produce compatible Ethernet products.[52] At the IEEE meeting later that month, the trio briefly described their still incomplete Ethernet standard and promised to release the complete specification at a later date. Through these announcements, the alliance not only offered Ethernet to IEEE 802 for adoption but also threatened to build Ethernet products—regardless of the presence of an alternative IEEE standard.[53] Not surprisingly, this uncompromising stance caused hostility among many IEEE 802 participants, who felt they were being placed in the position of merely ratifying the DIX group's technology.[54]

When the DIX group released its Ethernet specification—also called the Blue Book because of its blue cover—in September 1980, it provoked an intense debate about the technical merits of Ethernet.[55] Some participants quickly identified various weaknesses in the technology. The manufacturers of networks for industrial process control expressed concerns that Ethernet's randomly based CSMA/CD access method did not provide the determinism they believed critical for the smooth operation of real-time factory processes. As an alternative, they suggested a standard based on token-passing technology.[56] Other participants opposed Ethernet because of its lack of electrical safety, the possibility for electrical interference in a factory environment, and the difficulty of implementing its CSMA/CD mechanism on fiber optic and broadband cable.[57]

The DIX group, in turn, dismissed these objections. Xerox contended that it had been using Ethernet experimentally for several years, whereas several of the proposed token technologies were merely phantom concepts not yet in operation. The alliance further argued that electrical interference could prevent the token from circulating, a failure that would require the token's reinitialization. In their eyes, this made the token-passing method no longer deterministic.[58]

Yet the DIX group's counterarguments failed to prevent the rise of a strong token faction. Token technology was quickly embraced by Allen-Bradley, Apollo Computer, AT&T, Burroughs, Concord Data Systems, Fisher-Porter, GM, Gould, Honeywell, Modicon, and Prime. Many of these firms had strong positions in process control and factory automation; others offered broadband modems, while a few, such as Apollo and Prime, were already selling token ring networks.[59] This meant that a great number of participants were in favor of some form of token technology, not Ethernet.[60]

Although IBM did not officially endorse token technology, it clearly did not favor Ethernet.[61] As mentioned, IBM had already begun developing a token ring system at its Zurich laboratory, but its aversion to

Ethernet derived mainly from the latter's inability to serve the needs of its primary customers: the management information system (MIS) departments and data centers of large organizations.[62] Since these customers had to network very large numbers of nodes, often in the hundreds, they needed a network that not only guaranteed high reliability and availability but also allowed them to manage and monitor such large LANs.[63] They demanded central control over the network and needed to know what types of machine were connected to the network, where the nodes were located, and whether messages had arrived. In IBM's view, Ethernet completely failed to meet these customer requirements. Ethernet's bus topology, though convenient for adding a few nodes along a corridor in an engineering lab or a small office workgroup, failed to provide MIS managers with a central point of control. Like Jerome Saltzer and Kenneth Pogran of MIT, IBM found that this omission rendered Ethernet totally inadequate for managing and monitoring large networks and disabling individual nodes from one location.[64] IBM also found that Ethernet's randomly based CSMA/CD mechanism inherently failed to provide high predictability and availability. Even worse, in IBM's view the CSMA/CD mechanism performed poorly under heavy network loads.[65] Such deterioration might have had few consequences in the relatively small workgroup networks that DEC's and Xerox's customers were installing, but in the large enterprise networks of IBM's customers, rapid performance degradation was a serious handicap—especially since IBM had observed that users tended to reach the full capacity of their systems rather quickly.[66] In addition, IBM engineers regarded Ethernet's coaxial cable as quite inflexible and its method of connecting nodes to the wire as prone to failure.[67] This too was unacceptable to IBM's customers, who depended on high reliability in their large networks.

To IBM, a standard based on token technology appeared far better suited to meet these customer demands, especially a token ring technology wired in a star-based topology with several concentrators or hubs attached to it. Such a token ring technology would provide MIS managers with a far better way of monitoring and managing the network, as well as of attaching nodes to it.[68] In addition, since the token-passing method included a deterministic element, it provided much higher levels of reliability and availability and was far more likely than Ethernet to guarantee a given performance level and arrival time for messages.[69] Furthermore, IBM intended to use shielded twisted-pair (STP) wire, which was more flexible than Ethernet's coaxial cable and also allowed a more foolproof way of connecting nodes to the wire.[70] Finally, the token method made it possible to prioritize messages.[71] This also appeared to IBM to be a useful feature, since a message initiated from a terminal did not carry the same importance as a message initiated from a mainframe that cost several million dollars.[72] Yet Ethernet's CSMA/CD mechanism did not allow for such prioritization.

Of course, these features would make IBM's token ring more expensive than Ethernet, but they seemed warranted to IBM because they let token ring "do a job Ethernet simply did not do."[73] In fact, Robert Love, one of IBM's token ring engineers, summarized IBM's view of Ethernet as follows: "Ethernet did not quite solve the problem. It solved the simpler problem, and it solved it in a simple way. But it did not solve the problem that was critical to a very important part of our customer base."[74] Ethernet, which had been designed by Xerox PARC as a small workgroup LAN, appeared adequate to IBM for exactly this type of application, but inadequate for enterprise-wide networks—the primary application of its customers. IBM was therefore just as strongly committed to a token standard as it was firmly opposed to an Ethernet standard.

Giving up Ethernet in favor of IBM's token ring standard was not, however, acceptable to the DIX group. Of course, as Ethernet's sponsor Xerox had strong vested interests, while DEC and Intel, through their alliance with Xerox, had made firm commitments of their own to Ethernet and had already invested in the technology. Intel had spent a significant amount of money and labor on developing an Ethernet IC and was concerned that the state of the art in VLSI technology would be inadequate for the complexity of IBM's proposed token ring technology.[75] Furthermore, Xerox's and DEC's customers did not really need the advanced features of IBM's token ring. Xerox intended to network small offices of professionals, and DEC focused primarily on departments and engineering labs. Although many of these departments and labs were located within the same Fortune 500 companies as IBM's customers, they usually maintained smaller networks than IBM's MIS departments and operated quite independently from them. Besides, many of DEC's engineering customers had the technical expertise to manage the relatively small networks themselves. To DEC's customers, token ring's additional capabilities not only were unnecessary but also did not justify its expected higher price.

Xerox and DEC, as well as their allies, also preferred Ethernet because it was far closer to commercialization than token ring technology. In fact, in September 1980, when the DIX group presented an almost complete Ethernet specification, IBM had hardly begun the development of its token ring, and the technology's complexity appeared likely to prolong its development even further.[76] Whereas the development of a better network justified some market delays in IBM's view, delays were unacceptable to the Ethernet supporters. Xerox and DEC needed a LAN immediately for their Star workstation and VAX strategies, respectively;

they could not wait several years for the completion of IBM's token ring.[77]

Finally—although DEC and IBM preferred different technologies primarily because they wanted to serve different customer needs, rather than because they wished to exclude each other from their respective networks—they nevertheless had *strategic* reasons for not being too compatible with each other. By offering a different LAN than IBM, DEC hoped to prevent IBM's SNA protocol from penetrating the departmental minicomputer market, DEC's principal market segment. DEC calculated that, once departments had adopted Ethernet-based computers and installed coaxial cable, they would face high switching costs, because IBM's minicomputers required different communication protocols and wire. By driving Ethernet into the departments, DEC expected to lock in future minicomputer sales and exclude Big Blue from the departmental market.[78] Likewise, IBM hoped to turn LAN technology into a lucrative business—an outcome it had concluded would be more difficult to achieve in the Ethernet realm.[79] Hence neither the DIX group nor IBM had a strong desire to reconcile their differences and to join their antagonist's network. Despite their interest in an open standard, IBM and DEC, the two most important computer manufacturers of the 1980s, were in opposing camps.

In hindsight, the DIX group with its Ethernet, IBM with its token ring, and the vendors of factory systems with their token bus technology were the principal antagonists in IEEE 802, for they all eventually succeeded in standardizing their preferred technologies. But in 1980 there were even more potential contenders. One of Ethernet's most vocal opponents was Wang. Like Xerox, Datapoint, Zilog, and many other computer manufacturers, Wang vied for the office automation market, and it was a strong competitor.[80] Although it was well behind IBM, which had sales of $1.2 billion in the word processor market, with $470 million in revenues in 1980 Wang ranked second in this segment and was far ahead of Xerox, which ranked sixth with sales of $85.5 million.[81] Like Xerox and the other entrants in the office automation market, Wang was developing a network to connect its various computers into a homogeneous environment. Falsely believing that Ethernet was favored within IEEE 802 owing to its relatively high speed, Wang decided to leapfrog Xerox with a superior technology.[82] Its network, Wangnet, was to transmit at 12 Mbps (2 Mbps faster than Ethernet), and it would be a broadband LAN.[83] This meant that unlike Ethernet (a baseband LAN), Wangnet would be able to transmit voice and video in addition to computer data.[84]

In Graube's view, Wang participated constructively in the IEEE 802 meetings, but Liddle recalled that Wang made many unwarranted claims about the superiority of its planned (but as yet undeveloped) Wangnet; he believed that the firm participated primarily to slow down the adoption of Ethernet.[85] In fact, whereas Ethernet had already been developed and commercialized, Wang was just beginning to develop Wangnet.[86] Hence Wang had every reason to delay Xerox, as the proliferation of Ethernet would have spurred the sales of Xerox's office system while stalling those of Wang's products.[87] Although Wang never offered Wangnet to IEEE 802 for adoption, since it believed that the superiority of its network would be a competitive advantage in the office market, it heightened the level of divisiveness within IEEE 802 through its opposition to Ethernet.[88]

In his role as chair of IEEE 802, Graube also contacted Datapoint, which at the time had the largest installed base of LANs, but its vice president of engineering expressed no interest in submitting its network, ARCnet, for consideration as an IEEE standard.[89] In fact, Datapoint even declined to participate in the IEEE 802 meetings.[90] Jonathan Schmidt, one of the company's vice presidents, maintained that Datapoint's management simply did not understand the power of open standards: "[Before Ethernet] there was nothing that was open back in the 1970s. It was not in the normal psychology of that day to perceive the synergies of joining together with other companies to expand the market so much more that a smaller piece of a bigger pie would be better for you. That was just not a concept." But Datapoint also faced some constraints the other vendors did not. Because of the great success of the ARCnet system, Datapoint's cash flow had become dependent on it. Datapoint could not open ARCnet without risking increased competition and jeopardizing its margins and sales.[91] In addition, as a relatively small vendor with revenues of approximately $319 million in 1980, Datapoint was unlikely to push ARCnet through IEEE 802 unaltered.[92] Any modification, however, would have stranded its existing customer base. Datapoint could not adopt an open standard for the same reason. Besides, the company felt that its ARCnet was superior to Ethernet and did not want to give up this technological edge.[93] In this sense, Datapoint's technological and market lead was, paradoxically, something of a handicap: giving up that edge would be too costly, and it would expose Datapoint to the risk of being outflanked by an open standard (table 4.3).

ARCnet ultimately stagnated precisely because of Datapoint's decision to keep its network proprietary (see chapter 6). Although one might think that Datapoint made a strategic blunder by not participating in IEEE 802, the restrictive path dependencies it faced and the limited foresight available to its management vindicate the company. In 1980, the

TABLE 4.3

Key Differentiators in the Standardization
Strategies of IBM, DEC, Wang, and Datapoint

	IBM	*DEC*	*Wang*	*Datapoint*
Penchant for proprietary control	++	+	+++	+++
Restrictive path dependencies	+	+	+	+++
Vision of the power of open systems	+++	+++	+	+
Power to push own technology through IEEE 802	+++	++	+	+

extent to which open systems would succeed was still unclear. That open systems could prevail became obvious only in the mid-1980s as a result of the success not only of Ethernet but also of Sun Microsystems and the IBM PC. Though IBM and Sun adopted open strategies at about the same time that Datapoint ruled out such a move, their decisions were motivated by two economic factors that were absent in the case of Datapoint. First, both Sun and IBM lagged behind the leaders in workstations and microcomputers, respectively, and they used openness as means to catch up. Second, as a small start-up, Sun had little to lose by betting on openness. In contrast, Datapoint was not only a well-established $319 million company but also one poised at the cutting edge technologically and commercially. The potential risks of openness—stranding customers, increased competition, and lower profitability—therefore appeared to exceed its unproven benefits, at least in the short term. Datapoint's biggest "error" thus consisted of being a leading pioneer in an unsettled market—an error for which the company can hardly be blamed.

Wang's and Datapoint's refusal to submit their technology left Ethernet and token technology as the main contenders in the race for the IEEE standard. Like token technology, Ethernet quickly gathered support beyond the DIX group. Among its supporters were the start-up suppliers (primarily 3Com and U-B) that Metcalfe and his friends had already established to exploit the DIX group's forthcoming Ethernet standard. They had a strong vested interest in Ethernet's success and could not wait for the development of a token ring standard. Even more important, several minicomputer manufacturers, including Data General and H-P (in 1981 the second and third largest minicomputer firms, respectively) rallied behind Ethernet.[94] H-P, for instance, decided to embrace the DIX group's Ethernet proposal because its own experimentation with LANs had shown that such a technology would best serve the needs of its customers. Loughry emphasized that H-P did not adopt Ethernet because of the decision made by DEC, the market leader in minicomputers.[95] Nevertheless, sharing the same LAN with DEC had some advantages for H-P, since both vendors sold to a similar customer base. By adopting DEC's LAN, H-P could make its minicomputers transmit on the same cable, even though the two vendors employed different higher-level protocols. Hence its customers would not have to install a separate cable for H-P computers—a requirement that would have made them less likely to buy from H-P and more likely to purchase from market leader DEC. In this sense, H-P and Data General did exactly what standardization theory suggests they should have: as small vendors, they joined the network of the leading vendor in their market segment, namely DEC.

The rise of a strong Ethernet faction quickly led to a stalemate at the IEEE 802 meetings. The DIX group refused to make significant concessions and saw no reason to abandon Ethernet. On the other side, Ethernet remained unacceptable to the supporters of token technology, despite the DIX group's counterarguments. By late 1980, it was clear that the two factions were in a deadlock, unable to reach an agreement and unwilling to work out a compromise. The meetings came to consist largely of each group attacking its rivals' system while defending its own.[96]

Hopelessly divided, the participants eventually decided to take a vote. In a secret ballot taken in December 1980, token technology received fourteen votes in favor and twelve votes against, while Ethernet received ten votes in favor and sixteen against.[97] Neither technology was able to garner the two-thirds majority necessary for adoption. In anticipation of this deadlock, the representatives of DEC, Gould, and IBM had already discussed the possibility of developing more than one standard. In a further ballot, the opposing camps agreed to split the IEEE 802 group into several subgroups and to create a standard for each of the main factions: (1) an Ethernet standard for the DIX group and its allies (IEEE 802.3); (2) a Token Bus standard for the vendors of factory systems (IEEE 802.4); and (3) a Token Ring standard, mainly intended for IBM, which split away from its token allies and was able to get its "own" standard (IEEE 802.5).[98] Ethernet and Token Ring were now the two principal IEEE standards for the office market.[99]

As Robert Metcalfe later remarked, the split was a dark day in the history of standardization.[100] Though it certainly increased the range of available technological choices, the split entailed significant disadvantages for end users and suppliers alike. Any end user purchasing systems from both IBM and DEC—a likely scenario given their market size— would now need costly gateways. What was more, users would have to install two wires, since Ethernet and Token Ring operated with different topologies and cable types. This was a significant drawback because wiring was one of the largest cost factors for LANs (see chapter 7). To the supplier industry, the split meant that it would have to develop two different LAN chip sets.

These costs raise the question of whether the split was inevitable. On the surface, the intense battle and the uncompromising stance of both factions might have indicated that it was.[101] Yet the split actually hinged on various minor events that influenced the decisions of those vendors that could have voted either way. While IBM's preference for token ring was quite inflexible, DEC's position was more malleable. As a vendor of departmental computing resources, DEC did not necessarily need the enterprise-wide, high-cost network approach of IBM. But with its VAX strategy DEC was clearly aiming at larger networks and computing systems than Xerox, which had targeted only small workgroups. The technological needs of DEC's customers fell somewhere between a simple workgroup LAN (like Xerox's Ethernet) and an enterprise-wide network (like IBM's Token Ring).[102] Consequently DEC could have opted for either network. As Samuel Fuller, a key player in DEC's development and later its chief scientist, has acknowledged, DEC tested both technologies and concluded that both worked fine.[103] In fact, Fuller saw the technical differences between Ethernet and Token Ring as mere second- or third-order arguments.

Ultimately DEC's decision to support Ethernet resulted from a collection of small things. According to Fuller, while negotiating with Xerox in 1979, DEC did not contact IBM regarding a similar alliance, since it doubted that IBM would collaborate as openly as Xerox. Fuller also pointed out that Robert Metcalfe played an instrumental role in brokering the DIX alliance, thereby locking DEC into the Ethernet camp.[104] Without Metcalfe, DEC might not have contacted Xerox and thus might have attended the IEEE 802 meetings with an attitude more open to alternative technologies. In other words, under different historical circumstances, DEC might well have joined the token ring camp.

DEC's decision, however, was critical for the overall outcome. Although in the democratic IEEE group DEC's vote counted just as much as those of the other Ethernet supporters, its endorsement triggered a snowball effect that Ethernet's smaller supporters could never have initiated. Consider the following scenario. The other vendors might not have been able to push Ethernet through IEEE 802 without DEC. Without supporters, Xerox and the two start-ups backing Ethernet (3Com and U-B)—the firms with the greatest vested interest in Ethernet—would have had greater difficulty in having Ethernet adopted as a standard. In fact, without DEC

they would have been in a position similar to that of the proprietary
start-ups and vendors of office automation systems (such as Wang, Datapoint, Network Systems, and Nestar), who had no leverage at all within
IEEE 802. If DEC had joined the token ring alliance, the other
(mini)computer firms backing Ethernet—namely H-P, Data General, and
Siemens—might have had second thoughts about supporting Ethernet
because DEC's support for an alternative LAN would have made it much
more difficult for them to sell to the same customer base as DEC. Their
votes, however, were critical in preventing token technology from gaining a two-thirds majority. If only four out of the ten actual Ethernet
voters had defected to the token camp, token technology would have
obtained the two-thirds majority necessary for adoption as the IEEE's
only standard.

Even if H-P, Data General, and Siemens had joined Xerox and the two
start-ups, it is doubtful whether they could have replaced DEC adequately and sustained an Ethernet bandwagon in the way DEC did. With
minicomputer revenues of $573 million and $435 million, respectively,
Data General and H-P were considerably smaller than DEC, which had
sales of $2.068 billion in 1981.[105] Their smaller revenues might not have
sufficed to lure Intel into the Ethernet faction. Besides, H-P, Data General, and Siemens alone might have failed to provide a sufficient market
for Ethernet start-ups, a critical force behind Ethernet's later de facto
standardization. In fact, if DEC and IBM had agreed on a less complex—
and thus less delayed—token ring, this would have created a marketplace
much more attractive to start-up specialists than the market Xerox, H-P,
Data General, and Siemens provided.

DEC's importance therefore went far beyond casting a vote for Ethernet; it provided the rationale for most other vendors to rally behind
Xerox's LAN. This is only counterfactual reasoning, but it suggests that
the split might not have occurred if DEC had joined IBM in supporting
token ring.

A Final Skirmish

Despite the separation of the principal antagonists into subgroups,
the elaboration of the exact Ethernet specifications remained con-
tentious. H-P discovered various weaknesses in the DIX group's Ethernet
proposal.[106] It claimed that the DIX Ethernet version had some serious
grounding problems and that their specification was not sufficiently
explicit because of the lack of a transmitter specification. Such vagueness
represented a problem for H-P because it prevented vendors from build-

ing compatible products by just relying on the specifications.[107] H-P and the DIX group debated many other technical issues, such as preamble length, collision methods, high-level data-link control framing, and address lengths.[108]

These disagreements became so severe that they slowed progress in the Ethernet subgroup for almost a year.[109] Finally H-P openly defected from the DIX group's Ethernet version, endorsing the incompatible IEEE 802.3 version instead.[110] The DIX group in turn resisted some of the modifications suggested by H-P.[111] Intel insisted that it had progressed too far in its chip design to accommodate major changes.[112] The DIX group also believed that H-P was attempting to gain time by delaying the alliance.[113] The stalemate was not resolved until 1982, when the DIX group, in a clever strategic maneuver, approached the European Computer Manufacturers Association (ECMA) about creating a CSMA/CD-based standard.[114] Collaborating closely with Bull, as well as Siemens and Olivetti, DEC and Xerox drafted a CSMA/CD standard for the ECMA. Their draft stuck closely to the work of IEEE 802.3 but did not concede any major points considered critical by the DIX group. In the middle of 1982, when the ECMA approved the draft and nineteen companies announced their support of it, the IEEE 802.3 group, as the DIX alliance had expected, was forced to resolve its differences.[115] In December 1982, after some minor modifications, Ethernet received unofficial approval from the IEEE. Despite the long dispute, the DIX group's original Ethernet specification (Blue Book) had changed only marginally; yet it was not completely compatible with the final IEEE CSMA/CD standard.[116] In 1985 the IEEE ratified the Ethernet standard.[117]

The elaboration of the Token Ring standard progressed even more slowly because Token Ring's development had hardly begun in 1980 and the technology was far more complex.[118] As a result, the IEEE 802.5 subgroup did not complete its Token Ring draft before October 1984, that is, almost four years after the DIX group had released the Blue Book.[119] This delay was to play a significant role in the outcome of the later market battle between Token Ring and Ethernet, as it prevented Token Ring's swift commercialization and the rise of a large supplier community.

Standards and Market Structures

When IEEE 802 selected Ethernet and Token Ring, IBM and DEC, the two dominant computer manufacturers of the 1980s, saw their preferred technologies established as standards. Their prospects were in marked contrast to those of the smaller vendors—such as Wang,

Datapoint, H-P, and the various start-ups—which had no chance to standardize their technologies. This outcome is quite consistent with that predicted by standardization theory. As vendors with huge market shares, IBM and DEC simply carried more weight than some of the smaller players and could instigate far greater network effects in favor of the IEEE standards. In fact, a standard that neither IBM nor DEC supported would have made little sense and would even have endangered the success of an alternative IEEE standard.

But DEC and IBM also succeeded in forcing their technology through the IEEE because they employed clever standardization strategies. For instance, from the outset DEC built on multivendor support for its technology of choice—a critical requirement within the democratic IEEE 802. This contrasted sharply with the actions of some of the smaller players, who continued to pursue a strategy based on vertical integration and complete proprietariness, and thus in essence defeated themselves. Given its considerable clout, IBM did not undertake an alliance strategy as pronounced as that of DEC, but it nevertheless came up with a clever tactic to circumvent the democratic requirements of the IEEE. Realizing that it alone could not push token ring through the IEEE, it first sided with the vendors of factory automation systems, who also favored a token-passing LAN (albeit one based on a token bus). Once the participants had agreed to overcome the gridlock by creating several standards, it then defected from its allies and created its "own" Token Ring standard.

But events deviated from the predictions of standardization theory in that IBM and DEC, the large vendors, opted for an open standard, while some smaller vendors, including Datapoint and Wang, refrained from joining the larger vendors' network (see the introduction).[120] The previous discussion has identified a number of reasons for this countertheoretical fact. IBM and DEC were certainly more visionary than Wang and Datapoint, who did not understand the power of open standards and the increasing aversion of users to proprietary systems. Furthermore, IBM and DEC benefited from their greater power to push their preferred technologies through the IEEE without accepting many alterations. In fact, the uncompromising stance of both companies indicates that they were as unwilling to accept changes as Datapoint and Wang. But IBM and DEC could also afford to have an open LAN standard because they kept their higher-level protocols proprietary and because their business success did not really depend on their LANs, which ultimately were noncore businesses. In contrast, Datapoint, having already sold a large number of ARCnet systems, was locked into its own success, while Wang urgently needed a more capable LAN to stop Ethernet's ascendancy (table 4.3).

Finally, DEC opened its LAN to attract suppliers. Despite its relatively large size, DEC, like Xerox, lacked the necessary capabilities to produce all the necessary LAN components, especially ICs, at a competitive price. Instead of designing and manufacturing all Ethernet products in house, it made far greater sense to both firms to have specialized suppliers produce the parts it could not manufacture. They then could concentrate on their core businesses: workstations and laser printers for Xerox and minicomputers and profession-specific software applications for DEC. Because the DIX group did not make Ethernet an open standard only in order to increase network effects, but also to gather the necessary capabilities for its successful commercialization, this reasoning is a second deviation from standardization theory. In this sense, the capability theory explains the action of the DIX alliance as much as standardization theory.

Despite the widely shared interest in an open standard, the two largest computer vendors, IBM and DEC, failed to agree on a single standard. As we have seen, their decision to adopt incompatible standards originated primarily from different customer needs. IBM thought that it required a more reliable and complex technology than Ethernet could provide, whereas DEC was willing to trade greater simplicity for faster commercialization. Such incompatibility did not appear as a huge handicap to them, since their systems operated in quite different market segments and thus were often not interconnected.[121] Besides, in the early 1980s gateway technologies between IBM and DEC systems were emerging, making ex ante standardization less compelling.[122] Yet both had good reasons for not becoming too compatible with each other. By maintaining an incompatible LAN, DEC hoped to prevent IBM from penetrating its customer base, while IBM sought to build up a lucrative LAN business and wanted to avoid the competitive pressure it could foresee in the Ethernet market.[123]

In hindsight, the formation of IEEE 802 was the single most important event in the creation and evolution of the LAN industry: it had a vital impact on the structuring of both the standardization race and the marketplace itself. As most large computer vendors and start-ups adhered to one of the two IEEE 802 standards, imminent chaos in data communication was averted or at least mitigated, despite the failure to create a single de jure standard. In addition, by selecting Ethernet and Token Ring, IEEE 802 almost predetermined the outcome of the impending de facto standardization battle. With their adoption by most large computer manufacturers, the two technologies instantaneously gained vast markets and immediate legitimacy among customers, while attracting component and chip suppliers. For the same reasons, Ethernet's and Token Ring's de jure standardization greatly depressed the prospects of any proprietary LAN for becoming a de facto standard. A vendor of a proprietary LAN would have to not only vie with IBM, DEC, H-P, and Data General but also overcome the stigma of its proprietariness—an attribute most end users associate with high prices and potential lock-in. Their IEEE 802 status ensured that Ethernet and Token Ring were now the clear favorites in the standards race.

Yet the two standards were not equally positioned. Thanks to its hub topology, flexible STP wire, and more complex access method, Token Ring was clearly the IEEE's high-end LAN, whereas Ethernet was its low-end standard. But, as Ethernet's relatively high speed and its adoption by most minicomputer firms indicate, it certainly was not a low-end LAN in absolute terms. It was not really intended for low-cost microcomputers but was instead appropriate for midrange markets, such as minicomputers.

Aside from structuring the standards race, IEEE 802 had its greatest impact on the shaping of the incipient LAN industry. When LAN technology was emerging in the late 1970s, this incipient economic space could theoretically have been occupied either by the computer manufacturers or by specialized start-up vendors. But because of their control of the LANs' primary market, namely their own computers, the computer manufacturers were far better positioned before the formation of IEEE 802 to take over the LAN business. In fact, they controlled the computers' interfaces, the customers, and the distribution channels—and they clearly dominated the agenda at IEEE 802. From a pre–IEEE 802 perspective, LAN technology appeared as a natural extension of the computer manufacturers' core business. However, as most computer manufacturers joined IEEE 802 and adopted one of its standards, they voluntarily gave up this power and placed the start-ups, at least from a legal perspective, on an equal footing. The start-ups could now offer the computer manufacturers' technology and compete for their customer base, all the while remaining relatively well protected from any arbitrary manipulations. This equality created an attractive economic space for start-ups and laid the foundation for a quickly emerging, thriving supplier industry—and ultimately for the start-ups' final dominance, as narrated in the next chapter.

5 The Formation of the Ethernet Community

As the DIX group had expected, the open Ethernet standard quickly attracted suppliers after its swift standardization and adoption by most minicomputer firms. The first suppliers to offer Ethernet products were small start-ups, but the minicomputer vendors supporting it within IEEE 802, as well as several semiconductor firms, soon joined them. The economic space the Ethernet standard created was so attractive that by 1982 at least twenty firms had announced or even begun to manufacture products.[1] These suppliers all operated as autonomous firms; yet they were more than a cluster of unrelated companies adhering to the same standard. Rather they formed a *community,* with its own complex interactions, collaborations, and synergies. For instance, most founders of the start-ups knew each other and shared information. More important, the various firms specialized in different market segments, supplied each other with products, and collaborated within the IEEE 802.3 group to standardize new versions of Ethernet, all the while fiercely competing. In a word, the open Ethernet standard led to a complex, highly differentiated communal "ecosystem" among its suppliers.

The firms playing a pivotal role in the formation and structuring of the Ethernet community were the various start-ups established to exploit the IEEE standard. They not only expedited Ethernet's introduction into the market but also improved the technology, reduced its prices (with the help of the manufacturers of ICs), and drove it into several new markets, especially PCs, thereby ensuring its continued success in the late 1980s, when PCs began replacing minicomputers as Ethernet's main market. Most important, the fast-growing start-ups became the community's largest vendors (although in the mid-1980s DEC briefly became the sales leader). These start-up suppliers were, to a large extent, responsible for Ethernet's standardization success.

By focusing on the Ethernet community, this chapter examines Ethernet's adoption on only the supply side. Although its standardization success resulted from its adoption on both the supply and demand sides, this perspective has been chosen because of the difficulty of collecting widely diffused, historical data on the adoption of the standard by end users. Though narrow, this focus does not unduly limit the analysis, because the supply side serves as an accurate representation of the standard's entire adoption process. In fact, the sales and activities of the various vendors reflect the demand for Ethernet, and, as this chapter shows, it was the manufacturers that played the most critical role in setting the Ethernet bandwagon into motion.

The Pioneers: 3Com and Ungermann-Bass

Aside from its adoption by most minicomputer firms, Ethernet's main leverage in attracting suppliers was its openness. Its status as an IEEE standard meant that any firm could use the technology at any time on a nondiscriminatory basis. Although such openness indeed contributed to the rapid growth of the Ethernet community in the late 1980s, in 1980–82 the community was essentially established by a few insiders—that is, firms and individuals who had been closely involved with Ethernet's standardization in IEEE 802 or who were friends or acquaintances of those involved. Such insider knowledge positioned them well to take advantage of the Ethernet standard, initially kept secret by the DIX group.

The quintessential insider, of course, was Robert Metcalfe. Although Metcalfe was Ethernet's principal evangelist, as we have seen, his friends Ralph Ungermann and Charles Bass acted far more aggressively to bring a product to market, forming Ungermann-Bass in 1979 with plans to network the computers that then formed the core of the industry. Metcalfe, by contrast, remained committed to a vision of networked personal computers; it was a vision that lay at the heart of his view of the future and of the future he projected for his own firm, 3Com. Since the DIX alliance did not release their Ethernet specification until September 1980, Metcalfe restricted 3Com's initial activities primarily to consulting, although his firm did develop some prototype transceivers and a network software package called Unet.[2] Ungermann and Bass, on the other hand, in their drive to solve corporations' widespread data communication problems, started developing a product immediately after establishing their firm. Since the Ethernet standard was not yet available, they decided to make their initial LAN product compatible with Xerox's Experimental Ethernet while promising customers an eventual upgrade to the final standard.[3] They called their product line Net/One and began shipping it in 1979.[4]

Their swift action meant that Ungermann and Bass immediately had to seek venture capital.[5] The search began positively, as the two entrepreneurs received a firm commitment from Neil Brownstein of Bessemer Venture around the same time as they started their company. Brownstein was receptive to their proposal because he was familiar with the communication market as a result of his previous investment in Telenet, the provider of a nationwide packet-switching network. He could appreciate the market potential for high-speed LAN technology and the power of an open network standard. Brownstein even helped Ungermann and Bass write their business plan. Nonetheless, he insisted that the pair find additional investors, a charge that proved difficult.[6] The two entrepreneurs contacted numerous venture capitalists, but, as Ralph Ungermann recalled, "Everybody in the venture community turned us down."[7] Part of the problem was that the West Coast venture capitalists perceived Zilog's success as spotty and thus hesitated to back its founder in his new start-up.[8] But the duo faced another problem. In 1979, IEEE 802 had not yet been formed, nor had the DIX group officially announced Ethernet. According to Ungermann, the venture capitalists therefore "believed the computer companies would build the network that would interconnect each other's equipment and that there was no room for a standalone networking company."[9] In the absence of a ratified Ethernet standard, the venture capitalists did not perceive U-B's situation as different from that of Nestar or Network Systems, which were looking for capital at about the same time.

After an exhaustive search over the course of a year and a half, Ungermann and Bass finally managed to close the deal—thanks to their friend Robert Metcalfe. In 1979 and 1980, while Ungermann and Bass attempted to jumpstart their company and beat their friend to the market, Metcalfe was giving various presentations and lectures in his effort to promote Ethernet. As it turned out, one of these presentations, at a McGraw-Hill conference on data communication, was attended by James Swartz, a venture capitalist who operated with Fred Adler, another well-known venture investor. Like Brownstein, Swartz was familiar with the data communication field. He had already invested in a small broadband LAN start-up, Amdax, and had even been forced to step in as its CEO after Amdax's founder passed away. During this stint he attended many IEEE conferences on data communication and studied numerous research papers on LAN technology. Thus when Metcalfe presented a list of LAN vendors that included U-B, Swartz was well prepared to make an investment.

He decided to visit the two entrepreneurs, and, impressed with their vision and expertise, he committed funding the day after their first meeting.[10] In early 1980—the period during which IEEE 802 held its initial meetings—Ungermann and Bass received $1.5 million from Neil Brownstein and James Swartz, as well as Stewart Greenfield of Oak Investment Partners.[11] In later rounds, these financiers added a further $10 million; in June 1983 U-B went public, with a total valuation of $48 million.[12]

Armed with venture capital and a product compatible with Experimental Ethernet several months before the DIX group would make its technology public, U-B was now in a prime position in the race to commercialize Ethernet. In September 1980, when the DIX group released the Blue Book, U-B promptly began the development of compatible components, and it shipped its first product, a terminal server, in 1981. According to Ungermann, U-B reached the market "many, many months before anybody else."[13] The terminal server was a very basic Ethernet product. It simply switched (that is, connected) several terminals to a minicomputer or mainframe host. Reflecting on this early period, Metcalfe complained that U-B's focus on terminals and minicomputers "was not the high purpose for which Ethernet was invented." Rather, he had developed Ethernet to network personal workstations or computers. But since in 1980 the market opportunities to use Ethernet with personal computers were very limited, Metcalfe conceded that his friends "had found a real problem that [Ethernet] could solve."[14] As DEC, H-P, and Data General's support of Ethernet within IEEE 802 had already indicated, Ethernet's primary initial markets were minicomputers and terminals, not personal computers.

The DIX group's release of the Blue Book also encouraged Metcalfe to make the transition from consulting to manufacturing. Since 3Com's consulting business had not generated sufficient revenues for the development of hardware products, the firm first had to look for venture capital. Despite Ethernet's progressing de jure standardization and Metcalfe's personal charisma and status as Ethernet's inventor, the raising of capital proved difficult.[15] Neither Metcalfe nor his management team had ever started or managed a company.[16] Lack of management experience was not the only problem. Coming out of Xerox PARC, Metcalfe was insistent that Ethernet be applied to network personal computers or workstations, not minicomputers. In late 1980, however, the number of desktop computers was still very small. Neither IBM nor Sun Microsystems had introduced their PCs and workstations, respectively, and Ethernet's high initial costs of approximately $3,000 per node made it uneconomical to deploy with the popular but low-cost Apple II.[17] The lack of an obvious PC or workstation market forced 3Com's business plan to remain somewhat vague. In a document written for a venture capital briefing in October 1980, 3Com proposed to capitalize on Xerox's Information Outlet and to provide multivendor compatibility in local networks.[18] Given Xerox's ostensible absence from the computer market, this business plan was not very convincing. As 3Com investor Richard Kramlich later said, no one knew exactly what kind of market 3Com was going to be in.[19]

After a six-month search, however, 3Com found several venture capitalists willing to take the risk. On February 28, 1981—the very day it ran out of money—3Com received a total of $1.05 million from venture capitalists Kramlich, Jack Melchor, and Wallace Davis.[20] They invested partly because they shared Metcalfe's vision of the market potential for high-speed LAN technology and partly because they were impressed by Metcalfe personally and by the technical expertise of his team.[21] Gib Myers of the Mayfield Fund, who also invested in 3Com, was later quoted as saying, "Ethernet, at the time, was controversial. But in our business, when you meet a guy like Metcalfe who is clearly a leader and a guru in his field, you just say: 'Let's go with this horse.' He was a technical beacon, but he had the personality and the leadership skills, and you want someone like that when you are backing a small company in a new market."[22] The venture capitalists were clearly betting on 3Com's management team rather than on Ethernet's standardization.[23]

Metcalfe may have disliked the idea of applying Ethernet to minicomputers, but without a viable alternative, 3Com joined U-B in initially focusing on this very market. 3Com made its first products, some transceivers and controllers, compatible with DEC's minicomputer buses, the Unibus and Q-bus.[24] Shipped in 1981 for $550 and $2,500–$3,000, respectively, these transceivers and controllers were products even more basic than U-B's terminal server; they simply served as the interface between computers and the Ethernet cable and ensured proper transmission.[25] Although minicomputers were clearly Ethernet's largest market in the early 1980s, 3Com refrained from expanding its product line for this segment. Not only did Metcalfe's start-up have the handicap of lagging behind U-B, which had gone after this market wholeheartedly, but he also regarded minicomputers as moribund machines.[26] Ever since his experience at Xerox PARC, Metcalfe had become convinced that personal computers would inevitably replace minicomputers in the office environment.[27] The market strategy of 3Com was to wait for the widespread adoption of microcomputers, and so in 1980–81 Metcalfe decided not to follow U-B into the minicomputer market. Instead, he considered building Ethernet products for the Apple II and DEC's microcomputer. But when these plans failed to materialize, Metcalfe was forced to watch his start-up fall far behind U-B.[28] While 3Com's sales crept up to $1.7 million in 1982, those of U-B—which was by then fully engaged in the minicomputer LAN market—skyrocketed to $11.3 million.[29] This was a bitter moment for Ethernet's inventor, as Metcalfe himself vividly described:

> 3Com, coming out of Xerox PARC, was always aiming towards providing personal computer networks. But there were not any PCs to speak of in those days [1979–82]. So 3Com grew very slowly until 1983. U-B and Sytek, on the other hand, were ambitious and shrewd and wanted to get started sooner.[30] So they built these so-called general-purpose LANs whose purpose it was to switch terminals. Again, there weren't any PCs; there were only terminals. So they [U-B and Sytek] grew much more rapidly than 3Com. I mean they were down the street from 3Com. We watched them. It was horrifying. They bought up all these buildings, and they had these huge parking lots.[31]

It appeared in the early 1980s as if the father of Ethernet had been outmaneuvered by his own followers and friends.

The Growth of the Community

In 1981 3Com and U-B had a head start, but their exclusivity waned quickly as several other Ethernet insiders—as well as ex-employees of Ralph Ungermann's first start-up, Zilog—established Ethernet firms. The first start-up to rush into the market behind 3Com and U-B was Interlan, established in May 1981 in Chelmsford, Massachusetts, by Paul Severino, David Potter, and William Seifert, among others. Like the founders of 3Com and U-B, they were well aware of Ethernet and the network market. While Severino had been involved with networking at Prime Computer, a minicomputer firm in the Route 128 area, Potter had managed LAN hardware development in DEC's Distributed Systems Group, and Seifert had also worked on Ethernet development at DEC.[32] They all had intimate knowledge of the forthcoming Ethernet standard and of the efforts of the DIX group.

Four months later, in September 1981 in Silicon Valley, several ex-employees of Zilog—William Carrico, Judith Estrin, and Eric Benhamou—established another Ethernet start-up, Bridge Communications.[33] None of them had been directly involved with the DIX group or Ethernet's standardization within IEEE 802 in early 1980. But because Estrin and Benhamou had worked under Ungermann at Zilog and Estrin had been employed at U-B for a short period before starting Bridge Communications, they were well aware of the activities of their former boss and of Ethernet's standardization.[34] They started an Ethernet firm not only because they possessed ample technical expertise in networking but also because they believed that Ethernet would become the standard in the market. As Judith Estrin explained, Ethernet was a proven technology, and it was also backed by several large computer manufacturers, especially DEC, H-P, and Data General.[35] This legitimized the technology while providing a profitable market opportunity for nimble start-ups, especially since DEC's (transceiver) products were delayed in coming to market. Even more important to them, Ethernet was backed by Intel. Estrin noted that Intel's support was crucial because "the real key in anything of becoming the standard is having inexpensive semiconductors available."[36] Bridge Communications' founders regarded Ethernet's openness as great advantage. Although it deprived them of a protected market, it provided them with semiconductors, a ready market, and possibly additional complementary components supplied by other firms. Ethernet's openness thus reduced many of the risk factors that had plagued Nestar and the other pioneers.

In January 1982, a second group of former employees of Zilog—Kanwal Rekhi, Inder Singh, and Navindra Jain—founded Excelan. Though they had joined Zilog after the departure of Ralph Ungermann, they knew the founders of Bridge Communications and shared their colleagues' intimate knowledge of data communication. In fact Rekhi (who later replaced Singh as Excelan's CEO) had worked as a replacement engineer at Zilog on the improvement of Z-Net.[37] Interlan, Bridge, and Excelan were not the only start-ups rushing to exploit the Ethernet market, but together with 3Com and U-B they became the leading Ethernet start-ups of the early to mid-1980s.[38] For almost four years, no new start-ups would break into their ranks.

Since IEEE 802 had already selected Ethernet as a standard by the time these three start-ups were established, one might expect that they would have faced less difficulty in raising venture capital than had 3Com and U-B. According to Seifert, Interlan indeed encountered few obstacles in securing a total of $5.5 million in financing, partly because of Paul Severino's track record.[39] The founders of Bridge Communications and Excelan, in contrast, experienced far greater difficulty. Bridge co-founder Judith Estrin believes that many venture capitalists initially did not understand the nature of its technology, falsely believing that the start-up was attempting to develop a sophisticated modem.[40] The founders encountered a further setback during their negotiations with the venture capitalists, when a market research company released a well-publicized report that predicted Ethernet's failure because it was incapable of transmitting video and voice.[41] Estrin also recalled that their search for capital was hindered by their proposal to interconnect different LANs—hence the name Bridge Communications.[42] In the early 1980s the number of installed

LANs was far too small to provide a viable market for such a narrowly focused firm. Such a business strategy would become viable for a start-up only in the late 1980s, after the number of LANs had greatly increased. In the case of Excelan, many venture capitalists hesitated to invest because its founding team, three Indian engineers, lacked experience in American management techniques and did not have an established track record in the United States.[43] Bridge and Excelan thus confronted technology-, market-, and management-related questions similar to those that had dogged 3Com and U-B in their start-up phases.

Despite these concerns, Bridge and Excelan both eventually managed to obtain venture capital because some investors accepted the entrepreneurs' vision of Ethernet's edge in the standards race. In December 1981, the venture capital firms Weiss, Peck & Greer and Merrill, Pickard, Andersen & Eyre invested a total of $2 million in Bridge Communications in exchange for an equity stake of 60 percent.[44] Likewise, in October 1982 Excelan received funding from four firms: Bay Partners; Dougery, Jones & Wilder; Hambrecht & Quist; and Ventech Partners.[45] As in the case of 3Com and U-B, these venture capitalists had great confidence in the two start-ups' management teams.[46] But implicit in their investment decisions was their belief that Ethernet would become the dominant standard.[47] Ethernet had by now been adopted as an IEEE standard, and the uncertainty over whether Token Ring or Ethernet would prevail within IEEE 802 had ended. Besides, thanks to the backing of DEC and the minicomputer manufacturers, Ethernet had a good chance to become the de facto standard. Ethernet clearly was one of the strongest contenders in the standards race.

As these three firms joined 3Com and U-B in launching still more Ethernet products, the start-ups spearheaded the formation of the Ethernet supplier industry. Despite their leading role, the five start-ups did not long remain the only suppliers, for Ethernet's openness made it relatively easy to adopt the technology. The first vendors to follow were those that had championed Ethernet's standardization within IEEE 802. Since DEC, collaborating with the chip manufacturers Advanced Micro Devices Corporation (AMD) and Mostek, had developed a fairly sophisticated Ethernet IC, its entry was delayed; however, around 1983–84 DEC began shipping its first Ethernet products.[48] H-P, Ethernet's other major minicomputer proponent within IEEE 802, initially relied on U-B as an OEM supplier, but by the early 1980s it too had introduced its own products.[49] Like DEC, Intel experienced some product development delays, but by October 1982 it had some ICs on the market as well.[50]

In addition to these insiders, several firms without a direct link to Ethernet's standardization within the IEEE began offering products. Most important, by the middle of 1983 at least six additional chip manufacturers—namely AMD, Fujitsu, Mostek, National Semiconductor, Rockwell, and Seeq—were either developing or producing Ethernet chips.[51] Although no comprehensive, comparative survey could be found, a review of articles in the trade press at the time suggests that this level of involvement exceeded the number of semiconductor firms involved with any other (proprietary) LAN. Since semiconductors were to play such an instrumental role in reducing network costs, the chip manufacturers' support gave Ethernet a critical edge in the standards race.

Thus between 1979 and 1982 a small circle of Ethernet insiders—consisting of Metcalfe, some of his friends, ex-employees of Ungermann's Zilog, and Ethernet's proponents within the IEEE—spearheaded the formation of the Ethernet supplier industry by launching products or firms. In 1983 the trade press named twenty firms as either developing or manufacturing Ethernet products: four start-ups (3Com, U-B, Interlan, and Bridge Communications), eight computer manufacturers (DEC, H-P, Data General, Siemens, Tektronix, Xerox, ICL, and NCR), and seven chip manufacturers (Intel, AMD, Fujitsu, Mostek, National Semiconductor, Rockwell, and Seeq).[52] Barely two years after the DIX group had made its initial Ethernet announcement, the technology had already accumulated substantial supplier support.

Specialization, New Markets, and Increasing Product Variety

The twenty Ethernet start-ups acted quite autonomously. They all developed their own products, maintained their own distribution channels, and cultivated their own customer bases. Yet their adherence to the same standard also allowed for a rich communal "ecosystem" with complex interactions and synergies.

In 1981–82, when the Ethernet community consisted of only a small number of firms, the degree of specialization among these firms was relatively low and their product offerings were fairly homogeneous. As previously mentioned, in 1981 3Com and U-B, despite their different long-term market strategies, both focused on the DEC minicomputer-terminal market and offered only a few basic connectivity products, namely servers and boards for minicomputers. The first start-up to follow 3Com and U-B, Interlan, did not greatly expand the existing range of product offerings. Interlan's initial products, shipped in the middle of 1981, were controller and transceiver boards that, like those of 3Com, were made for DEC's Unibus and Q-bus and cost around $3,000.[53] In an attempt to diversify its product line, in the middle of 1983 Interlan announced a terminal server. Although this was a new product for the start-up, U-B had already created the product category in 1981.[54] By introducing the first controller boards for Data General minicomputers, the Nova and the Eclipse, Interlan was responsible for some innovations, thereby widening Ethernet's product and market range.[55] Ultimately, however, Interlan followed very closely in the footsteps of 3Com and U-B; it saw Ethernet's principal market as remaining in (DEC) minicomputers and so offered similar board and server products. Yet, thanks to its focus on the minicomputer market, Interlan eventually surpassed 3Com in sales, and with revenues of $18 million in 1984 it ranked second among the five start-ups.

In time, as the number of firms increased, the degree of specialization and differentiation within the Ethernet community increased as well. The entrepreneurs and firms had different ideas about the kinds of markets to which Ethernet should or could be applied, but they also specialized because the occupation of certain market segments by earlier entrants forced them to look for alternative markets. These different corporate specialization strategies allowed Ethernet to penetrate new markets, and its product variety greatly increased.

The firm with the broadest business focus among all the start-ups remained U-B; in fact, the company developed almost every conceivable product category. As the first entrant into the market and the leading Ethernet supplier, U-B did not encounter preoccupied niches and thus could choose its own territory. But U-B also pursued the broadest business focus because its mission of solving the widespread data communication problems of large organizations meant that U-B had to provide a "communication system capable of addressing an organization's *entire* local area networking needs."[56] U-B aimed to provide a network that could connect any type of information-processing equipment existing in large enterprises.

Naturally this implied a very broad product range. Because of the preponderance of terminal-based minicomputer and time-sharing systems in most large corporations in the early 1980s, U-B initially focused on various server and board products directed at this segment. But in the mid-1980s, as PCs proliferated throughout most large corporations and needed to be connected to mainframe and minicomputer systems, U-B also began shipping PC adapters.[57] Moreover, since large organizations often possessed subsidiaries and offices in distant locations, U-B started offering remote bridges and X.25 gateways, which could interconnect several LANs over a public network.[58] Many large organizations were spread over several buildings or even a campus, and so their networks grew far-flung. Consequently, U-B had to develop devices, such as repeaters and local bridges, that could extend a LAN's distance by interlinking several segments.[59] U-B even attempted to enter the factory automation market, although this initiative ended in failure.[60] Later, such all-encompassing networks became known as general-purpose LANs; although they included PCs, in the early to mid-1980s they consisted mainly of terminals and host computers (minis or mainframes) and often contained hundreds of nodes.[61]

As part of the same thrust, U-B began implementing Ethernet on cable types different from the original coaxial cable specified by the IEEE 802.3 standard. By doing so, U-B initiated a trend that would secure Ethernet's survival in the late 1980s, especially with its implementation over the telephone wiring.[62] U-B's first nonstandard Ethernet implementation was a 5-Mbps broadband version, introduced in March 1982. Since this version increased Ethernet's maximum distance from 2.5 to 16 kilometers and allowed for the transmission of voice and video, U-B could penetrate the long-distance campus- and enterprise-wide network market, an achievement entirely compatible with its business strategy.[63] In addition, in February 1984 U-B introduced the community's first fiber optic Ethernet version. Fully interoperable with U-B's baseband and broadband Ethernets, fiber optic Ethernet provided increased noise immunity, enhanced security, and greater long-distance coverage. As a result, it was mostly used for "backbone" connections, another critical segment in the network market of large organizations.[64] To deliver comprehensive networks, U-B thus developed a very broad product line and eventually offered items in almost every conceivable product category, including repeaters, local and remote bridges, gateways, adapters, boards, and servers.[65] Thanks to its head start and its focus on Ethernet's largest market during the early to mid-1980s, namely minicomputers and terminal-based systems, U-B solidified its market lead. With revenues of $72.2 million in 1985, it was by far the largest Ethernet start-up in the first half of the 1980s.

Like U-B, Bridge Communications focused on the general-purpose LAN market, but instead of developing an extensive product line, it specialized in producing powerful servers, such as communication, gateway, and network management servers.[66] In some cases, the servers of Bridge and U-B overlapped in their functionality or were introduced at approximately the same time.[67] But as a specialist Bridge could focus more narrowly and thus broaden its product variety beyond the offerings of U-B. In fact, it introduced some novel server types, such as a network management server, and throughout the mid-1980s it improved its product line by making its servers more powerful and by including more options

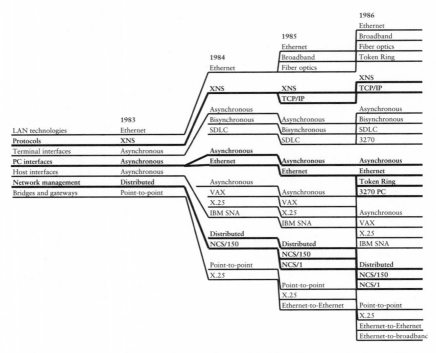

FIGURE 5.1   Expanding product variety of Bridge Communications. (From Bridge Communications 1986.)

in its existing server line.[68] As figure 5.1 illustrates, Bridge's products interoperated with an ever-increasing number of interfaces, protocols, and complementary products. The trade press reported that "Bridge Communications deftly outengineered U-B," while Judith Estrin was quoted as saying "We leapfrogged their [U-B's] technology."[69] In 1985, with sales of $30.5 million, Bridge ranked third among the five Ethernet start-ups. Hence Bridge, by specializing narrowly, contributed to the ever-increasing variety of products in the Ethernet system. This would be one of the principal strengths Ethernet would enjoy in its competition with the proprietary LANs.[70]

The next entrant, Excelan, addressed yet another niche within the general-purpose LAN market. As did U-B and Interlan, Excelan developed Ethernet boards (among other products), but because of its late entry into the market it had to find an unoccupied niche. Eventually Excelan settled on Ethernet boards for Unix-based minicomputers and workstations employed in engineering departments and the financial sector.[71] Because of its focus on Unix-based machines, Excelan was one of the first vendors to implement the TCP/IP protocol set, the emerging Internet standard, on its Ethernet boards; in contrast, the other board vendors relied on Xerox's XNS protocol, initially the higher-level protocol standard for the office market.[72] Excelan became a leader in TCP/IP— although with sales of $9.9 million in 1985 it ranked last among the start-ups discussed here.[73]

The start-up that pursued the most radical differentiation strategy was, however, Metcalfe's 3Com. While the other vendors accepted the minicomputer-terminal market as Ethernet's natural domain, Metcalfe was determined to apply his invention to personal computers and workstations. As a consequence, 3Com stagnated in 1980–81 because Ethernet's price was too high and its boards were too large to fit into a microcomputer; however, when IBM introduced its PC in August 1981, 3Com's long-awaited chance seemed to have arrived.[74] The PC's base price of $2,880 was moderately higher than that of the Apple II, thereby decreasing the cost differential between computer and network hardware that had prevented Ethernet from penetrating the Apple II segment.[75] And IBM vigorously marketed the machine to the corporate sector. The widespread deployment of hard disks and laser printers in offices meant that this market required far more networks than the home and educational markets, the traditional Apple strongholds.[76]

Despite these friendlier overall conditions, 3Com faced substantial technical and price obstacles in entering the PC market. In 1981, the "smallest complete [Ethernet] minicomputer interface [board] measured 100 square inches and drew 30 watts."[77] The IBM PC, in contrast, only allowed for a maximal interface size of 52 square inches and a power of 5 watts. 3Com also knew that to be competitive in the low-cost PC LAN market, it had to reduce Ethernet's minimum price—which at that time was approximately $1,800 for the controller, transceiver, and drop cable—to less than $1,000. At the outset, these obstacles seemed insurmountable, but after a long internal debate, 3Com decided to develop Ethernet products for the IBM PC.[78] 3Com's focus on IBM's microcomputer was ironic; in 1980 at the IEEE 802 meetings, 3Com had strongly refused to adopt IBM's Token Ring, and IBM had in turn rejected Ethernet. Thanks to the PC's openness, however, Ethernet could easily be applied to IBM's microcomputer.

To overcome the various price, power, and size obstacles, 3Com's engineers began redesigning the Ethernet board and developed a VLSI chip in collaboration with Seeq Technology.[79] By implementing Ethernet's controller function on a VLSI chip, 3Com was able to replace the functional equivalent of fifty standard ICs and to reduce power consumption to one-fifth of previous levels, while shrinking board size dramatically.

This size reduction in turn permitted Ronald Crane, an extremely skilled engineer at 3Com, to include a radically redesigned transceiver (which had previously been on a separate board) on the same controller board.[80] Putting the transceiver and controller functions on one board saved not only space but also the cost of a board package and the drop cable.[81] Thanks to the redesign and the use of a VLSI chip, Ethernet now fit into a PC—and its minimum price was $950 in the fall of 1982, when 3Com shipped its first PC boards.[82] Within roughly two years, Ethernet's per-node price had decreased by about two-thirds.[83] This drastic price reduction confirmed the thinking behind the formation of the DIX group and IEEE 802. ICs, though constituting a major upfront investment, allowed for steep reductions in network costs. As the following chapters show, the continuous price reductions in Ethernet technology resulting from an ample chip supply would play a critical role in Ethernet's eventual victory over Token Ring and the proprietary LANs.

In combination with its Ethernet version for the IBM PC, 3Com made another critical innovation. Instead of using Ethernet's original, 0.4-inch-thick RG-11 coaxial cable, 3Com decided to employ the thinner RG-58 coaxial cable. Its Ethernet version thus also became known as Thinnet or Thin Ethernet—as opposed to Thicknet or Thick Ethernet, the name given to the original Ethernet standard.[84] 3Com selected the nonstandard cable because it was significantly less expensive than the standard version, as well as easier to install and attach nodes to, thanks to BNC connectors.[85] As chapter 7 describes in greater detail, the two latter advantages removed critical bottlenecks inherent in Thicknet. As a result, Thinnet became the dominant Ethernet version in the PC market, while Thicknet continued to dominate the minicomputer market.

3Com's bet on the PC market paid off handsomely. Despite stiff competition from low-cost proprietary LANs, by 1985 the company had sold 100,000 PC adapter cards.[86] In the process, its sales shot up from $1.7 million in fiscal 1982 to $46.3 million in fiscal 1985, making it the second largest Ethernet start-up, surpassed only by U-B (see appendix B). To be sure, the PC market was initially not Ethernet's principal market, and 3Com's sales in 1985 still lagged far behind the $126.6 million combined sales of U-B, Interlan, Bridge Communications, and Excelan, which all continued to focus on the terminal-minicomputer LAN market. Nevertheless, the fast-growing PC business added a critical segment to Ethernet's market portfolio and would allow Metcalfe's firm to catch up with U-B.[87]

With these specialization and product differentiation strategies, the start-ups played the most prominent role in expanding Ethernet's markets and products. But the firm to amass the largest sales volume in the Ethernet community of the mid-1980s was DEC. Despite its delayed entry into the market, DEC quickly surpassed the sales volume of the start-ups, thanks to its extensive distribution channels and control of Ethernet's primary market—DEC minicomputers. By 1984 its sales had reached $58 million and by 1985 they totaled $173 million, clearly surpassing the combined $126.6 million in sales of U-B, Interlan, Bridge Communications, and Excelan, its principal competitors.[88] Following in DEC's footsteps, other minicomputer firms, such as H-P, introduced Ethernet products and became strong competitors.[89] DEC and the other minicomputer vendors may have failed to drive Ethernet into new markets, but they greatly expanded its market share.

The specialization and differentiation strategies of the various firms were instrumental in helping Ethernet achieve market success. As they specialized and diversified, they drastically augmented the scope of Ethernet product offerings. Only a few years after 3Com and U-B had shipped the first basic terminal server and board products, the Ethernet community's products encompassed PC adapter cards, gateway servers, network management servers, communication servers, repeaters, local and remote bridges, several VLSI chips, and fiber optic and broadband Ethernet versions, as well as a great variety of boards aimed at Sun workstations and the minicomputers of DEC, Data General, and H-P, among others. Of course, this broad product range appealed to end users, while putting enormous pressure on the vendors of proprietary LANs to offer similar product ranges.

In addition, the start-ups' various differentiation strategies meant that Ethernet was pushed into several new markets simultaneously. By the mid-1980s, it was no longer a pure minicomputer LAN technology but was also well accepted in PCs and workstations. Furthermore, the vendors' pursuit of several market directions at once reduced Ethernet's risk of being adversely affected by the ongoing changes in the computer industry. If the market approach of one vendor failed, the community was likely to include vendors with more successful approaches, so problems at one company would not retard Ethernet's adoption. Finally, the existence of several specialists spurred innovation, with not just one but several vendors generating improvements within the same product category.

Collaboration and Competition

Specialization and independent innovation were among the most salient characteristics of the Ethernet community, but the firms also shared information and collaborated even as they competed. The collaboration and interaction among the members of the community—individual engineers as well as firms—took many forms. The previous sections have mentioned the personal relationships that bound together the various founders. Another important platform for collaboration was IEEE 802.3. In fact, as vendors employed new cable types, new standardization efforts by IEEE 802.3 became necessary. In 1984, the trade press reported several ongoing standardization initiatives, including ones for broadband, fiber optic, and thin coaxial Ethernet.[90] In this sense, IEEE 802.3 temporarily united otherwise fiercely competitive Ethernet vendors and exerted great pressure on them to resolve their differences and come up with a single standard. Defiant vendors could attempt to delay standardization, but they could hardly opt out of an IEEE 802.3 standard. Aside from the collaboration it facilitated between firms, IEEE 802.3 also provided a venue for individual engineers from different firms to get to know each other and forge professional relationships.

Collaboration within the Ethernet community also took the form of division of labor among certain firms. For instance, most semiconductor firms developing Ethernet ICs in the early 1980s did not make products for the open market but instead collaborated closely with a particular Ethernet vendor—Seeq with 3Com, Fujitsu with U-B, and AMD and Mostek with DEC—designing their chips to meet the specific needs of that vendor.[91] In the case of the 3Com-Seeq collaboration, 3Com had an exclusive right to Seeq's IC for six months, after which it became available on the open market. In other cases, the firms resold each other's products. For example, in the early 1980s DEC, H-P, and Xerox relied on the start-ups, such as U-B, as OEM suppliers, while Bridge Communications, entrenched in the general-purpose LAN market and thus offering a product line aimed at minicomputers, began marketing 3Com's adapter cards as PCs proliferated throughout its customer base.[92] As another example, in October 1984 DEC and Vitalink, a start-up that joined the Ethernet community as the successor to a failing satellite data transmission business, entered into a cooperative marketing, development, and service agreement that lasted several years. Under this agreement, DEC licensed bridging technology to Vitalink, which used it as a basis for its remote bridging products; DEC also agreed to make referrals to Vitalink's sales personnel. In a later agreement, DEC became a direct reseller of Vitalink's products.[93] Such division of labor, collaboration, and specialization were possible because the Ethernet standard provided a common platform and ensured interoperability among the vendors' products. A firm did not need to develop an entire range of products, but could rely on other firms to supply complementary components.

Moreover, the various firms and their engineers cooperated on an informal, ad hoc basis. As we have seen, Ronald Crane of 3Com would regularly assist engineers at competing firms to implement the Ethernet standard to which they were all committed; even though their respective firms were trying to drive one another out of business, all realized that none could succeed if the Ethernet standard were to fail because of poor implementation.

Yet such collaboration did nothing to lessen the vigorous level of competition overall. Competition became so intense precisely because the open Ethernet standard removed any technological barriers among vendors, thereby allowing the firms to invade one another's turf. The many personal rivalries among the firms and their founders only spurred competition further. As several founders of Ethernet start-ups have pointed out in interviews, these rivalries were often so intense that firms competed far more vigorously even as they collaborated with each other.[94]

Whereas in the early 1980s 3Com, the community's lonely PC specialist, faced relatively little competition from *within* the community, the competition grew stiffest among those vendors focusing on the general-purpose LAN market.[95] Bridge Communications, Interlan, and U-B vied fiercely for the server market, while in the minicomputer-terminal board market U-B battled primarily with DEC.[96] Of course, such intense competition led to continuous price erosion and commodification. These trends ensured Ethernet's competitiveness in the standards race, yet they put enormous pressure on the vendors and were soon to claim the community's first victim: Interlan. Although by 1984 Interlan had grown to $18 million in annual sales and 153 employees, in 1985 its founders decided to sell the firm to Micom, a vendor of private branch exchange (PBX) systems, for several reasons.[97] Interlan, which had never developed its own VLSI chip, suffered from constant price erosion in its board business, with boards increasingly viewed as a commodity, while its server business, with its higher value added, required ever-greater investments.[98] Unable to sustain two separate business lines and starting to fall behind— in 1985 Interlan was surpassed in sales by 3Com and Bridge Communications—its founders decided to accept an offer of $47 million from Micom, which was eager to complement its PBX products with LAN technology.[99] Though the combined firm, Micom/Interlan, continued to offer Ethernet products, with the acquisition of Interlan the first Ethernet start-up lost its independence.

Micom's acquisition of Interlan anticipated a far bigger consolidation in the Ethernet supplier industry. In 1987, 3Com effectively acquired Bridge Communications for stock valued at about $235 million, although the move was formally announced as a merger.[100] In 1988, Tandem, the market leader in fault-tolerant computer systems, acquired U-B for $260 million.[101] And in early 1989, Novell, the dominant NOS vendor for PC

LANs, purchased Excelan in a stock swap valued at $152 million.[102] This consolidation, to a large extent, reflected the ongoing decline of mini-computers and the simultaneous rise of PCs. In fact, all the acquired firms (Bridge, U-B, and Excelan) had focused on the minicomputer and terminal market, while the acquirers (3Com and Novell) focused on the PC market—3Com on the hardware side and Novell on the software side. As the relative importance of minicomputers shrank, U-B and Bridge saw their rates of growth decrease. The faster-growing PC market, in contrast, allowed 3Com, which in 1987 had sales of $155.9 million, to surpass U-B as the largest Ethernet start-up; Novell enjoyed an even higher sales volume than 3Com. With this consolidation the Ethernet supplier industry changed dramatically. Of the initial five major Ethernet start-ups, by 1989 3Com remained the only independent firm.[103]

Standards and Industry Creation

By the mid-1980s, the DIX group's goal of attracting suppliers by creating an economic space through an open standard had been accomplished. Ethernet's openness and its adoption by most minicomputer firms encouraged numerous start-ups, as well as computer and semiconductor manufacturers, to begin producing components for it, thereby creating a dynamic, fast-growing supplier industry. Initially the industry was established by a handful of insiders, but gradually firms that could not trace any direct lineage to Ethernet's original standardization within IEEE 802 began offering products as well. By 1983 the Ethernet community already encompassed at least twenty vendors; by 1987 this number would increase to approximately two hundred.[104]

As we have seen, these suppliers quickly developed a highly differentiated community structure. The sharing of a common standard allowed them to specialize quite narrowly; they collaborated intensively on various occasions and supplied each other with complementary components. Individuals as well as firms maintained a dense web of communication. Yet the open standard also imposed stiff competition, making Ethernet a double-edged sword for the members of the community. On the one hand, the standard and the community that had evolved around it created direct and indirect synergies for the firms; they could rely on other firms for complementary goods, and the success of the community strengthened its individual members. On the other hand, Ethernet's openness removed technical barriers to entry, thereby exposing the firms to not only intertechnological but also intracommunal competition. As many interviewees pointed out, the firms competed far more intensely as they collaborated.

Yet the many independent specialists and the resulting highly differentiated community structure had only positive effects on Ethernet's competitiveness. Thanks to the firms' differentiation and specialization strategies, Ethernet penetrated several new markets simultaneously, including minicomputers, workstations, and PCs, as well as short-range, long-range, and backbone segments. The many suppliers allowed for specialization, created economies of scale, spurred trial-and-error learning, intensified price competition, and created incentives for firms to innovate. In fact, within the open Ethernet environment, innovation was the principal way for suppliers to avoid, at least temporarily, the continual downward price pressure. Most important, with various specialists pursuing different markets, Ethernet became less vulnerable to the market discontinuities that had devastated the systems of the early pioneers, including Nestar and Network Systems. Although the decline of the minicomputer market adversely affected Interlan, U-B, and Bridge Communications, it had little impact on the overall success of Ethernet. Ethernet's PC specialist, 3Com, as well as several new entrants, had already seized the microcomputer segment and therefore compensated for the other firms' stagnation. Clearly, Ethernet's large, diversified community was its main competitive advantage in the standards race.

The main foundation on which the community was built was, of course, Ethernet's standardization by IEEE 802. By opening Ethernet technology to any vendor on a nondiscriminatory basis, the IEEE standard created strong incentives for suppliers. By providing a complete and smoothly functioning standard specification and a ready market, IEEE 802 also removed critical burdens that had contributed to the fall of the pioneering firms. Unlike Nestar or Zilog, the Ethernet start-ups did not have to struggle to find customers, nor did they have to develop a complete technology on their own. Instead they could focus on product development and commercialization, while benefiting from Ethernet's wide degree of adoption. Besides, Ethernet's standardization made semiconductor firms far more eager to develop ICs—even if it meant doing so for a specific vendor—for they could always offer the same chip to other suppliers. The resulting ample chip supply removed another critical obstacle that had plagued the pioneers and would again affect the vendors of proprietary LANs. All of these advantages meant that the Ethernet start-ups had far better chances to succeed than the proprietary vendors.

Aside from IEEE 802, a second vital foundation for the Ethernet community has been identified here: venture capital. Though Ethernet's openness intensified price competition and removed legal barriers to entry, between 1979 and 1982 many venture capitalists were nevertheless quite willing to fund Ethernet start-ups, for several reasons. In 1980–82 the

Ethernet market was not yet a commodity market: only a few competitors existed, and DEC had experienced delays of several years in introducing its products. Nimble entrants therefore had a good chance to capture a strong position in the Ethernet market and perhaps secure a lasting competitive advantage. Besides, Ethernet's openness and its adoption by most minicomputer manufacturers led venture capitalists to envision a considerable market—another crucial criterion in venture capital investment decisions.[105] By funding several start-ups, the venture capitalists played a vital, enabling role in the evolution and structuring of the community. Their investment prevented the large computer manufacturers, mainly DEC and H-P, from monopolizing the Ethernet market—as did IBM in the Token Ring market, with problematic results. In addition, by investing in start-ups, venture capitalists helped Ethernet's product variety to expand. Though they were never at center stage, the venture capitalists ensured the community's ultimate diversity and highly differentiated structure.

However, the window of opportunity for venture capital investments in Ethernet firms was only a brief one. After the investment in Excelan in October 1982, venture capitalists cut back on funding new Ethernet start-ups: DEC was now entering the market; the existing start-ups had occupied the most attractive niches; and Ethernet technology was relatively stable. A start-up established after 1983 would thus have lacked significant competitive advantage. Venture capital investment in the Ethernet space resumed only in the mid- to late 1980s, when several technological discontinuities disrupted Ethernet technology and new network components were required. Thanks to its large technological community, Ethernet had an excellent chance to dominate the market. But, as chapter 6 makes clear, its ultimate success would also depend on the success of the competing communities and their technologies.

6 The Rise and Fall of Ethernet's Proprietary Competitors

Ethernet had attracted a large supplier community, but it was not the only viable LAN in the early to mid-1980s. Its initially high price and narrowly confined technological parameters at first prevented it from penetrating all possible market niches. This inability, in turn, created business opportunities for alternatives designed for those segments Ethernet could not serve. It was therefore not surprising that, concurrent with Ethernet's commercialization in 1980–81, several proprietary LANs were introduced, and these soon became potent competitors. In the price-sensitive PC LAN market, Ethernet faced stiff competition from numerous LANs that not only were less expensive but also dominated the Apple II market—a segment from which Ethernet was excluded by price and technological considerations. Apart from Datapoint and Nestar, leading companies in the micro-LAN segment included Apple, Applitek, Corvus, Davong, Digital Microsystems, Gateway Communications, IBM (with its PC Network), Orchid Technology, Tiara, and ViaNet. In the minicomputer LAN market, Ethernet faced fewer rivals, but it nevertheless competed against systems that were in some ways technologically better adjusted to the segment and that occupied niches it had initially failed to penetrate. Ethernet's principal competitors in this market segment were Proteon and Sytek.

Aside from these price, technological, and market advantages, the proprietary LANs challenged Ethernet by building supplier communities of their own. This made it possible for them—at least temporarily—to offer innovations, economies, and product variety on a par with Ethernet's, and thus gave them a fair chance in the standards race. Yet, despite these competitive advantages, none of the proprietary LANs succeeded in stopping Ethernet's ascendancy, and by the end of the decade they had all faded from the marketplace.

Each proprietary LAN disappeared for reasons that reflected its particular situation. But the common denominator among their failures was their inability to form supplier communities as powerful and dynamic as the Ethernet community "ecosystem." Their communities remained not only separate from each other but also much smaller than Ethernet's. They included far fewer independent manufacturers and in some cases comprised only a single innovating firm. These differences had considerable repercussions. The proprietary LANs suffered far more than Ethernet from various market discontinuities, as well as from the strategic blunders of their sponsors. In addition, their communities failed to develop highly differentiated communal "ecosystems" of their own. Specialization, collaboration, and division of labor could not extend over many firms, and there was little intra-technological competition to preselect the "fittest" vendor for the battle with Ethernet. As a result, the proprietary communities could not keep pace with the steep price reductions and everexpanding product variety of the Ethernet community. The proprietary LANs thus gradually lost their initial technical and price advantages and saw Ethernet invade their markets. In the following sections I analyze the rise and fall of Ethernet's four principal competitors—Corvus, Datapoint, Proteon, and Sytek—as representative of the fate of all the proprietary LANs.

The Commercialization and
Rise of the Proprietary LANs

Ethernet was quickly improved after its standardization by IEEE 802. By 1985, its prices had fallen drastically, thanks to the development of VLSI chips and vigorous competition. It was implemented on several new cable types, and its product variety had increased far beyond the initial, basic product offerings. But in 1980–81, Ethernet technology still had many shortcomings. Its high price excluded it from the Apple II market, the largest microcomputer segment before the introduction of the IBM PC. The short distances it covered and its bus topology made it unsuitable for large networks, and because it was a baseband network, the transmission of video and voice was impossible. These inadequacies prompted various start-ups to develop proprietary LAN technologies to address the market needs that Ethernet failed to satisfy.

One of these start-ups was Corvus, founded in 1979. As we have seen, although Corvus's core business originally lay in disk servers, the start-up was quickly forced to complement its disk business with a LAN. Introduced in March 1980 (that is, at about the same time as the first IEEE 802 meeting took place), Corvus's first attempt at a LAN product, CONSTELLATION, was an instant, but only temporary, success.[1] Within less than two years, Corvus had sold 2,750 networks connecting 12,000 microcomputers.[2] Although this made it the leading LAN vendor for the Apple II, Corvus immediately began looking for an alternative, because the CONSTELLATION network was obsolete almost from the very beginning. Designed simply to connect microcomputers to a standalone disk server, it covered too short a distance and operated at too low a speed to be a fully functional LAN.[3] In its search for a more powerful LAN, the disk vendor considered Ethernet, the recently released IEEE 802 standard. But like Nestar and 3Com, Corvus calculated that Ethernet's boards were too large to fit into an Apple II and its price per node too high.[4] Unable to take advantage of the IEEE standard, Corvus developed a second proprietary LAN, and its Omninet was introduced in May 1981.[5]

The technical compromises that Corvus was forced to make in order to deal with the cost restrictions imposed by the Apple II market indeed succeeded in making it the leader in a market from which Ethernet was excluded. Like Ethernet, Omninet employed a CSMA-based access method, but to hold down costs Corvus omitted Ethernet's collision detection (CD) scheme.[6] This omission seemed justifiable because performance studies had revealed that fewer than 1 percent of messages collided on a typical Ethernet network. Corvus therefore believed the CD scheme unnecessary, especially since it increased circuitry costs.[7] In a further attempt to save money, Corvus restricted Omninet's coverage to approximately 1.3 kilometers (compared with Ethernet's 2.5 kilometers) and kept its speed at 1 Mbps (compared with Ethernet's 10 Mbps).[8] Although the speed limitation decreased Omninet's life span and market penetration, this compromise also seemed acceptable, because the bus speed of the Apple II was far slower than Ethernet's transmission speed.[9] Finally, Corvus implemented Omninet on twisted-pair (RS-422) wire, which was not only easier to install but also less expensive than Ethernet's coaxial cable.[10] These compromises gave Omninet a six-to-one price advantage over Ethernet and made Corvus the leader in networking the Apple II market, the principal market for personal computer products prior to the introduction of the IBM PC.

Whereas the inability to apply Ethernet to the Apple II market had forced Corvus to chose a proprietary network, the start-ups Proteon and Sytek addressed Ethernet's principal market, minicomputers; therefore, they could theoretically have adopted Ethernet. Yet both companies found reasons to launch proprietary LANs instead. Proteon's decision was rooted in its staunch belief in the superiority of token ring technology. Established in 1972 by Howard Salwen in Westborough, Massachusetts, Proteon initially operated as a data consulting firm and only became involved with LAN technology in 1979, when the MIT researchers Jerome Saltzer, Kenneth Pogran, and David Clark developed their star-shaped token ring LAN.[11] In fact, to build the components of their network, these MIT researchers hired nearby Proteon as a "hands-on consultant that knew all the nuts and bolts—physical stuff that was not known by laboratory computer science professors who were more into computers." This contract had a significant effect on the firm. Salwen himself became deeply convinced of token ring's superiority and decided to commercialize a proprietary version when MIT showed no business interest in its LAN and IBM continually delayed Token Ring's standardization within IEEE 802.[12] In the process, Proteon made the transition from consulting to manufacturing and became one of the first specialized token ring vendors.[13]

Unveiled in June 1981, Proteon's token ring, called ProNet, clearly surpassed Ethernet technologically, despite the two products' similar parameters and market focus.[14] Like Ethernet, ProNet operated at 10 Mbps and cost approximately $3,000 per node.[15] However, because token ring's deterministic access method allowed it to transmit more rapidly than Ethernet, Proteon was able to market its LAN for swift file transfer instead of terminal-to-host switching, U-B's original application for Ethernet.[16] What was more, with its hub-based topology, ProNet had the upper hand in network management and installation and could accommodate much larger networks than bus-based Ethernet. Howard Salwen claimed that Proteon often "did 120-node networks" and that they "would go in [to customer sites] and replace Ethernets that just could not do that."[17] By surpassing the Ethernet standard in speed and network management capability, Proteon clearly competed on the basis of technological superiority. The start-up expected that this strategy would compensate for its proprietariness, allowing it to become a viable alternative to its principal competitor.[18]

Like Proteon, Sytek developed a proprietary system to focus on a niche in the minicomputer market that Ethernet was unable to satisfy in 1980–81. Established in Silicon Valley in June 1979 by Michael Pliner, a friend of Robert Metcalfe, and other former employees of Ford Aerospace and Communications Company, Sytek entered the emerging LAN business with a background similar to Proteon's.[19] It began as a consulting operation "with the primary purpose of performing data communications engineering and research services on a contract basis."[20] Given the widespread data communication problems that firms were experiencing at the time, its consulting operation (which included the development of customized network components) flourished, reaching $2.3 million in annual sales as early as 1981.[21] Such rapid growth convinced Sytek's founders of the market opportunity for a mass-produced LAN. After consulting several large organizations, they decided to develop a LAN for the general-purpose network market, the same market U-B was targeting.[22] But in contrast to U-B—soon to be their principal competitor— they decided to focus on long-distance networks spanning several miles. Since in 1980–81 Ethernet's maximum distance of 2.5 kilometers was too short for the far-flung networks they intended to build, Sytek's founders rejected it and opted to develop a proprietary LAN instead.[23] Sytek introduced its LAN, called LocalNet, in late 1981 and early 1982.[24]

Although LocalNet employed a CSMA/CD mechanism very similar to that of Ethernet, it differed in various respects from the standard. As in the case of Corvus's Omninet or Network Systems' HYPERchannel, most of these differences derived directly from different market foci.[25] Most important, unlike Ethernet, which was a baseband LAN, LocalNet was a broadband LAN. As such, it could cover far greater distances than Ethernet: up to 65 kilometers instead of 2.5 kilometers.[26] Broadband's multiple channels also permitted a user to divide its network into separate subsegments—say, individual LAN segments for the finance and engineering departments. Such subsegmenting bolstered network management and security—a critical feature for large networks, and, according to Pliner, one available in the Ethernet realm only later.[27] In addition, the broadband capability allowed for the transmission of data, video, and voice; Ethernet, in contrast, transmitted only computer data. Sytek's founders expected that its voice and video capability would boost LocalNet's adoption in the office market. As a result of these features, LocalNet was better adapted than Ethernet for the long-distance, general-purpose LAN market, despite a far lower transmission rate of 128 kbps.[28] Like Howard Salwen of Proteon, Sytek's founders believed that, by offering a technology ideally suited to a particular market niche, they could compete successfully with the open Ethernet standard. Corvus, Proteon, and Sytek, despite their different market foci, thus developed proprietary LANs for similar reasons. A nonstandard LAN allowed them to offer a superior technology, to penetrate market segments Ethernet initially could not serve, or both. It was cost issues and the dictation of technological parameters by a particular market niche, rather than an inherent drive to achieve a proprietary lock-in, that motivated the three start-ups.

In the early 1980s, the strategy paid off handsomely for all three vendors. Corvus quickly replaced Nestar as the leader in the Apple II market and expanded its total sales to $26.8 million in 1982.[29] It was thus in an excellent position to dominate the emerging PC LAN market, which required a price structure and network performance similar to those of the Apple II market. Whereas in late 1983 Proteon had installed only approximately fifty networks, in September 1982 Sytek claimed to have already sold over a hundred LocalNets.[30] According to the Yankee Group, a Boston-based market research firm, the 4,000 nodes attached to these hundred LocalNets represented nearly a quarter of all nodes networked in the United States.[31] Not surprisingly, Sytek, which had sales of $16.4 million in 1983, emerged as the third largest LAN start-up, trailing only Network Systems and U-B, but clearly surpassing 3Com, Interlan, Bridge Communications, and Excelan. Proprietariness clearly did not constitute a severe handicap in the nascent LAN market of the early 1980s. Addressing the "right" market segment with a well-tuned technology could compensate for the lack of a standard.

Community-Building Efforts by the Sponsors

To keep pace with Ethernet's continuing success, the sponsors of the proprietary LANs did not rely only on their technological superiority and price advantages; several also attempted to emulate the Ethernet community. By doing so, they hoped to match its gains in specialization, division of labor, utilization of multiple distribution channels, and simultaneous pursuit of different markets. They implemented various strategies, including licensing their technologies, forging strategic partnerships, and deploying off-the-shelf parts. By assembling sponsor communities for their respective technologies, they expected to increase their market momentum and to overcome their biggest handicap in the competition with Ethernet: their proprietariness.

To establish Omninet as a standard in the microcomputer market, Corvus primarily relied on a licensing strategy. According to a company spokesman, the firm began licensing its technology shortly after Omninet's market introduction in May 1981 to "anyone who was interested, including computer vendors, systems houses, and software houses."[32] By October 1981, Corvus had received letters of intent from four microcomputer vendors, and by 1983, after a 90 percent cut in its licensing fee, over twenty licensees had signed up, including Dictaphone, Fujitsu, NCR, Olivetti, and Onyx.[33] But the most important member of Omninet's community became Nippon Electric Corporation (NEC), which in 1984 developed a chip that quadrupled the network's speed to 4 Mbps.[34] According to Michael D'Addio, Corvus licensed Omninet to ensure its price leadership and ultimately to establish it as a standard in the microcomputer market. By boosting Omninet's installed base before Ethernet's entry into the market (3Com did not launch its PC Ethernet products before fall 1982), Corvus hoped to preempt the proliferation of Ethernet.[35]

Whereas Corvus restricted its community-building activities mainly to licensing, Sytek developed a far more comprehensive strategy. First, in an attempt to hold down networking costs, Sytek used as many off-the-shelf components as possible in its LocalNet. By adopting broadband technology, for instance, the company benefited from broadband's de facto standardization in the cable television industry.[36] As Pliner explained, "The cable and the [broadband] parts were easily available through your local radio/TV store. People knew how to install [broadband]. We used the same technology in the same type of installations you would use with cable TV." In a further attempt to benefit from third-party suppliers' components, Sytek adopted the CSMA/CD chip Intel had developed for Ethernet. Such dual utilization was possible because LocalNet's CSMA/CD mechanism was similar to that of Ethernet and because Intel's Ethernet chip was generic.[37] By thus reducing cabling and IC costs, Sytek addressed two of the most significant cost factors of LANs and expected to offer a superior technology for a reasonable price.

Sytek also forged strategic alliances with two large firms in an effort to match Ethernet's community effects. Its first alliance originated during its capital-raising phase. In order to make the transition to manufacturing, Sytek needed funding, but instead of accepting an offer from the venture capital firms Hambrecht & Quist and Continental Illinois Venture Corporation, in late 1981 it accepted $6 million from General Instruments (GI), the dominant manufacturer of broadband cable, known as "the IBM of the cable industry."[38] Sytek preferred GI to the venture capitalists because the cable manufacturer brought to the table services and assets the financiers were unable to provide. For instance, Sytek gained access to GI's Systems Group, with a field service staff of 350 spread over sixty cities.[39] Of course, this was of enormous value to the small firm, which, like most start-ups, struggled with providing adequate field support to a customer base scattered around the country. Furthermore, GI let Sytek use its manufacturing facilities and VLSI chip technology, both vital requisites to reduce costs and enhance product quality.[40] Finally, Sytek and GI decided to jointly develop a metropolitan area network (MAN), to be called Metronet. The two companies expected MANs to become a very substantial business, eventually outstripping LANs in market volume. Though this expectation never materialized, at the time it appeared that the joint development of Metronet could increase Sytek's cash flow in a way the venture capitalists could not match.[41] With these additional resources and capabilities at its disposal, Sytek had obtained far more than just capital from its investor.

Sytek's second strategic alliance resulted from Token Ring's continuing delays. As the technology's sophistication prolonged the development of the necessary ICs and delayed its commercialization, IBM grew increasingly frustrated. IBM was the leading PC manufacturer, and the PC LAN market was burgeoning. But the giant of the computer industry had no network to offer. Unwilling to concede the entire PC LAN business to other firms, in the middle of 1984 IBM's Entry System Division decided to plunge ahead with an intermediate proprietary LAN, called the IBM PC Network and aimed at networking its PCs, XTs, and ATs. The division preferred to outsource the production of the PC Network, and after an evaluation of several LAN vendors, it awarded Sytek the manufacturing contract, mainly because it was impressed with LocalNet's video and voice capabilities and long-distance coverage.[42] Although the IBM PC Network was not fully compatible with Sytek's LocalNet, the contract gave Sytek an enormous boost. The firm received a loan of $6 million, and it was estimated that the contract would add approximately $50 million to its revenues.[43] Furthermore, since IBM had granted Sytek the right to manufacture its own compatible PC Network, the start-up secured much-needed assistance in making the transition from the minicomputer LAN market, its core business, to the newer but more rapidly growing PC market.[44] The agreement had the added advantage of legitimizing Sytek's broadband technology. These expected benefits led some analysts to believe that Sytek could become to LANs what Microsoft had become to operating systems, and they prompted Bob Metcalfe to characterize the partnership as "the deal of the century."[45]

Many of these benefits indeed materialized when, in April 1985, IBM unveiled the Sytek-built IBM PC Network.[46] With the delivery of approximately 142,000 adapter cards to IBM, Sytek's revenues soared from $30.6 million in 1984 to $70.4 million in 1985.[47] To bolster its position as the architect of the PC Network, in the middle of 1985 Sytek launched a compatible but more powerful version—an especially desirable product, because IBM had artificially limited the network's performance in order to ensure market acceptance of its forthcoming Token Ring.[48] Pliner concluded that the partnership with IBM had a positive impact on Sytek: "We had substantial revenue growth with IBM as a partner. . . . IBM helped the company [Sytek] quite a bit in the 1985 and 1986 time frame because we learned to manufacture to IBM standards, which gave us a quality manufacturing group. And finally, we pushed the technology to the limits through IBM's R&D."[49] By allying with two large firms, Sytek seemed able to transcend the limited capability set that is intrinsic to a small start-up. GI provided capital, field service, and chip technology; IBM offered substantial revenue streams, as well as market legitimization for its broadband technology. With these partnerships Sytek appeared to succeed in avoiding the typical pitfalls of a proprietary vendor, namely having to develop all components itself and competing without allies. It looked as if the company had made some smart strategic moves to counter its principal competitors in the Ethernet community, especially U-B.

While Sytek developed the most comprehensive, as well as the most deliberate, community-building strategy, Datapoint's ARCnet, quite accidentally, attracted the largest and longest-lasting supplier community. As already mentioned, Datapoint was initially determined to keep ARCnet completely proprietary. However, when Datapoint contracted with Standard Microsystems Corporation (SMC) for the manufacture of an ARCnet chip, it had to grant SMC the right to offer the chip on the open market.[50] Once ARCnet had escaped Datapoint's proprietary control, several microcomputer and PC LAN vendors swiftly adopted it, including Nestar, Davong (like Corvus, a vendor of hard disk systems), and Tandy (an early leader in proprietary microcomputers, with annual sales of $1.7 billion).[51] Because of ARCnet's robustness, simplicity, readily available chip supply, and low price (in the early 1980s an adapter cost approximately $500, half of what 3Com's first Ethernet PC adapter cost), it was a good choice for those microcomputer and PC vendors who preferred not to develop their own proprietary LAN.[52] As a result of this adoption, ARCnet found its way into the PC market—which was much larger than the Datapoint market—and gathered a considerable community around itself. In 1989 the trade press estimated that at least fifteen vendors were offering ARCnet products.[53] Though no exact figures could be found, ARCnet's appeared to be the largest community among all the proprietary LANs.[54] Although the community did not include heavyweights such as IBM, its support for the technology was relatively well distributed, with several firms manufacturing ARCnet components. ARCnet thus came the closest of the proprietary LANs to emulating the Ethernet community, whose most significant characteristic was its many independent innovators and manufacturers.[55]

With these community-building efforts, the four proprietary LANs and their vendors remained potent competitors throughout 1983–85. Between Corvus's fiscal years 1983 and 1984, Omninet's installed base almost doubled from 60,000 to 117,000 nodes. Corvus boasted that its installed base exceeded that of its five major competitors in micro-LANs combined and that Omninet had effectively become the de facto standard in microcomputer LANs.[56] Though 3Com's shipment of a total of 100,000 Ethernet PC adapter cards by 1985 make this claim appear exaggerated, Omninet's penetration of the microcomputer market nevertheless appeared roughly equal to Ethernet's.[57]

Number of adapters

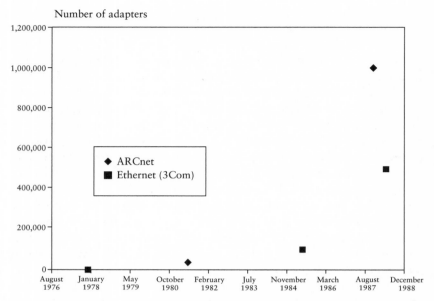

FIGURE 6.1   Comparison of installed bases: ARCnet total versus Ethernet shipments by 3Com, 1978–1988.

No exact data could be found for ARCnet's and Ethernet's installed base in the mid-1980s, but in 1989 the trade press claimed that between 1980 and 1987 more than one million ARCnet adapters had been sold.[58] In contrast, 3Com, the dominant Ethernet vendor for PCs, had sold only its 500,000th Ethernet adapter by April 1988.[59] If one assumes S-curve-shaped growth, ARCnet might have had an installed base of several hundred thousand nodes in 1985. If this estimate is correct, ARCnet may even have topped Ethernet in the microcomputer market (figure 6.1). Because of ARCnet's continued price advantage—an ARCnet board cost a third less than a comparable Ethernet board—it made particular inroads in small businesses, where price, not de jure status, was a critical factor in purchasing decisions.[60]

Likewise, between 1982 and 1984 Sytek's installed base in the general-purpose LAN market grew from 100 networks to 630 networks, connecting a total of over 97,000 user devices.[61] This compared with the approximately 1,000 Ethernet systems that its major Ethernet competitor, U-B, had installed by the end of 1984.[62] Though Sytek trailed U-B slightly in nodes, by 1985, as a result of the IBM contract, Sytek's sales had caught up with those of U-B, the largest Ethernet supplier, prompting Ralph Ungermann to recall that "Sytek was our most feared competitor [in 1984 and 1985], or let me rephrase that, the company we most often competed with."[63]

The proprietary LANs did not threaten to replace the Ethernet standard because their market share remained too small. Corvus's LAN sales of $11.6 million in 1984 lagged far behind the $52.3 million of U-B, the largest Ethernet specialist, and even behind those of Bridge Communications, which at $13.4 million was the fourth-ranked Ethernet start-up. Even Sytek, the third largest LAN start-up, earned only approximately 20 percent of the revenues of the five largest Ethernet start-ups and DEC combined. Despite this gap, it was clear that the proprietary LANs dominated important niches and would remain viable competitors throughout the mid-1980s.

The Fall of the Proprietary LANs

In the period between 1985 and 1989 the fortunes of the proprietary LANs and their sponsors shifted. While Ethernet continued to expand its installed base and market reach, its proprietary rivals increasingly lost market share and eventually disappeared altogether. The first LAN to fade away was Corvus's Omninet. Having dominated the Apple II market for the first half of the decade, in 1985–87 Omninet vanished as a major force in PC LANs. A couple of years later, Sytek's LocalNet followed it into oblivion.

Proteon and Datapoint's ARCnet fared somewhat better. In the mid-1980s, Proteon's sales stagnated, but in 1986, when the IEEE 802.5 Token Ring standard was finally released and Proteon offered compatible products, its fortunes revived (see appendix B). Thanks to Token Ring's growing market momentum in the late 1980s and Proteon's embrace of the fledgling internetworking market, sales grew to $120 million in 1992.[64] Even more impressive, with two million adapters sold by 1989, ARCnet had accumulated the third largest installed base, lagging behind only the two IEEE standards, Ethernet and Token Ring.[65] Yet neither ProNet nor ARCnet could keep pace with Ethernet. In the early 1990s ARCnet's sales stagnated, and the LAN dropped out as a major force in the office market, while by 1997 Proteon's sales had fallen precipitously, to $26.9 million.[66]

On the surface, Omninet floundered partly because a series of technological discontinuities undermined its competitiveness and that of its sponsor, Corvus. The first such discontinuity resulted from the continuous price erosion of hard disks. By the mid-1980s, the prices of the disks had fallen so steeply that it became economical to integrate them into PCs.[67] This integration weakened the disk sales of sponsor Corvus, but more importantly, it made the installation of a LAN purely for disk-sharing purposes less essential. Needless to say, this trend had a devastating effect on Omninet. As hard disks were integrated into PCs, Omninet, which had initially benefited from its tight linkage to Corvus's brisk sales of mass storage systems, lost one of the principal rationales for its adoption.

To make matters worse, Corvus was ill prepared to make the transition from disk sharing to file sharing, which now became the principal LAN application. Simply put, the problem was that file sharing required a far more complex NOS than disk sharing (see chapter 3). Although Corvus eventually offered an NOS capable of file sharing, it could not halt the ascendancy of Novell's NetWare, which was by far the best choice for file sharing. Even more important, Novell had designed NetWare to be compatible with any LAN hardware.[68] This was another blow to Corvus's Omninet. While Corvus, the disk vendor, had every incentive to make its NOS compatible only with its Omninet, in order to spur hard disk sales, users could employ almost any LAN hardware when running Novell's NetWare. This greater hardware flexibility, together with NetWare's inherent technical superiority, made Novell's NOS a far more attractive choice than Corvus's.

A second market discontinuity hit Corvus at least as hard as the obsolescence of disk sharing: the transition from the Apple II to the IBM PC standard in the early 1980s. As sales of the Apple II declined, Omninet began to lose its principal market. If Corvus could have smoothly entered the PC market, this trend would have had little effect on the firm. But Corvus, which had meticulously followed Apple's distribution channels and educational markets, faced great difficulty in penetrating the new PC LAN market. PCs were sold through different sales channels than Apple IIs, as well as to a different customer base, namely Fortune 1000 companies instead of educational institutions. Corvus attempted to reorganize its distribution channels but found it difficult to penetrate Fortune 1000 companies, which preferred Ethernet because of its status as an IEEE standard.[69]

Ethernet, Omninet's principal competitor, benefited from the rise of the PC in two more ways. The PC's higher price softened the price-related barriers to entry Ethernet had previously faced in the Apple II market, an advantage 3Com reinforced with its PC-based Ethernet version for less than $1,000.[70] And unlike Omninet, Ethernet enjoyed some modest network externalities when many departments of large organizations began interconnecting PCs with their minicomputers, which had initially been Ethernet's main market.[71] The transition from the Apple II to the PC standard thus destroyed Omninet's main market, the Apple II, while favoring Ethernet in the PC market.

Omninet failed for a third idiosyncratic reason, namely its inability to penetrate the minicomputer LAN market—the largest LAN segment in the early 1980s and Ethernet's stronghold. Omninet was blocked from the minicomputer segment partly because of its performance and partly because of its proprietariness. Its slower transmission speed and inferior access method were sufficient to compete with Ethernet in the Apple and PC markets; in fact, because of the accompanying cost savings, its lower performance indirectly gave Omninet at least an initial advantage. But its inferiority constituted a severe handicap for minicomputers and work-stations, whose higher computing power required comparably higher network speeds. And Omninet faced almost insurmountable obstacles in this segment because of Ethernet's official endorsement by most mini-computer vendors. In the words of Michael D'Addio of Corvus, "I think the IEEE 802 standard really made a big difference. I think that our strategic error was not to spend the time with the IEEE people or going to them too late and basically letting Ethernet run away as a standard. The end users did not really care [about installing a standard] but the Suns, the DECs and IBMs in the world did."[72] Its inability to compete in the minicomputer market meant that Omninet had a much smaller potential market than Ethernet. Whereas Ethernet was being deployed in the minicomputer, workstation, and PC LAN markets, Omninet had only the (moribund) Apple II and PC markets, in which it struggled to gain a foothold. With a smaller potential market, Omninet did not have any-thing near equal standing with Ethernet in the standardization battle.

Idiosyncratic reasons also contributed to the fall of Sytek's LocalNet. As previously noted, in the early 1980s baseband and broadband tech-nology were engaged in a close race to become part of the dominant design for LANs. Baseband had the advantages of lower cost and higher trans-mission speed, while broadband promised the transmission of video and voice, potentially important features in the office environment. After much confusion, the market eventually chose baseband, partly because of its cost advantage and partly because video applications were not widely available in computing in the early 1980s.[73] Since Sytek had based its product line entirely on broadband technology, it was stuck with a pre-dominant-design network and found itself outside the mainstream LAN market.

Like Omninet and LocalNet, Proteon's ProNet and ARCnet succumbed to Ethernet for various idiosyncratic reasons, such as limited life span and proprietariness. ARCnet suffered when the competitiveness of its sponsor Datapoint deteriorated owing to the rise of the IBM PC. In addition, in the early 1980s Datapoint was making some unfavorable headlines because of financial difficulties and the fact that a corporate raider was making a pass at the company.[74] John Murphy, ARCnet's chief architect, believed that "for anyone in charge of computers at a large company, it would have taken an enormous amount of courage to select ARCnet over Ethernet."[75] ARCnet was thus unable to penetrate large corporations and remained locked in to the small business market.

Yet, despite these many idiosyncratic reasons, the proprietary LANs ultimately succumbed to Ethernet because of a striking common disadvantage: their communities comprised only a single innovator, or if they included several manufacturers, the group was much smaller than the Ethernet community.

Among the four proprietary LANs examined here, Proteon's ProNet and Sytek's LocalNet gathered the weakest communities. Before Proteon switched to the Token Ring community by offering products compatible with the IEEE 802.5 standard, it kept its ProNet completely proprietary.[76] Hence the technological community built around ProNet included only a single innovator and manufacturer—Proteon. Likewise, LocalNet's supplier support did not extend far beyond its sponsor, Sytek. Although Sytek had pursued a clever partnering strategy, its main allies, GI and IBM, failed to provide the kind of support that Sytek had expected and that Ethernet enjoyed from its allies. In fact, Sytek and GI's plan to jointly produce a MAN never materialized, and IBM was never really committed to the PC Network because it considered it only a temporary solution. As a result, in 1986 when IBM introduced Token Ring, its principal LAN, it simply let the contract with Sytek expire (especially because the PC Network had, in the meantime, failed in the marketplace).[77] This meant that Sytek remained the principal supporter and innovator of LocalNet.[78] LocalNet's and ProNet's success therefore depended completely on the financial strength, technical capabilities, and distribution channels of Sytek and Proteon, respectively.

Omninet and ARCnet formed larger communities than LocalNet and ProNet, but these too failed to match the size and scope of the Ethernet community. The weak ties that linked these passive adopters of proprietary technologies to the proprietor firms meant that they could easily abandon their association with the technologies and switch their business commitments to another firm without substantial penalties when the proprietary technologies ceased to serve their interests. This was exactly what two leading licensees decided to do to Corvus and Omninet in the mid-1980s. Another sign of Omninet's weaker community was the fact that it attracted only one IC producer, NEC, while Ethernet had at least seven.[79] For these reasons, Corvus remained not only Omninet's strongest proponent but also its only innovator.

ARCnet's community support was more widespread than that of Omninet. Aside from Datapoint, several firms—including American Research, Aquila, Compex, Cubix, Performance Technology, Thomas-Conrad, and Tiara—actually manufactured ARCnet products and were responsible for product innovations, such as the increase in ARCnet's speed from 2.5 Mbps to 20 Mbps in the late 1980s.[80] ARCnet also attracted a few formal support groups, including the National Datapoint User Group and the ARCnet Trade Association, formed in 1987 mainly to support the battered technology.[81] Yet with only twenty-six vendors in 1989, the ARCnet community never matched the size and diversity of the Ethernet community, which comprised some two hundred vendors in 1987.[82] What was more, ARCnet, unlike Ethernet, did not have the many vendors who produced specialty products, such as bridges, routers, and terminal servers. In short, none of the proprietary LANs gathered a supplier community as large as that of Ethernet; most had only a sponsor or a proprietary community with a single innovator.

The communities' smaller size and dependence on a single innovator had severe repercussions. As described in the previous chapter, Ethernet's many suppliers quickly developed a highly differentiated communal "ecosystem" replete with helpful synergies. They collaborated, supplied each other with complementary goods, and specialized narrowly, knowing that customers could always purchase other necessary products from their competitors. In contrast, smaller size meant that the communal "ecosystems" of the proprietary LANs were not as conducive to innovation or adaptation to market shifts. There were fewer practitioners and firms with which to collaborate and communicate. And, with fewer innovators and manufacturers, the individual firms could not focus as narrowly on specific products as could the Ethernet specialists. Finally, the smaller number of manufacturers restricted the extent of intracommunal competition. The various communal interactions and activities that stimulated, united, and strengthened numerous firms in the Ethernet community were restricted to a single vendor or at best to a handful of firms in the sponsor communities of the proprietary LANs.

Competing with an impoverished "ecosystem" and fewer firms, the proprietary LANs and their communities were quickly outcompeted by the Ethernet community. The effects of the proprietary LANs' community disadvantage and Ethernet's simultaneous advantage surfaced in at least four areas. First, without support from numerous specialists, the proprietary LANs could not move into as many markets as Ethernet, nor could they overcome market discontinuities as smoothly as Ethernet. As noted in the previous chapter, because of the differentiation strategies of its many specialists, Ethernet quickly became entrenched in the minicomputer, PC, workstation, backbone, and long-distance LAN markets. Rather than evolving within a myriad of firms pursuing different market segments, the proprietary LANs, in contrast, remained closely tied to the markets their sponsors were pursuing. Because of the limited financial, technical, and marketing capabilities inherent in small firms, Corvus, Sytek, and Proteon could not pursue all possible market segments wholeheartedly but were forced to concentrate on a few niches. Omninet remained in the Apple II and PC markets, ProNet in the minicomputer market, and LocalNet in the long-distance general-purpose segment.

Such dependence on a single market undermined not only the proprietary LANs' potential market size, and thus their clout in the standards battle, but also their ability to overcome the various market shifts occurring in the computer industry. When the computer market shifted from the Apple II to the PC standard, Omninet depended entirely on the ability of its sponsor Corvus to follow this market shift. Bound by corporate path dependencies, however, Corvus could not instantly switch to the PC market; instead it had to readjust its technology and distribution channels in a time-consuming process.[83] Likewise, LocalNet's success in making the transition from the minicomputer terminal market to the PC market depended entirely on the capabilities of Sytek after IBM had dropped out of their partnership. As a relatively small firm, Sytek could not muster all the financial, marketing, and technical capabilities necessary to pursue the minicomputer and PC LAN markets simultaneously. In fact, in the mid-1980s—while Sytek attempted to escape the declining minicomputer market and diversify into the faster-growing PC market—its competitiveness in its established market, minicomputer terminals, deteriorated. In 1987, Ralph Ungermann remarked that "In 1984 and 1985, Sytek was the company we most often competed with. In the last couple of years, it [competition with Sytek] has dropped off dramatically."[84]

To be sure, the individual Ethernet firms also could not pursue several markets simultaneously or overcome market shifts without time-consuming adjustment processes. As described in chapter 5, most Ethernet firms specialized quite narrowly, and Ethernet's minicomputer specialists ultimately fell victim to the relative decline of this market segment just as Sytek and Proteon did. The Ethernet *community as a whole,* however, was quite immune to such *corporate* path dependencies. As its various independent firms specialized in different market segments, Ethernet was less susceptible to the market changes that plagued its proprietary rivals. When the decline of the minicomputer market undermined U-B, Interlan, and Bridge Communications, Ethernet was less seriously affected because its PC vendors, especially 3Com, ensured its continued success. The proprietary LANs lost the battle partly because they could not move into as many markets as Ethernet without support from numerous specialists, nor could they overcome market discontinuities smoothly.

The second way in which the proprietary LANs' community disadvantage affected their ability to compete was through their inability to match Ethernet's product variety and economies of specialization. As already described, the individual Ethernet suppliers did not have to produce all components but could specialize narrowly in certain product types because the sharing of a common standard guaranteed interoperability.[85] The concurrent specialization of numerous firms then led to vast economies of specialization and a great variety of products, ranging from minicomputer boards and PC adapters to remote and local bridges, repeaters, gateways, and management and terminal servers—all compatible with a multitude of interfaces and protocols. In contrast, the proprietary LAN vendors were competing without allies and had to design, produce, and constantly upgrade all their network components on their own. This not only deprived them of specialization economies but also strained them financially: many were small firms, and the number of network components kept expanding.

It is not that the proprietary LAN vendors did not attempt to provide a complete system; on the contrary, several vendors made valiant attempts to produce a comprehensive product line. For example, between 1983 and 1985 Corvus introduced an SNA gateway, a Macintosh network, a faster Omninet version, a new NOS, and connectivity strategies to DEC minicomputers, in addition to its Omninet, disk drives, and a workstation.[86] Even more ambitious, during the 1980s Proteon was one of the most innovative firms, developing a ProNet version for PCs; creating a precursor to the Fiber Distributed Data Interface (FDDI); launching IEEE 802.5 Token Ring products (including one of the first 16-Mbps Token Ring versions for telephone wire); and even flirting with the emerging internetworking market by developing multiprotocol routers—all the while continuously upgrading its system.[87] Despite these efforts, the proprietary LANs to a large extent failed to match Ethernet's extensive product variety, for the individual firms could not keep pace with the entire Ethernet community and support every conceivable product type and interface. As Howard Salwen of Proteon remarked,

> When you are on your own, you [have] to do everything. For example, hubs. Our system did not work with anybody's hubs except ours, the ProNet hubs. We also made a variety of connecting devices. We had an infrared device that could go from building to building. . . . We also did a microwave [connectivity device]. We started selling ProNet-80 [a precursor

to FDDI operating at 80 Mbps]. We did a lot of software. We had to do all of that ourselves. There was not anybody that would build an accessory for the Proteon system. Proteon did it all. And that is the big difference [in being proprietary versus open].[88]

In Salwen's view Proteon, as well as the other proprietary LAN vendors, failed partly because they had to offer a product range equivalent to the sum of the offerings of all the Ethernet specialists, many of which were far larger. This was an impossible task.

Eventually, the disadvantage in product variety led to two diverging and self-reinforcing processes. As most users adopted Ethernet, its market continued to expand, allowing for even greater specialization and increased product functionality. In contrast, the proprietary LANs' smaller product range deterred users, contracting the economic space for the specialists even further.

The Ethernet firms' drive to continually develop new specialty products also extended Ethernet's life span. As described in greater detail in the next chapter, in the mid- to late 1980s Ethernet's continued success was seriously threatened by its increasing inability to accommodate growing networks. In response to this threat, the Ethernet community brought forth many improvements. The collective effort eventually led to an Ethernet version for star-based telephone wire, a version that required a hub component. This innovation revived Ethernet's competitiveness while depriving the proprietary LANs, especially ARCnet, of their last technical edge. Jonathan Schmidt of Datapoint recalled that, as soon as he saw it operating over telephone wire, he knew Ethernet had won the final battle. The proprietary LANs, in contrast, failed to continue to improve rapidly enough and were soon eclipsed.[89]

Third, the proprietary LANs' community disadvantage meant that they could not keep pace with Ethernet's relentless price reductions. Although no exact price comparisons could be found, my own data indicate that Ethernet experienced some of the steepest price decreases. As a result, it ultimately became a very low-cost network and almost as inexpensive as ARCnet, the leading low-cost PC LAN (figure 6.2). Of course, the narrowing price gap reflected Ethernet's continuous adoption and market growth, which augmented economies of scale and learning effects. But Ethernet's price reductions also resulted from its larger number of IC vendors and more diverse community, which spurred price competition and economies of specialization. In this sense, the proprietary LANs lost the battle partly because the Ethernet community eliminated their initial price advantage.

Fourth, the proprietary LANs' community disadvantage meant that they were more susceptible to strategic errors and business failures than

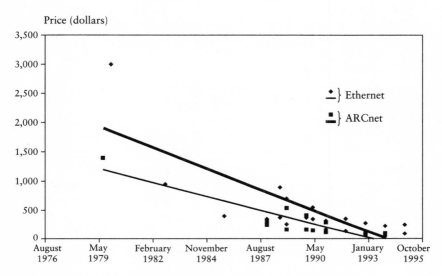

FIGURE 6.2   Price ranges of Ethernet and ARCnet, 1979–1995.

Ethernet vendors. As already noted, the decline and eventual disappearance of some of Ethernet's leaders had little effect on the technology per
se. In contrast, the disappearance of its sponsor had a devastating effect
on a proprietary LAN. For instance, in the early 1980s, when Corvus
made a serious strategic blunder—the introduction of a proprietary workstation called Concept only eight months after the introduction of the
IBM PC—the company had to report a loss of $10.6 million on sales of
$50.3 million in 1984.[90] Although this loss had no immediate impact on
Omninet's competitiveness, it ultimately destroyed the LAN, since the
financial loss weakened sponsor Corvus to the point that it had to sell its
storage business as well as its LAN business (the latter to CDC) in 1987.[91]
As an empty shell company, Corvus then filed for bankruptcy in 1988.[92]
Without a strongly committed sponsor, Omninet then vanished as well.

A similar fate befell Sytek's LocalNet. After the termination of the
IBM contract, Sytek's revenues declined from $91 million in fiscal 1986
to $60 million in 1987, and, having lost $1 million in the third quarter of
fiscal 1987, the firm had to lay off 46 of its 500 employees.[93] In 1989
Sytek's founders finally accepted an acquisition offer from GM Hughes;
like Omninet, LocalNet soon disappeared from the market because no
other firm existed to sustain its market presence.[94]

ARCnet fared somewhat better than Omninet and LocalNet during
the decline of its sponsor, Datapoint, thanks to its larger community.
However, lacking a designated sponsor and operating within a community

made up of relatively few small, independent manufacturers, ARCnet lacked the firms that could have nurtured its market growth in the same way as the Ethernet specialists did Ethernet's growth. Consequently it too faded away with the weakening of its sponsor. The lack of an open community created a risky linkage between firm success and technology success. When the sponsor failed, the proprietary technology disappeared as well.

Thus all four proprietary LANs and LAN vendors succumbed to Ethernet, primarily because they lacked large and dynamic supplier communities. The four adverse effects resulting from the so-called community disadvantage did not affect all four LANs in the same way, and some of these effects had few repercussions for particular LANs. For instance, LocalNet and ProNet penetrated the minicomputer market despite Ethernet's standardization by the IEEE, and ARCnet continued to exist for a few years even after the decline of Datapoint. However, without open communities of their own, they could not keep up with Ethernet's relentless price reductions, product expansions, and market growth. All eventually slid into oblivion.

The Disadvantages of Not Having an Open Community

In the early 1980s several proprietary LANs challenged Ethernet on the basis of various price and technological advantages, enabling them to penetrate market segments Ethernet was initially unable to serve. Yet despite their early market success, the proprietary LANs failed to prevent Ethernet from expanding its market share, and all eventually disappeared from the marketplace. On the surface, the four LANs appeared to have floundered for very different reasons, including market discontinuities, strategic errors, and the financial troubles of their sponsors. The common fundamental cause of their disappearance, however, was their lack of an open community. Although their sponsors tried various approaches to building Ethernet-like communities, Ethernet's proprietary rivals ultimately failed to build "ecosystems" with numerous firmly committed and independently innovating firms. Instead, their communities comprised only one firm or at most a few innovators—aside from the licensees, resellers, and distributors, who were only weakly committed to the proprietary LANs.

This so-called community disadvantage imposed four major handicaps in their competition with Ethernet. First, the lack of an open community limited their ability to move into several markets simultaneously and to overcome the discontinuities that obliterated their original markets. The financial resources and capabilities of the sponsors, mostly small start-ups, were too limited to cover all possible markets. As a result, each of the proprietary LANs became entrenched for the most part in a single principal market and was thereby highly vulnerable to market discontinuities, which required costly and time-consuming adjustments in technology and distribution channels. Second, the community disadvantage limited the proprietary LANs' product variety. Without much support from other vendors, the sponsors had to provide entire product ranges by themselves. This deprived them of important specialization economies while imposing a heavy financial burden, owing to the ever-increasing number of network components and the small volume in which each had to be manufactured. As a result, product variety was far smaller for the proprietary LANs than for Ethernet, making them less attractive to users. Third, the prices of the proprietary LANs did not fall as precipitously as those of Ethernet, for similar reasons. Fourth, the reliance on a single sponsor created a risky linkage between sponsor and LAN technology. When the sponsor ceased to exist, the technology vanished as well. Not surprisingly, those proprietary LANs (mainly ARCnet) that had the largest communities fared best in their competition with Ethernet—although even they could not avoid gradual decline.

In contrast, thanks to its open community Ethernet did not face such problems. Because several firms specialized in different products and market segments, Ethernet was naturally present in several markets and thus, as a technology, could overcome market shifts smoothly. Ethernet did not suffer greatly from the same computer industry shifts that weakened the proprietary LANs. Specialization among the many Ethernet vendors also boosted its product variety while generating steep price reductions. Because the Ethernet standard ensured interoperability among vendors' devices, firms could autonomously and simultaneously pursue innovations without having to coordinate their efforts. Such concurrent innovation activity led to rapid trial-and-error learning that no single firm could emulate. As a result, Ethernet overcame the initial technical and price advantages of its proprietary contenders and invaded their market niches. Finally, the open community effectively decoupled firm success and standard success. Although some Ethernet firms fell victim to the relative decline in the minicomputer market, Ethernet itself did not perish because it could rely on those vendors that focused on the PC LAN market.

Ethernet's community advantage, to some extent, reflected its standardization success and larger market size. Most LAN start-ups simply developed products for the network that promised the largest market. In this sense, status as an IEEE standard and the minicomputer vendors' adoption of Ethernet proved critical because they guaranteed Ethernet the largest market in the early 1980s and access to the distribution channels of the large manufacturers. But the community divergence between Ethernet and its proprietary competitors also resulted from different community-building efforts and ultimately from their different degrees of openness. In fact, none of the proprietary LAN vendors undertook the community-building efforts of Robert Metcalfe and the DIX group, who actively sought suppliers and prepared for Ethernet's economic success by making it an open standard. Without similar openness, the proprietary LANs exposed their licensees to the risk of unilateral, discriminatory actions by the proprietor and limited themselves to smaller markets, thanks to users' aversion to proprietary systems. The competition between Ethernet and its proprietary competitors confirms the thesis outlined in the first chapter. The sponsor communities of the proprietary LANs resulted in a structural disadvantage in the simultaneous pursuit of several markets and in the generation of innovations and price reductions.

Finally, network effects—derived from either physical network size or complementary goods—played a negligible role in this standardization struggle, for several reasons. Many early LANs, such as Corvus's Omninet, which was used for disk sharing, were rather small. Even some of the larger LANs, such as Sytek's LocalNet, failed to give rise to extensive network effects because most networks did not cross enterprise boundaries. Network effects were also limited because many complementary goods turned out to be competitively neutral. The leading NOS for file sharing, Novell's NetWare, supported almost any LAN hardware, while the specifications for many computer buses were in the public domain or could be obtained through clever reverse engineering.[95] Hence many of the network effects that played a decisive role in other standardization battles failed to create significant "tipping" effects in this stage of LAN standardization.

Ethernet's proprietary rivals therefore could not rely on their early market lead and domination of certain segments, such as the Apple II or long-range general-purpose LAN markets. Instead, they had to continue to compete on the basis of traditional cost and manufacturing advantages. Thanks to its community advantage, Ethernet had the clear edge in this respect. Interestingly, the absence of significant network effects actually prolonged the life cycle of the proprietary LANs. In the presence of strong network effects, the market might have "tipped" more rapidly toward the leader.

Given the historical circumstances, an open community was the best advantage Ethernet could possess in its competition with the proprietary LANs. With the disappearance of the proprietary LANs, the first phase in the standardization struggle had come to an end. By the mid- to late 1980s, Ethernet seemed to be the clear favorite to become the dominant standard.

7 The Battle Between Ethernet and Token Ring

Despite the continuous rise of Ethernet, the standardization battle was not yet over. Ethernet still had to face Token Ring, which was finally introduced in 1986. The battle between the two IEEE 802 standards had all the elements of a classic standardization struggle, as a superior and thus more expensive newcomer (Token Ring) challenged an inferior incumbent that had already amassed a large installed base (Ethernet). Standardization theory leaves little uncertainty about the expected outcome. The superior newcomer faces an uphill battle against the incumbent, whose large installed base and ample supply of complementary goods generate network effects that provide it with an almost insurmountable advantage. Without vast technical advantages, the superior entrant is most likely to lose the contest, allowing the inferior technology to solidify its lock-in.

In the end, Ethernet indeed prevailed over Token Ring—but for reasons quite different from those suggested by standardization theory. Contrary to the path dependency literature, Ethernet's victory did not result from its first-mover advantages and larger installed base, nor did it remain an inferior standard. Instead, Ethernet had to secure its victory with radical technological improvements, including a fundamental change in topology that effectively closed the technological gap between the two antagonists. Ethernet was unable to drive its victory home solely on the basis of its past momentum because, throughout the mid-1980s, network effects were still manifested on a relatively small scale: many users had not yet interconnected their LANs. In the absence of strong network externalities and their attendant high switching costs, in the late 1980s users were increasingly ready to switch to the Token Ring standard, whose technical superiority made it initially better suited to accommodate the increasingly large number of nodes within networks. However, once Ethernet had closed the gap and could handle the growing networks as effectively as Token Ring, users remained loyal to it because of its continuing price advantage over Token Ring.

On the surface, Ethernet's victory originated from its price advantage and technological improvements. However, another factor contributed to its success—one that was actually behind its price advantage and technological improvements and that had already led to its victory over the proprietary LANs. This was its large supplier community, which continuously produced new, improved Ethernet versions while vigorously driving down prices. As an open IEEE standard, Token Ring had a better chance to attract a large community than the proprietary LANs. Though it did attract suppliers, its community remained much smaller and less diverse than that of Ethernet—partly because of Token Ring's later entry and partly because of various community-restricting strategies adopted by IBM. Without an equivalent supplier community, Token Ring could not close the price gap—its main handicap—and even began falling behind technologically. As a result, the market "tipped" toward Ethernet.

Ethernet versus Token Ring: The Beginning of the Battle

In 1980 the DIX group and IBM, the principal proponents of Ethernet and Token Ring, respectively, chose quite different standardization strategies within IEEE 802. The DIX group was willing to trade technological complexity for speedy market introduction and relatively low cost. In contrast, IBM decided to spend more time to develop a sophisticated, high-end technology, one clearly superior to Ethernet. In IBM's view, the development of such a product warranted delays in market introduction. These standardization strategies propelled the two technologies on quite different trajectories, with the result that they had quite distinct strengths and weaknesses in early 1986, when IBM, after long delays, finally introduced Token Ring (table 7.1).[1]

Ethernet's biggest advantage over Token Ring at the outset of the battle was its large installed base and substantial market momentum. Whereas Token Ring completely lacked an installed base, by late 1985 approximately 30,000 Ethernet networks had been installed, connecting at least 417,000 nodes, and probably significantly more.[2] Thanks to this installed base, Ethernet dominated the minicomputer terminal market and enjoyed a strong presence in PC LANs. Furthermore, as we have seen, it had assembled a dynamic supplier community. By 1985, its principal vendors had shipped products with an accumulated value of at least

TABLE 7.1

Competitive Strengths and Weaknesses
of Ethernet and Token Ring, 1985–1986

	Ethernet	Token Ring
Relative strengths	Large installed base: approximately 30,000 networks and at least 417,000 nodes Large supplier community Low price	Technological superiority: Hub topology Network management features Implementation on telephone wire
Relative weaknesses	Significant technical shortcomings: Bus topology No network management features Cumbersome connectivity method	Huge gap in installed base Few integrated circuits High price

$511.5 million, and in 1987 the trade press estimated that its supplier community encompassed approximately two hundred vendors.[3] This support on both the demand side and the supply side made Ethernet the leading LAN at the time of Token Ring's market introduction.

Only one problem appeared to stand in the way of Ethernet's continued ascendancy: its technical inferiority. One of the LAN's most serious handicaps was its bus topology, which, as mentioned in chapter 2, had the potential to create severe problems in network management and troubleshooting. In the early 1980s, when networks were relatively small and did not require management in the true sense of the word, Ethernet's bus topology did not cause much trouble, nor did it jeopardize the technology's adoption. But the number of nodes per network gradually increased. By 1985, the average size of peer-to-peer networks (as opposed to the larger terminal-to-host networks) had increased to twelve nodes— up from three to four nodes in the early 1980s—and twenty- to thirty-node networks were quite common. By 1990, fifty-node networks would be typical.[4] As Jerome Saltzer and IBM had anticipated in the late 1970s and early 1980s, under these conditions Ethernet's bus topology did indeed become a serious handicap.[5] Without a central connection point, network administrators could not know the exact location and source of a failure on an Ethernet network, and thus they had to follow the wire as it meandered from office to office. Since the wire was often strung above ceilings and within conduits, access was difficult, and administrators often spent days crawling around, trying to find the trouble spot. As Thomas Bredt—the lead investor in SynOptics, which was to provide a critical solution to this problem—recalled, "[Texas Instruments gave me] these compelling case studies how they had to spend days when their [coaxial Ethernet] network would be shut down, searching through the ceilings—crawling through the ceilings—trying to locate where the devices were connected to the network and which ones were failing."[6] Ethernet's bus topology made troubleshooting in the continually growing networks a nightmare.

If Ethernet had been crash-proof, its topology might not have been so critical an issue. However, it was indeed susceptible to crashes, for a variety of reasons. As mentioned previously, Thick Ethernet, with its RG-11 coaxial cable, required a very cumbersome method of connecting a node to the wire: the network administrator actually had to pierce holes in the wire in order to attach a tap and external transceiver to it.[7] Bredt explained the process:

> The way [Thick] Ethernet worked was you strung a yellow cable about as thick as your thumbs through the crawl space in the ceiling or through the walls. And any place you wanted to attach a workstation to the Ethernet, you used what was known as a "vampire clamp." [This clamp] had prongs on two sides and you would position it on either side of this cable and then tighten it down so that it pierced to the cable. [This] made contact with the appropriate levels of the yellow cable to establish connectivity.[8]

Not only did this method require significant technical expertise and thus labor expense, it was also prone to failure.[9] In fact, piercing the wire with a connection tap was an unreliable technique, for it often failed to make a proper connection between the node and the wire. If an improper installation had brought down only the newly connected node, this might have been tolerable. But Ethernet's bus topology meant that a failure at a single node could stall the entire network.[10] And trying to locate such an improperly connected node on Ethernet's bus topology was very time consuming. As Bredt described it, "[Network administrators] had to individually pull things off, see if that one caused the problem, and put them back on."[11] As the number of nodes connected to a network grew—increasing the likelihood of a network failure while protracting the search process—this trial-and-error diagnostic method became increasingly unacceptable.[12] Ethernet's principal shortcomings thus were its problematic troubleshooting and connectivity methods—consequences of its bus topology and use of coaxial cable.

But Ethernet had additional technical shortcomings. The thick RG-11 coaxial cable of the original Ethernet standard was not only expensive and often not preinstalled in buildings but also stiff and thus difficult to bend around corners. This made wire installation difficult and in turn increased labor expenditures, which were already one of the largest cost

factors for network installations.[13] In addition, because Ethernet's connectivity method required considerable technical expertise, an untrained
end user was typically unable to hook up a new node. This became a significant handicap as Ethernet penetrated the office market.[14]

For all these reasons, it appeared by the late 1980s that Ethernet's life
cycle was likely to come to an end by the beginning of the new decade.
As corporate America increasingly depended on LANs to conduct business, and found itself connecting an ever-larger number of nodes, bus-
based Ethernet was no longer an adequate technology, especially for
network expansions and new installations. Of course, thanks to its large
installed base, Ethernet was not immediately going to disappear from the
corporate LAN-scape, but it was clear that administrators needed a more
sophisticated technology to accommodate their growing networks.[15]

Ethernet's shortcomings provided an excellent window of opportunity
for Token Ring, allowing its technological superiority to come into play.
In fact, having been designed by IBM from the start as an enterprise network, Token Ring eliminated most of Ethernet's deficiencies and was
thus far better suited to accommodate growing LANs. To begin with, its
shielded twisted-pair (STP) wire was more flexible and thus easier to install
than Thick Ethernet's coaxial cable. Token Ring also provided a more
foolproof way of connecting nodes to the wire, thereby reducing the risk
of network downtime resulting from improper installations.[16] Furthermore, Token Ring had an automatic bypass mechanism that prevented a
single malfunctioning node from stalling the entire network.[17] But most
important, with its star-shaped ring topology, including several hubs—or
what IBM called multistation access units (MAU)—Token Ring provided
central points to monitor the network and to enable and disable individual nodes.[18] This design greatly facilitated network management and
troubleshooting.[19] Network administrators did not need to crawl through
ceilings to locate a failure but could disable the node at the MAU whose
LED indicators conveniently revealed a malfunctioning node.[20] Since the
MAUs were often locked in wiring closets, network managers also
regained control over who could connect to the network; individual
users could not connect without the administrator's knowledge, as they
could on an Ethernet LAN. This added security also reduced the risk of
network failure.

IBM's decision in 1984 to implement Token Ring on telephone wire
strengthened its technical advantages even further. Initially IBM did not
intend to use telephone wire—which was in fact unshielded twisted-pair
(UTP) wire—for its Token Ring. UTP wire had greater physical constraints,
such as attenuation and susceptibility to crosstalk, than, say, coaxial
cable or STP wire; it therefore offered lower network performance in

terms of number of nodes and distance coverage. But certain defensive strategic moves that the company was forced to make ultimately led IBM to use the inferior telephone wire for its Token Ring. The first such move occurred in 1984, as IBM was receiving much criticism of Token Ring's continued delays from its customers, who hoped that the LAN would solve their communication problems by allowing them to integrate all their IBM equipment.[21] To appease its customers, in October 1984 the company announced a wiring specification for commercial buildings, the IBM Cabling System, which was based on STP wire—even as it continued to postpone the delivery of actual products.[22] By specifying a cabling system, IBM hoped that, if users went ahead and at least installed the wire, they would continue to wait for Token Ring, thereby guaranteeing its proliferation once IBM could ship products. But when most customers decided against the installation of a cabling system aimed specifically at IBM products, in late 1985 IBM decided to make the telephone wire of commercial buildings an integral part of the IBM Cabling System.[23] Users could now implement Token Ring on their regular telephone systems.

Using the telephone system for data communication offered tremendous advantages. UTP wire was easy to install and quite inexpensive.[24] Moreover, the telephone systems of commercial buildings were wired in a star topology owing to their use of PBXs. This meant that Token Ring's hub topology could easily be preserved. But most important, because telephone wiring was widely preinstalled in commercial buildings, users did not need to install a separate wire for their data communication needs. These advantages clearly surpassed telephone wire's inferior performance in terms of distance coverage and speed, and consequently the telephone system became the dominant wiring infrastructure for LANs in the late 1980s and early 1990s.[25]

Not surprisingly, Token Ring, which operated at 4 Mbps, quickly gained market share after its introduction in early 1986, despite a price disadvantage of approximately $300 or 70 percent over Ethernet.[26] The few estimates of Token Ring's initial market share ranged between 12 and 50 percent for the period 1987–88.[27] Of course, Token Ring took off briskly because of its technical superiority and openness. But it also benefited from IBM's extensive distribution channels, its close relationship with IBM systems, and the expectations of IBM's customers that they would receive a complete solution to the problem of integrating all their IBM computers.[28] As a result, Token Ring penetrated the Fortune 500 companies, as well as the banking and insurance industries, where IBM had long dominated.[29] It was well on its way to becoming the LAN with the second largest installed base.[30]

In late 1988, when IBM introduced a 16-Mbps version, Token Ring was poised to capture even greater market share. Though the 16-Mbps Token Ring initially operated only on STP wire, not on telephone wire, it outperformed the original 4-Mbps Token Ring and 10-Mbps Ethernet (which both operated at approximately the same actual throughput rate) by a factor of 3 to 3.5.[31] Of course, such a speed increase only reinforced Token Ring's reputation of providing a superior migration path for growing networks.[32] Backed by such market momentum, Token Ring now posed a serious threat to Ethernet. There was little doubt among analysts that Token Ring would become a dominant force in the 1990s, possibly replacing Ethernet as the leading standard.[33] It appeared that IBM's strategy of spending extra time on the development of a sophisticated technology had paid off.

Thus, although Ethernet appeared to have already "tipped" the market by the time of Token Ring's introduction in 1986, in fact the battle was far from over. The market was still relatively small compared with its final size, and Ethernet's technical weaknesses, which increasingly caused serious bottlenecks, provided Token Ring with a vital window of opportunity.[34] Not surprisingly, Token Ring succeeded in capturing significant market share within the first two years after its introduction. These developments structured the competitive situation for years to come. Though Ethernet would not vanish quickly owing to its large installed base and well-established supplier community, it clearly had to solve its technical problems if it was to defend its market lead into the 1990s. Token Ring, in turn, had to continue to increase its market momentum and especially to reduce its significant price disadvantage if it was to compete with Ethernet.[35] The battle would be decided by whether Ethernet would close the technology gap before Token Ring could close the price gap.[36]

The Closure of the Technology Gap by Ethernet

The efforts of the Ethernet community to improve its standard began well before the introduction of Token Ring. The community had already implemented the technology on wire types different from its original thick coaxial cable—namely on fiber optic, broadband, and thin coaxial cable—in the early 1980s. These cable variations all improved the standard and broadened its market appeal in various ways. In particular, Thinnet, which became Ethernet's main version in the PC LAN market, eliminated the cumbersome method of connecting nodes to the wire. In hindsight, however, all of the variations failed to solve Ethernet's shortcomings in network management, troubleshooting, and wiring structure, because they all preserved its bus topology and failed to take advantage of the ubiquitous telephone wire.[37] In other words, although these implementations provided improvements, they were pre-dominant-design variants, and none combined all the features that would make up Ethernet's later dominant design.

As a result, Ethernet caught up only when its community changed the bus topology to a star and implemented it on telephone wire, that is, used the same topology on the same wire as Token Ring. The new version owed its origin to two developments that began quite independently but came together in 1986–87: AT&T's attempt to use telephone wire for Ethernet and the efforts of a small start-up, SynOptics, to solve Ethernet's problematic wiring situation by using a hub.

Following in the footsteps of 3Com and U-B—which in the early 1980s had implemented Ethernet on nonstandard cable types, such as fiber optic, broadband, and thin coaxial cable—around 1984 AT&T introduced a 1-Mbps Ethernet version for UTP wire.[38] On this basis AT&T's version, later called Starlan, looked just like any other new Ethernet type, but AT&T's variant included an important modification. It operated not only on UTP wire installed exclusively for data networking, but also on the UTP wire used by the existing telephone systems in commercial buildings. Because such telephone systems typically employed a PBX, with the individual lines branching out from the PBX to the offices, the systems were already wired in a star topology. This meant that AT&T's Starlan, unlike the new Ethernet versions of 3Com and U-B, could function on a hub-based star topology and thus offered the same advantages in network management and troubleshooting as Token Ring.[39]

Not surprisingly, the ability to implement Ethernet on existing telephone wire made Starlan quite a success. In 1986, IEEE 802.3 ratified it as a standard, and Starlan quickly attracted numerous suppliers, including several semiconductor firms.[40] Their competing ICs allowed the prices of adapters to fall precipitously, from an initial $600 in 1986 to less than $300 in 1987, making Starlan the least expensive IEEE 802 standard. At the same time, AT&T's shipments of Starlan soared from fifty networks per week in the middle of 1986 to over five hundred units half a year later.[41] Thanks to Starlan, Ethernet finally appeared to be on track to match Token Ring's technological advantage.

Starlan's success was ironic. PBX vendors had proposed using existing low-bandwidth telephone wire for data communication as far back as the early 1980s.[42] But because of the low speed of telephone wire, they were forced to yield to the Ethernet and LAN vendors, who suggested an extra, high-speed wire, such as coaxial cable, dedicated to data communication.

Although it was the LAN vendors who prevailed at first, only a few years later they were obliged to concede that their proposition had been wrong.[43] As Ralph Ungermann put it, "When we started the LAN business, everyone said: 'Telephone wiring is stupid. What we need is this single, shared wire. Look how much simpler this is.' I railed against the PBX vendors at almost every single speaking engagement. But in reality, Ethernet wire was stupid, and it turned out that the PBX vendors had the right wiring and the right architecture."[44] Of course, this radical shift back to telephone wiring for data communication was rooted in the growing concerns about Ethernet's long-term viability and AT&T's desire to gain a presence in the fast-growing data communication market. But the shift also resulted from the tremendous improvements in chip technology that enhanced the ICs' ability to discern signals even as they rapidly deteriorated on low-speed telephone lines.[45]

Despite its market growth, Starlan's success was only short lived, and it failed to halt Token Ring's rise in 1987–88. With its 1-Mbps throughput rate, Starlan was not only considerably slower than Token Ring but also incompatible with 10-Mbps Ethernet.[46] This meant that users needed costly gateways if they were to connect Starlan with the other Ethernet versions.[47] Consequently, Starlan was never considered a fully equivalent sibling of Ethernet. As Frank Derfler wrote in *PC Magazine*, "People never accepted the 1-Mbps Starlan as sufficient for their data needs, despite its advantages in cost and convenience."[48] As a result, Starlan trailed Token Ring in the market by a considerable margin, even at its peak.[49] When the Ethernet community finally implemented Ethernet at its full speed on telephone wire for a price similar to that of Starlan, it rapidly faded away. Despite this short-lived success, Starlan, with its implementation on the hub-based telephone system, took Ethernet an important step toward its final dominant design—even though it would never exactly match Token Ring's capabilities because of its lower speed.

Immediately after Starlan's standardization in 1986, the Ethernet community attempted to increase its speed. Patricia Thaler of H-P recalled: "By the time we were done with [the Starlan standard], it was fairly clear to some of us that not only did it work at 1 Mbps [on UTP wire] but that there was a lot of slack in the budget [that is, the standard specification]."[50] In hindsight, Ethernet's subsequent speed increase to 10 Mbps on telephone wire resulted from the collective effort of the entire Ethernet community. Nevertheless, the first company to launch such a product was a new start-up, SynOptics.[51] Though the incumbent vendors followed with similar products shortly thereafter, SynOptics managed to remain a step ahead of its competitors and to dominate the market for hubs, the main product for this version.

Interestingly, the roots of SynOptics go back to the same organization that had produced Ethernet's bus topology in the first place: Xerox PARC. While still involved in winning the standards battle within IEEE 802, in 1980 PARC hired Ronald Schmidt, a Ph.D. in electrical engineering and computer science, to develop a high-bandwidth Ethernet version for fiber optic cable.[52] Schmidt quickly realized the drawbacks of Ethernet's bus topology and decided to implement his fiber optic version on a hub-based star topology instead, mainly to enhance reliability and network management capabilities.[53] Initially he and PARC were pursuing this project for pure research rather than commercialization purposes. But in the early 1980s, when PARC came under attack for the many innovations it had let escape to other Silicon Valley firms, Schmidt thought he could assist PARC by commercializing his innovation. In this endeavor he found support within, of all places, Xerox's real estate consulting unit. As he later recalled,

> They [the real estate unit] were pitching new technology in the office environment. They wanted some hot stuff to pitch and really [latched] onto it because at that time there was this cabling nightmare. You take pictures of computer rooms with lots of cables underneath there, and then you go into offices and there were cables all over the place. The promise of the fiber optics was that one cable could support all your bandwidth needs. So they really promoted that.

Yet—taking a similar attitude as it had in 1979 when the DIX alliance was formed—the management of Xerox rebuffed Schmidt's commercialization idea.[54] Xerox conceived of fiber optic Ethernet as niche product, and its management did not want to be in the business of producing LAN components.

Despite this setback, Schmidt eventually succeeded in marketing his fiber optic Ethernet—ironically with IBM's help! In October 1984, when IBM announced a cabling system for its forthcoming hub-based Token Ring, the IBM Cabling System, Schmidt realized that the topologies of Token Ring and his Ethernet version mirrored each other despite their different cable types and access methods. Determined to take advantage of this similarity, Schmidt modified his Ethernet so it could run not only on fiber optic cable but also on the STP wire of the IBM Cabling System. Although this modification allowed Schmidt—now joined by Andrew Ludwick, a Xerox executive assistant looking at new business opportunities and later the CEO of SynOptics—to promote the business proposition of having *one* cabling system supporting both Token Ring and Ethernet, Xerox management declined their renewed commercialization requests. But, in exchange for an equity position, Xerox allowed them to license the technology and to spin off a company of their own. Schmidt and Ludwick established their company, initially called Astra Communications, in Mountain View, California, in June 1985.[55]

By offering a structured (that is, hub-based) wiring approach for Ethernet, SynOptics tapped into an unsatisfied market need. In late 1985—when it shipped its first product, called LattisNet, a hub-based Ethernet version for both fiber optic cable and the IBM Cabling System—it was an immediate success, as Ronald Schmidt documents with the following example:

> We had these hubs in Texas Instruments' evaluation labs [for beta testing]. Well, on [their regular coaxial] Ethernet they had this financial system with which they were trying to close the books by Christmas Day. Up until a day and a half [before the deadline], their Ethernet was down because they had all these problems with the transceivers. One of them would short, and you did not know where it was until you basically went through every office— removing the ceiling tiles, going in there, and playing with it. They could not get their Ethernet up to close the books. But they had the IBM Cabling Systems going into the computer room and they said: "Well, why don't we try this SynOptics stuff and see if we could get it to work?" So, they rolled in, plugged it all in, and it came right up in five minutes. Well, that sold them![56]

As a result, SynOptics was profitable from the very beginning, and by April 1987 it had installed LattisNet in more than twenty customer sites, connecting approximately 20,000 nodes.[57] This was good news for SynOptics, but its LattisNet product still had a significant disadvantage. Though operating at Ethernet's full speed of 10 Mbps on a hub topology, it functioned only on the STP wire of the IBM Cabling System, not on the more ubiquitous telephone wiring.

This shortcoming was soon to interfere with the company's efforts to raise capital. In 1986, when Schmidt and Ludwick began looking for venture funding, they encountered great difficulty. Although SynOptics clearly offered a superior wiring approach for Ethernet, many venture capitalists turned the deal down because Ethernet on the IBM Cabling System appeared to be only a niche market owing to its small number of installations.[58] The deal also raised concerns because SynOptics had not yet implemented Ethernet on telephone wiring, and it was unclear whether this would be technologically feasible in the near future.[59] But most important, the venture capitalists doubted whether SynOptics had a sustainable competitive advantage. Since the hub, its principal product, was a relatively low-tech device, many financiers viewed the barriers to entry as quite low.[60] They feared that competitors could easily erode its first-mover advantages and undermine its profitability by offering similar products. To some extent, they were correct.[61] As mere connectivity points, the SynOptics hub products were not sufficiently high-tech and software-intensive to deter the incumbent LAN vendors—such as 3Com, H-P, and U-B—from marketing similar products. What many failed to envision, however, was that the hub could become a platform upon which high-value software and firmware could be deployed and that its head start, combined with rapid innovation, would permit SynOptics to outrun its competitors in the hub business.[62]

The venture capitalists' concerns were intensified as they investigated the business plan by talking to incumbent LAN vendors. Ronald Schmidt explained: "The venture capitalists talked to 3Com, and 3Com said: 'What they are doing, we can do with our hands tied behind our back and one eye blinded.' And then that gets out all in the [venture] community. So, you had to find people who would not think as part of the herd instinct."[63] To most venture capitalists SynOptics, though promising and profitable, did not look like the big winner it was soon to become, but like an unremarkable start-up with a small, indefensible market niche.

Amid these concerns, in August 1986 John Lewis of Paragon Partners and Thomas Bredt of Menlo Ventures, among others, nevertheless decided to invest.[64] Because of his earlier involvement with H-P as the engineering manager responsible for all of H-P's communication products, including Ethernet, Bredt immediately grasped the advantages of LattisNet's star topology:

> The SynOptics architecture was a simple point-to-point connection. You had total visibility in the wiring closet. You could look at all the lights in the panel and see exactly where everything was connected. And you could, just in the wiring closet itself, take things off, put them in, if you had to do that manually. So the whole troubleshooting, reliability, et cetera—the arguments were absolutely compelling. And the cost savings to use this hub approach as opposed to the wire-through-the-ceiling approach were compelling because of reduced maintenance. And given that the network was going to become the data communications highway for corporate America to run their business, it was critical to have a reliable architecture.[65]

For these reasons, Bredt and his co-investors believed that SynOptics had an important innovation for the leading LAN technology and that it could perhaps sustain its lead despite the market power of the incumbent Ethernet firms.

Having secured venture capital in the middle of 1986, SynOptics joined the other Ethernet vendors in their effort to increase Starlan's speed over telephone wire. Because of the various physical constraints of the UTP wire—including high attenuation, radio frequency emission, and electro-magnetic noise—a speed increase to 10 Mbps appeared to many observers far more difficult to achieve than Starlan or the SynOptics Ethernet version for the IBM Cabling System.[66] After extensive research, however, Schmidt made the, breakthrough, and in August 1987 SynOptics shipped the first proprietary 10-Mbps Ethernet product for the telephone network.[67] SynOptics' breakthrough meant that, only one and a half years after Token Ring's market introduction, Ethernet had caught up with its rival technologically. Like Token Ring, it now ran on widely installed telephone wire at its full speed and provided identical advantages in troubleshooting and network management.

Renewed Standardization and the Arrival of Intelligent Hubs

As the venture capitalists had expected, the exclusivity that SynOptics enjoyed quickly evaporated. In early 1988, barely six months after SynOptics had shipped the first product, H-P introduced a similar 10-Mbps Ethernet product for telephone wire; half a year later AT&T, David Systems, U-B, and Cabletron (soon to be SynOptics' fiercest competitor in the hub business [table 7.2]) followed with similar products.[68] Because of the hubs' low-tech nature and the advantages of the star-based topology, the list of Ethernet vendors with hub products continued to grow quickly and soon included a myriad of suppliers, including Gateway Communications, NetWorth, BICC Data Networks, Nevada Western, Chipcom, Digital Communications Associates, Fibermux, Lannet, and Racal Interlan.[69] At the same time, the hub market flourished. Sales at SynOptics, for instance, shot up from $1.6 million in 1986 to $40.1 million in 1988, while those of Cabletron, the second largest hub vendor, increased from $3.9 million to $24.9 million for the same period.[70]

Yet one significant drawback plagued users and vendors alike. Since in 1987 no standard existed, the vendors' products were all proprietary, unable to interoperate with each other.[71] This was a severe handicap for end users who had become accustomed to interoperability and standardization in Ethernet technology. The absence of a standard meant further that the semiconductor firms hesitated to develop ICs; as a result, Ethernet on telephone wire cost between $100 and $150 more per node than its coaxial sibling.[72] These cost and compatibility issues called for renewed standardization efforts by IEEE 802.

The first steps toward a 10-Mbps Ethernet standard for telephone wire, later called 10Base-T, occurred at about the same time as SynOptics shipped the first proprietary product. In 1987, while SynOptics rushed to market, Thaler of H-P, who later chaired the standards group, contacted engineers at competing firms to inquire whether they were interested in

TABLE 7.2

Hub Market Share, Selected Years

Year	Company	Hub shipments (in millions of dollars)	Market share (percentage)
1989	SynOptics	55.48	38
	U-B	40.88	28
	Cabletron	35.04	24
	Others	14.60	10
	Total	146.00	100
1990	SynOptics	117.67	41
	Cabletron	57.40	20
	U-B	51.66	18
	Chipcom	14.35	5
	AT&T	11.48	4
	David Systems	8.61	3
	Hewlett-Packard	8.61	3
	Others	17.22	6
	Total	287.00	100
1993	SynOptics	756.40	31
	Cabletron	439.20	18
	3Com	170.80	7
	Chipcom	170.80	7
	Others	902.80	37
	Total	2,440.00	100

SOURCES: 1989: Forrester Research Inc. (Cusack 1990); 1990: The Yankee Group (Brown 1991c); 1993: Dataquest (Clark 1994).

forming an IEEE 802.3 study group to evaluate possible technologies for a standard. Most agreed, and the group's first meeting was scheduled for August 1987.[73] At this meeting, H-P was the only firm to present a proposal, but at subsequent meetings in October and November SynOptics, AT&T, David Systems, 3Com, DEC, Wang, Micom/Interlan, Western Digital, and U-B all submitted their own proposals.[74] All the principal hub vendors had joined the standardization effort, despite their proprietary product offerings. Bredt explained the vendors' interest in joining IEEE 802 from SynOptics' perspective:

> When we [Menlo Ventures] initially made the investment, SynOptics had a patent on this architecture, which Xerox Corporation had filed for them. [The patent] basically would have precluded anyone else from implementing the hub on Ethernet. And so, in one sense, you might look at this patent and say: "That is a powerful barrier to entry. It will keep competitors away from

the door." Unfortunately, in the networking business it kind of works against you in that the IEEE will not allow any company to have a patent on something that is going to give that company an advantage if the technology covered by the patent is to become an industry standard.

So SynOptics had a dilemma. If we retained the patent rights and defended our exclusivity, we basically had to give up the idea of becoming the industry standard. On the other hand, if we wanted to have our technology adopted as the industry standard, we basically had to throw our patent on the pile and offer a free license to anyone.

So the reason we decided to go for the standard and give free license to the patent was, by becoming the standard, the market acceptance of this technology would be dramatically increased. In fact, had we kept the proprietary standard, I believe someone else would have gone to the IEEE and a different approach would have been adopted. And we would have been left in the dust.[75]

In other words, once H-P initiated a renewed standardization process, events followed a compelling logic. In order to avoid being outflanked by a standardized version, the vendors had no choice but to participate in the process. If they could no longer compete with proprietary offerings, they at least wanted to influence the IEEE's standardization process.

Although ten vendors had submitted proposals, there were only two competing technical approaches. While SynOptics and most other vendors, including H-P, favored a "pure" standard, written exclusively for star-based telephone wiring, 3Com and DEC, the market leaders in coaxial Ethernet, suggested a hybrid technology, that is, one that could intermix coaxial and telephone wire, as well as bus- and star-wired segments (figure 7.1).[76] Mainly concerned with their customers' investment in coaxial Ethernet, they justified their hybrid approach with three short-term cost advantages:

1. In their competitors' approach, every single node had to be wired to the hub individually; in their hybrid approach, in contrast, several nodes could be "daisy-chained" on a length of coaxial cable before being connected collectively to the hub over UTP wire. This approach saved wiring costs and, more important, allowed users to connect offices with several coaxial nodes to the telephone system without any modifications. This made the migration from coaxial Ethernet to telephone wire very simple.

2. Whereas their competitors' technology transmitted data only unidirectionally over a pair of UTP wires, their hybrid approach allowed for bidirectional signaling. In the eyes of 3Com and DEC, this saved the costs of extra wire installation in certain circumstances.

3. To protect the installed base of coaxial adapter cards from becoming completely obsolete, the approach of SynOptics and its allies allowed

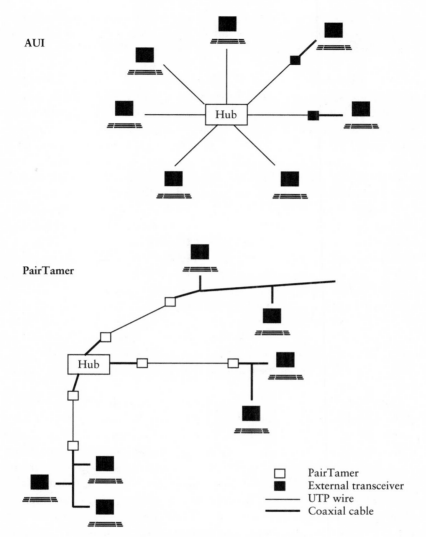

FIGURE 7.1   AUI approach versus PairTamer approach.

for the attachment of an external transceiver, called an access unit interface (AUI), to each node. This meant that users could continue to employ
their coaxial adapter cards, since the AUI interfaced with the UTP
wire.[77] Although this method indeed helped to protect users' investments
in coaxial adapter cards, in the view of 3Com and DEC it created extra
costs since it required an AUI for each coaxial node. In contrast, by

allowing users to daisy-chain several nodes over coaxial cable, the 3Com-
DEC approach did not require an AUI for each individual node and
thus reduced some of the AUI costs.[78]

These arguments, however, failed to convince SynOptics and the other
seven vendors. They objected to the 3Com-DEC hybrid solution in part
because, by using external transceivers or AUIs, it did not closely follow
the IEEE's traditional approach to the standardization of new variants.
Moreover, H-P, SynOptics, and their allies argued that the 3Com-DEC
technology created the potential for higher *long-term* cost by requiring
an extra device, the PairTamer, for connecting coaxial and UTP wire.[79]
Therefore the AUI group refused to abandon their proposal.

Though 3Com and DEC clearly had the lead in the marketplace, they
realized that they were in the minority within the democratic IEEE group,
and to avoid defeat at the ballot box they elected not to pursue their
approach further.[80] As a result, in March 1988 Thaler's study group
selected the AUI technology as the basis for the 10Base-T standard.
However, in a reconciliatory gesture, it also attested that the 3Com-DEC
approach complied fully with the existing thin coaxial or 10Base2 standard.[81] Despite such face saving, it was clear that the two leading Ethernet vendors had failed to impose their preferred technology as a standard
on the industry. This failure was to have significant effects on the structure of the Ethernet supplier industry, as it anticipated the rise of new
dominant firms.

Even after the resolution of this preliminary conflict, the elaboration
of the actual standard remained a thorny matter. Because of the booming
market in pre-standard products, even minor technical "decisions that
should have been relatively easy became painstaking."[82] Many differences revolved around the issues of drive voltage, link integrity, jitter, and
equalization.[83] It took the 10Base-T group about a year to finish the first
draft, which "was not directly compatible with any existing product."[84]
Although the draft was initially rejected (mainly for editorial reasons), in
late 1989 it passed the confirmation ballot.[85] On September 28, 1990, the
IEEE Standards Board ratified 10Base-T as part of the IEEE 802.3 specification set.[86] As an interoperability demonstration at the Interops trade
show in October 1990 proved, users could now mix and match 10Base-T
components from different vendors.[87]

The passing of the 10Base-T standard reinforced the booming pre-
standard market.[88] On the demand side, large numbers of users switched
from coaxial Ethernet to 10Base-T, making it the dominant Ethernet version by the mid-1990s.[89] On the supply side, the rapidly growing market
attracted a large number of hub, adapter, and IC vendors. In fact, in 1991

over a hundred vendors were offering 10Base-T adapter cards, and several semiconductor firms—including AMD, Intel, Micro Linear, and National Semiconductor, NCR—developed ICs.[90] The average 10Base-T adapter card now carried a suggested retail price of $365 and, according to Ronald Schmidt, the barriers to entry for low-end hubs dropped so dramatically that any vendor that could read an AMD part specification could develop hub products.[91] In short, the wide adoption of 10Base-T led to a virtuous circle of constant price erosion, market expansion, and commodification.[92]

Initially, SynOptics' head start had sufficed to keep it ahead of the competition. But in the late 1980s and early 1990s, these trends caught up with the hub pioneer, thereby changing its competitive situation drastically, as Thomas Bredt pointed out:

> [After winning the standardization battle] the challenge for the company was to out-execute the competition. . . . We were first to market with products . . . and being first to market means you are farther down the learning curve than the competition and you learn more because you have more customers, there is more feedback, you see more problems, you solve more problems. So that keeps you out in front for a period of time. Now, it is fair to say that over time I think the Hewlett-Packards and the larger companies are going to catch up to you and probably get down the learning curve as far as you are. So to make SynOptics a successful company, we knew—the management knew, the board knew—that we had to do more than just win the standardization battle. The next strategic question for the company was how to differentiate ourselves from the competition given that this product, which we pioneered, is now going to become a commodity.[93]

SynOptics, like many other vendors, countered the commodification trend by making its hubs more intelligent. In fact, to differentiate itself from the competition, SynOptics began adding software and firmware to its hubs, thereby making them capable of far more than just interconnecting the "spokes" of the network.[94] Most notably, SynOptics (as did some of the other hub vendors) complemented its hubs with network management software that provided statistical analysis, monitored the network, and reported various network activities, such as traffic, error conditions, number of collisions, faulty nodes, and broken cables.[95] In the early 1990s, sophisticated hubs even allowed network managers to monitor, as well as to enable and disable, individual nodes remotely from their desktop computers.[96] Of course, such features simplified network management tremendously, especially for large organizations, which often had networks spread over several buildings.[97] Aside from network management software, vendors integrated modules into their hubs to bridge, route, and intersect different cable types.[98] As a result, the hub market bifurcated into two segments. While low-end hubs continued to be simple, inexpensive connectivity devices and thus commodities, intelligent high-end hubs were now software-intensive high-tech platforms capable of managing the networks of entire departments and even corporations.

In addition to changing the hub market, the introduction of intelligent hubs considerably affected the structure of the industry and the race between Ethernet and Token Ring. Since in the early to mid-1990s high-end enterprise hubs comprised millions of lines of software code and cost hundreds of millions of dollars to develop, the barriers to entry rose dramatically.[99] This trend allowed SynOptics and Cabletron, the two early front-runners in the hub market, to consolidate their dominance and to become leaders in the LAN industry. With sales of $389 million and $290 million, respectively, in 1992, SynOptics and Cabletron, the two hub specialists, were approaching 3Com, the leading adapter card manufacturer and the largest specialized Ethernet firm, with sales of $423.8 million.[100] Thanks to the transition from coaxial Ethernet to 10Base-T and the rapidly growing LAN market, SynOptics and Cabletron even began surpassing U-B, the Ethernet market leader of the early and mid-1980s. In addition, the arrival of intelligent hubs in combination with 10Base-T meant that Ethernet was now fully adequate to accommodate the needs of growing networks. In 1990–91 large organizations no longer had any reason to switch from Ethernet to the more expensive, but technologically equivalent, Token Ring.

Thus the rapid growth of networks and its inability to provide an adequate technology seriously threatened the Ethernet standard in the period between 1986 and 1988. However, as Ethernet was implemented on star-wired telephone systems and its hubs were equipped with sophisticated software, it managed to narrow the technological gap. SynOptics spearheaded many of these improvements, but ultimately they resulted from a concentrated community effort, as other vendors initiated similar innovations independently and simultaneously. By closing the technology gap, Ethernet solidified its lead over Token Ring in the standards race. Ethernet still had a larger installed base than Token Ring and cost significantly less; as a result, it was able to retain its existing adopters while attracting most new users.

The Failure of Token Ring to Keep Pace with Ethernet

Having lost its technological edge in the middle of 1987, Token Ring was now under enormous pressure to close the price gap—its principal handicap—if it was ever to catch up with Ethernet's market momen-

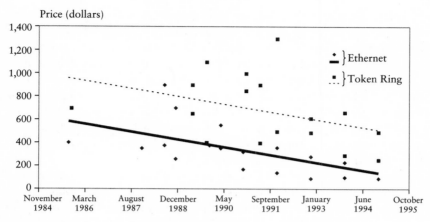

FIGURE 7.2   Price ranges of Ethernet and Token Ring, 1986–1995.

tum and installed base.[101] As the LAN market continued to grow and learning effects kicked in, Token Ring's prices indeed fell, but ultimately they failed to reach the level of Ethernet's (figure 7.2 and table 7.3). Token Ring had one significant and enduring drawback: the greater sophistication of the token access method inevitably made its chips, and thus the adapters that contained them, more expensive.[102] But most important, Token Ring's prices continued to lag because it did not attract a *supplier community* as competitive and dynamic as that of Ethernet.[103] Without equivalent community support, Token Ring lacked the socio-economic force that generated the price reductions and innovations that secured Ethernet's long-term competitiveness.

TABLE 7.3

Price Comparison Between Ethernet and Token Ring, Early 1993

LAN technology	Adapter card (dollars)	Hub interface (dollars)
4-Mbps Token Ring	650	150
16-Mbps Token Ring	650	150
10Base-T Ethernet	150	40–60*
Switched Ethernet	150	400–800*
Multiport routing	150	200–400*
100-Mbps Ethernet	250*	250*
100-Mbps FDDI	1,000	1,000

SOURCE: Lippis (1993:27).
*Projected 1993 prices.

Token Ring's trailing community support can to some extent be explained by its delayed market introduction.[104] Its protracted standardization process during the first half of the 1980s meant that most startups developing products for an IEEE standard had only one choice: Ethernet. Even as Token Ring was introduced, Ethernet remained their first choice because of its larger installed base. Of course, this put Token Ring at a great disadvantage. As its broader community support ensured further price reductions and thus continued market growth, Ethernet's momentum was continually reinforced.[105] In this sense, Ethernet benefited from considerable first-mover advantages.

But Token Ring also failed to attract a dynamic, competitive supplier community because various strategies implemented by IBM, Token Ring's dominant vendor, stymied rather than nurtured the formation of such a community. One such strategy can be seen in connection with the supply of Token Ring chips. To refute criticism that Token Ring was mainly an IBM technology, in 1982 IBM began collaborating with semiconductor firm Texas Instruments (TI).[106] TI was to produce "guaranteed IBM-compatible" Token Ring chips for independent vendors, since Big Blue did not intend to offer its own chips on the open market.[107] Though IBM's collaboration with TI was a positive step for the supplier community, IBM's role as kingmaker quickly backfired. When Token Ring's complexity delayed the introduction of TI's 4-Mbps Token Ring chips in 1985 and 1986, third-party vendors had no second source to which they could turn, and IBM refused to sell its own ICs.[108] To make matters worse, once introduced, TI's chips did not perform as well as those of IBM and were priced so high that third-party suppliers could not compete with IBM in the Token Ring market.[109] This supplier-unfriendly situation was repeated in 1988–89, when IBM introduced the 16-Mbps version of Token Ring. Again, TI was the only IC source for third-party suppliers, and it shipped its ICs many months after Big Blue.[110] Of course, this discrimination discouraged suppliers and in the process severely undermined Token Ring's competitiveness, which depended on an ample supply of ICs to achieve price reductions.

Moreover, IBM stymied the rise of a Token Ring community by casting doubt on the interoperability of its own products.[111] Though IBM collaborated with TI and adhered fully to the IEEE 802.5 Token Ring standard, it nevertheless implemented many more MAC-level management and control frame formats in its products than were specified by the IEEE standard. This meant that IBM's products included many features that were not part of the standard. A third-party supplier's Token Ring product, therefore—even if it fully implemented the IEEE 802.5 specifications—was "unable to recognize all the network-management and control messages issued by an IBM adapter." In addition, IBM's networking architecture required many proprietary, software-based interfaces and higher-level protocols, such as NetBios, to be implemented in its PCs.[112] Since IBM did not make all these software features public, it created much confusion about the full interoperability of its products. Before the introduction of Token Ring, independent suppliers could not know for certain whether their products would fully interoperate with those of IBM, and they could conduct compatibility tests only after IBM had released all its products. Even worse, the vendors felt that IBM could easily render their hardware products incompatible by simply manipulating its software.[113] Because of IBM's dominance, this was a serious concern to the independent suppliers.

IBM may have had good reasons to rely on such proprietary features, as they allowed it to increase the performance of its products and thus were part of a legitimate corporate differentiation strategy. But they also coincided with IBM's attempt in the late 1980s to regain control over the PC market through similar maneuvers.[114] One could therefore argue that IBM pursued a deliberate strategy of manipulating the interoperability of its Token Ring products in order to gain market share and to keep prices, as well as margins, high—a strategy that seemed to have succeeded.

These compatibility issues were eventually resolved, but in combination with the restricted chip supply they undermined the rise of a powerful supplier community for Token Ring.[115] By singling TI out as a "guaranteed IBM-compatible" IC vendor and by casting doubts on the interoperability of its products, IBM eliminated exactly the type of competition that drove Ethernet's adoption. Many potential vendors felt that they were systematically placed at a disadvantage and could not compete with IBM. Frustrated with IBM's secretive behavior, many adopted a wait-and-see attitude toward the development of Token Ring products. In 1986, for instance, U-B was quoted as saying that it was delaying the development of its own Token Ring chip until IBM's implementation had stabilized.[116] Worse, instead of developing Token Ring products and competing with IBM, many independent LAN vendors simply allocated most of their resources to Ethernet, whose rapid improvements promised a larger market than Token Ring, thereby spurring innovations and price advantages in the Ethernet realm. IBM's tight control of Token Ring—leading to a monopolistic chip supply and widespread compatibility concerns—thus undermined the third-party suppliers' competitiveness and consequently impaired the development of a diverse, dynamic Token Ring community.

It is not that Token Ring gathered no supplier community; it indeed attracted multiple suppliers. In late 1985, when IBM announced its plans to ship Token Ring products, several LAN specialists—including Nestar and the Ethernet vendors 3Com, U-B, and Excelan—announced their intention to follow with Token Ring products as well.[117] Moreover, Token Ring's market introduction in 1986 led to the establishment of at least one new Token Ring start-up specialist, Madge Networks in the United Kingdom, while Proteon, the previously established proprietary token ring specialist, added standardized products to its offerings.[118] By late 1989, the Token Ring community had grown to at least fifteen vendors (selling mainly Token Ring adapter cards for PCs), including 3Com, Madge, Proteon, Tiara, U-B, and Western Digital.[119] These vendors supported Token Ring because of its status as an IEEE 802 LAN standard, giving them full access to the technology. But they also developed products because IBM's support legitimized the standard by expanding its market. Token Ring appealed to the independent suppliers because it had become the second-largest LAN market, thanks to IBM's support and its status as an open standard.

Yet the rise of Token Ring suppliers could not conceal subtle but critical differences between the Token Ring and Ethernet communities. Token Ring did not attract an entire wave of start-ups in the way that Ethernet did in the early 1980s; and the two hundred Ethernet vendors in 1987 clearly outnumbered the roughly two dozen Token Ring vendors in 1989.[120] What was more, IBM dominated the Token Ring community in a manner that was unparalleled in the Ethernet community. With a worldwide market share of 57.7 percent in the 4-Mbps Token Ring adapter market and 92.6 percent in the 16-Mbps Token Ring market in 1990 (weighted average 78 percent), IBM left little space for independent vendors. Proteon and Madge, the two leading independent Token Ring start-ups, each had a market share of only about 10 percent in the 4-Mbps Token Ring market and thus could not match the revenues of the leading Ethernet suppliers, namely 3Com, U-B, SynOptics, and Cabletron.[121] The Token Ring community had not only fewer but also (with the exception of IBM) smaller firms; therefore it was more concentrated and less diversified than its Ethernet counterpart. IBM's effect on Token Ring was thus quite paradoxical. On the one hand, its adoption of the standard boosted Token Ring's market to a size it would have never reached without IBM's support. On the other hand, by dominating the market, Big Blue contracted the economic space for independent vendors, thereby impairing the rise of a large and diverse community.

Without a dynamic supplier community, Token Ring's competitiveness depended largely on IBM. IBM alone, however, could not keep pace with the many fast-growing Ethernet start-ups, all specializing in different products and market segments, and Token Ring's competitiveness began deteriorating. Its prices, as already mentioned, continued to exceed those of Ethernet, partly because of the more complex chip design, the lack of vigorous competition, and the smaller market and consequently smaller economies of scale. But prices also remained higher because IBM was more interested in sustaining a profitable business than gaining market share through aggressive forward pricing.[122] In addition, unlike many PC clone makers, Madge Networks—which surpassed Proteon in sales and emerged as the second-largest Token Ring vendor in the early 1990s—adopted a strategy of beating IBM not on the basis of price but by offering superior performance and quality. Of course, this tactic only solidified the premium prices charged in the Token Ring realm.[123] Since Token Ring served the high-end market, such as the MIS departments of large financial institutions, a high-price strategy made sense for both IBM and Madge. But it ultimately prevented Token Ring from becoming a fast-growing commodity market.[124]

A second sign of Token Ring's deteriorating competitiveness was its increasing inability to keep pace with technological advances. This first became apparent in 1988 and 1989, when IBM introduced the 16-Mbps Token Ring version but was unable to implement it on the crucial telephone wire until 1991.[125] This meant that, while the Ethernet community and most users were switching to telephone wire, 16-Mbps Token Ring was left out of the trend and hence lost much of its appeal.[126]

What was more, by the time IBM succeeded in making its 16-Mbps Token Ring operable on telephone wire, several new Ethernet start-ups, such as Kalpana and Grand Junction, had already taken Ethernet a step further by offering switching technology and a 100-Mbps Ethernet version, respectively.[127] These two innovations proved critical in removing Ethernet's growing speed bottlenecks.[128] As in the case of hubs, switching technology attracted a great number of start-ups, but all the incumbent Ethernet vendors rapidly offered switching products of their own.[129]

The introduction of Token Ring switches, in contrast, lagged several years behind that for Ethernet. In fact, switching technology was introduced only in 1994—and it never attracted as many start-ups as in the Ethernet realm.[130] This delay and the lagging supplier interest resulted partly from the higher throughput of 16-Mbps Token Ring, making speed increases less urgent, and partly from its greater technical complexity, complicating the implementation of switching.[131] In other words, Token Ring's greater complexity—which initially had been its principal advantage—now handicapped its further improvement. But most important, the smaller Token Ring market was simply not as attractive for start-ups as the Ethernet market. As Token Ring lacked similar start-up support, it began falling behind technologically, while Ethernet advanced rapidly

TABLE 7.4

Technological Evolution of Ethernet and Token Ring, 1970–1994

Year	Ethernet	Token Ring
1970–71		UC Irvine Ring
1973	Experimental Ethernet at PARC	
1979–80		Star-shaped token ring at MIT
1981	Thick Ethernet (10Base5)	Proteon's Pronet-10: proprietary 10-Mbps token ring LAN
1982	Thin Ethernet (10Base2)	
1985	SynOptics implements Ethernet at 10 Mbps on the STP wire of the IBM Cabling System	4-Mbps IEEE 802.5 Token Ring operates on the telephone wire and the STP wire of the IBM Cabling System
1986	Starlan: 1-Mbps Ethernet for telephone wire	
1987	SynOptics ships first 10-Mbps Ethernet product for telephone wire Standardization of 10Base-T begins	
1988		16-Mbps Token Ring for STP wire
1989	Arrival of intelligent hubs	
1990	Ratification of 10Base-T standard	
1991		16-Mbps Token Ring for UTP wire
1990–91	Switching	
1992–93	100-Mbps Ethernet	
1994		Switching

owing to its many start-up suppliers (table 7.4).[132] Put differently, thanks to its broad community support and new waves of start-up formation, Ethernet could progress at a much faster pace than Token Ring, which had to depend mainly on a single firm: IBM.

Token Ring's technological slowdown owing to its smaller community and lack of start-up support was apparent in at least one more instance. In the late 1980s, corporations increasingly interconnected their LANs over long distances, thereby forming private WANs. Such internetworking required new devices. Initially corporations used remote bridges, which were provided in the Ethernet realm mainly by start-up specialists, especially Vitalink, and in the Token Ring market chiefly by IBM.[133] As these WANs grew in size and complexity, however, bridging proved ineffective, causing a problem called broadcast storm.[134] Consequently, in the early 1990s users increasingly replaced their bridges with an alternative internetworking technology: multiprotocol routers.[135] Because bridging had created more and far earlier problems in Ethernet than in Token Ring owing to the latter's reliance on a different bridging method, the router start-ups Cisco and Wellfleet began focusing on solving *Ethernet's* bridging bottlenecks and thus became integral members of the Ethernet community.[136] Having encountered fewer bridging problems in Token Ring, IBM, in contrast, continued to rely on remote bridges as its principal internetworking tool.[137]

Thus, in the early 1990s, when it became clear that routers would be the more effective internetworking technology than bridges for *both* Ethernet *and* Token Ring, Ethernet users, thanks to Cisco and Wellfleet, had already switched more rapidly to routing than had IBM's Token Ring users.[138] Though Cisco and Wellfleet did support Token Ring in their multiprotocol routers, Werner Bux of IBM and Jon Bayless claimed that Cisco's and Wellfleet's support gave Ethernet a clear edge in the dawning internetworking era.[139] IBM eventually adopted an internetworking strategy based on routing as well, but, as in switching, it lagged several years behind the efforts of the Ethernet community.[140] Once again, a conglomeration of many swiftly acting start-up specialists proved far more powerful than a single (though large) firm in solving bottlenecks in the system. Supplier support mattered far more in the race for the LAN standard than any initial technological advantage.

Eventually, Token Ring's price gap and technological slowdown propelled Ethernet and Token Ring on two diverging, self-reinforcing courses. Despite further absolute market growth, Token Ring could not avoid a vicious circle of relatively fewer new customers, fewer innovations, and higher prices. In contrast, a virtuous circle of increased market share, more innovations, and lower prices continued to solidify Ethernet's technological lead and market dominance. Before 1990, these two self-reinforcing circles diverged only modestly; in 1989 2.2 million Ethernet adapters were shipped versus 1.4 million Token Ring adapters.[141] In the mid-1990s, their momentum and divergence accelerated, however. With an accumulated installed base of 10 million adapters in 1993, Token Ring now trailed far behind Ethernet, which had an installed base of 25 million adapters.[142] By 1995, the market had almost completely "tipped" toward Ethernet: only 3.8 million Token Ring adapters, compared with 23.7 million Ethernet adapters, were sold that year.[143] Ethernet's lead had increased from a ratio of 1.6:1 in 1989 to 6.2:1 in 1995.

The "tipping" resulted mostly from these two self-reinforcing processes, but a couple of additional developments contributed to the large absolute gap. First, in the early 1990s the installed base of corporate PCs exploded, reaching fifty million units in 1994, up from thirteen million in 1987. What was more, the percentage of PCs networked within corporations increased from 8 percent in early 1987 to roughly 60 percent in 1994.[144] This mass of networked corporate PCs meant that the market could "tip" in a way that a smaller market could not. Second, in the late 1980s and early 1990s many corporations began interconnecting the LANs proliferating through their workgroups and departments. Standardization now increasingly mattered, because conversion was quite costly in terms of gateways and throughput deterioration. Of course, the pressure for standardization favored market leader Ethernet.[145] In this sense, the LAN market eventually displayed the typical characteristics of network technologies—namely increasing rates of return and network effects—as described by the economic theory of standardization.

Market Structure, Firm Creation, and the Elimination of Network Bottlenecks

With Ethernet's victory over Token Ring in the early 1990s, the standardization battle in LANs finally came to an end after a decade of fierce competition. Superficially, the battle between Ethernet and Token Ring confirms the tenets of standardization theory: first-mover Ethernet prevailed over Token Ring despite its initial inferiority. Upon closer examination, however, two deviations between theory and actual outcome are revealed. First, Ethernet was unable to lock in its victory solely on the basis of its past momentum and larger installed base; instead, it had to secure that victory with tremendous technological improvements, including a radical change in topology, all the while maintaining its initial price advantage. In fact, if it had remained inferior technologically, it might well have lost the battle. Similarly, Token Ring's initial rapid market growth indicates that it did not lose because it was locked out by Ethernet's network effects, but because it failed to close the price gap while losing its initial technological edge. In other words, Ethernet secured its victory with traditional cost and performance advantages instead of reliance on network externalities.

Past momentum and network effects played a relatively negligible role in the outcome partly because many LANs initially remained "unconnected islands" and partly because the life cycle of the Ethernet standard was about to end in the mid-1980s. Without a central point of control and network management features, the original coaxial Ethernet standard was unable to provide an adequate migration path for the growing networks. As a result, users were increasingly willing to switch to Token Ring, which, having been designed as an enterprise LAN, was better suited for expanding networks. To defend its market lead, Ethernet was forced to overcome its technological handicaps. As Ethernet caught up with Token Ring, in a second deviation from the theory, it did not remain an inferior lock-in, but eventually surpassed Token Ring technologically.

Whereas users based their adoption decisions mainly on Ethernet's price advantage, on a more profound level, Ethernet's victory and Token Ring's defeat originated primarily from a striking divergence in community building. As we have seen, the two hundred Ethernet vendors in 1987 were matched by only one or two dozen for Token Ring—of which many were also leading Ethernet suppliers. In other words, Token Ring's introduction in 1986 did not trigger a firm-creation process similar to that resulting from Ethernet's commercialization in the early 1980s. To some extent, the disparity in communities originated from Token Ring's delayed commercialization and hence smaller market. But IBM clearly exacerbated the problem with its penchant for market dominance and manipulative behavior. Without vigorous competition and an ample IC supply, the battle between Token Ring and Ethernet became, to a large extent, a battle between IBM and the diverse Ethernet community, with its myriad specialized, independent start-up suppliers. Despite its gigantic size, IBM, like the proprietary LAN vendors, could not keep pace with the steep price reductions and the vast technical improvements of which the numerous Ethernet specialists were capable. By the time IBM launched an innovation, such as a router or a switch, the Ethernet specialists had already solved the corresponding problem in their own realm. In this sense, the battle between Ethernet and Token Ring confirms the thesis that a large supplier community with its diverse capability set tends to outcompete a single firm, even one as big as IBM—especially in a system technology with many components and potential bottlenecks that continually require new product innovations.

As the case of Token Ring shows, some minor disadvantages, such as technological inferiority or a short market delay, do not appear as severe handicaps in a standards race. Ethernet prevailed over its rival despite significant initial technological shortcomings, and Token Ring had a fair chance at the outset of the battle despite its delay in coming to market. What matters far more in standardization races is to have the "right" market conditions in place—that is, conditions that foster innovation, competition, and the formation of new firms. In LAN technology this meant, to a large extent, the pursuit of a community-friendly strategy based on open standards. As the case of Token Ring shows, de jure open-ness does not by itself meet this criterion, as such status does not automatically lead to a vibrant supplier community. Like Ethernet, IBM's Token Ring technology was backed by an open IEEE standard. But as we have seen, the quasi-proprietary strategy that IBM pursued in its LAN business prevented a vibrant technological community from growing up around the standard and eventually led to Token Ring's loss of market dominance. What is more important than formal status is that sponsors live up to the spirit of their commitment.

In fact, a community must be nurtured and constructed; it requires an unconditional commitment to full interoperability by its principal proponents, as well as an absence of monopolistic control and the opportunity for many firms to build a profitable business. DEC and Xerox, Ethernet's main sponsors within IEEE 802 in the early 1980s, pursued such a community-friendly strategy from the beginning. They were committed to the attraction of suppliers and did not intend to monopolize the Ethernet market. Both provided a market for start-ups; both purchased components from the fledgling companies; and both licensed their technology. As a result of their efforts to nurture a supplier community, both lost their leadership in the marketplace rather quickly. But because networking was not their core business, this outcome was not so grave.

IBM, in contrast, had a more "selfish" plan. From the outset, IBM intended to develop a lucrative Token Ring business and undermined the rise of a Token Ring community by controlling the chip supply and manipulating the interoperability of its products. Instead of nurturing a supplier community and winning the standardization race, IBM preferred to reap high profits, to control the market, and to avoid the commodification that plagued the Ethernet suppliers. Although this strategy was viable as long as Token Ring remained superior to Ethernet in large networks, from a standardization perspective it became an obstacle when Token Ring lost its technological edge. In this sense, the creation of open standards with the goal of nurturing a supplier base was the decisive factor in setting the "right" conditions in the battle for the LAN standard.

The lack of a community was a handicap because a diverse group of suppliers tends to have a larger capability set than an individual firm, even one as large as IBM. But it was also a handicap because of the very nature of LAN technology. In fact, LAN technology is not just a network technology in the sense that it interconnects remote users or user devices; it is also a network in that it consists of multiple discrete components that must operate in conjunction to make the system work. As we have seen, in LAN technology the system consists of adapters, routers, bridges, gateways, hubs, and switches. If the system is to perform efficiently, all the components of the system must operate in sync, that is, they must support relatively equal levels of performance (such as throughput rate). But quite often, and partly due to the bottom-up construction of networks, the components of the system do not operate in sync, thereby creating bottlenecks in parts of the network. Such unequal performance puts great strain on a single network sponsor, as it must continuously move from bottleneck to bottleneck to keep the system running. In contrast, a market structure that decentralizes the elimination of such bottlenecks to many firms is far more powerful, allowing several firms to work on such network bottlenecks simultaneously.

This characteristic of the LAN network was also behind the most salient historical patterns of the LAN industry: recurring waves of start-up formation and the emergence of new industrial leaders at points of technological discontinuity caused by the introduction of new network components. In fact, in an open system the continuous occurrence of network bottlenecks creates excellent opportunities for new firms to enter the market. As new components are frequently required to eliminate a bottleneck, the barriers to entry are temporarily lowered. This creates a relatively level playing field for start-ups with technologies or components capable of solving the bottleneck. If a start-up has some first-mover advantage and is able to execute strongly, it has a fair chance to become a new industry leader, for the overall size of the network and the inefficiency created by the bottleneck can propel its market growth tremendously.

This phenomenon first became apparent in the rise of SynOptics. The creation of the original coaxial Ethernet standard in 1980–81 had provided an economic space for a first wave of Ethernet start-ups, including 3Com, U-B, Interlan, Bridge Communications, and Excelan. As these firms occupied the new economic space, the barriers to entry increased considerably, with the consequence that the rate of start-up formation dropped in the period between 1983 and 1985. But the growing bottleneck centered on wiring structure and effective management of Ethernet networks created a technological discontinuity in the Ethernet system that generated a new economic space and temporarily lowered the barriers to entry, thereby creating an excellent entry point for the start-ups SynOptics and Cabletron. As the hub market took off, these start-ups grew with it and eventually became new industry leaders. In contrast to events in other industries, they did not replace the incumbent leaders, such as 3Com, but instead coexisted with them thanks to the many market segments the various LAN devices created.

This pattern of waves of firm creation at technological discontinuities was not confined to hubs but occurred on other occasions as well. As the networks grew, new components—such as bridges, routers, and switches—became necessary either to solve critical bottlenecks or to add new functionality to the networks. Like the hub, each of these components represented a technological discontinuity and created a business opportunity for start-ups. As in the case of SynOptics and hubs, small start-ups backed by venture capital quickly exploited these niches. Vitalink, for instance, occupied the remote bridge market; Cisco and Wellfleet, the market for multiprotocol routers; and Kalpana, Grand Junction, and a myriad of other start-ups, the switching business. As their components helped solve critical bottlenecks in the fast-growing LAN market, all these start-ups had the potential to become industry leaders. Some failed to grow with the market or were acquired by incumbent LAN firms, but others succeeded in defending their niches and went on to significant success. Cisco clearly epitomizes this model, but the rise of new leaders in the fiber optics market follows a similar pattern. This recurrent pattern of bottleneck creation, firm creation, and bottleneck elimination is clearly one of the reasons that the data networking industry has been so dynamic and so beneficial to Silicon Valley and its venture capitalists.

8 *Implications*

What theoretical lessons can be drawn from the story of Ethernet's rise to the status of market standard within the LAN industry? As we have seen, any answer to that question must begin with the importance of Ethernet's supplier community. Clearly, an array of factors contributed to the victory of Ethernet's proponents in the race for the LAN standard. Its standardization by the IEEE was followed by its adoption by most minicomputer manufacturers, by relatively early commercialization, and by vast technical improvements and relentless price reductions. Various weaknesses of its competitors also contributed to this outcome. All these factors influenced and reinforced each other in complex ways. For instance, without rapid technological improvements and a radical topology change that allowed Ethernet to accommodate rapidly growing networks, its constant price decreases would have been futile. Without its adoption by most minicomputer firms, Ethernet might not have attracted so many suppliers early on—an outcome that, in turn, would have undermined its progress and further adoption.

Yet in one way or another Ethernet's large supplier community was the reason most of these factors contributed to the success of the technology. A direct consequence of its high degree of openness and the deliberate strategy of the DIX group, and the underlying advantage that it enjoyed throughout its rise, its community was the most fundamental reason that Ethernet progressed so rapidly and users adopted it so extensively. The community's many specialists generated the steep price reductions, the large product variety, and the many technical improvements that made Ethernet the most versatile network of the late 1980s and early 1990s. The community's support also enabled Ethernet to move into several markets simultaneously while remaining unaffected by corporate path dependencies, thus avoiding fallout from the market shifts that plagued the proprietary LANs. Its vibrant community also made Ethernet's success independent of the success of individual vendors. When several early start-up suppliers vanished, Ethernet did not disappear, as did the proprietary LANs during the decline of their sponsors. In short, Ethernet's community was the underlying socioeconomic force that produced the many advantages necessary for its victory.

As the term "community" suggests, the various Ethernet suppliers were not merely a cluster of autonomous firms. Instead they interacted with each other and created various communal synergies. The sharing of a standard encouraged community members to collaborate on many occasions. Of course, this created new knowledge and advanced the technology, which, in turn, positively contributed to the success of its vendors. Aside from such direct interaction and collaboration, the Ethernet vendors benefited from each other indirectly. U-B's entry into the minicomputer market, for example, facilitated 3Com's penetration of the PC LAN market when corporations began linking their PCs and minis. And the second-wave Ethernet start-ups, SynOptics and Vitalink, built on the existing infrastructure laid out by the first wave, while their innovations fed back to all vendors. The Ethernet vendors also nurtured each other through various forms of division of labor and specialization. In several instances, they resold each others' products, and even more important, they relied on their peers to supply complementary products. Thanks to the standard, no single firm needed to offer the entire product range, because its customers could employ products from other specialists. Users, for instance, could purchase PC adapter cards from 3Com, communication servers from Bridge Communications, hubs from SynOptics, and remote bridges from Vitalink. In this sense, the Ethernet standard created a platform for interaction and communication and allowed for symbiotic relationships among its adherents.

Yet the Ethernet community did not act as a collusive entity, nor were relationships among its members entirely "cozy." Instead, Ethernet suppliers competed fiercely with each other. In fact, they competed to a far greater extent as they collaborated. Competition was spurred by various personal animosities among the entrepreneurs who founded the firms, but it grew so intense mainly because the open Ethernet environment failed to impose high costs on switching from one supplier to another, and it is such costs that often cushion proprietary vendors. Furthermore, the Ethernet community failed to ensure the success of all its vendors. By the late 1980s, four of its most important early start-up vendors— Interlan, Bridge Communications, U-B, and Excelan—had ceased to exist as independent firms. Interlan fell victim to the stiff competition of U-B and Bridge, while 3Com in turn swallowed Bridge in an acquisition.

Hence the Ethernet community was a double-edged sword for its members. Ethernet's success potentially benefited all vendors because it enlarged the market and cemented standardization success, but openness and intense competition exposed its adherents to constant competitive pressure and weeded out weaker firms. In this sense, all the firms assisted Ethernet in achieving success, but Ethernet's success failed to help all the firms committed to it.

The advantages Ethernet derived from its large, diversified community become most clearly visible when one compares its victory with the fate of its competitors. Without support from other specialists, the sponsors of the proprietary LANs had fewer possibilities for interaction and collaboration with other firms and were forced to develop and upgrade their entire product lines internally. Given the ever-increasing number of network components, this was an onerous burden, and one that led to reduced product variety and relatively smaller price declines. By the same token, each new market or technological discontinuity seriously imperiled the continued success of the proprietary LANs because strong corporate path dependencies prevented their sponsors from pursuing all possible markets and from reacting as swiftly as could the favorably prepositioned Ethernet specialists. Even IBM, with its gigantic capability set and extensive distribution networks, could not keep pace with the Ethernet community. Though IBM generated many product innovations—including a 16-Mbps Token Ring version, bridges, and switches—it typically lagged behind similar product innovations in the Ethernet realm. As a result, IBM failed to close the price gap while gradually falling behind technologically. Without a similar community, Ethernet's competitors simply could not keep pace with the leader.

Ethernet's community advantage did not originate only from its greater market success, thereby reflecting the natural outcome of a self-reinforcing process. Instead, it originated from the deliberate strategy of its proponents to build such a community, as well as from the market opportunities Ethernet provided. DEC and Xerox actively sought suppliers, since they depended on semiconductor firms for ICs and intended to outsource the manufacturing of many network components. Such reasoning led them to create an open standard, which in combination with DEC's built-in market created an attractive economic space for start-ups. Put differently, the Ethernet standard attracted so many start-ups because its openness and the DEC market allowed them to build a thriving business without any discriminatory threats, one of the fundamental requirements for a supplier community. Besides, many start-ups were established by individuals who had been involved in Ethernet's standardization within IEEE 802 or who were friends of those involved in the process. The early founders began as a tightly knit community of Ethernet insiders. In this sense, Robert Metcalfe, with his relentless lobbying efforts, was a critical catalyst in the initiation of the Ethernet community.

Neither IBM nor the proprietary LAN vendors undertook similar community-building efforts, nor were their LANs supported by a charismatic leader and a community of insiders. Though IBM adopted an open standard, its community strategy was more ambiguous. Not only did it implement many proprietary features in Token Ring that obscured interoperability, it also attempted to carve out a lucrative business for itself, not for the suppliers. Hence the Token Ring market was not as attractive for start-ups as the Ethernet market, despite their identical de jure openness. In the case of the proprietary LANs, many sponsors deliberately kept third-party suppliers out of their systems, although some tried to imitate the efforts of the DIX group by licensing their technologies and by encouraging the growth of supplier communities. Yet without de jure status they could not give the same assurance of nondiscrimination to suppliers as the DIX group. Ethernet's sponsors undertook the most community-friendly policies, and as a result Ethernet gained the broadest and deepest community support and prevailed in the standards battle.

Ethernet and Standardization Theory

Although generalizations derived from particular historical studies entail the risk of overstating their applicability to other situations, a few general implications of Ethernet's rise seem clear. First, standardization is a far more socially constructed process than standardization theory would suggest. In some senses, LAN standardization proceeded along the lines the theory would predict. When the DIX group succeeded in pushing Ethernet through IEEE 802, Ethernet gained a critical small advantage that led to a self-reinforcing process of ever-increasing adoption by users and manufacturers and continuous improvements and price reductions. As Ethernet pulled away and its contenders increasingly fell behind, the market "tipped."

Though this summary suggests that standardization theory is well able to explain the outcome, Ethernet's victory did not result only from such a mechanistic process; instead it depended on many social events usually neglected by standardization theory. In 1979–80, the DIX group and IEEE 802 spent almost two years negotiating Ethernet's openness and de jure status. Even after its standardization by the IEEE, Ethernet entrepreneurs still had to convince many skeptical venture capitalists to invest in their firms. In addition, the various manufacturers regularly convened within IEEE 802 to bargain over improvements. Only rarely does a firm succeed in setting a technological standard by itself; instead, in most cases, successful standardization means that firms must collaborate and agree on a technology in some form. And in order to make that technological standard dominant in the marketplace, they must also persuade customers to adopt their technology and entice suppliers to manufacture the necessary components. Standards do not just happen or result from a mechanistic "tipping" process; they are agreed upon in negotiations involving a large number of firms, entrepreneurs, institutions, and users.

Such social events did not underlie only LAN standardization; a careful reading of accounts of other standards battles reveals similar events. For instance, JVC, sponsor of the VHS standard, took pains to rally large manufacturers such as Matsushita around its technology. This, in turn, helped it to outrun Sony, which was slower to gather allies for its Beta system.[1] Similarly, IBM may not have explicitly negotiated with other firms when it created the PC standard, but by publishing the PC specifications and by allowing Microsoft and Intel to license the operating system and microprocessor of its microcomputer, it implicitly invited other firms to join its standard. The defeat of the OSI standard by TCP/IP supporters does not invalidate the claim that standards are socially constructed. It means only that the relatively small TCP/IP community acted far more swiftly in getting its technology adopted than the OSI community, which consisted mainly of large government and standardization bodies.

To say that standards in many technological fields and their corresponding markets are socially constructed is not to propose the radically constructivist view that such standards are solely social constructions. Ethernet's victory did not result merely from social negotiations, regardless of its price and technology parameters. Rather it evolved from market-mediated processes in which its price and technological advantages—as well as its openness and the social participations that its openness invited—played a critical role. Price and technological parameters greatly influenced the stance of its supporters.

Another clear implication of what we have seen in the LAN industry is that standardization theory may overstate the role of small events, randomness, and consumer expectations vis-à-vis the role of systematic forces in standardization. Various small events indeed played a significant role in the success of Ethernet technology. If Metcalfe had not promoted Ethernet so strongly in 1979–80, the DIX group might not have coalesced as rapidly as it did, and DEC, despite its experimentation with CSMA technology, might have joined IBM in supporting Token Ring, which initially was superior in some respects. Under this scenario Token Ring, not Ethernet, would likely have become the industry standard. In another example, if Zilog had not spun off so many start-ups, Ethernet might have lacked its broad entrepreneurial base, the core of its early community.

However, the outcome of LAN standardization to a large extent resulted from systematic forces, rather than random events. Despite Metcalfe's role in forging the DIX alliance and initiating the Ethernet community in 1979–80, CSMA/CD was not an obscure technology, but rather had amassed substantial support within the scientific and entrepreneurial communities. In fact, both DEC and H-P had experimented with CSMA/CD before joining the DIX group and IEEE 802. Besides, several start-ups, such as Corvus, Sytek, and Zilog, employed a proprietary version of it in their products. This meant that even without Metcalfe's efforts, latent support for CSMA/CD technology existed at the IEEE 802 meetings. Furthermore, once the IEEE and most minicomputer firms had adopted Ethernet, its continued rise was almost assured because of its support by an open community—also a systematic, not a random, advantage.

Conversely, Ethernet's competitors did not lose because of small events, but for systematic reasons and because they made the wrong strategic decisions. Some of the earliest LAN technologies were clearly inferior, and various proprietary LAN vendors, such as Datapoint, Corvus, and Sytek, opted quite consciously for a proprietary strategy—a vital strategic error in a market based on communication. Likewise, Token Ring's market introduction was not delayed for random reasons, but because IBM was willing to spend a few additional years at the IEEE to develop a "perfect" standard.

The power of systematic forces and strategic decisions is far greater than that of small, random events. If a random event and a systematic advantage are initiated within the same period, the latter is most likely to overpower the effects of the former. What is more, a systematic advantage may override the effects of a small event that occurred earlier but that has not yet been fully magnified. In this way, standardization must not be regarded as purely the result of random events, but instead as a playing field on which actors have ample space to initiate systematic advantages, thereby annihilating the effects of small, random events.

One might counter that the role of small events may have been underrepresented in the rise of Ethernet because of the small number of network externalities within the LAN industry, making it less "tippy" than other network industries. However, the standardization of PC technology and of videos shows that technologies with the most community-friendly policies and the greatest number of suppliers typically prevailed over technologies that lacked such assets, even when they were favored by some small events.

Standardization theory may also overstate the tendency for inferior technologies to become locked in by path dependencies. Ethernet did not decay to an inferior lock-in, but instead gradually improved and eventually surpassed Token Ring technologically. Several factors fostered Ethernet's continuous improvement.

From a technical point of view, the Ethernet standard proved mutable. While Ethernet's CSMA/CD mechanism remained its stable core, it was relatively simple to implement it on different cable types, to alter its topology, and to increase its speed. Ethernet also mutated quite smoothly because the institutional design of the IEEE was sufficiently flexible to standardize new variants of the original Ethernet standard. New Ethernet standards were simply added to the existing ones. But most important, rapid technological change—and thus the constant threat of obsolescence—forced the Ethernet community to improve its standard, especially since LANs did not create many network externalities early on. If Ethernet had remained rigid and thus had become increasingly obsolete, the costs of switching to a different technology would have greatly decreased. In this sense, Ethernet's various bottlenecks and large installed base created considerable incentives for innovations within the Ethernet community, as well as enormous profit opportunities for innovative firms and venture capital investors. Under conditions of rapid technological evolution, the costs of switching to a superior technology may quickly dwindle, permitting users to abandon an inferior standard.

However, this does not mean that we live in the best of possible worlds, as Liebowitz and Margolis claim in their paraphrase of Voltaire's Dr. Pangloss.[2] When Token Ring finally reached the market, users did not immediately abandon Ethernet, since Token Ring was not technologically superior by orders of magnitude. Switching and transaction costs might effectively shield a mildly inferior technology from being dislodged, but not a strikingly inferior one.

Finally, as the LAN case reveals, standardization theory needs to consider how community structures affect supply structures. Given rapidly changing markets and modular product systems, a single firm is unable to produce the same economies and innovations as a community comprising several innovating firms and manufacturers. An open community entails too many systematic advantages over less open communities to be ignored.

In short, the superior power of open communities implies that the creation of an open technological standard and the assembly of a large supplier community may well represent the best strategy for a firm attempting to establish its technology as the market standard, especially if its competitors are also considering such a move. If a firm insists on a proprietary standard, it risks being outflanked by competitors who opt for openness and thereby attract an open community. Despite the claim of standardization theory that open standards decrease a firm's profitability owing to increased competition and potential appropriability problems, this seems not to be the case. As the analysis of the LAN industry illustrates, open standards develop their own dynamic and can reward their sponsors with a market whose size is increased by orders of magnitude. And as the case of SynOptics shows, some nonstandard features added on top of the standard may nevertheless allow the sponsor to appropriate substantial profits. But, as IBM's floundering Token Ring strategy reveals, firms pursuing such a strategy must strike a careful balance between competition-stifling and competitively neutral value-added measures.

Policies and Prospects

The superior power of open communities under certain conditions has some potential policy implications, especially in light of the recent antitrust debate centered on Microsoft. It is possible that a de facto standard sponsored by a single firm may be assumed a priori to be inferior. Economic efficiency (in terms of prices, innovations, and product variety) could thus likely be improved if several independent innovators were to develop and upgrade a standard like the Windows operating system. But before declaring Microsoft inefficient and forcing it to release its source code, we need to know much more about the conditions under which the presumption of the superior power of open systems holds true, and especially under what conditions such standards increase innovation rates without causing balkanization. An operating system with millions of lines of code might exhibit far more technological indivisibilities and interrelatedness than LAN hardware (which, after all, was a relatively simple module) and might therefore be less prone to independent innovation. As the case of the Linux operating system indicates, however, an operating system can indeed thrive under such conditions.

Beyond these immediate public policy implications, the analysis of the creation and evolution of the LAN industry also provides important insights into recent fundamental developments characterizing the future prospects of the computer industry and the global economy as a whole. To begin with, the examination of the LAN industry sheds light on the recent rise of open systems.

Until the late 1970s, most standards in the computer industry were proprietary, as most computer manufacturers relied on vertically integrated systems to lock in their customers. But since the early 1980s, the computer market has increasingly shifted toward open standards. Though Sun Microsystems and the IBM PC drove this shift, the IEEE LAN standards were among the earliest open standards available to users and vendors. Not surprisingly, the shift toward openness began in communication technology. Most customers no longer tolerated proprietary solutions in this realm, since these aggravated their problem of making their incompatible computers share data and peripherals. Once a few vendors began to offer open solutions in one part of the system, the others quickly lost their prerogative of setting proprietary standards. New entrants such as Sun began using openness as a competitive weapon, with the result that users increasingly insisted on openness and now shy away from proprietary systems unless these present compelling advantages. LAN standardization by IEEE 802 was an important catalyst in the shift toward open standards.

Before the DIX group consciously attempted to build a technological community around an open technological standard, this strategy had rarely been employed. In fact, between the 1960s and the 1980s, IBM and the other computer vendors largely pursued a strategy of vertical integration, and IBM fiercely fought the manufacturers of plug-compatible mainframes. Though DEC, the leading minicomputer manufacturer in the 1970s, relied to a greater extent on outside suppliers, ultimately it too attempted to manufacture as many components in house as possible.[3] Today, however, the assembly of a community of engineers and suppliers around a technological standard has become a common tactic in standardization struggles. In 1996–97, when U.S. Robotics and Rockwell vied to set the standard for 56-kbps modems, both tried to sign up as many Internet service providers, computer and modem manufacturers, and vendors of remote access switches as possible.[4] The signing up of vendors can in part be a strategy to influence end users' expectations favorably by signaling that the firms that employ a particular technology will likely prevail in the standards race. But such a strategy is also aimed at generating and enlarging the necessary pool of capabilities and complementary assets necessary for winning the standards race. It is a community-based strategy.[5]

In another instance, while under severe attack from Microsoft, in late 1997 Netscape opened the source code of its previously proprietary browser Navigator.[6] This strategic move was completely at odds with the dictates of existing standardization theory. By opening Navigator's source code, Netscape gave away the crown jewel of one of its major products. Any firm could now copy Navigator and resell it under a different brand name. Netscape calculated, however, that an open-source strategy would enlarge the pool of software engineers and hackers working on and improving Navigator. Any software engineer or programmer connected to the Web could now debug Navigator's code and create new features that Netscape could then harness for its own browser products. By tapping into the collective knowledge and creativity pool of thousands of programmers scattered around the globe, Netscape expected it could boost its R&D capabilities by leaps and bounds, effectively turning the Internet into a virtual R&D lab. Its browser product would advance far more rapidly if both Netscape and non-Netscape programmers worked on it.[7] At the time of this writing, Netscape's strategy has not worked out very well; its browser has continued to lose market share to Microsoft's Internet Explorer. From today's perspective, the move came too late, and Microsoft's control of the PC market proved to be too strong. But by opening the source code, Netscape's management signaled that it intended to take advantage of a community-based strategy.

The most recent and perhaps most pronounced example of the power of a technological community, however, is Linux, a Unix-based operating system that, like Netscape's Navigator, is open-source code and competes directly with Microsoft's Windows NT/Windows 2000.

The story of Linux and its community began in 1991, when Linus Torvalds, a Finnish computer science student, could not afford his own Unix-based workstation and decided to develop a Unix-based operating system for a less expensive 386 PC. He posted the kernel of his experimental operating system on an Internet newsgroup for comments. A few others downloaded the program, modified it, and sent it back to Linus. What began as an individual project quickly began to take on a life of its own. An ever-increasing number of programmers and hackers scattered all around the globe and communicating with each other only through e-mail were drawn into the project. They all contributed new code to Linus's operating system, now dubbed Linux, which grew from its initial 10,000 lines of code to over 1.5 million lines.[8] It is estimated that by 1998 thousands of programmers had contributed code to Linux.

As we have seen, the early Ethernet adopters and entrepreneurs were a tightly knit community of like-minded individuals—mostly friends and acquaintances of Robert Metcalfe and Ralph Ungermann, and individuals involved in the early activities of the DIX group. They all were attempting to make Ethernet the standard and to grow their companies in the face of competition from the established computer manufacturers. But the Linux programmers created a community with an even more pronounced counterculture. Most of these programmers were not driven by money; they all worked voluntarily and without remuneration on the development of Linux, driven primarily by the personal satisfaction of writing code and the desire to impress peers with a good hack.[9] In fact, since Linux is open-source code, nobody owns the copyright to any of its code, including altered code, and the software is available on the Internet to anybody for free. No one can build a company on it in the way that Bill Gates did based on his proprietary MS-DOS and Windows. Although these structural forces prevent them from benefiting financially from their efforts, many members of the Linux community disdain the power, control, and greed they believe that Gates and Microsoft exemplify. Instead, they embrace what they view as far more egalitarian values, such as cooperation, technological progress, and the open sharing of new ideas and software. In this sense, they cherish values that characterized the early period of the personal computer revolution in the 1970s and that they see as having been betrayed by Gates, for example when he complained about the piracy of Microsoft's proprietary software in an open letter to the software community. Undermining Microsoft is not a declared goal of the Linux community, but Linux programmers definitely see themselves as part of a community that is challenging the status quo in the software industry.

The power that such a community can exert is also manifested in the way that Linux has frequently been adopted within organizations. As in effect a countercultural movement, Linux did not find much support from those in charge of MIS departments. It did not have an official vendor and thus (until start-up firms began offering it) did not have a support apparatus—or anyone to sue if things went wrong. But farther down the management hierarchy, network administrators, Web masters, and computer maintenance technicians—in short, the people who do the actual work—began installing Linux without the knowledge of those at the top. They did so because Linux is stable, free, and easy to modify, and because it has substantial grass-roots support from the Linux community—all significant advantages, especially for smaller organizations. In fact, the community often can offer better support than a designated vendor. A Linux user experiencing a problem can simply post a message in a Linux newsgroup or on a Linux bulletin board and expect to receive an answer within a few hours or days. It is not unusual for a Linux hacker somewhere in the world to write code to address that specific situation, and many Linux adopters within corporations also write code in their spare time. As an increasing number of networks and Web sites began relying on Linux, MIS departments gradually have accepted the software because it has become too valuable for them to abandon it.

Linux and its community have now gained significant momentum. Though Linux was a patchwork created by a loosely formed community of hackers, the collaborative efforts of thousands of programmers have made it a very powerful operating system. In fact, any modification or feature an individual or a group of hackers develops must now undergo peer review by others within the community, and only the best hacks are integrated into the operating system's kernel. As a result, Linux has become one of the best pieces of server software available, surpassing even Microsoft's NT in certain respects.[10] Linux's user base continues to expand; according to IDC, in 2000 Linux already had a market share of 27 percent in the server operating system market, compared with 41 percent for Microsoft.[11] Though the number of Linux desktop computers is still tiny when compared with Windows' total installed base, Linux undeniably has a strong grass-roots following, which could spread to the desktop as well.[12]

Even more important, Linux has begun attracting start-ups and gathering corporate support. Several start-ups—such as Red Hat, Caldera, and LinuxCare—have been formed, providing either documentation or service and support.[13] In 1998–99 even established computer and software vendors—including IBM, Intel, H-P, Netscape, Oracle, Informix, Corel, Compaq, and Dell—were drawn into the Linux community.[14] Of course, they support Linux because they intend to cater to one of the fastest-growing server segments, but they also perceive it as potential means to escape Microsoft's reign.[15] In fact, owing to its ready availability and the absence of any ownership rights, Linux frees its adopters from any proprietary levy (the so-called Microsoft tax) and theoretically allows all its vendors to build a thriving business. This prospect provides a far more egalitarian, fertile basis for a vendor community than the Microsoft world, in which Microsoft appropriates the biggest share of the profits.[16] Linux's more community-friendly approach could potentially allow it to draw in an ever-increasing number of vendors, thereby creating a self-reinforcing process and ultimately displacing the Microsoft standard.

It is still far too early to predict the ultimate effect of Linux on Microsoft, although Linux has already slowed the proliferation of Windows NT.[17] Whatever the final outcome, from today's perspective Linux appears to have real potential to undermine Microsoft's almost invincible hegemony and to boost competition and choice. If Linux continues to grow and even starts moving down into the desktop market, the Linux community may have far more serious effects on Microsoft's competitiveness than the antitrust efforts of the Justice Department.

One thing is clear. The significance of what can be learned about the role of technological communities formed around open standards extends well beyond the battle for the LAN standard. The community phenomenon and the power of open systems were among the most important phenomena in the social structure of technological innovations in the computer industry of the late 1990s. Though their promise for the future has not yet been entirely fulfilled, their influence on the future development of the computer and software industry is now better understood.

List of Interviews

Name	Title/role	Affiliation	Date(s) of interview(s)
Bayless, Jon	Venture capitalist, investor in Proteon	Sevin Rosen Ventures	3/17/1998
Bredt, Thomas	Venture capitalist, investor in SynOptics	Menlo Ventures	7/19/1995
Breyer, James	Venture capitalist	Accel Partners	3/22/1996
Brownstein, Neil	Venture capitalist, investor in Ungermann-Bass	Bessemer	4/8/1998
Burton, Craig	Senior Vice President	Novell	3/6/1995
			6/4/1996
			6/7/1996
Bux, Werner	Designer of Token Ring	IBM, Zurich	10/28/1998
Carano, Bandel	Venture capitalist	Oak Investment	10/9/1996
Charney, Howard	Founder	3Com, Grand Junction	7/14/1995
			7/16/1995
Cooper, Eric	Founder, CEO	Fore	12/10/1996
Crane, Ronald	Engineer	3Com	5/17/1995
			10/1/1996
D'Addio, Michael	Founder, CEO	Corvus	4/2/1996
			7/12/1996
Davidow, William	Venture capitalist	Mohr Davidow Ventures	3/8/1996
Davis, Wally	Venture capitalist, investor in 3Com	Mayfield	3/6/1998
Doll, Dixon	Venture capitalist	DMV, Accel	4/26/1995
			2/2/1996
Donnan, Robert	Chairman, IEEE 802.5	IBM	1/26/1996
Dougery, John	Venture capitalist, investor in Excelan		3/20/1998
Estrin, Estrin	Founder	Bridge Communications	4/24/1995
Farber, David	Inventor of Token Ring	UC Irvine	1/31/1997
Friend, Marc	Venture capitalist	U.S. Venture Partners	2/24/1995
Fuller, Samuel	Vice President, Chief Scientist	DEC	2/23/1996
Galin, Robert	Chairman, 1Base5 (Starlan)	Intel	6/5/1995
Gill-Robertson, Jennifer	Venture capitalist	Sevin Rosen Ventures	2/24/1995
Graube, Maris	Chairman, IEEE 802	Tektronix	10/5/1995
			2/9/1996
			2/4/1997

Name	Role	Company	Date
Hoel, Sonja	Venture capitalist	Menlo Ventures	2/14/1995
Kramlich, Richard	Venture capitalist, investor in 3Com	New Enterprise Associates	7/17/1995
Krause, William	CEO	3Com	6/9/1995
Liddle, David	Head, Systems Development Division	Xerox	6/21/1995
Loughry, Donald	Chairman, IEEE 802.3 (10 years) and IEEE 802 (6 years)	Hewlett-Packard	2/25/1996
Love, Robert	Designer of Token Ring	IBM	2/5/1996
Mahoney, David	Founder, CEO	Banyan	12/8/1995
Metcalfe, Robert	Founder, inventor of Ethernet	3Com	5/10/1996
			6/12/1996
Morgridge, John	CEO	Cisco	11/8/1995
Nikora, Leo	Systems Product Marketing	Microsoft	6/12/1996
			7/16/1996
Pliner, Michael	Founder	Sytek	7/3/1995
Rekhi, Kanwal	Founder	Excelan	6/15/1995
Rodgers, David	Ethernet Product Development	DEC	6/28/1995
Saal, Harry	Founder, CEO	Nestar	5/8/1995
Saltzer, Jerome	Professor	MIT	1/30/1997
Salwen, Howard	Founder, CEO	Proteon	7/5/1995
Schmidt, Jonathan	Vice President, Advanced Product Development	Datapoint	5/15/1995
Schmidt, Ronald	Founder, CTO	SynOptics	6/5/1995
Seifert, William	Founder	Interlan, Wellfleet, Agile	6/28/1995
Shustek, Leonard	Founder	Nestar	6/23/1999
Stephenson, Larry	Founder	Gateway Communications	6/19/1995
Swartz, James	Venture capitalist, investor in Ungermann-Bass	Accel Partners	6/22/1995
Thaler, Patricia	Chair, 10Base-T Group	Hewlett-Packard	6/20/1995
Ungermann, Ralph	Founder, CEO	Ungermann-Bass	4/26/1995
			4/28/1995
			12/14/1995
Valentine, Donald	Venture capitalist, investor in Cisco	Sequoia	6/26/1995
Verhalen, Andrew	Venture capitalist	Matrix	2/10/1995
Wythes, Paul	Venture capitalist	Sutter Hill Ventures	1/4/1995

APPENDIX B

Annual Sales and Revenues of Selected LAN Companies

	1976	1977	1978	1979	1980	1981	1982	1983
IBM (r)	16,304	18,133	21,076	22,863	33,043	33,199	41,890	45,937
Datapoint (r)	72	103	162	232	319	449	508	540
DEC (r)	736	1,059	1,437	1,804	2,368	3,198	3,881	4,272
Xerox (r)	4,210	5,190	6,018	6,996	8,197	8,691	8,459	8,606
Intel (r)	226	283	399	661	855	789	900	1,122
Wang (r)	97	134	198	322	543	856	1,159	1,538
Network Systems (r)	0.1	1.0	6.7	8.2	13.1	18.4	28.6	47.0
Nestar (s)[1,2]	—	—	n/a	0.3	0.8	2.3	4.3	6.2
Ungermann-Bass (r)	—	—	—	0.0	0.4	3.8	11.3	25.4
3Com (s)	—	—	—	—	0.0	0.1	1.7	4.7
Interlan (s)[5]	—	—	—	—	—	n/a	2.5	6.7
Bridge Communications (r)	—	—	—	—	—	—	0.0	3.2
Excelan (r)	—	—	—	—	—	—	0.0	0.5
Proteon (s)	n/a	n/a	n/a	n/a	n/a	n/a	n/a	1.8
Sytek (r)[9]	—	—	—	n/a	1.3	2.5	6.6	16.4
Corvus (s)[11]	—	—	—	—	2.2	10.3	2/26.8	6.1/47.7
Novell (s)	—	—	—	—	n/a	n/a	n/a	3.8
Gateway (r)	—	—	—	—	—	0.0	0.0	0.1
SynOptics (r)	—	—	—	—	—	—	—	—
Cabletron (s)	—	—	—	—	—	—	—	n/a
Chipcom (r)	—	—	—	—	—	—	—	n/a
Vitalink (s)	—	—	—	—	n/a	n/a	n/a	n/a
Cisco (s)	—	—	—	—	—	—	—	—
Wellfleet (r)	—	—	—	—	—	—	—	—
Fore (r)	—	—	—	—	—	—	—	—

SOURCES: Annual reports and Standard & Poor's reports.
NOTE: In millions of dollars for corresponding fiscal year. n/a, Not available; (r), revenues; (s), sales.

1984	1985	1986	1987	1988	1989	1990	1991	1992	1993
45,937	50,056	51,250	54,217	59,68	62,710	69,018	64,792	64,523	62,716
600	520	325	312	331	313	267	265	255	208
5,584	6,686	7,590	9,389	11,475	12,742	12,943	13,911	13,931	14,371
9,002	8,955	9,781	10,866	16,441	17,635	17,973	17,830	17,410	16,933
1,629	1,365	1,265	1,907	2,875	3,127	3,921	4,779	5,844	8,782
2,185	2,352	2,643	2,724	2,914	2,868	2,461	2,091	1,896	1,247
71.2	90.1	108.8	120.5	131.5	154.1	178.3	210.3	219.1	215.6
10.0	n/a	<10.0	[3]						
52.3	72.2	108.7	143.8	[4]					
16.7	46.3	94.0	155.9	251.9	385.9	419.1	398.6	423.8	617.2
18.0	14.0[6]								
13.4	30.5	46.2	[7]						
5.2	9.9	22.0	39.0	65.9	[8]				
5.4	n/a	19.4	22.3	40.6	52.7	73.9	94.7	120.3	103.4
30.6	70.4	91.0	60.0	n/a	[10]				
11.6/50.5	53.3	42.1	36.1	25.4	[12]				
17.4	45.2	96.9	182.8	281.2	421.9	497.5	640.1	933.4	1123
1.7	5.6	11.7	12.8	16.7	25.3	25.0	23.5	20.8	10.4
—	0.2	1.8	6.1	40.1	77.3	176.0	248.3	388.8	
n/a	n/a	3.9	9.5	24.9	54.8	104.7	180.5	290.5	418.2
n/a	n/a	2.8	6.9	9.8	17.1	28.4	48.0	87.3	
n/a	3.5	10.1	18.5	37.4	57.2	66.8	[13]		
—	n/a	n/a	1.5	5.5	27.7	69.8	183.2	339.6	649
—	—	n/a	n/a	0.3	2.9	10.2	35.9	85.1	180.1
—	—	—	—	—	—	0.0	0.0	0.2	4.9

Notes

INTRODUCTION

1. Saltzer 1997.
2. Sirbu and Hughes 1986:5; Bell 1995.
3. Bell 1988.
4. The VAX computers were to range from microcomputers to mainframes, although minicomputers, long DEC's strong suit, would remain the primary constituent of the line (Bell 1988:18f, 43ff).
5. *Datamation* 1982:102; Sirbu and Hughes 1986:4.
6. Barney 1983; Sirbu and Hughes 1986.
7. Sirbu and Hughes 1986:5.
8. Liddle 1995.
9. Barney 1983:113; Metcalfe 1991.
10. Sytek 1984:29; Metcalfe 1991.
11. *Data Channels* 1981a; 3Com 1984:5; Charney 1995.
12. Ungermann-Bass 1983a:3; Ungermann 1995.
13. Ungermann had worked on data communications projects at Collins Radio in Cedar Rapids, Iowa, in the mid-1960s, whereas Bass had experience with the ALOHANET (*Network World* 1988a:29; Ungermann 1995).
14. Ungermann-Bass 1979.
15. Ungermann 1995.
16. Ibid.
17. Like Metcalfe and Ungermann, in the summer of 1979 Pliner established his own start-up, Sytek. Whereas 3Com and U-B adopted Ethernet, Sytek developed a proprietary LAN technology (see chapter 6).
18. Corvus 1982:9; D'Addio 1996. Corvus did not manufacture its own disk drives but purchased them from IMI; it then added intelligent controllers, software, and other firmware. The chief designer of these value-added components was Mark Hahn of H-P, whom D'Addio had hired as the company's chief technologist (Greitzer 1981:12; D'Addio 1996).
19. Lettieri 1981:23; Corvus 1982:15.

20. Cashien 1982; D'Addio 1996.
21. Lettieri 1981:23; Saal 1995; D'Addio 1996.
22. Corvus 1982:10.
23. Metcalfe 1992a; D'Addio 1996.
24. Corvus 1982:15.
25. Corvus 1986:6.
26. Katz and Shapiro 1985:424ff, 1994:93ff.
27. Shapiro and Varian 1999:183.
28. Katz and Shapiro 1986:822.
29. Katz and Shapiro 1985:424. For a critical analysis of indirect network externalities see Liebowitz and Margolis (1994, 1995a), who argue that indirect network externalities are peculiar network externalities and do not constitute market failure. As Ronald Coase (1960) pointed out long ago, however, externalities can cause market failure. Such a failure arises when "consumers do not consider the effects on others when they adopt a new technology" (Gilbert 1992:5). For instance, since new users are not directly rewarded for the social benefits their adoption renders to incumbent users, some may forgo adoption, leading to inefficient underutilization of the network. Similarly, consumers who join a new network do not bear the full costs of leaving users of existing networks "stranded," thus causing inefficient overutilization of the newcomer technology (Farrell and Saloner 1987:10f). This suggests that networks may not be of the optimal size. Without policy intervention, networks may be too large or too small.

Furthermore, network externalities give rise to a severe coordination problem. Let us assume that (1) a novel network technology emerges, (2) all users have to decide in the same period whether to adopt it, and (3) all users would be better off if they adopted it. Because the network benefit to an individual user depends on the other users' adoption, users must coordinate their actions. If preferences are well known, then all users will adopt the network. But if information about their eagerness for adoption is imperfect (for instance, when users cannot communicate their preferences), coordination becomes difficult. With incomplete information, a user is prone to wait for others to adopt first so she can avoid losing her investment if the other users do not follow her adoption. As all potential users delay adoption, the network never gets off the ground, even though its success would be socially beneficial. This coordination problem resulting from incomplete information especially plagues markets with many buyers and sellers, resulting in diffused decision making (Farrell and Saloner 1985, 1987:10f; Greenstein 1993a:38ff).

Adoption processes stretching over several periods further exacerbate the coordination problem. Lagged adoption means that early adopters bear overproportionate costs because initially they are deprived of the full network benefits, which arise only as the network grows. As a result, potential early adopters postpone or even forgo adoption, thus preventing the network from growing (Farrell and Saloner 1985, 1987:13ff). Farrell and Saloner (1987:13) termed this coordination problem a "penguin effect," referring to the fact that hungry penguins, eager to get into the water to hunt for fish, gather on the edge of ice floes and jostle others to try to get them to dive in first, to see whether a predator is lurking nearby. Of course, conventional goods whose value does not depend on other users' consumption do not pose such coordination problems.

Finally, the notion of network externalities means that the adoption of a network depends on its adopters' expectations. Since the value of a network derives from mutual adoption, an actor considering joining a network must form expectations about the final network size. Often these predictions become self-fulfilling. If most adopters expect a technology to become the dominant standard, they adopt it, thereby establishing that technology as standard (Katz and Shapiro 1985, 1994). Thus expected, rather than real, advantages may govern the adoption process. It is assumed that expectations indeed helped the IBM PC to get off to a flying start. IBM's reputation and the PC's openness simply made users and software developers believe that the IBM PC would succeed, even though from a technical point of view it was a rather unremarkable product (Metcalfe and Miles 1994; Cringely 1996:137f). As Ronald Crane of 3Com later said: "Everybody thought that [the IBM PC] would become significant. And because they all thought it was going to be significant, they all developed products for it. So, having the belief created the reality; that is, any product that everyone [supported] with hardware and software was by definition going to be a successful product. It just took the three magic letters, I-B-M, written on the front [of the machine] to get everybody to line up and say, 'Yep, I think this one is going to be a go'" (Crane 1995). Again, a conventional good does not give rise to such a phenomenon.

30. Arthur 1988, 1989.

31. Shapiro and Varian 1999:175.

32. According to Arthur (1988:590f), increasing rates of return arise not only from network externalities but also from learning by using, scale economies in production, and technological interrelatedness.

33. David 1985; Arthur 1988, 1989.

34. Arthur 1994. The decreasing or constant rates of return inherent in conventional goods prevent such self-reinforcing processes and hence "tipping."

35. Gabel 1991:27ff; Cusumano et al. 1992.

36. Katz and Shapiro 1994:106.

37. See also De Bijl and Goyal (1995) for the role of consumer heterogeneity in sustaining two networks.

38. David 1985; Arthur 1988, 1989; Grindley 1995, 9.

39. David and Greenstein 1990:6.

40. David 1985; Arthur 1988, 1989.

41. David 1985; David and Greenstein 1990:5.

42. Economists often cite as examples of lock-in the persistence of the QWERTY keyboard and the (initial) inferiority of the IBM PC as compared with Apple's systems (David 1985; David and Greenstein 1990:5). Although Liebowitz and Margolis (1990, 1995b) have debunked QWERTY's inferiority and proposed that an (intermediary) actor could earn rents by coordinating the migration to a superior standard, from a theoretical perspective the phenomenon of lock-in to an inferior standard appears a real possibility.

43. See Greenstein (1993b) and Gandal (1994) for a statistical corroboration of the incumbent's dvantage and network effects and Postrel (1990) for one based on historical accounts.

44. Carano 1995; Grove 1996:30ff.

45. Shapiro and Varian 1999.

46. Saloner 1990:137.

47. Besen and Farrell 1994:121. Although the literature is not conclusive, most analysts believe that price competition is less intense in a proprietary system than in an open system in which several vendors compete (Besen and Farrell 1994:121). For a contrasting view, see Matutes and Regibeau (1987, 1988) and Economides (1988). They argue that compatibility allows for the possibility of mixing and matching components from different vendors and therefore of building high-value, customized systems. This freedom increases the users' willingness to pay a premium (David and Greenstein 1990:16).

48. Grindley 1995:4ff.

49. Katz and Shapiro 1986; David and Greenstein 1990:13.

50. Besen and Farrell 1994:122ff; Grindley 1995:39ff.

51. Although sponsoring allows for strategic actions, sponsored standardization processes preserve many characteristics of their unsponsored counterparts. In fact, the network effects inherent in system technologies uphold the markets' "tippiness" and sensitivity to small events (David and Greenstein 1990:13; Besen and Farrell 1994:118). Besides, sponsoring does not mitigate the possibility of a victory by an inferior technology (Cusumano et al., 1992; Langlois 1992).

52. Gabel 1991:13f.

53. Curry and Kenney 1999.

54. Bresnahan and Chopra 1990:105ff; see also Metcalfe and Miles 1994: 249.

55. Gabel 1991:13f; Langlois and Robertson 1992.

56. Matutes and Regibeau 1987, 1988; Economides 1988.

57. David and Greenstein 1990:14–15.

58. Ibid.:15; Besen and Farrell 1994:126ff.

59. Besen and Saloner 1989, 178ff; Besen and Farrell 1994:121ff.

60. Besen and Farrell 1994:121.

61. Saloner 1990.

62. Cringely 1996:300ff; Grove 1996: 37–52; Moschella 1997:16f.

63. Garud and Kumaraswamy 1993. See Hall and Barry (1990) for a history of Sun Microsystems.

64. Gabel 1991:23ff.

65. Ibid.:26ff.

66. Gabel 1991; Langlois 1992.

67. Original contributions to the dominant-design theory go back to a handful of Harvard and MIT economists under the leadership of William Abernathy and James Utterback, who took an interest in the relationships between technological evolution and industry structure; see Abernathy and Utterback (1978) and Utterback and Abernathy (1975). In their view, tech-

nological innovation and industry structure evolve in two phases. The first, the so-called pre-dominant-design period, begins with the introduction of a radical technological innovation, a product such as the automobile or the minicomputer. Since the exact product design requirements are very often not clear at the outset, but must be determined through an evolutionary trial-and-error process, firms experiment with the new technology and produce many product variations. Hence the rate of product innovation is quite high during this first stage. In addition, since firms compete on the basis of frequent product innovation, not cost advantages, incumbency does not necessarily offer any particular competitive advantage. As a result, new firms can easily enter the market, and the industry remains fragmented, with a high rate of firms entering and exiting. The period prior to the emergence of a dominant design thus is a time of great product experimentation, flux, and industry fragmentation (Nelson 1994:53). Once the market has selected a dominant product design, however, thereby initiating the second (or dominant-design) period, fundamental changes in industry structure and innovation process take place. There is an industry shakeout, and those firms that do not adhere to the prevailing product specification vanish. Firms that can survive begin to compete on the basis of cost advantages, with the result that the innovation process shifts from product innovation to incremental process innovations. For instance, once Bell Laboratories and Texas Instruments had invented the transistor and the integrated circuit, respectively, the semiconductor industry spent a great deal of time and capital to improve the processes to produce these very components. Because achieving a cost advantage often requires high-volume, capital-intensive production methods, the market position of incumbent firms solidifies, and entry becomes increasingly difficult. Consequently, the industry structure becomes more concentrated, and the surviving firms tend to be large ones (Nelson 1994:53). In other words, the market selects a dominant design, and as a result the industry becomes concentrated in a few large firms that adhere to and continue to support it until a new, radical product innovation appears and renews the cycle.

Many scholars developing subsequent models have focused on the impact of technological discontinuities on firm success. Tushman and Anderson (1986), for instance, have developed a model that distinguishes between competence-destroying and competence-enhancing technological innovations. Competence-destroying innovations can undermine the ability of large, existing firms to compete, creating opportunities for new firms to enter the field, whereas competence-enhancing technological innovations can strengthen the market position of the incumbent leaders. And some innovations may not only enhance or destroy a firm's competence, but also conserve or disrupt its linkages to its customers. Even innovations that do not appear to modify the underlying technology of individual components and thus seem competitively benign can have a devastating effect on a firm, for innovations may change a product's architecture in very subtle ways, requiring new technological capabilities. Thus, in the seemingly innocuous shift from 5¼-inch to 3½-inch disks and disk drives, the once-dominant firms failed to recognize the changes in customer needs underlying these size modifications. Their shortsightedness gave rise to new industry leaders while causing the decline of the previously dominant disk manufacturer (Tushman and Anderson 1986; Abernathy and Clark 1985; Henderson and Clark 1990; Christensen 1992, 1993).

68. Suarez and Utterback 1995:421.

69. Gabel 1991; Cusumano et al. 1992; Langlois 1992; Grindley 1995.

70. Gabel 1991; Cusumano et al. 1992:77; Liebowitz and Margolis 1995b: 218.

71. Langlois 1992.

72. Cusumano et al. 1992.

73. For example, in July 1975 Sony refused to license Beta to Hitachi, insisting that it had not perfected Beta sufficiently (Cusumano et al. 1992:71).

74. Wade 1995, 1996. Various scholars, however—including Granovetter (1985), Tushman and Rosenkopf (1992), Kenney and Florida (1993), and Rosenkopf and Tushman (1994)—have noted that technological evolution is embedded within a social or organizational context.

CHAPTER 1 • TECHNOLOGICAL COMMUNITIES AND OPEN STANDARDS

1. Crane 1995.

2. Porac 1994:412.

3. Von Hippel 1988.

4. Such as Wade (1995, 1996).

5. For instance, von Hippel (1988).

6. See, for example, Hughes (1983, 1987) and Pinch and Bijker (1987).

7. Saxenian 1994.

8. Lundvall 1992; Nelson 1993.

9. Constant 1987.

10. Lynn et al. 1996.

11. Wade 1995:112.

12. See, for example, the contributions in Montgomery (1995) and Foss and Knudsen (1996).

13. Richardson 1972:888.

14. Arguably, the paper by Wernerfelt (1984) had the most critical impact on the emergence of the capability approach in strategic management. Wernerfelt has claimed that a firm derives its strategic advantage (that is, consistently high returns over a long period) from what he calls firm-internal resources. Wernerfelt defines resources as both tangible and intangible assets, such as brand names, in-house technological knowledge, skilled personnel, machinery, or particular organizational and managerial procedures (Wernerfelt 1984: 172). Hence, Wernerfelt shares with Penrose the belief that firms must build their competitive advantage in a painstaking process. But he differs from Penrose in considering a much broader set of resources to confer economic advantages. His approach is now known as the "resource-based" view of the firm.

Wernerfelt's notion that firm-internal resources could deliver a strategic advantage does not appear to be a revolutionary insight, but it certainly was at odds with the dominant paradigm in strategic management in the 1980s, the "competitive forces approach." Based on the works of Michael Porter (1980) and on the structure-conduct-performance paradigm of industrial organization, the competitive forces approach argues that the profit potential of firms primarily originates from the competitive structure of the industry in which the firm competes. According to this paradigm, profitability depends on the following factors: (1) entry barriers, (2) threat of substitution, (3) bargaining power of buyers and suppliers, and (4) rivalry among industry incumbents (Teece et al. 1997:511). In this framework, a firm earns profits primarily by impeding or evading the industry's competitive forces, which tend to erode profits. Wernerfelt's resource-based view of the firm also clashed with the "strategic conflict" approach of strategic management, which emerged in the 1980s in the works of Dixit (1980), Schmalensee (1983), and Shapiro (1989) (Teece et al. 1997:511). Based on game-theoretical tools, this approach argues that a firm's competitive advantage arises from clever strategic maneuvers rather than from an increase in its long-term efficiency, as Wernerfelt and the capability theory claim.

In the early 1990s, several scholars of strategic management—such as Prahalad and Hamel (1990), Leonard-Barton (1992), and Teece et al. (1997)—adopted Wernerfelt's resource-based view of the firm but emphasized a somewhat different firm-internal factor in sustaining strategic advantage. Pioneering a paradigm known as the (core) competence or capability view of the firm, they argued that firms do not derive their competitive advantage from (superior) products or technologies. A competitive advantage results instead from the *underlying capabilities* or *competencies* to manufacture and innovate superior products at lower unit costs, as well as to adjust swiftly to changing market and technological conditions and to generate new capabilities. These competencies and capabilities, in turn, may lie in a firm's collective learning processes, bodies of knowledge, skills, and experiences; that is, they are embodied in the skills of employees, in a firm's collective technological know-how, and in its organizational and managerial processes. Consequently, competencies or capabilities are hard to identify, often intangible, nontradable, and knowledge-related; they must be built within the firm (Prahalad and Hamal 1990:81ff; Leonard-Barton 1992:112ff). In short, competencies and capabilities constitute the underlying foundation from which firms generate competitive products on a consistent basis.

15. Teece et al. 1997.

16. Ibid.:518ff.

17. Ibid.

18. For a more detailed discussion about the determinants of vertical integration, employing capabilities, production and transaction costs, see Langlois and Robertson (1995: 20–45).

19. Langlois 1992:13.

20. See also Kogut and Zanden 1992.

21. Foss 1996.

22. This definition does not take into account the many subtle differences among competencies, capabilities, and resources that the scholars of strategic

management have elaborated. The definition also subsumes all resources and competencies under the concept of "capability," not just those that are unique, as do many capability approaches in strategic management. This study refrains from incorporating only unique assets and skills (that is, those that render a strategic advantage) because this approach embodies the risk of becoming tautological. There is indeed an inherent risk to identifying competitive-advantage-rendering resources and competencies on the basis of an actually realized competitive advantage and then assuming that these competencies have created this competitive advantage. However, the study accepts the notion that capabilities must be unique in order to render a competitive advantage.

23. Gabel 1991:10ff; Borrus and Zysman 1997.
24. Ibid.:148.
25. Borrus and Zysman 1997.
26. David and Greenstein 1990:4; Gabel 1991:10ff.
27. To limit the scope of the analysis, I refrain from developing a community type for cases (B) and (D) in figure 1.1, since they are quite similar to (A) and (E), respectively.
28. Williamson 1985.
29. Von Hippel 1988.
30. Dorfman 1987:87ff.
31. Carlton and Hill 1997.
32. See, for example, Langlois and Robertson (1995:124ff) for various types of institutional forms.
33. Teece et al. 1997:528.
34. Dorfman 1987:103ff; Riffkin and Harrar 1988.
35. Cusumano et al. 1992.
36. Of course, this discussion goes back to Ronald Coase (1937). Other classical contributions are Schumpeter (1942), Chandler (1977, 1990), and Williamson (1985).
37. Chandler 1977.
38. Lazonick 1991.
39. Langlois and Robertson 1995. Whereas the first condition is often fulfilled at the beginning of an industry's life cycle, the reasoning behind the latter condition is more elaborate. Langlois and Robertson (1995:135) define an innovation as systematic "if change in one part of the system (one stage of production, for example) necessitates corresponding change in other parts." A systematic innovation may therefore make certain stages obsolete while requiring redirection of resources and renegotiations among resource owners in other stages.
40. In the sense of Williamson (1985).
41. Langlois and Robertson 1995:38f. As evidence, Langlois and Robertson cite Morris Silver (1984), who has suggested that Ford's development of mass production and the assembly line process made it difficult to communicate precise specifications to tool makers in advance, forcing Ford to integrate vertically to maintain sufficient flexibility (Langlois and Robertson 1995:53).
42. Langlois and Robertson 1992.
43. Nonaka and Takeuchi 1995.

44. Teece et al. 1997.

45. See Nelson (1991) for a discussion of firm heterogeneity.

46. Note here the incongruence of the argument in terms of firm and technology success. Whereas the well-positioned firms of the open community move the technology into the new direction, thus ensuring its continuous success, the community's ill-positioned firms may lack the necessary capabilities to make the transition and hence may perish like the sponsor of the sponsor community.

47. Langlois and Robertson 1995.

48. Gabel 1987.

49. Teece 1986. Assets are co-specialized if the exploitation of one asset depends on the use of other assets. For example, without its wide distribution network, Coca Cola would find it difficult to introduce a new variety of drink in the soft drink market.

50. For instance, if a small firm lacks the cospecialized asset of strong distribution channels, it will not able to benefit from its innovation.

51. Garud and Kumaraswamy 1993.

52. Cohen and Levinthal (1990) call these investments "absorptive capacity."

53. Gabel 1991:13ff.

54. Gabel 1991; Gomes 1998.

CHAPTER 2 • THE INVENTION OF THE LAN

1. Flamm 1988:46ff.

2. See Stern (1981:133), Augarten (1984:125), Moreau (1984:54), Flamm (1988:48), Smith (1989:295), and Eklund (1993:451) for the prices and sizes of particular mainframe models.

3. Braun and Macdonald 1982:99.

4. Juliussen and Petska-Juliussen 1994:317.

5. Flamm 1988.

6. Dorfman 1987:44ff.

7. Ibid.:53ff.

8. Dorfman 1987:53ff; Flamm 1988:80ff.

9. Dorfman 1987:110.

10. Riffkin and Harrar 1988:318; Langlois 1992:7.

11. Flamm 1988:128; Riffkin and Harrar 1988:318f.

12. Braun and Macdonald 1982.

13. Dorfman 1987.

14. Ibid.:103ff; Flamm 1988:127.

15. Dorfman 1987:61.

16. Ibid.:104ff.

17. Juliussen and Petska-Juliussen 1994:317. Note that the total installed base of connectable devices in both minicomputer and mainframe environments was considerably higher thanks to their use of terminals.

18. Dorfman 1987:107ff.

19. Among these firms were DEC, Data General, H-P, Prime Computer, Honeywell, Wang, and Tandem (Dorfman 1987:109ff).

20. Ibid.:109.
21. Braun and Macdonald 1982:88.
22. Freiberger and Swaine 2000:17ff.
23. The first microcomputer, the Altair, cost $379; the Apple II, between $1,000 and $3,000; and the original IBM PC, $2,880 (Chposky and Leonsis 1988:220; Langlois 1992:10; Cringely 1996:62).
24. Freiberger and Swaine 1984.
25. Ibid.; Langlois 1992:10ff.
26. Juliussen and Petska-Juliussen 1994:317.
27. Bell 1988:6ff, 7.
28. See Kenney (1992) for a history of Wang.
29. Saxenian 1994; Kenney and von Burg 1999.
30. Hellige 1994:52.
31. The first family of compatible mainframes was the IBM 360 system, introduced in 1964 (Flamm 1988:96ff).
32. Moreau 1984:77; Abbate 1994:43; O'Neill 1995:78.
33. Even with today's intercorporate links (for example, over the Internet), corporations pay considerable attention to the issue of firewalls.
34. According to Hellige (1994:52), the idea of making computers capable of communication so they could be networked came quite early. Even before the creation of the ENIAC computer some were thinking about data transfer. Also, a few network attempts occurred before SAGE. For example, in 1952, Teleregister Corporation developed the first flight reservation system, called "Magnetronic Reservisor," which linked all American Airlines offices in New York via telex lines to a central magnetic drum storage device (Hellige 1994: 52). Another early event was IBM's introduction of an off-line Data Transceiver in 1954 that allowed users to punch cards over telephone lines (Moreau 1984:128). Yet these earliest network attempts remained on a relatively small scale and had little impact on the further networking evolution.
35. Augarten 1984:196–205; Flamm 1988:53, 87f.
36. Flamm 1988:88.
37. Norberg and O'Neill 1996:73.
38. Augarten 1984:205ff; Moreau 1984:128.
39. Augarten 1984:204ff.
40. SABRE was actually designed by IBM, the main contractor for SAGE (Ibid.:208ff).
41. Augarten 1984:208f; Moreau 1984:125.
42. Flamm 1988:89.
43. This mode was called batch processing because the operator typically ran several programs in one batch in order to economize on expensive mainframe computing time.
44. This presented an especially big bottleneck in the debugging of programs (Corbato 1993:1376ff). See also Augarten (1984:254), Moreau (1984: 108ff), Hafner and Lyon (1996:25), and Norberg and O'Neill (1996:76).
45. Users, however, were often deprived of this illusion during peak hours, since a system shared up to its capacity tended to slow down noticeably. See

Flamm (1987:55), Abbate (1994:16ff), and Norberg and O'Neill (1996:74) for the development of time-sharing.

46. Kenney and von Burg 1999.

47. Corbato 1993:1377.

48. Farber 1997; Saltzer 1997. Phone lines typically supported transmission speeds of no more than 9.6 kilobits per second (kbps) (Mier 1984b:131). In other words, they operated at a transmission speed approximately a thousand times slower than the later Ethernet standard.

49. Abbate 1994:21; Norberg and O'Neill 1996:105; Brownstein 1998.

50. Hafner and Lyon 1996:160f.

51. Dorfman 1987:62f; Norberg and O'Neill 1996:109–18.

52. No exact figures for early network growth could be found. Note, however, that between 1958 and 1968 AT&T's annual sales of modems (a good proxy for network installations) soared from 1,000 to approximately 85,000 units (Abbate 1994:21).

53. Hafner and Lyon 1996:20ff.

54. O'Neill 1995:77; Norberg and O'Neill 1996:9ff.

55. Norberg and O'Neill 1996:157.

56. The principal proponent within ARPA for such a research community was J. C. R. Licklider, IPTO's first director (Norberg and O'Neill 1996).

57. Roberts 1988:151; Hart et al. 1992:670; Hafner and Lyon 1996:166, 228; Zakon 1999.

58. Kahn 1987:136.

59. Salus 1995; Hafner and Lyon 1996.

60. Packet switching was invented in 1962 by Paul Baran at the request of the Air Force, which sought a network architecture that could survive a nuclear strike. Although Baran's concept pleased the Air Force, political considerations within the defense complex prevented the realization of such a network in the mid-1960s (Abbate 1994:27). Thus packet switching remained untested before its implementation for the ARPANET (Kahn 1987:136; Hellige 1994:62; Norberg and O'Neill 1996:171).

61. If ARPA had connected the nodes by using the circuit-switching method, it would have paid for telephone lines that were idle most of the time (Abbate 1994:27). In fact, design studies by ARPA had shown that the costs of having a dedicated line between two nodes would have surpassed the expected cost savings from sharing computer resources among several research centers (Abbate 1994:23; O'Neill 1995:77). A telephone connection between Boston and Los Angeles, for instance, would have cost $30 per hour, while a computer hour cost only $10–$20 (Abbate 1994:22f).

62. Abbate 1994:45ff.

63. O'Neill 1995:78.

64. Sheldon 1994:678; Saltzer 2000.

65. Jerome Saltzer of MIT, an early LAN pioneer, recalled that as soon as MIT attached its second computer to the ARPANET (sometime around 1971), a majority of the packets coming out of either machine were headed for the other one. MIT soon had five machines on the ARPANET, and most

of the traffic was still local. In this sense, the ARPANET was clearly used as a LAN (Saltzer 2000).

66. Mayne 1986:251; Farber 1997.

67. A computer bus is a circuit over which electronic signals are transmitted to the various parts of the computer.

68. Farber 1997.

69. Dzubeck 1986:16; Mayne 1986:169ff; Stallings 1987:155f; Madron 1988:13.

70. Hutchinson 1988:115. In fact, token ring's proponents would argue that the technology's deterministic feature allowed it to transmit closer to its nominal rate than could Ethernet.

71. Farber 1975:45, 1997. Although David Farber is usually credited with the development of the first operational token ring LAN, loop technologies were commonly used for terminal networks. In addition, several researchers before him had explored loop and ring technologies for data networks. For instance, Farmer and Newhall (1969) of Bell Laboratories presented one of the first notions of a ring-based data communication network (Farber 1997). Though the concept contained some local loops, their loop network was primarily intended for communication over long distances using telephone lines. Hence it was not a pure LAN. Another early account of loop topology was that of Pierce (1972), also at Bell Laboratories. But, similar to Farmer and Newhall's concept, the so-called Pierce Ring was primarily intended for regional and national communication, although it did contain some local network elements. Since Bell Laboratories had no interest in local network technology, it did not pursue these concepts further (Hellige 1994:68; Hutchinson 1988:114), and therefore no pure, operational token ring LAN existed before Farber's UC Irvine Ring.

72. Farber 1975.

73. Farber 1972, 1997.

74. Needham and Herbert 1982:3.

75. Wilkes and Wheeler 1979.

76. Hopper 1978.

77. Stallings 1987:154.

78. Cooke 1988:66.

79. Stallings 1987:154.

80. Saltzer 1997.

81. Saltzer and Pogran 1979:179f; Saltzer et al. 1981. See Freiberger and Swaine (1984) for a description of the microcomputer revolution. In 1979 MIT anticipated taking delivery of a hundred desktop computers (Saltzer and Pogran 1979:188).

82. Saltzer and Pogran 1979:180ff.

83. Ibid.:184.

84. Ibid.:183. The notion of a wiring center and central switches was well known in the telephone industry. Because Saltzer, before developing a LAN, had experimented with central telephone switches and also used a star topology to connect terminals and computers, he was well prepared to deploy

this topology in his LAN (Saltzer 1997). Datapoint's ARCnet, introduced in 1977, also used a hub-based star topology (see chapter 3).

85. The idea of using central points of connection was born when Saltzer and Pogran experimented with their own Ethernet. In fact, in the mid-1970s Pogran had visited Metcalfe at PARC. Though he learned that PARC's Ethernet was effective, Pogran also discovered that maintenance of the network was already proving problematic. Indeed, some of the stories about tracking down problems in PARC's system were positively alarming. Therefore, when building an Ethernet at MIT, Pogran devised an arrangement that took advantage of the wiring closets on each floor. As a result, he was able to isolate each floor from the rest of MIT's Ethernet (Saltzer 2000). This idea evolved into the hub topology when Saltzer and Pogran built their token ring network.

86. Early researchers experimenting with token ring technology were responsible for variations not only in topologies and access methods, but also in devices and methods for connecting stations to the wire and for moving data from the computer to the wire. This additional dimension is not, however, considered here.

87. Smith and Alexander 1988:23ff.

88. Ibid.:33, 49.

89. Uttal 1978:88.

90. Smith and Alexander 1988:48; emphasis added.

91. See Smith (1977a–c) and Connell (1979) for a discussion of the "office of the future" from the perspective of the late 1970s.

92. As part of its effort to acquire computer technology, in 1969 Xerox bought Scientific Data Systems (SDS) for the then-exorbitant price of $900 million. SDS, however, served the engineering and scientific markets and lacked strong research facilities (Smith and Alexander 1988:33, 43, 49).

93. Smith and Alexander 1988:49.

94. Perry and Wallich 1985:62; Smith and Alexander 1988:50.

95. Pake 1985:54.

96. Smith and Alexander 1988:56.

97. See Kenney and von Burg (1999) for these institutions.

98. Taylor had been with IPTO between June 1966 and March 1969 and had been instrumental in initiating the design studies for the ARPANET (Norberg and O'Neill 1996:16, 159).

99. Perry and Wallich 1985:64; Thacker 1988:268.

100. PARC's time-sharing minicomputer system was called MAXC (for Multiple Access Xerox Computer) (Perry and Wallich 1985:64).

101. Wang, one of Xerox's stiffest competitors and a leader in OA, chose to base its office architecture on central time-sharing systems.

102. PARC used the term "personal computer" in a general way to circumscribe a single-user computer, "not distinguishing as we do today PCs from workstations, nor PCs from non-Wintel computers like Macintoshes" (Metcalfe 1994:83).

103. Thacker 1988:270. Intel had invented the first microprocessor in 1971, and many industry observers believed that the prices of ICs would

continue to fall dramatically. In a 1972 guest editorial in *Software—Practice and Experience,* Butler Lampson predicted that "within five years, it would be possible to build a system comparable to a 360/65 [IBM mainframe] in computing power for the manufacturing cost of perhaps $500" (Thacker 1988:271).

104. Smith and Alexander 1988:84f; Thacker 1988:270.

105. Lampson 1988:315ff.

106. J. Schmidt 1995.

107. Smith and Alexander 1988:93; Thacker 1988:274.

108. As these component costs would have translated into a retail price of $25,000 to $45,000 (in 1973 dollars), the Alto was really more of a workstation than a personal computer (Bell 1988). See Cringely (1996:83) for the lower estimate and Lampson (1988:296) and Metcalfe (1994:83) for the higher estimate.

109. Thacker 1988:282.

110. Pake 1985:56.

111. In the mid-1980s, Apple's laser printer, the LaserWriter, still cost approximately $7,000 (Cringely 1996:221).

112. Thacker 1988:282.

113. Though Harvard had rejected Metcalfe's dissertation on ARPANET's packet switching method just before he moved to PARC, he was well versed in network technology. At MIT he had "built ARPANET interface hardware and operating system software for a DEC PDP-10, connecting it to ARPANET's sixth IMP." In addition, Metcalfe was an ARPANET "facilitator," that is, "a roving technical expert for new ARPA sites wanting to join the network" (Metcalfe 1994:82).

114. Thacker 1988:274.

115. Metcalfe 1994:83.

116. Cringely 1996:84.

117. Metcalfe 1994:83.

118. This idea had been proposed by Charles Simonyi, whose network prototype was nicknamed SIGnet (Simonyi's Infinitely Glorious Network) (Metcalfe 1994:83).

119. Thacker 1988:274. According to Farber (1997), Metcalfe, while developing Ethernet, was aware of the UC Irvine Ring and could have adopted its technology. However, Metcalfe decided to try something different (http://thetech.org/revolutionaries/metcalfe/).

120. Metcalfe 1994:83.

121. The random delay was intended to prevent simultaneous retransmission.

122. Metcalfe and Boggs 1976:398; Metcalfe 1994:83ff.

123. Metcalfe 1994. Carrier sense refers to the fact that a node listens to the medium before transmitting. Multiple access means that as soon as the cable is found to be silent, any station connected to it can begin transmitting. Collision detection refers to the fact that the transmitting device continues to listen to the cable; if it detects a collision, it backs off immedi-

ately (Kolman 1988:89). Metcalfe liked to compare Ethernet's transmission mechanism to a cocktail-party conversation in which participants would immediately back off if they started talking at the same time. While developing PARC's network, Metcalfe drew inspiration from the ALOHANET, a packet-switching, radio-based WAN in Hawaii, which used a similar, though simplified, transmission method (Abbate 1994:96f; Metcalfe 1994:82).

124. In other words, they contended that Ethernet effectively transmitted at a far lower throughput rate than its nominal rate—in sharp contrast to token ring technology, whose deterministic nature allowed for a transmission speed close to its nominal rate (Brohm 1985; Suby 1986; Bard 1989; Glass 1989; Hunter 1989a).

125. Metcalfe 1994:87.

126. Metcalfe 1996c.

127. Ibid.

128. Saltzer 1997.

129. Thacker 1988:279.

130. The transceiver performed vital functions. It split messages from the computer into packets, transferred them to and from the cable, and scanned the cable for packets addressed to its computer. It also recovered data under less than ideal conditions, such as cable attenuation and impedance distortions, and isolated the station "from the buildup of dangerous voltages" (Metcalfe 1994:85).

131. Metcalfe 1994:84f.

132. Metcalfe and Boggs 1976:399.

133. Metcalfe was fond of saying that the round-off from 2.94 to 3 Mbps was larger than ARPANET's total speed of 50 kbps (Metcalfe 1994:85).

134. On December 13, 1977, on behalf of Xerox, Metcalfe, together with David Boggs, Charles Thacker, and Butler Lampson, was granted U.S. patent 4,063,220 for Ethernet (Metcalfe 1994:88).

135. Perry and Wallich 1985:67; Metcalfe 1994:84.

136. Metcalfe 1994:87.

137. Pake 1985:58.

138. Smith and Alexander 1988.

139. Metcalfe 1994:88.

140. In addition to Ethernet, PARC developed several high-level network protocols, including EEFTP, which kept track of transmitted packets and controlled the transfer of files between Altos. Metcalfe also developed a set of internetworking protocols that became known as PUP (PARC Universal Packet). Based on PUP—which originated from the Transmission Control Protocol/Internet Protocol (TCP/IP), the later Internet standard—PARC then developed XNS (the Xerox Network System), which became the de facto high-level protocol standard in the office market of the early 1980s (Metcalfe 1994).

141. Farber 1997.

142. Cooper 1996.

CHAPTER 3 • PIONEERS: THE BEGINNING OF COMMERCIALIZATION

1. See Comerford (1980), Frisch (1980), *Computer Decisions* (1981), and Klee and Verity (1982) for the amorphousness of, and users' confusion in, the new LAN market.

2. Freiberger and Swaine 1984.

3. Network Systems 1983a:14.

4. In 1970 5,700 mainframes and 6,060 minicomputers were sold; in 1975 6,700 mainframes and 26,990 minicomputers were shipped. In 1975 the mainframe market was worth $4.960 billion as compared with minicomputer shipments valued at $1.484 billion (Juliussen and Petska-Juliussen 1994:317).

5. Network Systems 1980:4f, 1983a:9.

6. The proprietariness also resulted from the rapid pace of technological progress, which made it difficult to adjust new models to achieve backward compatibility. See Saloner (1990) for a theoretical discussion of the vendors' proprietariness.

7. Network Systems 1983a:10f.

8. Between 1960 and 1977, annual unit shipments of mainframes had increased from 1,790 to only 8,900 (Juliussen and Petska-Juliussen 1994: 317).

9. Network Systems 1983a:9.

10. Network Systems 1983b:4.

11. Network Systems 1983a:6. Network Systems' principal customers were the data centers of large corporations, such as United Airlines, Chevron, and Union Bank of Switzerland (Network Systems 1980, 1982:4, 1983b:4).

12. Network Systems 1980:2, 1982:4, 1983a:6.

13. Network Systems 1983a:10. In 1980, Network Systems estimated that approximately 4,000 data centers worldwide had more than one mainframe. Yet to use its marketing resources most effectively, the company concentrated its efforts on only the top 1,500 data centers (Network Systems 1980:3).

14. Ungermann 1995.

15. Slater 1987:179f; Langlois 1992:9, 17ff. For instance, the TRS-80, Osborne I, and Kaypro computers all used Zilog's Z-80 processor, an improved but compatible version of Intel's 8080 microprocessor.

16. *Financial Times* 1977; LeBoss and Marshall 1981:97.

17. Ungermann 1995.

18. Faggin 1978.

19. Faggin 1978.

20. Estrin 1995.

21. Estrin and Carrico 1981.

22. *Business Week* 1979b.

23. Saal 1995.

24. Hafner and Lyon 1996:26. The leading microprocessors were quite powerful. According to Faggin (1978:29), "Zilog's Z8000 16-bit microproces-

sor had in many cases a higher throughput than [DEC's PDP-11/45 mini-computer], itself near the top of the minicomputer range."

25. Hard disks, for instance, remained prohibitively expensive for the low-cost microcomputers, which cost as little as $600 (the minimum price of a TRS-80) and $1,300 (the minimum price of an Apple II (Weyhrich 1991).

26. Saal 1995.

27. Saal 1995; Shustek 1999. Before joining Nestar, Leonard Shustek was a faculty member at Carnegie-Mellon University. Shustek regarded Jim Hindes and Nick Fortis as other co-founders of Nestar.

28. Saal 1995.

29. Nestar 1983:1.

30. See Wilson (1985) and Bygrave and Timmons (1992) for a discussion of venture capital investments.

31. Saal 1995.

32. Saal 1981:110; Cashien 1982.

33. Malone 1981:132ff; Cashien 1982.

34. Stritter and Shustek 1981:175; Saal 1995.

35. Cashien 1982; Saal 1995. Saal (1995) commented on Apple's disinterest in networks: "Some people at Apple were interested in Nestar to get Apple into the business world. Other individuals, the prime example [of whom] was Steve Jobs, did not want to go into that direction and viewed this as the wrong thing. They [the microcomputers] were called personal computers because they were personal. And he viewed anything which tied machines together [as something that] was going to lead to some kind of uniformity, some kind of central control, some kind of mainframe-like, IBM-dominated universe."

36. These numbers were provided by Leonard Shustek in 1995.

37. Estrin and Carrico 1981.

38. Estrin 1995; Ungermann 1995.

39. Rekhi 1995.

40. Ungermann 1995.

41. *Data Channels* 1983j:1.

42. The industry sales figure for 1984 includes data for DEC, Network Systems, Ungermann-Bass, Proteon, Nestar, Sytek, Corvus, Interlan, 3Com, Bridge.

43. Petrovsky 1988:9; Saal 1995.

44. Saal 1995.

45. Malone 1981:132ff; Cashien 1982; http://wwwhost.ots.utexas.edu/ethernet/enet-faqs/ethernet-faq.

46. Nestar 1983. See also Saal 1981:110, 1995; Stritter and Shustek 1981: 171; Cringely 1996:62. The price-performance comparison between Cluster/One and Ethernet reveals some general rules governing cost/performance relationships between computers and LANs. Generally the price structure of computers determines the price and thus the performance parameters of their associated LANs. The higher the price and performance of a computer, the higher the tolerable network costs. And the higher the tolerable network

costs, the higher the network's sophistication and performance. Conversely, the lower the price of a computer, the lower the tolerable network costs and thus the level of network performance. As the following sections show, these correlations made the barriers between the various LAN market segments quite impervious.

47. Saal 1995.

48. Ibid.

49. Ibid.

50. Ibid.

51. Saal 1981.

52. Burton 1995, 1996; Charney 1995.

53. Saal 1995.

54. Cashien 1982.

55. The trade press estimated that by 1985 approximately 30,000 Ethernet networks had been installed, and the proprietary LANs had a market share of approximately 20–40 percent (see chapter 6) (Goldstein 1985:60).

56. Saal 1995.

57. Nestar shared only OSI layers 1 and 2 with Datapoint's ARC system. Since Datapoint kept the higher-level protocols of the ARC system proprietary, Nestar's PLAN and Datapoint's ARC could share only the cable; they remained unable to communicate seamlessly with each other (Saal 1995).

58. Pearson et al. 1982:67ff.

59. Nestar 1983.

60. Saal 1995.

61. Network Systems 1980:2, 1983a:4, 1983b:8.

62. Network Systems 1980:3, 1983a:10f.

63. Among Network Systems' few competitors were Ungermann-Bass, Masstor, and Computer Network Technology, founded by Network Systems alumni (Gross 1984; Johnson 1984).

64. Johnson 1984:42.

65. The first public offering took place in November 1980 and netted $15 million; the second offering, in February 1981, raised another $1.7 million (Network Systems 1980:2).

66. Network Systems 1984:9; Shustek 1995.

67. Over distances of 2,000 feet, HYPERchannel's throughput deteriorated slightly (Network Systems 1980:3ff).

68. Mayne 1986:42.

69. Network Systems 1980:3ff.

70. Mayne 1986:42; Juliussen and Petska-Juliussen 1994:317; Cringely 1996:83.

71. My own computation on the basis of Juliussen and Petska-Juliussen (1994:317).

72. Gross 1984:40. When initially introduced, HYPERbus operated only at 6.3 Mbps (Network Systems 1981:5).

73. Network Systems 1981:5; Gross 1984:40.

74. Network Systems 1983a:8.

75. Saal 1995. In 1997, Network General was acquired by McAfee Associates, now called Network Associates.

76. Datapoint's original name was Computer Terminal Corporation (Wood 1994).

77. Since each incompatible computer system required its own terminal, it was not uncommon for individual computer users to have multiple terminals in their offices (Hafner and Lyon 1996:41).

78. Wood 1994; J. Schmidt 1995.

79. Datapoint 1978:24; Wood 1994:64; J. Schmidt 1995.

80. Datapoint's early development of an intelligent terminal suggests that the Texas-based firm competed at the forefront of the microcomputer revolution—although it is not usually credited with involvement in the invention of the microcomputer. In fact, neither Langlois (1992) nor Freiberger and Swaine (1984) mention Datapoint's intelligent terminal in their accounts of the commercialization of the microcomputer. Instead, they recognize the Altair as the first microcomputer. See Gardner (1976) and Rogers and Larsen (1984) for Datapoint's pioneering role.

81. J. Schmidt 1995.

82. Surden 1977; J. Schmidt 1995.

83. As chapter 4 explains, Xerox made a radical break from this business model when it opened Ethernet to the IEEE.

84. Because the term "network" had a negative connotation in the 1970s, Datapoint initially refrained from calling its LAN ARCnet (J. Schmidt 1995).

85. During the IEEE 802 standardization process, Ethernet's speed was upgraded to 10 Mbps (see chapter 4).

86. *Business Week* 1979b.

87. J. Schmidt 1995.

88. Peterson 1997.

89. The original ARCnet architecture allowed for up to ten (active) hubs (Murphy 1982:158ff; Shea 1983:33).

90. Murphy 1982:158ff; Shea 1983:33; J. Schmidt 1995.

91. Ibid. However, Ethernet's higher price resulted partly from its higher speed of 10 Mbps.

92. Chakravarty 1981:188; Davis 1982a:17.

93. Granovetter 1985; Garud and Jain 1995.

94. Saal 1995.

CHAPTER 4 • THE STANDARDIZATION OF LAN TECHNOLOGY

1. *Business Week* 1980.

2. Sirbu and Hughes 1986:4f; Bell 1995.

3. DEC was unaware of Jerome Saltzer and Kenneth Pogran's star-shaped token ring when selecting its LAN (Sirbu and Hughes 1986:5).

4. Sirbu and Hughes 1986:5; Rodgers 1995.

5. Sirbu and Hughes 1986:5.

6. Crane 1995; Galin 1995.

7. Crane 1995.

8. Sirbu and Hughes 1986:5. See Shoch et al. (1981) for the evolution of Ethernet between the late 1970s and 1981.

9. Metcalfe 1992a.

10. To attach nodes to the cable, Ethernet users actually had to put holes into the cable. (See chapter 7 for a detailed description of the process.)

11. *Data Channels* 1981i; Davis 1982a. The Star workstation was the commercial version of PARC's Alto and the linchpin of Xerox's product line for the office of the future.

12. Liddle 1995.

13. Price 1982:61; Liddle 1995.

14. Catalano 1985.

15. Liddle 1995.

16. Wilson 1987a:110.

17. Rodgers 1995.

18. Rodgers 1995.

19. The layering approach common in data communication makes the transmission of data on the wire completely independent from the higher-level protocols.

20. *Business Week* 1978.

21. As mentioned in chapter 2, in 1969 Xerox purchased Scientific Data Systems, a computer company targeting engineering and scientific customers (Smith and Alexander 1988:30f). SDS, however, quickly failed.

22. Batt 1981; Rodgers 1995.

23. Liddle 1995.

24. In the sense of Williamson (1985).

25. *Electronic News* 1980a:16.

26. Rodgers 1995; Fuller 1996.

27. Rodgers 1995.

28. Saxenian 1994:97; Rodgers 1995.

29. Rodgers 1995.

30. Williamson 1985.

31. Sirbu and Hughes 1986.

32. Loughry 1996.

33. McDermott 1976:76; Loughry 1996.

34. Sirbu and Hughes 1986:9; Graube 1995.

35. Graube 1995.

36. Stallings 1984:27; Sirbu and Hughes 1986:10. Sirbu and Hughes (1986:10) claim that IEEE 802 was initiated by the semiconductor firms, who were troubled by an increasing number of requests for custom VLSI chips for proprietary LANs. My research, however, has failed to substantiate their claim that the chip manufacturers approached the IEEE, which then contacted Graube. According to Graube (1997), he approached the IEEE on his own initiative. Likewise, Donald Loughry (1996) of H-P does not recall the semiconductor firms playing a major role in initiating IEEE 802.

37. According to Graube (1995), approximately twenty-five persons from AT&T alone attended the first meeting. Strictly speaking, the participants did not represent their employers in a legal way, since the IEEE confers mem-

bership on individuals, not companies. However, because the firms often
paid for the costs involved with attending the meetings, which took place all
over the United States, they clearly expected a return (Pitt 1987:20; Graube
1995).

38. Sirbu and Hughes 1986:7; Hellige 1994:67; Loughry 1996.

39. Loughry 1996.

40. Sirbu and Hughes 1986:20.

41. Bux 1998.

42. Love 1996. See, for example, Solomon (1979:101ff), Weil (1982:
278ff), and Fransman (1990:194f) for customers' frustration at being locked
in to IBM's mainframes. The importance of being able to operate in a multivendor environment became evident later with the rise of IBM PC clones.
While many customers used IBM Token Ring adapters to network their IBM
PCs, many users of PC clones employed non-IBM Token Ring adapter cards
(Love, 1996).

43. Sirbu and Hughes 1986:15f.

44. Love 1996.

45. Bux 1998.

46. Sirbu and Hughes 1986:10.

47. Graube 1995. As mentioned in chapter 2, the OSI Model divided the
entire communication process into seven layers or steps. LAN technology
occupied layers 1 and 2.

48. Stallings 1984:28.

49. Parker and Shapiro 1983:162.

50. Graube 1982:61f.

51. Crane 1995; Graube 1995.

52. *Electronic News* 1980b; Sirbu and Hughes 1986. According to Graube
(1995), DEC, Intel, and Xerox had not played leading roles in IEEE 802
before their announcement.

53. Xerox set the license fee for Ethernet at $1,000, a nominal fee intended
largely to cover administrative expenses (*Electronic News* 1980b:1; Hoard
1984:34; Liddle 1995).

54. *Electronic News* 1980a; Sirbu and Hughes 1986:11; Crane 1995.

55. *Data Channels* 1980a, 1980c. This Ethernet specification also became
known as Ethernet Version I (Mier 1984b:132; http://wwwhost.ots.utexas.edu/
ethernet/enet-faqs/ethernet-faq).

56. Saxton and Edwards 1981; Sirbu and Hughes 1986:7.

57. Sirbu and Hughes 1986:12.

58. Sirbu and Hughes 1986:12.

59. *Data Channels* 1980c; Sterry 1981:97; Sirbu and Hughes 1986:8, 13.

60. As the following discussion shows, there was a division within the
token faction. Whereas some vendors, primarily the vendors of factory
automation systems, preferred a token bus technology, others, especially
IBM, preferred a token ring. However, before these two factions split, they
stood united against Ethernet.

61. Sirbu and Hughes 1986.

62. Love 1996; Bux 1998.

63. Bux 1998.
64. Love 1996.
65. Bux 1981; Peden and Weaver 1988; Liddle 1995.
66. Sirbu and Hughes 1986; Bux 1998.
67. Saltzer 1997; Bux 1998.
68. Bux 1998. Unlike Saltzer and Pogran's token ring, IBM's had multiple hubs.
69. Love 1996; Bux 1998.
70. Glass 1989:365ff.
71. Bux 1981; Peden and Weaver 1988; Liddle 1995.
72. Potter 1985:321; Love 1996.
73. Love 1996. The token ring technology IBM was suggesting was to be more expensive specifically because of the more complex access method, the priority levels, and the hub device.
74. Love 1996.
75. Sirbu and Hughes 1986.
76. Goldstein 1985; Salwen 1995; Donnan 1996.
77. Valigra 1981:28f; Sirbu and Hughes 1986:13; Liddle 1995.
78. Rodgers 1995.
79. Bux 1998.
80. See Uttal (1978, 1981), *Business Week* (1979a, 1979b, 1979c, 1980, 1981), Cohen (1979), Blumenthal (1981), and Verity (1981) for the similar OA strategies of Wang, Datapoint, and Xerox. I have extensively analyzed Zilog in a previous chapter.
81. Third-ranked Lanier Business Products had sales of $192.5 million (*Datamation* 1982:117).
82. Metcalfe 1991.
83. Levy 1981; Lundquist 1981:31; McLellan 1981.
84. Liddle 1995. A baseband network is one that provides a single channel for communication across the wire. In contrast, in a broadband network the cable is virtually divided into several different channels, each with its own unique carrier frequency, allowing multiple communication sessions to take place simultaneously (http://wwwhost.ots.utexas.edu/ethernet/enet-faqs/ethernet-faq).
85. Graube 1995; Liddle 1995.
86. Wangnet became available only between mid-1981 and early 1982 (*Data Channels* 1981h; Liddle 1995).
87. Wang succeeded insofar as the intense debate about the relative merits of broadband and baseband LANs in the early 1980s created much confusion among LAN customers, thereby slowing down market growth (Bentley, 1983; *Computer Decisions*, 1982; Foley, 1984; Klee and Verity, 1982).
88. Wangnet never became a major force in the LAN market, partly because Wang's office system (to which it was coupled) never succeeded in the wake of the PC's ascendancy, and partly because the market preferred baseband to broadband LANs.
89. As mentioned in chapter 3, by 1981 Datapoint had installed over 2,000 ARCnets, whereas Xerox had installed a mere 35 Ethernets.

90. Graube 1995.

91. J. Schmidt 1995.

92. Graube 1995.

93. J. Schmidt 1995.

94. *Datamation* 1982:117.

95. Loughry 1996.

96. Graube 1995.

97. Saxton and Edwards 1981:101. In 1982, the following thirteen vendors supported Ethernet: Data General, DEC, Fujitsu America, H-P, Intel, Interlan, National Semiconductor, Siemens AG, Tektronix, 3Com, U-B, and Xerox (Hoard 1982b:1). Strong supporters of token passing were IBM, Honeywell, and Modicon (*Data Channels* 1980c).

98. *Data Channels* 1981b; Sirbu and Hughes 1986:13; Graube 1995, 1997.

99. As previously mentioned, given this book's focus on office LANs, the evolution of Token Bus is not considered further.

100. Metcalfe 1991.

101. Bresnahan and Chopra (1990) have argued that in the field of factory LANs Boeing and General Motors, as the two largest *end users,* had sufficient clout to enforce standardization single-handedly. Market concentration in the ubiquitous office market was, however, much smaller, and as a result no organization existed that could have forced IBM and DEC to reconcile their differences.

102. Saltzer 1997.

103. Fuller 1996.

104. Samuel Fuller 1996.

105. Datamation 1982:117.

106. Loughry 1996.

107. *Data Channels* 1982l; Liddle 1995; Loughry 1996. H-P's concerns were legitimate, as Ethernet was first commercialized by individuals who possessed considerable inside knowledge (see chapter 5).

108. Seifert 1991:315f.

109. Metcalfe 1991.

110. The DIX group's upgraded Ethernet specification also became known as Ethernet Version 2 (http://wwwhost.ots.utexas.edu/ethernet/enet-faqs/ethernet-faq).

111. *Data Channels* 1982a, 1982b, 1982l; Davis 1982a:17.

112. Metcalfe 1991.

113. Hoard 1984:32f; Metcalfe 1991.

114. Because the ECMA merely requires member firms to have manufacturing facilities in Europe, it included American corporations, such as DEC, Xerox, IBM, and Honeywell (Sirbu and Hughes 1986:16).

115. Hoard 1982b:9; Sirbu and Hughes 1986:16f.

116. Seifert 1991:321; Graube 1995. The DIX group's Ethernet specifications and the IEEE 802.3 Ethernet standard differed in the construction of the packet headers and in a sublayer called MAC (http://wwwhost.ots.utexas.edu/ethernet/enet-faqs/ethernet-faq).

117. Graube 1995. The IEEE Ethernet standard operated at a throughput rate of 10 Mbps; spanned 500 meters per unrepeated segment and a maximum distance of 2.5 kilometers (500 meters per segment); and allowed for 100 devices per unrepeated segment and a total of 1,024 nodes (Mier 1984b: 134; http://wwwhost.ots.utexas.edu/ethernet/enet-faqs/ethernet-faq).

118. Donnan 1996; Bux 1998. Token Ring's standardization also conflicted with the controversial patent rights claimed by Olof Soderblom (*Data Channels* 1982c; *Infosystems* 1983).

119. Bartik 1984:125; Love 1996.

120. However, several smaller players—especially H-P, Data General, and several start-ups—joined the DEC network.

121. Bresnahan and Greenstein 1992:13ff.

122. Fuller 1996. For instance, in 1980 DEC announced an SNA protocol emulator that allowed DEC's PDP-11 computers to emulate an IBM 3790 cluster controller, thereby communicating interactively with an IBM host (Saxton and Edwards 1980:83). In 1983, DEC introduced a PDP-11-based gateway for $27,000 to link DECnet-based PDP-11 and VAX-11 computers with IBM computers (Kar, 1981; *Data Channels* 1982f, 1983c; Davis 1982d).

123. Bux 1998.

CHAPTER 5 • THE FORMATION OF THE ETHERNET COMMUNITY

1. Nelson 1983:138.

2. 3Com 1984:5; Charney 1995; Crane 1995.

3. Bass et al. 1980; Ungermann-Bass 1984:7; Ungermann 1995.

4. See Bass et al. (1980) for a description of U-B's initial Net/One product.

5. Ungermann (1998) has said that he left Zilog in November 1978 and began looking for capital at about that time.

6. Brownstein 1998.

7. Ungermann 1995.

8. Brownstein 1998.

9. Ungermann 1995.

10. Swartz 1995.

11. *Electronic News* 1980c; Ungermann-Bass 1986b.

12. Hofmeister 1988:54. Interestingly, in 1983 U-B acquired Amdax (*Data Channels* 1983h; *Electronic Business* 1983b).

13. Ungermann 1995. See also *Electronic Business* (1983b) for U-B's lead. Among U-B's earliest Ethernet customers were H-P and Xerox. Xerox alone accounted for about 21 percent of U-B's sales in 1982 (*Data Channels* 1981g, 1982g; *Electronic Business* 1983a, 1983b).

14. Robert Metcalfe 1993b:50.

15. Charney 1995.

16. Metcalfe had spent his entire life in a university and research environment. The other founding members of the company's management team were similarly inexperienced. Howard Charney, a fraternity brother of Metcalfe's at MIT, was a patent attorney with an MIT undergraduate degree in mechanical engineering who had gained some high-tech experience while

working for disk drive firms in Silicon Valley. David Spiller, a neighbor of Metcalfe's, was a top administrator with San Mateo County, and Ken Morris was a business expert on China (Charney 1995).

17. Davis 1981a:52; Mier 1984b:136; Liddle 1995.

18. 3Com 1980.

19. Richman 1989:38. Metcalfe exacerbated the problem of attracting capital by initially refusing the offer price set by a group of West Coast venture capitalists. Whereas Metcalfe expected financing in the range of $20 per share because of 3Com's ongoing consulting business, the investors were unwilling to pay more than $13 per share (Wilson 1985). Attempting to break the hold of the Silicon Valley venture capitalists, Metcalfe turned to the Boston venture community and managed to elicit an offer of $21 per share. The Boston firm, however, never seemed willing or able to close the deal, and Metcalfe was eventually forced to return to the Silicon Valley venture community (Wilson 1985:177ff).

20. Wilson 1985; Charney 1995.

21. Kramlich reasoned that his involvement with Apple Computer had alerted him to "the logic of going from personal computer to network. Resource sharing was going to be the wave of the future" (Kramlich 1995). See also Kirsner (1998:234).

22. Kirsner 1998:234.

23. As part of the deal, William Krause, an experienced manager at H-P, joined the start-up. In June 1982, Krause became 3Com's CEO (Richman 1989:44).

24. Cortino 1981; *Data Channels* 1981a, 1981f; Davis 1981a; *Electronics* 1981; Crane 1995. DEC employed the Unibus and Q-bus in its popular PDP-11 and VAX minicomputers, among other machines.

25. *Data Channels* 1981a, 1981f. Metcalfe had built transceivers at Xerox PARC with David Boggs (see chapter 2).

26. Charney 1995; Metcalfe 1996a.

27. As mentioned in chapter 2, Xerox PARC first developed its own time-shared minicomputer system before it discarded this system in favor of personal workstations.

28. See chapter 3 for Nestar's difficulty in employing Ethernet for the Apple II.

29. During 1982, large end users—including Boeing, Control Data, RCA, and Texas Instruments, as well as several large universities—accounted for approximately 35 percent of U-B's revenues. OEMs and systems integrators—such as Fairchild Camera and Instrument, H-P, and Xerox—made up another 46 percent. Sales to Xerox alone accounted for about 21 percent of U-B's revenues in 1982 (*Electronic Business* 1983b).

30. Sytek addressed a market similar to that of U-B, but with a proprietary technology (see chapter 6).

31. Metcalfe 1996a.

32. Brinton 1981a:97; Davis 1981b:90; *Network World* 1988b; and Wellfleet 1991:27.

33. Bridge Communications 1985b:23ff.

34. Estrin had worked for Zilog from September 1976 to January 1981; Benhamou, from October 1977 to May 1981; and Carrico, Bridge Communications' CEO, from March 1979 to July 1981, responsible for the development and market introduction of Zilog's Z-Net. Estrin was employed at U-B in a product marketing position from February 1981 to June 1981 (Bridge Communications 1985a:23f).

35. Estrin 1995.

36. Ibid.

37. Excelan 1987:20; Rekhi 1995.

38. Additional early start-ups offering Ethernet products included TCL, started by Tat Lam, who had helped Metcalfe and Boggs to build the first Ethernet transceivers at PARC (see chapter 2); Gateway Communications, which was established in 1981 and which switched from a proprietary LAN to Ethernet; Technology Concepts, which developed software to connect Ethernet to DECnet and which was founded by Stuart Wecker and Michael Begun, who had both previously been architects of DECnet; and Communication Machinery, a supplier of Ethernet boards (Edwards 1982; Mier 1984a:46; Gateway Communications 1985:17; Metcalfe 1994:85; Stephenson 1995).

39. Severino 1984:277; Seifert 1995. Before starting Interlan, Severino had served as a vice president of engineering at Data Translation, a supplier of data acquisition and image processing products for personal computers. Prior to that, he had been a member of the original engineering staff of Prime Computer (Davis 1981b:90; Wellfleet 1991:26). Interlan's lead investor, Russell Planitzer of J. H. Whitney, had previously managed Prime's corporate marketing program (Brinton 1981a:100).

40. Estrin 1995.

41. Marshall 1981; *Computer Decisions* 1982; Estrin 1995.

42. Estrin 1995.

43. Rekhi 1995.

44. Hofmeister 1989:42.

45. *Data Channels* 1983e; Excelan 1987:25.

46. Estrin 1995; Dougery 1998.

47. Dougery 1998.

48. Davis 1982c:146; Hindin 1982:89; Rodgers 1995; Seifert 1995.

49. *Data Channels* 1982g; Thaler 1995; Loughery 1996.

50. *Data Channels* 1982h; Metcalfe 1992a.

51. Hindin 1982:89; Nelson 1983:138.

52. Nelson 1983:138. A fifth start-up established at that time (but one not mentioned in the press) was Excelan.

53. Brinton 1981a, 1981b; *Data Channels* 1981c; Davis 1981b; Severino 1984:283. Interlan shipped these boards mainly to OEM vendors, such as Calma (a vendor of CAD/CAM systems), Daisy Systems, and Convergent Technologies (*Data Channels* 1983f; Severino 1984:282; Seifert 1995).

54. *Data Channels* 1983g; Seifert 1995.

55. Davis 1981b; *Data Channels* 1983f.

56. Ungermann-Bass 1983b:13; emphasis added.
57. Ungermann-Bass 1984:7; Ungermann 1995.
58. *MIS Week* 1982; *Electronic News* 1984; Ungermann-Bass 1984:7.
59. U-B introduced its initial local and remote bridges in 1982, its base-band repeaters in 1983, and its PC adapters in 1984 (*Data Channels* 1983i; Ungermann-Bass 1984:7). A repeater is a device that amplifies and reshapes the waveform of the signal. It is commonly used to extend the distance of a LAN and to connect two network segments. Since a repeater does not look at the packets' addresses, unlike a bridge it cannot be used to reduce network traffic between two segments. A (local) bridge connects two (local) segments and transmits traffic between them, allowing users to extend the maximum distance of the network. Unlike a repeater, a bridge typically monitors the address of each packet and does not forward traffic across itself if the sending and receiving nodes are on the same segment; bridges were therefore often used to reduce network traffic (Derfler and Freed 1993:157; Sheldon 1994: 93ff; http://wwwhost.ots.utexas.edu/ethernet/enet-faqs/ethernet-faq).
60. Hyde 1985a; Kurita 1985; Ungermann 1995. In collaboration with Fujitsu of Japan, U-B also developed the first Ethernet chip, introduced in 1982 (Davis 1982b; Ungermann 1995).
61. The average general-purpose LAN built by Bridge Communications, one of U-B's competitors, encompassed about 200 nodes (Bridge Communications 1985b:4). The largest network that U-B had built by 1986 served more than 7,000 users (Ungermann-Bass 1986a:1).
62. U-B was not the only Ethernet firm to use nonstandard wire types. In late 1982, 3Com introduced an Ethernet version that used a different coaxial cable than that defined in the original IEEE specifications (see Chapter 5).
63. *Data Channels* 1982k; *MIS Week* 1982.
64. Ungermann-Bass 1984:2,7.
65. *MIS Week* 1982; *Data Channels* 1983a; Ungermann-Bass 1984:7; Ungermann 1995.
66. Bridge Communications 1985a:18f.
67. Whereas the communication servers primarily connected host computers to the network, the gateway servers allowed users to interconnect multiple LANs, either locally or over long distances. The network management servers enabled LAN administrators to monitor, configure, and control the network. Bridge Communications introduced its communication and gateway servers in November 1982 and its management server line in August 1984 (Bridge Communications 1985a:18f).
68. See, for example, Bridge Communications (1985a:17ff), *Data Channels* (1985d), Dix (1985b), and Greenstein (1985).
69. Hofmeister 1989:42.
70. Thanks to its gateway servers and initial vision of interconnecting LANs, Bridge gradually moved toward the internetworking market, a segment that Cisco eventually occupied (Greenstein 1985; Estrin 1995).
71. Rekhi 1995.
72. Mier 1984a:46.
73. Metcalfe 1996a.

74. Metcalfe 1992a.

75. Chposky and Leonsis 1988:220.

76. Since the IBM PC was one of the first microcomputers to use a sixteen-bit microprocessor, it also matched Ethernet's high speed more closely than did the Apple II (Crane 1995). D'Addio (1996), however, has pointed out that Ethernet's speed of 10 Mbps was, at least initially, overkill.

77. Birenbaum 1983:276.

78. Ibid.; Charney 1995.

79. 3Com collaborated with Seeq, an Intel spinoff, because the ICs of Intel, the DIX group's designated chip supplier, would not be ready until October 1982 (*Data Channels* 1982h; Metcalfe 1992a).

80. Before joining 3Com, Crane worked at Xerox PARC and was responsible for upgrading Experimental Ethernet to match the Blue Book specification. He joined 3Com immediately after the DIX group released the Blue Book in September 1980 (Crane 1995).

81. Birenbaum 1983:276; Metcalfe 1983:179; Crane 1995.

82. 3Com 1984:15.

83. Davis 1981a:52.

84. *Data Communications* 1984b; Sheldon 1994:338ff; Crane 1996. In the terminology of IEEE 802, Thicknet also became known as 10Base5 and Thinnet as 10Base2. The "10" stands for the signaling speed (10 megahertz) and "Base" for baseband; the last number indicates the maximum length of an unrepeated cable segment in hundreds of meters (http://wwwhost.ots.utexas.edu/ethernet/enet-faqs/ethernet-faq).

85. Sheldon 1994:338ff; Crane 1995, 1996.

86. 3Com 1985:1.

87. Like U-B, 3Com developed a comprehensive product line, but one mainly intended for PCs. It not only produced LAN hardware (PC adapter cards) but also developed file servers, network operating systems, and network applications like e-mail (3Com 1984; Metcalfe 1996a). In addition, 3Com introduced some Ethernet adapters for Sun workstations, although the workstation maker quickly implemented Ethernet on its own motherboards (Metcalfe 1992b).

88. Markels 1986:39. By October 1985, DEC had sold a total of 35,000 Ethernet connections (Lewis and Harris 1985:113).

89. Thaler 1995. Unfortunately no figures for their sales volumes could be found.

90. *Data Communications* 1984b; Jones 1985. The broadband IEEE Ethernet standard also became known as 10Broad36, and the fiber optic standard as 10BaseF (http://wwwhost.ots.utexas.edu/ethernet/enet-faqs/ethernet-faq).

91. Hindin 1982:89ff.

92. Bridge Communications 1985a:19.

93. Vitalink 1989:22.

94. Estrin 1995; R. Schmidt 1995.

95. 3Com became the dominant Ethernet supplier in the PC LAN market for several reasons. First, in contrast to 3Com, the other Ethernet start-ups

were late in recognizing the potential of the PC LAN market. Moreover, according to Howard Charney (1995), because of its collaboration with Seeq (from which it licensed the exclusive rights to the company's Ethernet chip for six months), 3Com knew all the idiosyncrasies of the chip, which had caused some difficulties for other vendors (Charney 1995). Finally, 3Com had excellent manufacturing facilities, allowing it to be very competitive on price (Metcalfe 1996a).

96. Wilson 1987a:110; Estrin 1995.
97. Severino 1984:277, 282.
98. Seifert 1995.
99. *Data Channels* 1985b; Estrin 1995; Seifert 1995.
100. Barney 1988:56; Hofmeister 1989:40.
101. Fisher 1988; Moad 1988:26.
102. *Wall Street Journal* 1989; Rekhi 1995.
103. Of course, the other vendors did not stop marketing products. U-B, for instance, operated autonomously within Tandem and continued to be an innovative Ethernet supplier (Ungermann 1995; see chapter 7).
104. Killorin 1987.
105. Many entrepreneurs and venture capitalists believed that the firms they were establishing would grow to annual revenues of \$30–\$50 million, a significant underestimation of the market.

CHAPTER 6 • THE RISE AND FALL OF ETHERNET'S
PROPRIETARY COMPETITORS

1. The CONSTELLATION network cost \$200 to \$300 per node and connected up to 64 microcomputers to a hard disk (Corvus 1981:15, 1982:5, 15).
2. Corvus 1982:9ff, 15.
3. Cashien 1982; D'Addio 1996.
4. Lettieri 1981:23; Saal 1995; D'Addio 1996.
5. Corvus 1982:10.
6. Hahn and Belanger 1981:126; Mier 1984b:140. See chapter 2 for a description of the CD function.
7. Williams 1981.
8. Corvus 1982:15; Mier 1984b:140.
9. Lettieri 1981:23.
10. Hahn and Beranger 1981:127.
11. Valovic 1987a:83; Salwen 1995. Proteon's original name was Proteon Associates, but on July 29, 1983, its name was changed (Proteon, 1991:5). By the late 1970s, the company had grown to thirty employees and served as a consultant for not only various corporations but also several government agencies, including NASA, the Department of Transportation, and the National Security Agency (Salwen 1995).
12. Salwen 1995.
13. Valovic 1987a:83.
14. Proteon 1991:4. Proteon's token ring was much simpler than the system IBM was developing (Salwen 1995), and it is proof that a (simpler) IEEE token ring standard could have been introduced concurrently with Ethernet.

15. Valovic 1987a.
16. *Data Channels* 1981d; Salwen 1995.
17. Salwen 1995. ProNet could connect up to 255 nodes (Valovic 1987a: 86).
18. Proteon received at least $2.4 million in venture capital in late 1983, followed by $6.5 million in a second round in March 1985. Its investors included Kleiner, Perkins, Caufield & Byers of Palo Alto; Sevin Rosen of Dallas; and Bayless Borovoy of Sunnyvale (*Data Communications* 1984a:101; *San Jose Mercury* 1985).
19. Sytek 1984:5f.
20. Sytek 1984:11.
21. Sytek 1984:10.
22. See chapter 5 for a definition of the general-purpose LAN market.
23. Pliner 1995. As mentioned in chapter 5, the Ethernet community eventually produced a broadband Ethernet version that extended Thicknet's distance. In 1980–81, when Sytek developed its LAN, this Ethernet version was not yet available.
24. Sytek 1984:11; Trifari 1982:33ff.
25. Pliner 1995.
26. Sytek 1984:2.
27. Pliner 1995. LocalNet had a predecessor. While at Ford Aerospace and Communications, at least one of Sytek's founders, Kenneth Biba, had co-developed a network, FordNet, that had characteristics similar to those of LocalNet, namely a CSMA/CD access method and broadband capability (Biba and Yeh 1979:199ff).
28. Pliner 1995.
29. Lavien 1981.
30. Sytek 1984; Salwen 1995.
31. Mead 1982:112.
32. Greitzer 1981.
33. Lavien 1981:65; Lettieri 1981:23; *Data Channels* 1982d; Corvus 1983.
34. *Data Channels* 1984a; D'Addio 1996.
35. D'Addio 1996.
36. Mier 1984b:132.
37. Pliner 1995 (in which quote appears); Mier 1984b:138.
38. *Data Channels* 1982j; Posner 1984. In 1982 GI had sales of $825 million (Mead 1982:110). Initially GI bought a 37 percent stake in Sytek, a share it increased in 1985 to 57 percent (Johnson 1982; Mead 1982; Posner 1984; *Data Channels* 1985g).
39. Mead 1982:110; Posner 1984:110.
40. Mead 1982:110ff.
41. Johnson 1982; Mead 1982:110; Posner 1984:109; Pliner 1995.
42. Berg 1984; Pliner 1995.
43. Berg 1984; Nee 1985.
44. Sytek 1984:16; *Data Channels* 1985e.
45. Berg 1984; Metcalfe 1996a (in which quote appears).
46. *Data Channels* 1985f.

47. Dix 1985a; *MIS Week* 1986.

48. *Data Channels* 1985f:5. In contrast to Token Ring, which transmitted at a speed of 4 Mbps and could connect up to 260 nodes (on UTP wire), the PC Network operated at 2 Mbps and connected up to 72 nodes (*Data Channels* 1985e).

49. Pliner 1995.

50. *Data Channels* 1982b; J. Schmidt 1995.

51. Chakravarty 1981; *Data Channels* 1981e; Manuel 1981:40f.

52. Chakravarty 1981; *Data Channels* 1981e; Miller 1983; Saal 1995; Ungermann 1995.

53. DiDio 1989a:25.

54. *Data Channels* 1984b.

55. In the late 1980s and early 1990s ARCnet even gained institutional support. In 1987, a user and vendor support group called the ARCnet Trade Association was formed, and in 1992 ARCnet even became an American National Standards Institute (ANSI) standard (Brown 1989; DiDio 1989a:25; Breidenbach 1990:19).

56. Corvus 1983:1, 1984.

57. 3Com 1985:1ff. Michael D'Addio, who left Corvus in 1985, today believes that Omninet had a total installed base of approximately 300,000 nodes prior to his departure. If that was the case, the original claims by Corvus would not have been exaggerated.

58. Sivula 1989:54. In 1985, when Novell began supporting ARCnet on NetWare, it sold over 300,000 ARCnet adapters within the first year. In 1988 the production of ARCnet chips jumped to 800,000 units per year (Stott 1998:7).

59. 3Com 1988:7.

60. Sivula 1989:54. In the late 1980s it was estimated that ARCnet controlled approximately 30 percent of the small business segment (Sivula 1989:54).

61. Sytek 1984:3.

62. Hyde 1985b:88. To compare the installed base of U-B and Sytek, note that U-B's fiscal 1984 ended in December whereas that of Sytek ended in May.

63. Kerr 1987a:30.

64. Salwen 1995.

65. DiDio 1989a; Sivula 1989:54; Karlin 1990; Doyle 1994. By 1998, over seven million ARCnet chips had been produced (Stott 1998:7).

66. *Info Canada* 1993; Doyle 1994.

67. Christensen 1993:546. The integration of hard disks into PCs occurred during 1983–84. One of the first PCs to include an internal hard disk was the IBM PC XT, introduced in March 1983 (Patterson 1997; Chposky and Leonsis 1988:220).

68. Burton 1996; D'Addio 1996. Initially, Novell's core business was microcomputers, with LANs as a by-product. In the early to mid-1980s, when the company almost went bankrupt, in a brilliant strategic move it decided to abandon its computer hardware business altogether and focus

on network software, mainly NOSs. As a pure network software vendor, Novell had no disincentive to support all vendors' LAN hardware (Burton 1996).

69. D'Addio 1996. Omninet's accumulated installed base in the educational market failed to generate any network externalities, which might have assisted Corvus in extending its dominance from the Apple II market to the PC market. Network effects remained absent because Apple's educational market and the PC's corporate market were completely separate and because Omninet's main application, disk sharing, created only "unconnected islands"—smaller networks not connected to one another.

70. Metcalfe 1992a. Whereas the Apple II cost approximately $1,000–$2,000, the original IBM PC sold for $2,880, the PC XT for $4,995, and the PC AT for $5,795. The PC included an Intel 8088 microprocessor, 64K of memory, and a 160K floppy disk drive. The XT, introduced in March 1983, included an Intel 8088 microprocessor, 128K of memory, a 360K floppy disk drive, and a 10-megabyte hard disk. Finally, the AT, introduced in August 1984, included an Intel 80286 microprocessor, 512K of memory, a 1.2-megabyte floppy disk drive, and a 20-megabyte hard disk (Chposky and Leonsis 1988:220f).

71. Beaver 1986.

72. D'Addio 1996.

73. Hoard 1982a; Klee and Verity 1982:115ff; Parker and Shapiro 1983: 159; Pliner 1995.

74. Dooley 1982; J. Schmidt 1995. Between February and May 1982, Datapoint's stock price dropped from $50 to $12, and five executives were forced out in the midst of charges of illegal insider trading (*Data Channels* 1982m).

75. Stott 1998.

76. Salwen 1995.

77. *Data Channels* 1986a; Watt 1986. Underscoring IBM's lack of commitment to the PC Network was its decision to artificially limit its performance. By late 1985, IBM had sold only between 1,000 and 1,200 PC Networks or approximately 10,000 adapter cards, a mere 7 percent of what Sytek had delivered to IBM (Dix 1985a:22).

78. *Data Channels* 1986c.

79. D'Addio 1996.

80. Greenfield 1989a; Sivula 1989:53; Karlin 1990. In May 1989, a list of manufacturers of ARCnet adapter cards included twenty-six firms (Greenfield 1989a).

81. Cross 1988; Brown 1989; Breidenbach 1990:19f.

82. DiDio 1989a:25.

83. Salwen 1995.

84. Kerr 1987a:30.

85. Ungermann 1998.

86. *Data Channels* 1983b, 1984a, 1985a, 1985c; *Computerworld* 1984b: 83; Corvus 1984:8; Burke 1985; D'Addio 1996.

87. Valovic 1987a; Salwen 1995. FDDI is a network standard for fiber optic cable developed by the ANSI X3T9.5 committee (Sheldon 1994:358).

88. Salwen 1995.

89. J. Schmidt 1995. In the late 1980s, ARCnet's speed was increased from 2.5 Mbps to 20 Mbps (Sivula 1989:53). Though this speed exceeded Ethernet's transmission rate, the improvement came too late to reverse ARCnet's decline.

90. *Computerworld* 1984a. Employing Motorola's 68000 32-bit microprocessor, the Concept computer used a proprietary operating system, though it supported CP/M-based programs. It cost $4,995 and was targeted at medium-size and Fortune 1000 companies (*Computer Business News* 1982; *Electronic News* 1982; *Wall Street Journal* 1982).

91. D'Addio 2000.

92. *Data Communications* 1988. As early as 1986, Corvus had to lay off 20 percent of its employees (Petrovsky 1986).

93. Kerr 1987a:30.

94. *Data Communications* 1989a.

95. Salwen 1997.

CHAPTER 7 • THE BATTLE BETWEEN ETHERNET AND TOKEN RING

1. Several other vendors developed Token Ring products as well, but IBM was the principal Token Ring vendor.

2. Goldstein 1985:60. The 417,200 Ethernet nodes include the accumulated shipment of adapters by 3Com (100,000 nodes by 1985), as well as the 1985 shipments by DEC (173,000 nodes), U-B (70,300 nodes), Bridge Communications (49,600 nodes), Interlan (16,800 nodes), and Excelan (7,500 nodes) (3Com 1985; Markels 1986, 31). Because the 417,200 shipped nodes do not include the pre-1985 installations of DEC, U-B, Bridge, Interlan, and Excelan, as well as the shipments of any other vendors, Ethernet's total installed base was probably significantly higher.

3. Killorin 1987. The figure of $511.5 million includes the combined accumulated revenues of 3Com, U-B, Bridge, Interlan, and Excelan, as well as DEC's LAN hardware sales in 1984 and 1985 (Markels 1986:39).

4. Salwen and Marshall 1990:42.

5. Bredt 1995; Love 1996.

6. Bredt 1995.

7. http://wwwhost.ots.utexas.edu/ethernet/enet-faqs/ethernet-faq.

8. Bredt 1995.

9. It was estimated that moving a station on Thick Ethernet—a frequent need in an office environment—could cost between $500 and $1,000 (Kerr 1987b:34).

10. Crane 1996; http://wwwhost.ots.utexas.edu/ethernet/enet-faqs/ethernet-faq.

11. Bredt 1995. Thin Ethernet (see chapter 5), with its BNC connectors, greatly simplified the process of connecting a station to the cable. However, Thin Ethernet continued to operate on a bus topology and thus did not eliminate Ethernet's fundamental topology problem (Jones 1985:79).

12. In 1989, Infonetics, a market research company, calculated that every hour of LAN downtime cost a Fortune 1000 company more than $30,000 in lost productivity (Saal 1990).

13. Jones 1985; Ross 1986:154; J. Schmidt 1995. According to Ross, in 1986 thick coaxial cable cost between $1.75 and $2.00 per foot, compared with $0.57–$1.11 for thin coaxial cable, $0.15 for broadband coaxial, and $1.18 for fiber optic cable.

14. Jones 1985:79.

15. *Data Communications* 1987; Estrin 1987; Greenfield 1989b:37; Anderson and Woods 1990a:49; Davis 1990:70; Brown 1991a.

16. Lally 1986:71; McMaster 1986:109.

17. Brohm 1985:27f.

18. IBM's 8228 MAU connected only eight nodes, but several MAUs could be interconnected (Dzubeck 1986).

19. Bux 1989:240.

20. Brohm 1985:28; Barlin 1989:45.

21. Braue 1985:22.

22. Bartik 1984; Stenzler-Centonze 1984; Jeffery 1986:34.

23. *Data Communications* 1985b. According to Jeffery (1986:35), fewer than 20 percent of IBM's most loyal customers installed the IBM Cabling System.

24. Derfler and Freed 1993:122ff; http://wwwhost.ots.utexas.edu /ethernet/ enet-faqs/ethernet-faq. In 1986, a foot of UTP cable cost between $0.10 and $0.15 (Ross 1986:154).

25. Token Ring on UTP cable supported only 72 nodes and spanned only 100 meters; the version on STP wire could handle 260 nodes and spanned 300 meters (*Data Communications* 1985b). *Data Communications* (1985b) surmised that, by supporting fewer nodes on UTP wire, IBM made a concession to the few customers who had installed the original, STP-based IBM Cabling System. But since UTP wire had a higher attenuation level and was more susceptible to external noise, crosstalk, and radiation interference, it indeed posed greater physical constraints than STP wire (Bates and Abramson 1986:223f).

26. Token Ring initially had a throughput rate of 4 Mbps. But since it transmitted at close to its nominal speed, whereas Ethernet's actual throughput rate deteriorated drastically under heavy network loads, many claimed that the two LANs operated at a similar speed. See Brohm (1985), Suby (1986), Killat et al. (1988), Bard (1989), Glass (1989:368), and Hunter (1989a) for these claims. See Boggs et al. (1988) and Callahan and Bradley (1989) for refutation of the claim that Ethernet's speed deteriorated under heavy loads. In late 1985, a Token Ring adapter cost approximately $695, while an Ethernet adapter was approximately $400 (*Data Communications* 1985b:62; Goldstein 1985).

27. See Bush (1988), DiDio (1988), Callahan and Bradley (1989), *Data Communications* (1989b), Glass (1989:363), Hindin (1989), and Valovic (1987b) for Token Ring's growing momentum. Valovic (1987b) quotes a

report by Forrester Research that estimated Token Ring's market share among Fortune 1000 companies at 22 percent, compared with 33 percent for Ethernet. In mid-1988, Dataquest estimated that Token Ring had a U.S. market share (all types of connections, including host, terminal-to-host, and PCs) of 12 percent, compared with 57 percent for Ethernet (Callahan and Bradley 1989:128). But for 1988 Dataquest estimated that Token Ring had a market share (in departments) of 20 percent, compared with 40 percent for Ethernet (Bush 1988:79). According to Forrester Research, in 1989 just under one million Ethernet adapters were shipped in the United States, compared with 500,000 Token Ring adapters (Davis 1990:70).

28. *Business Week* 1984; Crane 1996; Love 1996. As late as 1993, Lippis (1993) wrote that many SNA-specific applications, such as 3270 emulation packages, ran only on Token Ring LANs.

29. Bux 1998.

30. Greenfield 1989b:37; Davis 1990:70; Brown 1991a.

31. Hunter 1989a:37; Love 1996. Performance tests conducted by Network World/Infonetics in early 1990 revealed that 16-Mbps Token Ring improved network response time by only between 3 and 25 percent over 4-Mbps Token Ring (Salamone 1990b:1). By 1991, however, the 16-Mbps Token Ring products had improved dramatically. Performance tests now showed that 16-Mbps Token Ring had an actual throughput rate of approximately 15 Mbps, that is, 3 to 3.5 times faster than Ethernet (McGiffert 1991:43f).

32. Salamone 1990b:1.

33. Greenfield 1989b:37; Davis 1990:70; Brown 1991a.

34. In 1989 a total of approximately 1.5 million Ethernet and Token Ring adapters were shipped, compared with 27.5 million in 1995 (Davis 1990:70; *Electronic News* 1996:43).

35. Love 1996.

36. Despite the many heated debates about the relative merits of Ethernet's and Token Ring's access methods, the decisive parameters were topology and cable type. This was because the latter factors influenced network management and troubleshooting, the most critical "reverse salients" of LANs in the mid-1980s, whereas access method determined only LAN speed, which at that time was not yet a serious bottleneck.

37. The only Ethernet variation to deviate from the bus topology was fiber optic Ethernet. However, as discussed later in this chapter, it remained a niche technology.

38. Mier 1984b:141; *Data Communications* 1985b.

39. Levin 1985:54; Madron 1990:195. Although the transition from Ethernet's original bus topology to the hub-based star topology might appear to be a radical change, as pointed out in chapter 2, such a topology would have been possible from the beginning because Ethernet was defined as an "unrooted tree," branching out at any point. AT&T was the originator of Starlan. The traditional LAN vendors were initially very skeptical of implementing a high-speed Ethernet network on telephone wire designed for voice

transmission, because of its low bandwidth (Thaler 1995). But thanks to its large telephone switching centers, AT&T was more inclined to think in terms of centralized, star-based wiring structures than the LAN vendors.

40. Thaler 1995. The Starlan standard also became known as 1Base5. Aside from AT&T, important Starlan supporters were H-P and Intel (Thaler 1995; R. Schmidt 1995).

41. Gibson 1986; Donohue 1987:27; Madron 1988:132.

42. Hindin 1981.

43. See *Electronic Business* (1983a) and Ungermann-Bass (1983b:7f) for the competition between LAN and PBX vendors in the early 1980s.

44. Ungermann 1995.

45. Bridge and Stern 1986:48; Stallings 1986:40.

46. *Data Communications* 1984c; Jones 1985; Levin 1985.

47. In contrast, relatively inexpensive repeaters or bridges sufficed to connect the different Ethernet versions operating at 10 Mbps (Crane 1996).

48. Derfler 1988:189.

49. In 1987, AT&T shipped 48,000 Starlan adapters, compared with the 166,000 Token Ring adapters sold by IBM (Petrovsky 1988:9).

50. Thaler 1995.

51. Orlov 1988:41; Campbell 1990:35.

52. Ronald Schmidt was a Ph.D. graduate of the University of California, Berkeley, and had spent several years at prestigious industrial research labs, including AT&T Bell Laboratories, Hewlett-Packard's Palo Alto Research Laboratories, and the Hughes Research Laboratory in Malibu, California (Borsook 1988:113).

53. Schmidt et al. 1983; Borsook 1988:113.

54. R. Schmidt 1995.

55. Ibid.; SynOptics 1988:6.

56. Fallon 1985; SynOptics 1988:6, 18ff; R. Schmidt 1995 (in which quote appears).

57. Howe 1987:56; SynOptics 1988:4.

58. Bredt 1995.

59. Anderson and Woods 1990a:64; Bredt 1995.

60. To underline the low-tech nature of the initial SynOptics hubs, note that Ronald Crane, then with 3Com, constructed a similar device within a few weeks (Crane 1995).

61. Bredt 1995; R. Schmidt 1995.

62. Bredt 1995.

63. R. Schmidt 1995.

64. Ibid.; SynOptics 1988:33.

65. Bredt 1995.

66. Schmidt 1988.

67. Borsook 1988; R. Schmidt 1995. Because of the less robust UTP cable, the SynOptics product allowed for a maximal workstation-to-hub distance of only 110 meters (Kolman 1988:96; Madron 1990:168). On bus-based Thin Ethernet, the relatively short distance of 185 meters per segment had sometimes caused problems, especially in cubicle-based offices. But the

110-meter workstation-to-hub distance of the SynOptics product did not lead to similar difficulties because 97 percent of all telephones were located within 55 meters of a wiring closet, and 99 percent within 70 meters (*Data Communications* 1984b:50; Kolman 1988:94ff; Crane 1996). Patricia Thaler (1995) claims that H-P developed a product before SynOptics. According to the trade press, however, SynOptics was the first company to ship such a product (Howe 1987; Borsook 1988:114; Mulqueen 1988:72; Campbell 1990:35).

68. Mulqueen 1988:72.

69. Davis 1990:71; Johnson 1990:16f.

70. Located in Rochester, New Hampshire, Cabletron was established in 1983 and initially focused on selling and installing cable for building LANs. As a result of its close relations with LAN users, Cabletron could appreciate their networking needs and expanded into auxiliary network devices, such as network testing devices and ultimately hubs (Cabletron 1990; Hyatt 1991:40; *Upside* 1996:62). Bredt (1995) surmised that Cabletron was able to grow its hub business so rapidly because it knew many users who had previously purchased Ethernet systems.

71. Terrie 1991:43.

72. Mulqueen 1988:74; Hunter 1989b; Campbell 1990:35. To some degree, the extra costs also originated from the additional hub device.

73. Anderson and Woods 1990b; Thaler 1995.

74. Derfler 1988:189; Kolman 1988:98; Campbell 1990:35.

75. Bredt 1995.

76. To be more precise, the 3Com-DEC approach allowed users to replace an arbitrary coaxial segment with UTP wire. At each intersection of a coaxial and a UTP segment, users had to install a special device, called a PairTamer, to convert the signals (Derfler 1988; Kolman 1988:97; Mulqueen 1988; Crane 1996). But to accommodate the telephone system's star topology, this so-called PairTamer approach simultaneously allowed for a hub, which they called the MultiConnect Repeater. Oddly enough, this hub did not connect directly with the UTP wire, but required the installation of a PairTamer within the wiring closet to interconnect the coaxial cable with the telephone system (Derfler 1988:204ff).

77. Hence the technology of SynOptics, H-P, and the other vendors became known as the AUI approach.

78. Derfler 1988; Kolman 1988; Weiss and Sirbu 1990:119.

79. Ibid.; R. Schmidt 1995; Crane 1996; Metcalfe 1996a.

80. Thaler 1995; Metcalfe 1996b.

81. Kolman 1988:98; Anderson and Woods 1990b; Campbell 1990:35; Thaler 1995.

82. Anderson and Woods 1990b (in which quote appears); Campbell 1990:38; Davis 1990:71. In 1989, 500,000 Ethernet adapter cards—or over 40 percent of the total number of such cards shipped—were made for UTP wire.

83. Jitter refers to signal distortion; equalization refers to the balance of the amplitude of an electronic circuit.

84. Anderson and Woods 1990b:52.

85. Thaler 1995.
86. Anderson and Woods 1990b:52.
87. Johnson 1990:24; Thaler 1995.
88. Despite the installation of over 500,000 pre-standard nodes, few backward compatibility problems surfaced. Repeaters and modules inserted within hubs sufficed to ensure seamless interconnection of pre- and post-standard segments (Mulqueen 1988:74; Anderson and Woods 1990a:52; Davis 1990:71).
89. Campbell 1990:38; Metcalfe 1996a.
90. Davis 1990:71; Johnson 1990:15ff; Terrie 1991:43ff.
91. R. Schmidt 1995; see also Brown 1991c:1f; Terrie 1991:44; Bredt 1995.
92. Davis 1990:71.
93. Bredt 1995.
94. R. Schmidt 1995. Ralph Ungermann (1995) claimed that U-B pioneered intelligent hubs before SynOptics. In 1989, U-B had a market share in intelligent hubs of 28 percent, compared with 38 percent for SynOptics and 24 percent for Cabletron (Cusack 1990:45).
95. DiDio 1989b.
96. Herman 1991:63.
97. DiDio 1989b; Patch 1991.
98. Greenfield 1990:15ff; Brown and Molloy 1991.
99. R. Schmidt 1995.
100. Because of its focus on the PairTamer approach, 3Com had missed the hub market. In fact, in 1987–90, the firm found itself at several crossroads. It was the leading Ethernet adapter manufacturer, but it also had the chance to take over the hub business owing to the hubs' low-tech nature and its extensive distribution channels. In addition, because of its merger with Bridge Communications, which was on the brink of developing a multiprotocol router, it had an excellent chance to become the leader in this segment, by far the largest and most lucrative market. Under the leadership of CEO William Krause, however, 3Com missed out on these additional business opportunities and thus remained locked in adapters, a commodity product.
101. Love 1996.
102. Lippis 1993; Bux 1998.
103. Lippis 1993:27.
104. Metcalfe 1993c.
105. The lonely exception to the trend was Proteon, which attempted to push a (proprietary) token ring into the market (see chapter 6) (Salwen 1995).
106. Love 1996; Bux 1998; Carlo and Hughes 1989:26. Despite Token Ring's openness, full interoperability between IBM and non-IBM Token Ring chips was not automatically guaranteed because vendors often implemented additional proprietary features and protocols in their products (Mier 1986:48).
107. Mier 1986:48. Ralph Ungermann (1996) claimed that IBM first collaborated with U-B on the development of a Token Ring IC before it switched to TI. See Strauss (1984:82) for the close relationship between IBM and U-B in the mid-1980s.

108. According to Howard Salwen (1995) and Derfler and Greenfield (1992), TI remained the sole source of Token Ring ICs for many years. Only in the early 1990s did Chips and Technologies emerge as a second vendor of Token Ring chips (Greenfield 1992). U-B also finally developed its own IC, but it too was not sold on the open market (Glass 1989:374).

109. *Data Communications* 1985a:46f; Mier 1986:48f; Salwen 1995; Ungermann 1995.

110. Greenfield 1989b:40; Hunter 1989a:1; Salamone 1990b:36.

111. Metcalfe 1993c.

112. Mier 1986:49 (on which quote appears), 50f.

113. Mier 1986.

114. Gabel 1991; Langlois 1992.

115. According to Jon Bayless (1998), the compatibility issues disappeared fairly rapidly. But Carlo and Hughes (1989) have written that, as late as November 1989, "variation in vendor implementation [was] still very much an issue." In December 1988 the Token Ring vendors created the Open Token Forum to perform interoperability tests. IBM, however, refused to join the group (Carlo and Hughes 1989; *Network World* 1989:18). See also Metcalfe (1993c).

116. Mier 1986:49.

117. *Data Channels* 1986b; Haber 1986:42. Many vendors of Token Ring—such as 3Com, Cabletron, and U-B—were entrenched Ethernet suppliers. They wished to expand into Token Ring to satisfy all their customers' networking needs.

118. Salwen 1995.

119. Greenfield 1989b:37.

120. Killorin 1987; also compare the vendor lists of Terrie (1991) and Hurwicz (1991). Whereas Terrie (1991) lists fifty-one firms offering 10Base-T adapter cards and mentions a total of one hundred vendors, the list of Hurwicz (1991) comprises only nineteen vendors of Token Ring adapters.

121. *Network World* 1991. In their fiscal 1989, for example, the Ethernet vendors 3Com and SynOptics had revenues of $385.9 million and $104.7 million, respectively, while Proteon had sales of only $52.7 million.

122. Bux 1998.

123. *Network World* 1991; Reier 1995.

124. In 1991, IBM slashed prices of its 4-Mbps Token Ring adapters by 49 percent (from $772 to $395) and those of its 16-Mbps adapters by 6.5 percent (from $957 to $895). However, these reductions did not suffice to match the price of 3Com's best-selling EtherLink II adapter (less than $300) (Brown 1991b:52).

125. Salamone 1990b; Hurwicz 1991; Greenfield 1992; Love 1996.

126. Greenstein 1991. Unlike IBM, Proteon had already offered a 16-Mbps Token Ring for UTP wire in the fall of 1989 (Tunick 1990:85).

127. Bhardwaj 1990; Verhalen 1995. Kalpana was an early switching technology vendor. In 1992–93, Grand Junction—which was established by ex-employees of 3Com, including Howard Charney—was one of the first

firms to introduce 100-Mbps Ethernet technology (Kramer 1990; Semilof 1992; Verhalen 1995).

128. Verhalen 1995. Switching means that nodes on an Ethernet network do not need to share and contend for the wire, but that, similar to circuit switching, two nodes are directly connected. Hence several conversations can take place at once at a speed of 10 Mbps. Switches are often implemented in hubs (http://webopedia.internet.com/Networks/Network_Protocols/ Ethernet/switched_Ethernet.html).

129. Charney 1995; Verhalen 1995.

130. Klett 1994; Saunders 1994:87. The first companies to introduce switching technology for Token Ring were IBM, Chipcom, and start-up Centillion (Klett 1994).

131. Klett 1994.

132. Lippis 1993:27f.

133. See the preface for a definition of bridging.

134. Broadcast storm describes a condition in which devices on the network are generating traffic that by its nature causes the generation of even more traffic. The inevitable result is a massive degradation of performance or complete loss of the network as the devices continue to generate more and more traffic. Broadcast storms were often caused in an Ethernet network if loops were formed—a fault whose likelihood increased as the networks became more complex (Sheldon 1994:105f; http://wwwhost.ots.utexas.edu/ ethernet/enet-faqs/ethernet-faq).

135. Like a bridge, a router connects two network segments. But because routers work at OSI layer 3, they forward packets more directly to the destination than remote bridges, which broadcast packets over all possible links. The multiprotocol element means that the router is able to handle multiple higher-level protocols (Sheldon 1994:756; http://wwwhost.ots.utexas.edu/ ethernet/enet-faqs/ethernet-faq).

136. IBM used a bridging method called source routing in its Token Ring, whereas the Ethernet vendors employed a method called a transparent spanning tree (*Data Communications* 1989c).

137. Bux 1998.

138. Bayless 1998.

139. Ibid.; Bux 1998.

140. Bux 1998.

141. Anderson and Woods 1990a:49.

142. Metcalfe 1993d.

143. *Electronic News* 1996:43.

144. Mulqueen 1987:110; Wilson 1987b:112; Labate 1994:190. According to Seither (1989:17), only 6 percent of all PCs were connected to a LAN in early 1989.

145. In late 1990, only three vendors—U-B, IBM, and CrossComm— offered Ethernet–to–Token Ring bridges. IBM's and U-B's bridges cost $7,445 and $5,250, respectively. Routers with Ethernet–to–Token Ring conversion capability cost considerably more (Salamone 1990a:41).

CHAPTER 8 • IMPLICATIONS

1. Cusumano et al. 1992.
2. Liebowitz and Margolis 1990, 1995b.
3. Saxenian 1994.
4. Motter 1997.
5. In 1997–98, the two factions in the modem battle were forced to resolve their differences and to create a single standard.
6. Clark 1998; Cusumano and Yoffie 1998:138ff.
7. Cusumano and Yoffie 1998:138ff.
8. Calderbank 1998; McHugh 1998.
9. *The Economist* 1998.
10. Ibid.; Gomes 1999.
11. Shankland 2001.
12. Castelluccio 1998; Harmon 1998.
13. Darrow and Burke 1998; Glascock and Semilof 1998; Hafke 1998; O'Shea 1999; Pendery 1999.
14. Glascock and Semilof 1998; Young 1998; Musthaler 1999.
15. Harrison 1998.
16. Curry and Kenney 1999.
17. Shankland 2001.

APPENDIX B • ANNUAL SALES AND REVENUES
OF SELECTED LAN COMPANIES

1. Source for 1979–84: Leonard Shustek.
2. 1986: Saal (1995).
3. Acquired by DSC.
4. Acquired by Tandem.
5. According to William Seifert, founder of Interlan.
6. Acquired by Micom.
7. Merged with 3Com.
8. Acquired by Novell.
9. 1985: Howe (1986:47); 1986 and 1987: Kerr (1987a:32).
10. Acquired by GM Hughes.
11. LAN sales/total sales.
12. Out of business.
13. Acquired by Network Systems.

References

Abbate, Janet Ellen. 1994. "From ARPANET to Internet: A History of ARPA-Sponsored Computer Networks, 1966–1988." Unpublished doctoral dissertation, University of Pennsylvania. Ann Arbor: University Microfilms International.

Abernathy, William, and Kim Clark. 1985. "Mapping the Winds of Creative Destruction." *Research Policy*, Vol. 14: 3–22.

Abernathy, William, and James Utterback. 1978. "Patterns of Industrial Innovation." *Technology Review* (June–July): 40–47.

Anderson, Rick, and Kevin Woods. 1990a. "10Base-T Ethernet: The Second Wave." *Data Communications* (November 21): 49–64.

———. 1990b. "The Road to 10Base-T." *Data Communications* (November 21): 52.

Arthur, Brian. 1988. "Competing Technologies: An Overview." In Giovanni Dosi, Christopher Freeman, Richard Nelson, Gerald Silverberg, and Luc Soete (eds.), *Technical Change and Economic Theory*, 590–607. London: Pinter.

———. 1989. "Competing Technologies, Increasing Returns, and Lock-In by Historical Events." *The Economic Journal* (March): 116–131.

———. 1994. *Increasing Returns and Path Dependence in the Economy*. Ann Arbor: University of Michigan Press.

Augarten, Stan. 1984. *Bit by Bit: An Illustrated History of Computers*. New York: Ticknor & Fields.

Bard, Chris. 1989. "Ethernet versus Token Ring." *Electronics and Wireless World*, Vol. 95 (1640) (June): 608–609.

Barlin, David. 1989. "A Home-Brewed Remedy for High Token Ring Installation Costs." *Data Communications*, Vol. 18 (15) (November 21): 45–48.

Barney, Clifford. 1983. "1983 Award for Achievement: Robert M. Metcalfe." *Electronics* (October 6): 112–115.

———. 1988. "Sales and Profit Gains Ease the Pain of the 3Com/Bridge Merger." *Electronic Business* (November 15): 54–56.

Bartik, Jean. 1984. "IBM's Token Ring: Have the Pieces Finally Come To-gether?" *Data Communications* (August): 125–139.

Bass, Charlie, Joseph Kennedy, and John Davidson. 1980. "Local Network Gives New Flexibility to Distributed Processing." *Electronics* (September 25): 114–122.

Bates, Richard, and Paul Abramson. 1986. "You Can Use Phone Wire for Your Token Ring LAN." *Data Communications* (November): 223–229.

Batt, Robert. 1981. "User Education Paramount. Local Nets: Standards Not the Only Issue." *Computerworld* (May 4): 105–121.

Bayless, Jon. 1998. Personal Communication (March 17).

Beaver, Jennifer. 1986. "Micros and Minis: Tighter Ties." *Computer Decisions* (October 21): 30–34.

Bell, Gordon. 1988. "Toward a History of (Personal) Workstations." In Adele Goldberg (ed.), *A History of Personal Workstations*, 4–47. New York: ACM Press.

———. 1995. Personal e-mail Communication (April 29).

Bentley, Terry. 1983. "Weighing the LAN Sides: Baseband vs. Broadband." *Data Management* (June): 21–26.

Berg, Eric. 1984. "A Small Company Gets Big I.B.M. Lift." *New York Times* (August 16): D5.

Besen, Stanley, and Joseph Farrell. 1994. "Choosing How to Compete: Strategies and Tactics in Standardization." *Journal of Economic Perspectives*, Vol. 8 (2) (Spring): 117–131.

Besen, Stanley, and Garth Saloner. 1989. "The Economics of Telecommunications Standards." In R. Crandall and K. Flamm (eds.), *Changing the Rules: Technological Change, International Competition, and Regulation in Telecommunications*, 177–220. Washington, D.C.: Brookings Institution.

Bhardwaj, Vinod. 1990. "Can Fast Packet Switching Give Ethernet New Life?" *Data Communications* (August): 81–88.

Biba, Kenneth, and Jeffry Yeh. 1979. "FordNet: A Front-End Approach to Local Computer Networks." *Proceedings of the LACN Symposium* (May): 199–215.

Birenbaum, Larry. 1983. "The IBM PC Meets Ethernet." *BYTE* (November): 272–280.

Blumenthal, Marcia. 1981. "Datapoint Looking Ahead to Integrated Office Systems." *Computerworld* (May 4): 105, 116, 117.

Boggs, David, Jeffrey Mogul, and Christopher Kent. 1988. "Measured Capacity of an Ethernet: Myths and Reality." *Computer Communications Review*, Vol. 18 (4) (August): 222–234.

Borrus, Michael, and John Zysman. 1997. "Globalization with Borders: The Rise of Wintelism as the Future of Industrial Competition." *Industry and Innovation*, Vol. 4 (2) (December): 141–166.

Borsook, Paulina. 1988. "An Engineer Scores with 'Low-Class' Technology: Twisted-Pair Ethernet." *Data Communications* (June): 113–114.

Braue, Joseph. 1985. "IBM Token Ring: Brass or Gold?" *Computer Decisions* (November 19): 20–23.

Braun, Ernest, and Stuart Macdonald. 1982. *Revolution in Miniature: The History and Impact of Semiconductor Devices*. Cambridge: Cambridge University Press.

Bredt, Thomas. 1995. Personal Communication (July 19).

Breidenbach, Susan. 1990. "ARCnet Community Fights for Recognition." *Network World*, Vol. 7 (18) (April 30): 19–22.

Bresnahan, Timothy, and Amit Chopra. 1990. "The Development of the Local Area Network Market as Determined by User Needs." *Economics of Innovation and New Technology*, Vol. 1: 97–110.

Bresnahan, Timothy, and Shane Greenstein. 1992. "Technological Competition and the Structure of the Computer Industry." Center for Economic Policy Research Publication No. 315. Stanford University.

Bridge, Robert, and Ken Stern. 1986. "Getting the Most from Existing Twisted-Pair Transmission Media." *Telecommunications* (December): 45–58.

Bridge Communications. 1985a. Securities and Exchange Commission S-1 Form. Mountain View, Calif.

———. 1985b. Annual Report. Mountain View, Calif.

———. 1986. Annual Report. Mountain View, Calif.

Brinton, James. 1981a. "Market Forms for Local-Net Bridges." *Electronics* (July 28): 97–100.

———. 1981b. "Boards Hook DEC Machines to Ethernet." *Electronics* (November 30): 175–177.

Brohm, Edwin. 1985. "Token-Passing Ring Networks." *Computerworld*, Vol. 19 (36a) (August 28): 27–28.

Brown, Bob. 1989. "Will ARCnet Be an Endangered Species?" *Network World*, Vol. 6 (23): 9–10, 58.

———. 1991a. "IBM Token-Ring Had Major Impact in First Five Years." *Network World*, Vol. 8 (6) (February 11): 2, 6.

———. 1991b. "IBM Pares Prices of 4Mbit/sec Token Ring Cards." *Network World*, Vol. 8 (23) (June 10): 2, 52.

———. 1991c. "LAN Hub Vendors Rush to Bolster Management Tools." *Network World*, Vol. 8 (18): 1, 61.

Brown, Bob, and Maureen Molloy. 1991. "Next Generation of Local Net Hubs Adds Flexibility." *Network World*, Vol. 8 (49) (December 9): 1, 44.

Brownstein, Neil. 1998. Personal Communication (April 8).

Burke, Steven. 1985. "Corvus Says PC-NOS Eases Net Use." *Infoworld* (November 25): 11.

Burton, Craig. 1996. Personal Communication (July 6).

Bush, John. 1988. "A Formula for Curing Those LAN Cabling Blues." *Data Communications* (November 15): 79–89.

Business Week. 1978. "Xerox Plunges into a Digital Network Race." (November 27): 38.

———. 1979a. "Wang Labs Challenges the Goliaths." (June 4): 100–104.

———. 1979b. "Xerox's Bid to Unlock the Office of the Future." (December 24): 47.

————. 1979c. "Datapoint Leapfrogs into the Office." (December 10): 93–96.

————. 1980. "Wang's Game Plan for the Office." (December 15): 84–86.

————. 1981. "Xerox's Bid to Be No. 1 in Offices." (June 22): 77.

————. 1984. "Linking Office Computers: The Market Comes of Age." (May 14): 140–148.

Bux, Werner. 1981. "Local-area Subnetworks: A Performance Comparison." *IEEE Transactions on Communication,* Vol. COM-29 (October): 1465–1473.

————. 1989. "Token Ring Local Area Networks and Their Performance." *Proceedings of the IEEE,* Vol. 77 (2) (February): 238–256.

————. 1998. Personal Communication (October 28).

Bygrave, William, and Jeffry Timmons. 1992. *Venture Capital at the Crossroads.* Boston: Harvard Business School Press.

Cabletron. 1990. Securities and Exchange Commission Form S-1. Rochester, N.H.

Calderbank, Diana Alison. 1998. "Linux Movement's Founder." *Computer Reseller News* (December 7) (820): 135–136.

Callahan, Paul, and Bob Bradley. 1989. "New Token Ring versus Ethernet: Counterpoint." *Data Communications* (January): 127–134.

Campbell, Greg. 1990. "10BaseT: The UTP Standard Arrives. *LAN Technology* (June): 34–38.

Carano, Bandel. 1995. Personal Communication (March 6).

Carlo, Jim, and John Hughes. 1989. "Token Ring Compatibility: It's Time to Plug and Play." *Data Communications* (November 21): 26–34.

Carlton, Jim, and Christian Hill. 1997. "Apple Moves to Shut Down Cloners of Mac Line." *Wall Street Journal* (September 3): A3 (W).

Cashien, Jerry. 1982. "Nestar's Local Area Net Has Measurable Track Record." *Small Systems World* (September): 12.

Castelluccio, Michael. 1998. "Looking-Glass Software." *Management Accounting,* Vol. 79 (12) (June): 60–63.

Catalano, Frank. 1985. "Hewlett-Packard Focuses on the Office Spectrum." *Electronic Business* (August 1): 46–55.

Chakravarty, Subrata. 1981. "Elephant Walk." *Forbes* (October 21): 188–192.

Chandler, Alfred. 1977. *The Visible Hand: The Managerial Revolution in American Business.* Cambridge, Mass.: Belknap Press.

————. 1990. *Scale and Scope: The Dynamics of Industrial Capitalism.* Cambridge, Mass.: Belknap Press.

Charney, Howard. 1995. Personal Communication (July 14).

Chposky, James, and Ted Leonsis. 1988. *Blue Magic: The People, Power, and Politics Behind the IBM Personal Computer.* New York: Facts on File.

Christensen, Clayton. 1992. "The Innovator's Challenge: Understanding the Influence of Market Environment on Processes of Technology Development in the Rigid Disk Industry." Unpublished doctoral dissertation, Harvard University. Ann Arbor: UMI Dissertation Services.

———. 1993. "The Rigid Disk Drive Industry: A History of Commercial and Technological Turbulence." *Business History Review*, Vol. 67 (Winter): 531–588.

Clark, Don. 1998. "Netscape to Share Browser Program Code." *Wall Street Journal* (January 23): B6 (W).

Coase, Ronald. 1937. "The Nature of the Firm." *Economica*, Vol. 4 (November): 386–405.

———. 1960. "The Problem of Social Cost." *Journal of Law and Economics*, Vol. 3: 1–44.

Cohen, Ted. 1979. "In the Valley of the Giants." *Forbes* (December 10): 70–72.

Cohen, W. M., and D. Levinthal. 1990. "Absorptive Capacity: A New Perspective on Learning and Innovation." *Administrative Science Quarterly*, Vol. 35: 128–152.

Comerford, Richard. 1980. "Standards Push Starts on Short-Run Data Net." *Electronics* (March 27): 40–41.

Computer Business News. 1982. "Corvus Introduces 'Personal Workstation.'" (May 10): 10.

Computer Decisions. 1981. "LCN: Local Confusion About Networks." (August): 52–55.

———. 1982. "Ethernet Criticized." (January): 12–19.

Computerworld. 1983. "Board Connects DG Minis to Ethernet." (March 14): 83.

———. 1984a. "Corvus Systems Reports Quarterly Revenue Decline of $9.3 Million." (August 20): 102.

———. 1984b. "Corvus Unveils Local-Area Net for Apple Mac." (November 5): 83, 91.

Connell, John. 1979. "The Office of the Future." *Journal of Systems Management* (February): 6–10.

Constant, Edward. 1987. "The Social Locus of Technological Practice: Community, System, or Organization?" In Wiebe Bijker, Thomas Hughes, and Trevor Pinch. (eds.), *The Social Construction of Technological Systems*, 223–243. Cambridge, Mass.: MIT Press.

Cooke, Stephanie. 1988. "Cambridge Does It Again: New 100 Mbps Fast Ring Ousts Ring." *Data Communications* (June): 64–66.

Cooper, Eric. 1996. Personal Communication (December 10).

Corbato, F. 1993. "Time Sharing." In Anthony Ralston (ed.), *Encyclopedia of Computer Science*, 2d ed., 1376–1380. New York: Van Nostrand Reinhold.

Cortino, Julie. 1981. "3Com Ethernet Controller Fits DEC Units." *MIS Week* (November 4): 17.

Corvus. 1981. Annual Report. San Jose, Calif.

———. 1982. Securities and Exchange Commission Form S-1. San Jose, Calif.

———. 1983. Annual Report. San Jose, Calif.

———. 1984. Annual Report. San Jose, Calif.

———. 1986. Annual Report. San Jose, Calif.

Crane, Ronald. 1995. Personal Communication (May 17).

———. 1996. Personal Communication (October 1).

Cringely, Robert. 1996. *Accidental Empires: How the Boys of Silicon Valley Make Their Millions, Battle Foreign Competition, and Still Can't Get a Date.* New York: HarperCollins.

Cross, Thomas. 1988. "ARCnet Survives, and Battle Moves on." *Computerworld* (January 25): S7.

Curry, James, and Martin Kenney. 1999. "Beating the Clock: Corporate Responses to Rapid Change in the PC Industry." *California Management Review* Vol. 42 (Fall): 8–36.

Cusack, Sally. 1990. "Report Says Smart Hubs Will Spin into New Decade." *Computerworld* (January 8): 45, 53.

Cusumano, Michael, and David Yoffie. 1998. *Competing on Internet Time.* New York: Free Press.

Cusumano, Michael, Yiorgos Mylonadis, and Richard Rosenbloom. 1992. "Strategic Maneuvering and Mass-Market Dynamics: The Triumph of VHS over Beta." *Business History Review*, Vol. 66 (Spring): 51–94.

D'Addio, Michael. 1996. Personal Communication (April 2).

———. 2000. E-mail (October 2).

Darrow, Barbara, and Steven Burke. 1998. "Linux to Find Home in Small, Midsize Market." *Computer Reseller News* (November 23) (818): 224.

Data Channels. 1980a. "Ethernet Specifications Announced as IEEE Considers Standard for Local Network." Vol. 7 (11) (November): 2.

———. 1980b. "Xerox Unveils First Commercial Products for Ethernet." Vol. 7 (13) (December): 1–2.

———. 1980c. "Different Systems Contend for Endorsement of IEEE Local Network Committee." Vol. 7 (13) (December): 2.

———. 1981a. "Brief Bits." Vol. 8 (6) (March 16): 7.

———. 1981b. "IEEE Local Net Committee Endorses Both Token and Ethernet Type Standards." Vol. 8 (1) (January 5): 2.

———. 1981c. "Interlan Markets Ethernet Products for DEC Computers." Vol. 8 (25) (December 4): 3.

———. 1981d. "Proteon Markets Pronet, a Local Area Token Net for DEC Equipment." Vol. 8 (21) (October 9): 2.

———. 1981e. "Tandy Introduces Local Networking for TRS-80 via Datapoint's ARCnet." Vol. 8 (20) (September 25): 1.

———. 1981f. "3Com Introduces Ethernet Controllers for DEC Equipment." Vol. 8 (22) (October 23): 6.

———. 1981g. "Ungermann-Bass to Manufacture Ethernet Network Interface Units." Vol. 8 (11) (May 11): 8.

———. 1981h. "Wang Introduces Local Area Net." Vol. 8 (14) (July 6): 1.

———. 1981i. "Xerox Reveals Higher-Level Protocols for Ethernet, Encourages Others to Use Them." Vol. 8 (26) (December 18): 1–2.

———. 1982a. " . . . And Hewlett-Packard Endorses IEEE Standard over Ethernet." (February 8): 6.

———. 1982b. " . . . As Many Differences Remain." Vol. 9 (3) (February 8): 5.

———. 1982c. " . . . As Patent Controversy Threatens Token-Passing Local Area Network Standard." Vol. 9 (19) (September 20): 1.

———. 1982d. "Corvus Systems." Vol. 9 (10) (May 17): 6.

———. 1982e. "Datapoint Local Net Chips to Be Sold on Open Market." Vol. 9 (11) (May 31): 5.

———. 1982f. "Sytek, General Instruments Take Aim at Metropolitan Area Network Market." Vol. 9 (9) (May 3): 1.

———. 1982g. "Hewlett-Packard Signs OEM Deal for Ungermann-Bass Ethernets." Vol. 9 (24) (November 29): 8.

———. 1982h. "Intel Finally Takes Wraps off Its Ethernet Chips; New Chips Designed to Handle Physical, Data Link Layers of CSMA/CD Nets." Vol. 9 (21) (October 18): 1.

———. 1982i. "Markets Baseband Local Area Network That Can Be Upgraded to Broadband." Vol. 9 (14) (July 12): 7.

———. 1982j. "DEC Announces Initial Ethernet Products." Vol. 9 (11) (May 31): 4.

———. 1982k. "Ungermann-Bass Adds Broadband Version to Its Net/One Local Area Network." Vol. 9 (5) (March 8): 8.

———. 1982l. "Xerox Denies Ethernet's Reported Move to Conform with IEEE's Local Net Standard." Vol. 9 (3) (February 8): 5.

———. 1982m. " . . . As Company Ousts 5 Executives." Vol. 9 (11): 5.

———. 1983a. "Ungermann-Bass Inc." Vol. 10 (7) (April 4): 7.

———. 1983b. "Corvus Announces SNA Gateway for Omninet." Vol. 10 (11) (May 30): 2.

———. 1983c. "DECnet/SNA Gateway Available for $26,995." Vol. 10 (4) (February 21): 8.

———. 1983d. "Digital Microsystems Upgrades Proprietary Hardware for Hinet." Vol. 10 (4) (February 21): 2.

———. 1983e. "Excelan Debuts with Ethernet-Based Front End Processors." Vol. 10 (2) (January 24): 1.

———. 1983f. "Interlan Controller Opens Ethernet to Data General's Minis." Vol. 10 (5) (March 7): 3.

———. 1983g. "Interlan Links Pact with Calma for Ethernet Controllers." Vol. 10 (June 27): 3.

———. 1983h. "Ungermann-Bass Finally Announces Amdax Buy." Vol. 10 (2) (January 24): 1.

———. 1983i. "Ungermann-Bass Introduces LAN Board for PCs." Vol. 10 (20) (October 3): 4.

———. 1983j. "Zilog Discontinues Z-Net, Plans 'Standard' LAN Replacements." Vol. 10 (17) (August 22): 1–2.

———. 1984a. "Corvus Systems Inc. and NEC Corp." Vol. 11 (24) (November 26): 6.

———. 1984b. "Datapoint Accommodates Industry Standards in ARCnet." Vol. 11 (21) (October 15): 8.

———. 1985a. "Corvus Systems Inc." Vol. 12 (41) (December 4): 4.

———. 1985b. "Micom Chairman Resigns on Eve of Major LAN Announcement." Vol. 12 (32) (October 2): 7.

―――. 1985c. "LAN Firms Increase Capabilities by Leaps and Bounds: Corvus." Vol. 12 (41) (December 4): 4.

―――. 1985d. "New Bridge Ethernet Gateway Facilitates Hybrid Networks." Vol. 12 (May 1): 3.

―――. 1985e. "Sytek Unveils First in Series of IBM PC Network Links." Vol. 12 (22) (July 24): 5.

―――. 1985f. "Sytek Unveils Improved Network Control Center as It Halts Plans for an Interactive Data Network" (July 10): 4–5.

―――. 1985g. "General Instrument Increases Stake in Sytek." Vol. 12 (19) (July 3): 5.

―――. 1986a. "Life Without IBM: Sytek Marks International and Defense Arenas." Vol. 13 (24) (June 25): 4.

―――. 1986b. "3Com Enters Token-Ring Market with New Networking Products." Vol. 13 (30) (August 6): 1.

―――. 1986c. "Sytek Bringing PC Network Under Its Own Wing." Vol. 13 (10) (March 12): 2.

Data Communications. 1984a. "IBM Rival Girds Himself for Local Network Fray." (July): 101–102.

―――. 1984b. "Proliferating Permutations of the Ethernet 'Standard.'" (December): 48–52.

―――. 1984c. "CSMA/CD Net Has Aggregate Data Rate of 1 Mbps." (August): 203–204.

―――. 1985a. "Inside IBM's Token-Ring Plans." (February): 46–50.

―――. 1985b. "Tip of Token Ring Iceberg Bared; IBM Now Embracing Twisted-Pairs." (November): 62–64.

―――. 1987. "Token Ring Overtaking Ethernet." (July): 15.

―――. 1988. "Former LAN Giant Corvus Bankrupt." (August): 82.

―――. 1989a. "Sytek Slides into GM Subsidiary." (April): 78–79.

―――. 1989b. "Token Ring Base Growing, and Growing More Critical." (June 21): 47–51.

―――. 1989c. "Token Ring Bridge Standard Still Years Away." (November 21): 13.

Datamation. 1982. "Datamation 100." Vol. 28 (6) (June): 98–226.

Datapoint. 1978. Annual Report. San Antonio, Texas.

David, Paul. 1985. "Clio and the Economics of QWERTY." *American Economic Review*, Vol. 75 (2): 332–337.

David, Paul, and Shane Greenstein. 1990. "The Economics of Compatibility Standards: An Introduction to Recent Research." *Economics of Innovation and New Technology*, Vol. 1: 3–41.

Davis, Dwight. 1981a. "3Com Unveils Controllers, Links Future to Ethernet". *Mini-Micro Systems* (December): 52–54.

―――. 1981b. "Start-up Firm Joins Growing Ethernet Activity." *Mini-Micro Systems* (October): 90–93.

―――. 1982a. "Xerox Moves to Bolster Embattled Ethernet." *Mini-Micro Systems* (February): 17–18.

―――. 1982b. "Ungermann-Bass/Fujitsu Deal Promises First Ethernet Chips." *Mini-Micro Systems* (June): 26–32.

———. 1982c. "Ethernet Spec Spawns Diverse Group of Interface Products." *Mini-Micro Systems* (May): 143–151.

———. 1982d. "DECnet Phase IV to Add Ethernet Connections, SNA Gateway." *Mini-Micro Systems* (June): 58–62.

———. 1990. "LAN Vendors Covet Lowly Telephone Networks." *Electronic Business* (April 30): 70–72.

De Bijl, Paul, and Sanjeev Goyal. 1995. "Technological Change in Markets with Network Externalities." *International Journal of Industrial Organization*, Vol. 13: 307–325.

Derfler, Frank, Jr. 1988. "Making Connections—Fast Performance over Telephone Wire." *PC Magazine* (September 13): 189–211.

Derfler, Frank, Jr., and Les Freed. 1993. *How Networks Work*. Emeryville, Calif.: Ziff-Davis Press.

Derfler, Frank, Jr., and David Greenfield. 1992. "Poised for an Explosion." *PC Magazine* (October 13): 333–368.

DiDio, Laura. 1988. "Token Ring LANs Gaining Momentum." *Network World*, Vol. 5 (17) (April 25): 17, 42.

———. 1989a. "ARCnet Quietly Takes Its Place in History." *Network World* (December 4): 25, 27.

———. 1989b. "Smart Wiring Hubs Offer LAN Control." *Network World*, Vol. 6 (49) (December 11): 19–20.

Dix, John. 1985a. "Sytek Rests on Thin IBM Ice." *Computerworld* (November 25): 19–22.

———. 1985b. "Bridge Unwraps Communications Tools for TCP/IP Nets." *Computerworld* (July 22): 19.

Dixit, Avinash. 1980. "The Role of Investment in Entry Deterrence." *Economic Journal*, Vol. 90: 95–106.

Donnan. Robert. 1996. Personal Communication (January 26).

Donohue, James. 1987. "By Creating Competition, Starlan Lowers Network Prices." *Mini-Micro Systems* (February): 27–35.

Dooley, Ann. 1982. "High Hopes for Datapoint?" *Computerworld*, Vol. 16 (25) (June 6): 29–32.

Dorfman, Nancy. 1987. *Innovation and Market Structure: Lessons from the Computer and Semiconductor Industries*. Cambridge, Mass.: Ballinger.

Dougery, John. 1998. Personal Communication (March 20).

Doyle, T. C. 1994. "Left for Dead, ARCnet Shows Signs of Life." *Computer Reseller News* (August 22) (592): 143–144.

Dzubeck, Francis. 1986. "IBM's Token Ring Strategy." *Administrative Management* (February): 16–17.

Economides, Nicholas. 1988. "Desirability of Compatibility in the Absence of Network Externalities." *American Economic Review*, Vol. 79 (December): 1165–1181.

The Economist. 1998. "Revenge of the Hackers." Vol. 348 (July 11): 63–64.

Edwards, Morris. 1982. "Gateways Open Ethernet to DEC Systems." *Infosystems* (July): 100.

Eklund, Jon. 1993. "Digital Computers: History. Contemporary Systems." In Anthony Ralston (ed.), *Encyclopedia of Computer Science*, 440–466. New York: Van Nostrand Reinhold.

Electronic Business. 1983a. "Ralph Ungermann Bets on Multi-Network Strategy." (March): 134.

———. 1983b. "Public Spotlight: Ungermann-Bass Inc." (August): 178.

Electronic News. 1980a. "DEC, Intel, Xerox Form Local Data Com Net Team." Vol. 26 (May 19): 1, 16.

———. 1980b. "Xerox, Intel, DEC Release Specs for Ethernet Systems." Vol. 26 (October 6): 1, 35.

———. 1980c. "Ungermann-Bass Obtains Venture Capital Funding." Vol. 26 (March 17): 42.

———. 1982. "68000-Based Home CPU Introduced by Corvus Sys." Vol. 28 (April 26): 59.

———. 1984. "Ungermann Unveils Network Gateway." Vol. 30 (July 30): 56.

———. 1996. "Data Net." Vol. 42 (January 29): 43.

Electronics. 1981. "Ethernet Kit Speeds Evaluation." (September 8): 216.

Estrin, Judith. 1987. "The Future of Local Area Networks." *Telecommunications* (August): 68–69.

———. 1995. Personal Communication (April 24).

Estrin, Judith, and William Carrico. 1981. "Local Network Enlists Z80s for Distributed Processing." *Electronics* (February 10): 149–153.

Excelan. 1987. Securities and Exchange Commission Form S-1. San Jose, Calif.

Faggin, Federico. 1978. "How VLSI Impacts Computer Architecture." *IEEE Spectrum* (May): 28–31.

Fallon, Mary. 1985. "Astra Times Debut for Maximum Advantage." *San Jose Mercury* (December 16): 10E.

Farber, David. 1972. "Networks: An Introduction." *Datamation* (April): 36–39.

———. 1975. "A Ring Network." *Datamation* (February): 44–46.

———. 1997. Personal Communication (January 31).

Farmer, W. D., and E. E. Newhall. 1969. "An Experimental Distributed Switching System to Handle Bursty Computer Traffic." ACM *Symposium on Problems in the Optimization of Data Communications Systems* (October 13–16): 4–33.

Farrell, Joseph, and Garth Saloner. 1985. "Standardization, Compatibility, and Innovation." *Rand Journal of Economics*, Vol. 16 (Spring): 70–83.

———. 1987. "Competition, Compatibility and Standards: The Economics of Horses, Penguins and Lemmings." In Landis Gabel (ed.), *Product Standardization as a Tool of Competitive Strategy*, 1–21. Amsterdam: Elsevier Science (North-Holland).

Financial Times. 1977. "Zilog Aims to Lead the Micro World." (June 13): 8.

Fisher, Lawrence. 1988. "Tandem Computers to Buy Ungermann-Bass." *New York Times* (February 17): 37.

Flamm, Kenneth. 1987. *Targeting the Computer.* Washington, D.C.: Brookings Institution.

———. 1988. *Creating the Computer: Government, Industry, and High Technology.* Washington, D.C.: Brookings Institution.

Foley, Mary Jo. 1984. "The LAN Issue of the 80s: Broadband vs. Baseband? Marketing." *Electronic Business* (July 10): 198–200.

Foss, Nicolai. 1996. "Higher-Order Industrial Capabilities and Competitive Advantage." *Journal of Industrial Studies,* Vol. 3 (1): 2–20.

Foss, Nicolai, and Christian Knudsen. 1996. *Towards a Competence Theory of the Firm.* London: Routledge.

Fransman, Martin. 1990. *The Market and Beyond: Cooperation and Competition in Information Technology Development in the Japanese System.* Cambridge: Cambridge University Press.

Freiberger, Paul, and Michael Swaine. 1984. *Fire in the Valley: The Making of the Personal Computer.* Berkeley, Calif.: Osborne/McGraw-Hill.

———. 2000. *Fire in the Valley: The Making of the Personal Computer,* 2d ed. New York: McGraw-Hill.

Frisch, Ivan. 1980. "Planning Local-Area Nets Harder Than It Looks." *Computerworld* (November 24): SR 3–6.

Fuller, Samuel. 1996. Personal Communication (February 23).

Gabel, Landis. 1987. "Open Standards in the European Computer Industry: The Case of X/Open." In Landis Gabel (ed.), *Product Standardization as a Tool of Competitive Strategy,* 91–123. Amsterdam: Elsevier Science (North-Holland).

———. 1991. *Competitive Strategies for Product Standards.* London: McGraw-Hill.

Galin, Robert. 1995. Personal Communication (June 5).

Gandal, Neil. 1994. "Hedonic Price Indexes for Spreadsheets and an Empirical Test for Network Externalities." *RAND Journal of Economics,* Vol. 25 (1): 160–170.

Gardner, David. 1976. "Microprocessors are 'Old Stuff' to Him." Reprinted from *Datamation* (January).

Garud, Raghu, and Sanjay Jain. 1995. "The Embeddedness of Technological Systems." Paper presented at the conference on Embeddedness of Strategy, University of Michigan.

Garud, Raghu, and Arun Kumaraswamy. 1993. "Changing Competitive Dynamics in Network Industries: An Exploration of SUN Microsystems' Open Systems Strategy." *Strategic Management Journal,* Vol. 14: 351–369.

Gateway Communications. 1985. Securities and Exchange Commission Form S-1. Irvine, Calif.

Gibson, Stanley. 1986. "Starlan Earns High Marks." *Computerworld* (May 12): 19, 24.

Gilbert, Richard. 1992. "Symposium on Compatibility: Incentives and Market Structure." *Journal of Industrial Economics,* Vol. 40 (1): 1–8.

Glascock, Stuart, and Margie Semilof. 1998. "Linux Groundswell Continues to Grow." *Computer Reseller News* (October 5) (810): 1, 8.

Glass, Brett. 1989. "The Token Ring." *BYTE* (January): 363–376.

Goldstein, Mark. 1985. "IBM Throws Its Hat into the Ring." *Industry Week* (October 28): 60–61.

Gomes, Lee. 1998. "H-P to Market Its Own Strain of Java." *Wall Street Journal* (March 20): A3.

———1999. "Upstart Linux Draws a Microsoft Attack Team." *Wall Street Journal* (May 21): B1(W).

Granovetter, Mark. 1985. "Economic Action and Social Structure: The Problem of Embeddedness." *American Journal of Sociology*, Vol. 91: 481–510.

Graube, Maris. 1982. "Local Area Nets: A Pair of Standards." *IEEE Spectrum* (June): 60–64.

———. 1995. Personal Communication (May 10).

———. 1997. Personal Communication (February 4).

Greenfield, David. 1989a. "Anchoring ARCnet." *LAN Magazine* (May).

———. 1989b. "Multivendor Token Ring Networks Come of Age." *Data Communications* (November 21): 37–43.

———. 1990. "Intelligent Hubs Provide Benefits—But Not for Free." *Data Communications* (June 21): 15–18.

———. 1992. "Token Ring Closes in on Ethernet." *Data Communications* (January 21): 47–51.

Greenstein, Irwin. 1985. "Bridge Unveils Router For Linking Ethernets." *MIS Week* (March 6): 54.

———. 1991. "MIS Heads for the Wiring Closet with 10BaseT LANs." *Networking Management*, Vol. 9 (February): 48–53.

Greenstein, Shane. 1993a. "Markets, Standards, and the Information Structure." *IEEE Micro* (December): 36–51.

———. 1993b. "Did Installed Base Give an Incumbent Any (Measurable) Advantages in Federal Computer Procurement?" *RAND Journal of Economics*, Vol. 24 (1): 19–39.

Greitzer, John. 1981. "Customer Requests Trigger Move to Local Nets." *Computer Business News* (June 22): 12.

Grindley, Peter. 1995. *Standards Strategy and Policy*. Oxford: Oxford University Press.

Gross, Stephen. 1984. "Hyperchannel Takes Network Systems into Hyperspace." *Electronic Business* (June 15): 40–44.

Grove, Andrew. 1996. *Only the Paranoid Survive*. New York: Currency Doubleday.

Haber, Lynn. 1986. "IBM's Token Ring Network Signals Start for LAN Vendors." *Mini-Micro Systems* (January): 38–42.

Hafke, David. 1998. "David Challenges Goliath in OS Field." *Computer Reseller News* (December 7) (820): 1, 6.

Hafner, Kaie, and Matthew Lyon. 1996. *Where Wizards Stay Up Late*. New York: Simon & Schuster.

Hahn, Mark, and Phil Belanger. 1981. "Network Minimizes Overhead of Small Computers." *Electronics* (August 25): 125–128.

Hall, Mark, and John Barry. 1990. *Sunburst: The Ascent of Sun Microsystems*. Chicago: Contemporary Books.

Harmon, Amy. 1998. "For Sale: Free Software." *New York Times* (September 28): C1.

Harrison, Ann. 1998. "In Linux We . . . " *Software Magazine*, Vol. 18 (12) (September): 32–34.

Hart, Jeffrey, Robert Reed, and Franáois Bar. 1992. "The Building of the Internet." *Telecommunications Policy* (November): 666–689.

Hellige, Hans Dieter. 1994. "From SAGE via ARPANET to Ethernet: Stages in Computer Communications Concepts Between 1950 and 1980." *History and Technology*, Vol. 11: 49–75.

Henderson, Rebecca, and Kim Clark. 1990. "Architectural Innovation: The Reconfiguration of Existing Product Technologies and Failure of Established Firms." *Administrative Science Quarterly*, Vol. 35: 9–30.

Herman, James. 1991. "Smart LAN Hubs Take Control." *Data Communications* (June 21): 62–75, 142–143.

Hindin, Eric. 1989. "Ethernet-to-Token Ring: The Gap Begins to Narrow." *Data Communications* (April): 47–50.

Hindin, Harvey. 1981. "Controlling the Electronic Office: PBXs Make Their Move." *Electronics* (April 7): 139–148.

———. 1982. "Dual-Chip Sets Forge Vital Link for Ethernet Local-Network Scheme." *Electronics* (October 6): 89–103.

Hoard, Bruce. 1982a. "Bass Calls Baseband vs. Broadband Battle 'Passé.'" *Computerworld* (May 17): 26.

———. 1982b. "Thirteen Vendors Endorse IEEE Local-Net Standard." *Computerworld*, Vol. 16 (50) (December 13): 1, 9.

———. 1984. "After the Storm: Interview with David Liddle." *Computerworld* (March 14): 31–38.

Hofmeister, Sallie. 1988. "Big or Bust." *Venture* (April): 52–56.

———. 1989. "Two Men and a Merger." *Venture* (January): 40–43.

Hopper, Andrew. 1978. "Data Ring at Computer Laboratory, University of Cambridge." In *Computer Science and Technology: Local Area Networking*. Washington, D.C.: National Bureau of Standards Special Publication (April): 11–16.

Howe, Charles. 1986. "Back to the Roots." *Datamation,* Vol. 32 (6) (March 15): 45–48.

———. 1987. "Manhunt on for Missing Link: 10-Mbit/s Ethernet via Phone Wire." *Data Communications* (April): 54–56.

Hughes, Thomas. 1983. *Networks of Power*. Baltimore: Johns Hopkins University Press.

———. 1987. "The Evolution of Large Technological Systems." In Wiebe Bijker, Thomas Hughes, and Trevor Pinch (eds.), *The Social Construction of Technological Systems*, 51–82. Cambridge, Mass.: MIT Press.

Hunter, John. 1989a. "Token Ring vs. Ethernet: The Battle Continues." *Network World*, Vol. 6 (7) (February 20): 1, 37–41.

———. 1989b. "New Twists in Ethernet Not Just Token Advances." *Network World*, Vol. 6 (45): 1, 59–66.

Hurwicz, Mike. 1991. "Beware of Hidden Factors in Buying 16M Token Ring." *Network World* (December 30/January 6): 1, 25, 29–32.

Hutchinson, David. 1988. *Local Area Network Architectures*. Wokingham, U.K.: Addison-Wesley.

Hyatt, Joshua. 1991. "Born to Run." *Inc.* (January): 36–50.

Hyde, Anne. 1985a. "Factory Networks: The Promise Remains Unfilled." *Electronic Business* (September 15): 89–90.

———. 1985b. "The Networked Plans of Mr. LAN." *Electronic Business* (March 1): 88–100.

Info Canada. 1993. "ARCnet Waning in Market Shift." Vol. 18 (11): 23, 27.

Infosystems. 1983. "Xerox and IBM Gain in Standards Battle." (January): 18–20.

Jeffery, Brian. 1986. "A Look at IBM's Token-Ring Network." *Computerworld*, Vol. 20 (2): 33–36.

Johnson, Jan. 1982. "GI Goes Hi Tech Shopping." *Datamation* (December): 80–83.

———. 1984. "A High-Speed Race." *Datamation* (April 15): 42–49.

Johnson, Johna Till. 1990. "Ethernet Arrives on Twisted-Pair." *Data Communications* (September 21): 15–24.

Jones, Keith. 1985. "Cheapernet Makes Local Area Networking More Affordable." *Mini-Micro Systems* (January): 74–83.

Juliussen, Egil, and Karen Petska-Juliussen. 1994. *The 7th Annual Computer Industry 1994–95 Almanac.* Austin, Texas: Reference Press.

Kahn, Robert. 1987. "Networks for Advanced Computing." *Scientific American* (October): 136–143.

Kar, Saroj. 1981. "Closing the Gap: Compatibility with SNA." *Computerworld* (March 18): 89–91.

Karlin, Geof. 1990. "ARCnetplus is Twice as Fast as Ethernet." *Computer Technology Review*, Vol. 10 (10) (August): 8.

Katz, Michael, and Carl Shapiro. 1985. "Network Externalities, Competition, and Compatibility." *American Economic Review*, Vol. 75 (3): 424–440.

———. 1986. "Technology Adoption in the Presence of Network Externalities." *Journal of Political Economy*, Vol. 94 (August): 822–841.

———. 1994. "Systems Competition and Network Effects." *Journal of Economic Perspectives*, Vol. 8 (2) (Spring): 93–115.

Kenney, Charles. 1992. *Riding the Runaway Horse: The Rise and Decline of Wang Laboratories.* Boston: Little, Brown.

Kenney, Martin, and Richard Florida. 1993. *Beyond Mass Production.* New York: Oxford University Press.

Kenney, Martin, and Urs von Burg. 1999. "Technology, Entrepreneurship, and Path Dependence: Industrial Clustering in Silicon Valley and Route 128." *Industrial and Corporate Change*, Vol. 8 (1): 67–103.

Kerr, Susan. 1987a. "Is there Life after IBM?" *Datamation* (April 1): 30–32.

———. 1987b. "The Era of Twisted Pair Begins to Dawn on Ethernet." *Datamation* (September 15): 30–34.

Killat, U., H.-A. Muscate, and B. Wolfinger. 1988. "A Performance Analysis of the IEEE 802.5 Token Ring Protocol." *Philips Journal of Research*, Vol. 43 (5/6): 532–553.

Killorin, Eric. 1987. "Will Token Ring or Ethernet Dominate?" *Telecommunication Products and Technology* (March): 34–39.

Kirsner, Scott. 1998. "The Legend of Bob Metcalfe." *Wired* (November): 182–186, 232–234, 246–247.

Klee, Kenneth, and John Verity. 1982. "Battle of the Networkers." *Datamation* (March): 114–127.

Klett, Stephen. 1994. "Token Ring Switching Gathers Steam." *Computerworld* (July 25): 59.

Kogut, Bruce, and Udo Zander. 1992. "Knowledge of the firm, combinative capabilities, and the replication of technology." *Organization Science* 3:383–397.

Kolman, John. 1988. "A New Twist for Ethernet." *PC Tech Journal* (September): 87–98.

Kramer, Matt. 1990. "Startup's Switch Designed to Boost Ethernet Networks." *PC Week*, Vol. 7 (10) (March 12): 39.

Kramlich, Richard. 1995. Personal Communication (July 17).

Kurita, Shohei. 1985. "Factory Networks in the LAN of the Rising Sun." *Electronic Business* (September 15): 100.

Labate, John. 1994. "The Battle for Your PC Network." *Fortune* (October 31): 189–196.

Lally, Patrick. 1986. "Token Ring LANs in Multivendor Environment." *Telecommunications* (March): 71–76.

Lampson, Butler. 1988. "Personal Distributed Computing: The Alto and Ethernet Software." In Adele Goldberg (ed.), *A History of Personal Workstations*, 293–335. New York: ACM Press.

Langlois, Richard. 1992. "Creating External Capabilities: Innovation and Vertical Disintegration in the Microcomputer Industry." *Business and Economic History*, Vol. 66 (Spring): 93–1–50.

Langlois, Richard, and Paul Robertson. 1992. "Networks and Innovation in a Modular System: Lessons from the Microcomputer and Stereo Component Industries." *Research Policy*, Vol. 21: 297–313.

———. 1995. *Firms, Markets and Economic Change: A Dynamic Theory of Business Institutions*. London: Routledge.

Lavien, Andrew. 1981. "Local Area-Net Prices Coming within Reach." *Electronic Business* (October): 65–66.

Lazonick, William. 1991. *Business Organization and the Myth of the Market Economy*. Cambridge: Cambridge University Press.

LeBoss, Bruce, and Martin Marshall. 1981. "Zilog, at Six, Hews to Master Plan." *Electronics* (January 13): 97–98.

Leonard-Barton, Dorothy. 1992. "Core Capabilities and Core Rigidities: A Paradox in Managing New Product Development." *Strategic Management Journal*, Vol. 13: 111–125.

Lettieri, Larry. 1981. "Local Area Network Links Micros via Custom Interface." *Mini-Micro Systems* (June): 18–23.

Levin, David. 1985. "AT&T's Starlan: A Better Mousetrap." *Systems/3X World* (October): 54–56.

Levy, Walter. 1981. "Wangnet: A Bold Step Forward?" *Mini-Micro Systems* (November): 247–254.

Lewis, Geoff, and Marilyn Harris. 1985. "Rivals Roll Out the Red Carpet for Big Blue's Latest." *Business Week* (October 28): 112–113.

Liddle, David. 1995. Personal Communication (June 21).

Liebowitz, S. J., and Stephen Margolis. 1990. "The Fable of the Keys." *Journal of Law and Economics*, Vol. 33 (April): 1–25.

————. 1994. "Network Externality: An Uncommon Tragedy." *Journal of Economic Perspectives*, Vol. 8 (2): 133–150.

————. 1995a. "Are Network Externalities a New Source of Market Failure?" *Research in Law and Economics*, Vol. 17: 1–22.

————. 1995b. "Path Dependence, Lock-in, and History." *Journal of Law, Economics, and Organization*, Vol. 11 (1): 205–226.

Lippis, Nick. 1993. "Troubled Times for Token Ring." *Data Communications* (January): 27–28.

Loughry, Donald. 1996. Personal Communication (March 25).

Love, Robert. 1996. Personal Communication (February 5).

Lundquist, Eric. 1981. "Wang Labs Pushes Communications Offerings." *Mini-Micro Systems* (August): 26–31.

Lundvall, Bengt-Ake (ed.). 1992. *National Systems of Innovation*. London: Pinter.

Lynn, Leonard, Mohan Reddy, and John Aram. 1996. "Linking Technology and Institutions: The Innovation Community Framework." *Research Policy*, Vol. 25: 91–106.

Madron, Thomas. 1988. *Local Area Networks*. New York: Wiley.

————. 1990. *Local Area Networks*, 2d ed. New York: Wiley.

Malone, Joe. 1981. "The Microcomputer Connection to Local Networks." *Data Communications* (December): 132–135.

Manuel, Tom. 1981. "'Old' Local Net Wins Big New Backer." *Electronics* (September 22): 40–41.

Markels, Alex. 1986. "LAN Market Growth Takes Five Before Big Push." *MIS Week* (March 17): 31–39.

Marshall, Martin. 1981. "Ethernet Gets Two Bad Report Cards." *Electronics* (November 30): 88–90.

Matutes, Carmen, and Pierre Regibeau. 1987. "Standardization in Multi-Component Industries." In Landis Gabel (ed.), *Product Standardization as a Tool of Competitive Strategy*, 23–28. Amsterdam: Elsevier Science (North-Holland).

————. 1988. "Mix and Match: Product Compatibility Without Network Externalities." *Rand Journal of Economics*, Vol. 19 (Summer): 221–234.

Mayne, Alan. 1986. *Linked Local Area Networks*. New York: Wiley.

McDermott, Jim. 1976. "The IEEE 488 Bus Plays a Major Role in Programmable Instrument Systems." *Electronic Design*, Vol. 24 (November 22): 76–80.

McGiffert, Brian. 1991. "16 Mbps Token-Ring Adapters Outpace Ethernet." *Network World* (January 14): 43, 46, 55.

McHugh, Josh. 1998. "For the Love of Hacking." *Forbes* (August 10): 94–100.

McLellan, Vin. 1981. "Strategy Behind 'Wangnet.'" *Datamation* (January): 48–52.

McMaster, David. 1986. "IBM's Token Ring: What Are the Alternatives?" *Mini-Micro Systems* (September): 105–116.

Mead, Tim. 1982. "Sytek Opened a Door for General Instruments." *Electronic Business* (September): 110–112.

Metcalfe, J. S., and Ian Miles. 1994. "Standards, Selection, and Variety: an Evolutionary Approach." *Information Economics and Policy*, Vol. 6: 243–268.

Metcalfe, Robert. 1983. "Controller/Transceiver Board Drives Ethernet into PC Domain." *Mini-Micro Systems* (January): 179–190.

———. 1991. "Let the Ethernet Chips Fall Where They May." *Network Computing* (November 1).

———. 1992a. "EtherLink: The Hot Product That Made Ethernet." *Network Computing* (February 1).

———. 1992b. "OK, So Don't Put LANs on Your Systems' Motherboards." *Infoworld*, Vol. 14 (19) (May 11): 39.

———. 1993a. "The Future of LANs." *Infoworld*, Vol. 15 (21) (May 24): 67–70.

———. 1993b. "What Ralph Ungermann Ought to Start Next." *Infoworld*, Vol. 15 (47) (November 22): 50.

———. 1993c. "Looking Out for No.2: IBM LAN on Upswing." *Infoworld*, Vol. 15 (4) (January 25): 46.

———. 1993d. "Washing LAN Upgrade Worries Down the Drain." *Infoworld*, Vol. 15 (49) (December 6): 63.

———. 1994. "How Ethernet Was Invented." *IEEE Annals of the History of Computing*, Vol. 16 (4): 81–88.

———. 1996a. Personal Communication (May 10).

———. 1996b. Personal Communication (June 12).

———. 1996c. E-mail (April 12).

Metcalfe, Robert, and David Boggs. 1976. "Ethernet: Distributed Packet Switching for Local Computer Networks." *Communications of the ACM*, Vol. 19 (7): 395–403.

Mier, Edwin. 1984a. "Who's on Board for Ethernet?" *Data Communications* (May): 46–47, 62.

———. 1984b. "The Evolution of a Standard Ethernet." *BYTE* (December): 131–142.

———. 1986. "Question: How Open Is IBM's Much-Touted Token Ring?" *Data Communications* (January): 47–52.

Miller, Frederick. 1983. "Packing the Disks with More Data." *Infosystems* (July): 78–80.

MIS Week. 1982. "Ungermann-Bass Broadband Ties into Baseband Version." (March 3): 13.

———. 1986. "Sytek Says It's Covered Despite Close IBM Ties." (March 17): 30.

Moad, Jeff. 1988. "User Demands for Standards Said to Spur Tandem—U-B Deal." *Datamation* (April 1): 26–30.

Montgomery, Cynthia. 1995. *Resource-Based and Evolutionary Theories of the Firm: Toward a Synthesis*. Boston: Kluwer.

Moreau, René. 1984. *The Computer Comes of Age.* Cambridge, Mass.: MIT Press.

Moschella, David. 1997. *Waves of Power: Dynamics of Global Technology Leadership 1964–2010.* New York: Amacom.

Motter, Paul. 1997. "USCOMIX." *Upside* (May): 91–97, 134–141.

Mulqueen, John. 1987. "LAN Industry Booms amid Fear of Coming Shake-out." *Data Communications* (March): 109–121.

———. 1988. "SynOptics Turns Skeptics into Believers in Twisted-Pair Wiring." *Data Communications* (December): 71–80.

Murphy, John. 1982. "Token-Passing Protocol Boosts Throughput in Local Networks." *Electronics* (September 1982): 158–163.

Musthaler, Linda. 1999. "Linux Gathers Critical Mass Needed to Compete with NT." *Network World,* Vol. 16 (6) (February 8): 35.

Nee, Eric. 1985. "Sytek Revamps, 2 Execs Leave." *MIS Week* (April 10): 25.

Needham, R. M., and A. J. Herbert. 1982. *The Cambridge Distributed Computing System.* London: Addison-Wesley.

Nelson, Jim. 1983. "802: A Progress Report." *Datamation* (September): 136–152.

Nelson, Richard. 1991. "Why Do Firms Differ, and How Does It Matter?" *Strategic Management Journal,* Vol. 12: 61–74.

———(ed.). 1993. *National Innovation Systems.* Oxford: Oxford University Press.

———. 1994. "The Coevolution of Technology, Industrial Structure, and Supporting Institutions." *Industrial and Corporate Change,* Vol. 3 (1): 47–63.

Nestar. 1983. Business Plan. Palo Alto, Calif.

Network Systems. 1980. Annual Report. Brooklyn Park, Minn.

———. 1981. Annual Report. Brooklyn Park, Minn.

———. 1982. Annual Report. Brooklyn Park, Minn.

———. 1983a. Securities and Exchange Commission Form S-1. Brooklyn Park, Minn.

———. 1983b. Annual Report. Brooklyn Park, Minn.

———. 1984. Annual Report. Brooklyn Park, Minn.

Network World. 1988a. "We Build Big Networks." Vol. 5 (51) (December 19): 29–37.

———. 1988b. "Start-up Pro Talks of LAN Challenge." Vol. 5 (3) (January 18): 11–12.

———. 1989. "IBM Exec Discusses Firm's LAN Strategy." Vol. 6 (June 5): 17–18.

———. 1991. "IBM Maintains Token-Ring Dominance." Vol. 8 (13) (April 1): 19.

Nonaka, Ikujiro, and Hirotaka Takeuchi. 1995. *The Knowledge-Creating Company.* New York: Oxford University Press.

Norberg, Arthur, and Judy O'Neill. 1996. *Transforming Computer Technology: Information Processing for the Pentagon, 1962–1986.* Baltimore: Johns Hopkins University Press.

O'Neill, Judy. 1995. "The Role of ARPA in the Development of the ARPANET, 1961–1972." *IEEE Annals of the History of Computing*, Vol. 17 (4): 76–81.

Orlov, Mikhail. 1988. "Ethernet over Twisted-Pair: Is It Right for Your Network?" *Telecommunications* (December): 39–41.

O'Shea, Dan. 1999. "That Linux Mystique." *Telephony* (January 25): 58–59.

Pake, George. 1985. "Research at Xerox PARC: A Founder's Assessment." *IEEE Spectrum* (October): 54–61.

Parker, Richard, and Sydney Shapiro. 1983. "Untangling Local Area Networks." *Computer Design* (March): 159–172.

Patch, Kimberly. 1991. "A Guide to Wiring Hubs: Smart, Smarter, Smartest." *Network World*, Vol. 8 (10) (March 11): 1, 36–46.

Patterson, Jason. 1997. "The History of Computers during My Lifetime— The 1970s." Retrieved April 1997 from the World Wide Web: http://www. reflections.com.au/~jason/Articles/HistoryOfComputers/1970s.html.

Pearson, W., G. Ellis, J. Whitnell, C. Payne, and S. Dillon. 1982. "3-in-1 Local Network Links Personal Computers." *Electronics* (December 29): 67–70.

Peden, Jeffery, and Alfred Weaver. 1988. "Are Priorities Useful in an 802.5 Token Ring?" *IEEE Transactions on Industrial Electronics*, Vol. 35 (3) (August): 361–365.

Pendery, David. 1999. "Curtain to Rise on Multifaceted Linux Support Company." *Infoworld*, Vol. 21 (6) (February 8): 8.

Penrose, Edith. 1980. *The Theory of the Growth of the Firm*, 2d ed. Oxford: Blackwell.

Perry, Tekla, and Paul Wallich. 1985. "Inside the PARC: The 'Information Architects.'" *IEEE Spectrum* (October): 62–75.

Peterson, Gordon. 1997. E-mail (September 23).

Petrovsky, Mary. 1986. "Corvus Systems Inc. Lays Off 20 Percent of Its Work Force." *Infoworld* (November 20): 12.

———. 1988. "Local Net Firms See Safety in Mergers." *Network World* (July 25): 9, 18.

Pierce, J. R. 1972. "Network for Block Switching of Data." *Bell System Technical Journal*, Vol. 51 (6): 1133–1145.

Pinch, Trevor, and Wiebe Bijker. 1987. "The Social Construction of Facts and Artifacts: Or How the Sociology of Science and the Sociology of Technology Might Benefit Each Other." In Wiebe Bijker, Thomas Hughes, and Trevor Pinch (eds.), *The Social Construction of Technological Systems*, 51–82. Cambridge, Mass.: MIT Press.

Pitt, Daniel. 1987. "Standards for the Token Ring." *IEEE Network Magazine*, Vol. 1 (1) (January): 19–22.

Pliner, Michael. 1995. Personal Communication (July 3).

Porac, Joseph. 1994. "On the Concept of 'Organizational Community.'" In Joel Baum and Jitendra Singh (eds.), *Evolutionary Dynamics of Organizations*, 403–424. New York: Oxford University Press.

Porter, Michael. 1980. *Competitive Strategy*. New York: Free Press.

Posner, Bruce. 1984. "Big Deal." *Inc.* (January): 109–112.

Postrel, Steven. 1990. "Competing Networks and Proprietary Standards: The Case of Quadraphonic Sound." *Journal of Industrial Economics*, Vol. 39 (December): 169–185.

Potter, David. 1985. "IBM: Their Leadership Role in Local Networks." In *Localnet '85*, 319–323. London: Online Pinner.

Prahalad, C. K., and Gary Hamel. 1990. "The Core Competence of the Corporation." *Harvard Business Review* (May–June): 79–91.

Price, Margaret. 1982. "Xerox's New Office Systems Game Plan." *Industry Week* (August 9): 58–61.

Proteon. 1991. Securities and Exchange Commission Form S-1. Westborough, Mass.

Reier, Sharon. 1995. "Bland Ambition." *Financial World*, Vol. 164 (13) (June 6): 56–59.

Rekhi, Kanwal. 1995. Personal Communication (June 15).

Richardson, G. B. 1972. "The Organisation of Industry." *Economic Journal* (September): 883–896.

Richman, Tom. 1989. "Who's in Charge Here?" *Inc.* (June): 36–46.

Riffkin, Glenn, and George Harrar. 1988. *The Ultimate Entrepreneur: The Story of Ken Olsen and Digital Equipment Corporation*. Chicago: Contemporary Books.

Roberts, Lawrence. 1988. "The ARPANET and Computer Networks." In Adele Goldberg (ed.), *A History of Personal Workstations*, 143–165. New York: ACM Press.

Rodgers, David. 1995. Personal Communication (June 28).

Rogers, Everett, and Judith Larsen. 1984. *Silicon Valley Fever*. New York: Basic Books.

Rosenkopf, Lori, and Michael Tushman. 1994. "The Coevolution of Technology and Organization." In Joel Baum and Jitendra Singh (eds.), *Evolutionary Dynamics of Organizations*, 403–424. New York: Oxford University Press.

Ross, William. 1986. "Making the Data Connection with Twisted-Pair Cable." *Telecommunications* (September): 154–160.

Saal, Harry. 1981. "Local Area Networks." *BYTE* (October): 92–112.

———. 1990. "LAN Downtime: Clear and Present Danger." *Data Communications* (March 21): 67–72.

———. 1995. Personal Communication (May 8).

Salamone, Salvatore. 1990a. "Getting from Ethernet to Token Ring by Bridge." *Network World* (December 31–January 7): 1, 39–44.

———. 1990b. "16M vs. 4M Token-Ring: Fourfold Improvement?" *Network World*, Vol. 7 (7) (February 12): 1, 36, 58–60.

Saloner, Garth. 1990. "Economic Issues in Computer Interface Standardization." *Economics of Innovation and New Technologies*, Vol. 1: 135–156.

Saltzer, Jerome. 1997. Personal Communication (January 30).

———. 2000. E-mail (November 2).

Saltzer, Jerome, and Kenneth Pogran. 1979. "A Star-Shaped Ring Network with High Maintainability." *Proceedings of the LACN Symposium* (May): 179–190.

Saltzer, Jerome, David Clark, and Kenneth Pogran. 1981. "Why a Ring?" *IEEE Seventh Data Communications Symposium* (October): 211–217.

Salus, Peter. 1995. *Casting the Net: From ARPANET to Internet and Beyond.* Reading, Mass.: Addison-Wesley.

Salwen, Howard. 1995. Personal Communication (July 7).

———. 1997. Personal Communication (October 7).

Salwen, Howard, and Alan Marshall. 1990. "16-Mbit/s Token Ring LANs and UTP: Perfect Together." *Data Communications* (September 21): 41–50.

San Jose Mercury. 1985. "Helping Computers to Communicate." (June 3): 5D.

Saunders, Stephen. 1994. "LAN Switching Comes to Token Ring." *Data Communications* (January): 87–90.

Saxenian, AnnaLee. 1994. *Regional Advantage: Culture and Competition in Silicon Valley and Route 128.* Cambridge, Mass.: Harvard University Press.

Saxton, W. A., and Morris Edwards. 1980. "DEC Closes in on Networking Goal." *Infosystems* (April): 83–84.

———. 1981. "Xerox's Communications Legacy." *Infosystems* (July): 100–101.

Schmalensee, Richard. 1983. "Advertising and Entry Deterrence: An Exploratory Model." *Journal of Political Economy*, Vol. 91 (4): 636–653.

Schmidt, Jonathan. 1995. Personal Communication (May 15).

Schmidt, Ronald. 1988. "Developing Ethernet Capability on Unshielded Twisted Pair." *Telecommunications* (January): 52–56.

———. 1995. Personal Communication (May 6).

Schmidt, Ronald, Eric Rawson, Robert Norton, Stephen Jackson, and Douglas Bailey. 1983. "Fibernet II: A Fiber Optic Ethernet." *IEEE Journal on Selected Areas in Communications*, Vol. 1 (5) (November): 702–711.

Schmookler, Jacob. 1966. *Invention and Economic Growth.* Cambridge, Mass.: Harvard University Press.

Schumpeter, Joseph. 1942. *Capitalism, Socialism, and Democracy.* New York: Harper.

Seifert, Richard. 1991. "Ethernet: Ten Years After." *BYTE* (January): 315–321.

Seifert, William. 1995. Personal Communication (June 28).

Seither, Mike. 1989. "Novell's LAN Strategy Begins to Bud with NetWare 386." *Systems Integration* (July): 17–18.

Semilof, Margie. 1992. "100-Mbps Ethernet? Start-up Says 'Yes.'" *Communications Week* (October 5): 1.

Severino, Paul. 1984. "Statement of Paul Severino, CEO, Interlan, Westford, Mass." Climate for Entrepreneurship and Innovation in the U.S.: Hearings Before the Joint Economic Committee Congress of the United States (August 30 and 31). Printed for the use of the Joint Economic Committee. Washington, D.C.: U.S. Government Printing Office.

Shankland, Stephen. 2001. "Linux Catching Up to Microsoft in Server Market." C-Net news.com http://news.cnet.com/news/0-1003-200-4979275. html?tag=mn_hd (February 28).

Shapiro, Carl. 1989. "The Theory of Business Strategy." *Rand Journal of Economics*, Vol. 20 (1): 125–137.

Shapiro, Carl, and Hal Varian. 1999. *Information Rules*. Boston, Mass.: Harvard University Press.

Shea, Ellen. 1983. "Surveying the LANscape." *Office Administration and Automation* (February): 32–34, 106.

Sheldon, Tom. 1994. *Encyclopedia of Networking*. New York: Osborne/ McGraw-Hill.

Shoch, John, Yogen Dalal, Ronald Crane, and David Redell. 1981. *Evolution of the Ethernet Local Computer Network*. Xerox Office Products Division.

Shustek, Leonard. 1995. Fax (November 12).

———. 1999. Personal Communication (June 23).

Silver, Morris. 1984. *Enterprise and the Scope of the Firm*. London: Martin Robertson.

Sirbu, Marvin, and Kent Hughes. 1986. "Standardization of Local Area Networks." Paper presented at the 14th Annual Telecommunications Policy Research Conference, Virginia.

Sivula, Chris. 1989. "A New Rival to Ethernet and Token Ring?" *Datamation* (December 1): 53–58.

Slater, Robert. 1987. *Portraits in Silicon*. Cambridge, Mass.: MIT Press.

Smith, Douglas, and Robert Alexander. 1988. *Fumbling the Future: How Xerox Invented, Then Ignored, the First Personal Computer*. New York: Morrow.

Smith, Harold. 1977a. "The Century 21 Office." *Management World* (July): 25–27.

———. 1977b. "Managing Tomorrow's Office." *Management World* (June): 29–31.

———. 1977c. "The Office of the Future: Closer Than You Think." *Management World* (May): 3–6.

Smith, Richard. 1989. "A Historical Overview of Computer Architecture." *Annals of the History of Computing*, Vol. 10 (4): 277–303.

Solomon, Laurence. 1979. "IBM versus the PCM's." *Datamation* (February): 100–103.

Stallings, William. 1984. "IEEE Project 802." *Computerworld* (February 13): In Depth 27–41.

———. 1986. "The IEEE 802 Local Network Standards." *Telecommunications* (March): 40–48.

———. 1987. *Local Networks: An Introduction*, 2d ed. New York: Macmillan.

Stenzler-Centonze, Marjorie. 1984. "IBM's LAN: To Wait Is the Question." *Mini-Micro Systems* (August): 125–126.

Stephenson, Larry. 1995. Personal Communication (June 19).

Stern, Nancy. 1981. *From ENIAC to UNIVAC*. Bedford, Mass.: Digital Press.

Sterry, Richard. 1981. "Ring Nets: Passing the Token in Local Network Circles." *Data Communications*, Vol. 10 (12): 97–100.

Stott, Martha. 1998. "Two Decades of Networking." In *ARCnet: The First 20 Years*. CD-ROM. ARCnet Trade Association.

Strauss, Paul. 1984. "PC Network Threatens Small Firms That Thrived till Now." *Data Communications* (October): 77–84.

Stritter, Edward, and Leonard Shustek. 1981. "Local Network Links Personal Computers in a Multiuser, Multifunctional System." *Electronics* (June 16): 171–175.

Suarez, Fernando, and James Utterback. 1995. "Dominant Design and the Survival of Firms." *Strategic Management Journal*, Vol. 16: 415–430.

Suby, Carol. 1986. "IBM's Token Ring Takes Center Stage." *Electronic Business* (February 1): 33–34.

Surden, Esther. 1977. "Datapoint Concept Links Dedicated Processors." *Computerworld*, Vol. 11 (49) (December 5): 1, 6.

Swartz, James. 1995. Personal Communication (June 29).

SynOptics. 1988. Securities and Exchange Commission Form S-1. Mountain View, Calif.

Sytek. 1984. Securities and Exchange Commission Form S-1. Mountain View, Calif.

Teece, David. 1986. "Profiting from Technological Innovation: Implications for Integration, Collaboration, Licensing, and Public Policy." *Research Policy*, Vol. 15: 285–305.

Teece, David, Gary Pisano, and Amy Shuen. 1997. "Dynamic Capabilities and Strategic Management." *Strategic Management Journal*, Vol. 18 (7): 509–533.

Terrie, David. 1991. "Competition Driving 10Base-T Card Prices Down." *Network World* (October): 43–96.

Thacker, Charles. 1988. "Personal Distributed Computing: The Alto and Ethernet Hardware." In Adele Goldberg (ed.), *A History of Personal Workstations*, 267–289. New York: ACM Press.

Thaler, Patricia. 1995. Personal Communication (June 20).

3Com. 1980. Ethernet Product Plans (October 6). Menlo Park, Calif.

———. 1984. Securities and Exchange Commission Form S-1. Mountain View, Calif.

———. 1985. Annual Report. Mountain View, Calif.

———. 1987. Annual Report. Mountain View, Calif.

———. 1988. Annual Report. Mountain View, Calif.

Trifari, John. 1982. "Sytek Ties IBM CPUs to Minis, Micros via Broadband." *Mini-Micro Systems* (July): 33, 38, 41.

Tunick, Diane. 1990. "Token Ring Cards Move 16 Mbps over UTP." *Data Communications* (June 21): 85–88.

Tushman, Michael, and Philip Anderson. 1986. "Technological Discontinuities and Organizational Environments." *Administrative Science Quarterly*, Vol. 31: 439–465.

Tushman, Michael, and Lori Rosenkopf. 1992. "Organizational Determinants of Technological Change." *Research in Organizational Behavior*, Vol. 14: 311–347.

Ungermann, Ralph. 1995. Personal Communication (April 26 and April 28).

———. 1996. Personal Communication (December 14).

———. 1998. E-mail (December 4).

Ungermann-Bass. 1979. "Net/One Customer Prospect List." (December). Santa Clara, Calif.

———. 1983a. Securities and Exchange Commission Form S-1. Santa Clara, Calif.

———. 1983b. Annual Report. Santa Clara, Calif.

———. 1984. Annual Report. Santa Clara, Calif.

———. 1986a. Annual Report. Santa Clara, Calif.

———. 1986b. Securities and Exchange Commission Form S-1. Santa Clara, Calif.

Upside. 1996. "An Interview by Eric Nee with Craig Benson and Bob Levine." (January): 60–69.

Uttal, Bro. 1978. "Xerox Is Trying Too Hard." *Fortune* (March 13): 84–94.

———. 1981. "Xerox Xooms Toward the Office of the Future." *Fortune* (May 18): 44–52.

Utterback, James, and William Abernathy. 1975. "A Dynamic Model of Process and Product Innovation." *OMEGA—The International Journal of Management Science,* Vol. 3 (6): 639–656.

Valigra, Lori. 1981. "Xerox's 'Star' Shines on Professionals." *Mini-Micro Systems* (June): 23–33.

Valovic, Tom. 1987a. "An Interview with Howard Salwen, Chairman of Proteon." *Telecommunications* (September): 83–95.

———. 1987b. "Local Area Networks: Strategic Developments and Trends." *Telecommunications* (October): 46–50.

Verhalen, Andrew. 1995. Personal Communication (February 10).

Verity, John. 1981. "Xerox's Office Assault." *Datamation* (July): 36–49.

Vitalink. 1989. Securities and Exchange Commission Form S-1. Fremont, Calif.

Von Hippel, Eric. 1988. *The Sources of Innovation.* New York: Oxford University Press.

Wade, James. 1995. "Dynamics of Organizational Communities and Technological Bandwagons: An Empirical Investigation of Community Evolution in the Microprocessor Market." *Strategic Management Journal,* Vol. 16 (Summer): 111–133.

———. 1996. "A Community-Level Analysis of Sources and Rates of Technological Variation in the Microprocessor Market." *Academy of Management Journal,* Vol. 39 (5): 1218–1244.

Wall Street Journal. 1982. "Corvus Systems Unveils Desk-Top Computer." (April 26): B12.

———. 1989. "Novell and Excelan to Merge." (June 22): A3.

Watt, Peggy. 1986. "Sytek Offers Local Network Link, Sells Upgraded Net Adapter Card." *Computerworld* (March 10): 19, 22.

Weil, Ulric. 1982. *Information Systems in the 80's.* Englewood Cliffs, N.J.: Prentice Hall.

Weiss, Martin, and Marvin Sirbu. 1990. "Technological Choice in Voluntary Standards Committees: An Empirical Analysis." *Economics of Innovation and New Technology,* Vol. 1: 111–133.

Wellfleet. 1991. Securities and Exchange Commission Form S-1. Bedford, Mass.

Wernerfelt, Birger. 1984. "A Resource-Based View of the Firm." *Strategic Management Journal*, Vol. 5: 171–180.

Weyhrich, Steve. 1991. Retrieved January 4, 1998, from the World Wide Web: http://www.hypermall.com/History/AHO4.html.

Wilkes, M. V., and D. J. Wheeler. 1979. "The Cambridge Digital Communication Ring." In *Proceedings of the LACN Symposium* (May): 47–60.

Williams, Tom. 1981. "Interface Board Sets Up Local Network for Dissimilar Computers." *Electronic Design* (May 14): 35.

Williamson, Oliver. 1985. *The Economic Institutions of Capitalism*. New York: Free Press.

Wilson, John. 1985. *The New Ventures: Inside the High-Stakes World of Venture Capital*. Reading, Mass.: Addison-Wesley.

———. 1987a. "Suddenly the Heavyweights Smell Money in Computer Networks." *Business Week* (April 27): 110–111.

———. 1987b. "The Nerve-Racking Job of Setting Up a Network." *Business Week* (April 27): 112–114.

Wood, Lamont. 1994. "The Man Who Invented the PC." *Invention & Technology* (Fall): 64.

Young, Bob. 1998. "Face Off—Linux vs. Windows NT: Which Is Better for the Enterprise?" *Network World*, Vol. 15 (14) (November 16): 53.

Zakon, Robert. 1999. "Hobbes' Internet Timeline v.4.1." Retrieved July 20 from the World Wide Web: http://info.isoc.org/guest/zakon/Internet/History/HIT.htlm.

Index

Page numbers followed by letters *f*, *n*, and *t* refer to entries in figures, notes, and tables, respectively.

Balkanization, 45–46
Baran, Paul, 231n60
Baseband networks, 149, 157, 242nn84,87
Bass, Charles, 6, 23, 82, 86, 126–28
Batch processing, 56–57, 230n43
Bayless, Jon, 193, 214
Bay Networks, xiv
Bay Partners, 132
Begun, Michael, 246n34
Bell, Gordon, 102, 112
Bell Laboratories, 49, 225n67, 232n71
Benhamou, Eric, 86, 130, 246n34
Berkeley Computer Corporation, 69
Bessemer Venture, 127
Beta video system of Sony, 12, 19, 20, 39, 203, 226n73
Biba, Kenneth, 250n27
BICC Data Networks, 180
Blue Book of Ethernet, 112, 121, 128
Boeing, 243n101
Boggs, David, 73, 74, 235n134, 245n25
Borrus, Michael, 34
Bredt, Thomas, 170–71, 179, 181–82, 185, 214
Breyer, James, 214
Bridge Communications, 92, 133, 138, 139, 140, 143, 155, 160, 197, 200–201, 247nn61,67; acquisition of, 141, 142, 201; annual sales and revenues, 218–19; founding of, 6, 130–32; new products developed by, 135–36; Sytek competition with, 150
Bridges, remote, xv, 134, 192–93, 198, 247n59
Broadband networks, 140, 149, 151, 157, 174, 242nn84,87, 248n90, 250n23
Broadcast storm, 193, 260n134
Brownstein, Neil, 127, 128, 214
Bull (company), 121
Burroughs, 48, 108, 112
Burton, Craig, 214
Business Week, 100
Bus topology, 72–73, 113, 170–71, 175, 177
Bux, Werner, 110, 193, 214

Cablenet, 101t
Cabletron, 180, 181t, 186, 190, 197, 218–19, 257n70
Caldera, 210
Cambridge Ring, 64, 102
Cambridge University, 64, 76
Capabilities, 21, 29–46, 226–27n14, 227–28n21; dynamic, 32; external, 32; geographic space and, 29–30; higher-

order, 32–33; overview of concept, 30–33
CAP computers, 64
Carano, Bandel, 214
Carnegie-Mellon University, 68–69
Carrico, William, 86, 130, 246n34
Carrier Sense Multiple Access with Collision Detection. *See* CSMA/CD
Centram, 101t
Chandler, Alfred, 40–41
Charney, Howard, 214, 244–45n16
Chipcom, 180, 181t, 218–19
Ciena, xiv
Circuit switching, 59
Cisco, xiii–xiv, 77, 193, 198, 218–19
Citibank, 88
Clark, David, 64, 148
Client/server-based computing, 53, 82
Cluster/One, 84, 86–89, 97, 101t, 237–38n46
Codelink-20, 101t
Codelink-100, 101t
Codenoll Technology, 101t
Commodore, 52
Compaq, 40, 53, 210
Compatibility, 15–16
Competence-destroying and -enhancing innovations, 225n67
Competition, 26, 27, 139–42
Competitive advantage. *See* Strategic (competitive) advantage
Competitive forces approach, 227n14
Compex, 159
Computer buses, 72–73, 103, 113, 148, 170–71, 175, 177, 255n37; defined, 232n67
Concept computers, 163, 253n90
Concord Data Systems, 101t, 112
Constant, Edward, 29
CONSTELLATION, 7, 101t, 147, 249n1
Contel Information Systems, 101t
Contelnet, 101t
Continental Illinois Venture Corporation, 151
Control Data, 80
Cooper, Eric, 214
Corel, 210
Corvus, 7–8, 23, 89, 145, 153, 166, 204, 221n18, 252n69; annual sales and revenues, 218–19; attempts to improve product line, 161; community-building efforts of, 150–51; demise of, 8, 155–57, 158–59, 160, 163; founding of, 7; network name and year of introduction, 101t; rise of, 146–47, 149–50